Certified Information Security Manager Exam Prep Guide

Aligned with the latest edition of the CISM Review Manual to help you pass the exam with confidence

Hemang Doshi

BIRMINGHAM—MUMBAI

Certified Information Security Manager Exam Prep Guide

Group Product Manager: Vijin Boricha
Publishing Product Manager: Preet Ahuja
Senior Editor: Shazeen Iqbal
Content Development Editor: Romy Dias
Technical Editor: Nithik Cheruvakodan
Copy Editor: Safis Editing
Project Coordinator: Shagun Saini
Proofreader: Safis Editing
Indexer: Manju Arasan
Production Designer: Joshua Misquitta

First published: November 2021

Production reference: 1241121

Published by Packt Publishing Ltd.
Livery Place
35 Livery Street
Birmingham
B3 2PB, UK.

ISBN 978-1-80107-410-0

www.packt.com

To my mother, Jyoti Doshi, and to the memory of my father, Hasmukh Doshi, for their sacrifices and for exemplifying the power of determination.

To my wife, Namrata Doshi, for being my loving partner throughout our life journey together, and to my 6 year-old daughter, Jia Doshi, for allowing me to write this book.

To my sister, Pooja Shah, my brother-in-law, Hiren Shah, and my nephew, Phenil Shah, for their love, support, and inspiration.

To my in-laws, Chandrakant Shah, Bharti Shah, and Ravish Shah, for their love and motivation. To my mentor and guide, Dipak Mazumder, for showing me how talent and creativity evolve.

To the extremely talented editorial team at Packt, including Preet Ahuja, Neil D'mello, Shazeen Iqbal, and Romy Dias, for their wonderful support throughout the journey of writing this book.

– Hemang Doshi

Contributors

About the author

Hemang Doshi is a chartered accountant and a Certified Information System Auditor with more than 15 years' experience in the field of information system auditing/risk-based auditing/compliance auditing/vendor risk management/due diligence/system risk and control. He is the founder of CISA Exam Study and CRISC Exam Study, dedicated platforms for those studying for the CISA and CRISC certifications, respectively. He has also authored a few books on information security.

I wish to thank those people who have been close to me and supported me, especially my wife, Namrata, and my parents.

About the reviewers

When **George McPherson** was pulled through the ranks and pinned as a 21-year-old Sergeant in the U.S. Army over 20 years ago, he learned two things about himself. He could accomplish anything he put his mind to, and he would always pull others up if he was in a position to do so. George prides himself on integrity, an insane work ethic, attention to detail and (his greatest super-power) outside-the-box creativity. With 25 years in the technology industry, the first 18 in telecoms and the last 7 in cybersecurity, George has had the opportunity to work in industries such as the military, telecoms, local government, healthcare, and electric utilities.

George has over 20 professional certifications, including the CISM certification.

I would like to thank my beautiful wife, Audrey, whose constant support and sacrifice fuel my success.

Upen Patel is an IT professional with 20 years' experience, holding numerous professional IT certifications including CISM, CISA, CDPSE, CRISC, CCSP, CISSP, and Splunk Certified Architect. Upen attained a B.Sc. in geology from York College (CUNY), an M.Sc. in environment engineering from NYU Polytechnic Institute, and an M.Sc. in security and information assurance from Pace. Upen has held several positions, including cloud architect and security engineer, risk assessment expert, CyberArk consultant, and Splunk architecture consultant. He has worked on the implementation of many large public cloud projects on Azure and AWS and developed an automated DevRiskOps process in public. He has also implemented a large Splunk SIEM solution.

I would like to thank my family for their motivation and support.

Table of Contents

2

Practical Aspects of Information Security Governance

Section 2: Information Risk Management

3
Overview of Information Risk Management

4

Practical Aspects of Information Risk Management

5

Procedural Aspects of Information Risk Management

Section 3: Information Security Program Development Management

6

Overview of Information Security Program Development Management

7
Information Security Infrastructure and Architecture

8
Practical Aspects of Information Security Program Development Management

9

Information Security Monitoring Tools and Techniques

Section 4: Information Security Incident Management

10
Overview of Information Security Incident Manager

11
Practical Aspects of Information Security Incident Management

Preface

ISACA's **Certified Information Security Manager (CISM)** certification indicates expertise in information security governance, program development and management, incident management, and risk management. Whether you are seeking a new career opportunity or striving to grow within your current organization, a CISM certification proves your expertise in these work-related domains:

- Information security governance
- Information risk management
- Information security program development and management
- Information security incident management

Who this book is for

This book is ideal for IT risk professionals, IT auditors, CISOs, information security managers, and risk management professionals.

What this book covers

Chapter 1, Information Security Governance, is an overview of information security governance.

Chapter 2, Practical Aspects of Information Security Governance, discusses information security strategies.

Chapter 3, Overview of Information Risk Management, covers basic elements of risk management.

Chapter 4, Practical Aspects of Information Risk Management, covers tools and techniques for risk management programs.

Chapter 5, Procedural Aspects of Information Risk Management, covers risk communication and security training awareness.

Chapter 6, Overview of Information Security Program Development Management, discusses basic elements of information security program development and management.

Chapter 7, Information Security Infrastructure and Architecture, discusses information security infrastructure and architecture.

Chapter 8, Practical Aspects of Information Security Program Development Management, discusses various controls and countermeasures.

Chapter 9, Information Security Monitoring Tools and Techniques, emphasizes the importance of monitoring tools and techniques.

Chapter 10, Overview of Information Security Incident Manager, discusses basic elements of information security incident management.

Chapter 11, Practical Aspects of Information Security Incident Management, covers business continuity and disaster recovery processes.

To get the most out of this book

This book is completely aligned with the CISM Review Manual of ISACA. It is advisable to follow these steps during your CISM studies:

1. Read this book.

2. Complete ISACA's QAE book or database.

3. Refer to ISACA's CISM Review Manual.

CISM aspirants will gain a lot of confidence if they approach their CISM preparation by following these steps.

Download the color images

We also provide a PDF file that has color images of the screenshots and diagrams used in this book. You can download it here: `https://static.packt-cdn.com/downloads/9781801074100_ColorImages.pdf`.

Get in touch

Feedback from our readers is always welcome.

General feedback: If you have questions about any aspect of this book, email us at customercare@packtpub.com and mention the book title in the subject of your message.

Errata: Although we have taken every care to ensure the accuracy of our content, mistakes do happen. If you have found a mistake in this book, we would be grateful if you would report this to us. Please visit www.packtpub.com/support/errata and fill in the form.

Piracy: If you come across any illegal copies of our works in any form on the internet, we would be grateful if you would provide us with the location address or website name. Please contact us at copyright@packt.com with a link to the material.

If you are interested in becoming an author: If there is a topic that you have expertise in and you are interested in either writing or contributing to a book, please visit authors.packtpub.com.

Share your thoughts

Once you've read *Certified Information Security Manager Exam Guide*, we'd love to hear your thoughts! Scan the QR code below to go straight to the Amazon review page for this book and share your feedback.

https://packt.link/r/1801074100

Your review is important to us and the tech community and will help us make sure we're delivering excellent quality content.

Section 1: Information Security Governance

This part is about the management and governance of information security. It covers 24% of the CISM certification exam.

This section contains the following chapters:

- *Chapter 1, Information Security Governance*
- *Chapter 2, Practical Aspects of Information Security Governance*

1
Information Security Governance

Governance is an important aspect of the **certified information security manager (CISM)** exam.

In this chapter, we will cover an overview of **information security governance** and aim to understand the impact of good governance on the effectiveness of information security projects.

You will learn about assurance functions such as **governance**, **risk**, and **compliance** (**GRC**), and details about the various roles and responsibilities of the security function. You will also be introduced to the best practices for obtaining the commitment from the senior management of an organization toward information security.

The following topics will be covered in this chapter:

- Introducing information security governance
- Understanding GRC
- Discovering the maturity model
- Getting to know the information security roles and responsibilities
- Finding out about the governance of third-party relationships

- Obtaining commitment from senior management
- Introducing the business case and the feasibility study
- Understanding information security governance metrics

Let's dive in and discuss each one of these topics in detail.

Introducing information security governance

In simple terms, **governance** can be defined as *a set of rules to direct, monitor, and control an organization's activities*. Governance can be implemented by way of policies, standards, and procedures.

The information security governance model is primarily impacted by the complexity of an organization's structure. An organization's structure includes objectives, its vision and mission, different function units, different product lines, hierarchy structure, leadership structure, and other relevant factors. A review of organizational structure will help the security manager to understand the roles and responsibilities of information security governance, as discussed in our next topic.

The responsibility of information security governance

The responsibility for information security governance primarily resides with the **board of directors** and **senior management**. Information security governance is a subset of the overall enterprise governance. The board of directors is required to make security an important part of governance by way of monitoring key aspects of security. Senior management holds the responsibility to ensure that security aspects are integrated with business processes.

The involvement of senior management and the steering committee in discussions and in the approval of security projects indicates that the management is committed to aspects relating to security. Generally, a steering committee consists of senior officials from different departments. The role of an information security steering committee is to provide oversight on the security environment of the organization.

It is very important for a CISM aspirant to understand the steps for establishing the governance, as we will discuss in the next section.

Steps for establishing the governance

For effective governance, it should be established in a structured manner. A CISM aspirant should understand the following steps for establishing governance:

1. First, determine the **objectives** of an information security program. Most often, these objectives are derived from risk management and the acceptable level of risk that you are willing to take. One example of an objective for a bank may be that the system should always be available for customers – that is, there should be *zero* downtime. Information security objectives must also align with and be guided by the organization's business objectives.

2. The next step is that the information security manager develops a **strategy** and **requirements** based on these objectives. The security manager is required to conduct a gap analysis and identify the strategy to move to the desired state of security from its current state of security. The desired state of security is also termed as the **security objectives**. This gap analysis becomes the basis for the strategy.

3. The final step is to create the road map and identify specific actionable steps to achieve the security objectives. The security manager needs to consider various factors such as time limits, resource availability, the security budget, laws and regulations, and other relevant factors.

These specific actions are implemented by way of security policies, standards, and procedures.

Governance framework

The **governance framework** is a structure or outline that supports the implementation of the information security strategy. They provide the best practices for a structured security program. Frameworks are a flexible structure that any organization can adopt as per their environment and its requirements. Governance frameworks such as **COBIT** and **ISO 27000** are both examples of widely accepted and implemented frameworks for security governance.

Let's look a bit closer at an example of information security governance in the next section.

The aim of information security governance

Information security governance is a subset of the overall **enterprise governance** of an organization. The same framework should be used for both enterprise governance and information security governance for better integration between the two.

The following are the objectives of information security governance:

- To ensure that security initiatives are aligned with the business's strategy and support organizational objectives.
- To optimize security investments and ensure the high-value delivery of business processes.
- To monitor the security processes to ensure that security objectives are achieved.
- To integrate and align the activities of all assurance functions for effective and efficient security measures.
- To ensure that residual risks are well within acceptable limits. This gives comfort to the management.

We will now go through the key aspects from the perspective of the CISM exam, and in our next topic, we will discuss important aspects of GRC. A CISM aspirant should understand why it is important to integrate all GRC functions.

Key aspects from the CISM exam perspective

The following are some of the key aspects from the CISM exam perspective:

Question	Possible answer
Which approach (that is, top-down or bottom-up) is more effective for governance?	In a top-down approach, policies, procedures, and goals are finalized by senior management, and hence policies and procedures are directly aligned with business objectives. A bottom-up approach may not directly address management priorities. The effectiveness of governance is best ensured by a top-down approach.
What is the important aspect from a senior management perspective in an information security strategy?	Business priorities, objectives, and goals.
What is a governance framework?	A governance framework is a structure that provides the outline to support the processes and methods.

Table 1.1 – Key aspects from the CISM exam perspective

Questions

1. The effectiveness of information security governance is best indicated by which of the following?

    A. Security projects are discussed and approved by a steering committee.

    B. Security training is mandatory for all executive-level employees.

    C. A security training module is available on the intranet for all employees.

    D. Patches are tested before deployment.

    Answer: A. Security projects are discussed and approved by a steering committee.

    Explanation: The involvement of a steering committee in the discussion and approval of security projects indicates that the management is committed to security governance. The other options are not as significant as option *A*.

2. An information security governance model is most likely to be impacted by which of the following?

    A. The number of workstations.

    B. The geographical spread of business units.

    C. The complexity of the organizational structure.

    D. The information security budget.

    Answer: C. The complexity of the organizational structure.

    Explanation: The information security governance model is primarily impacted by the complexity of the organizational structure. The organizational structure includes the organization's objectives, vision and mission, hierarchy structure, leadership structure, different function units, different product lines, and other relevant factors. The other options are not as significant as option *C*.

3. Which of the following is the first step in implementing information security governance?

    A. Employee training.

    B. The development of security policies.

    C. The development of security architecture.

    D. The availability of an incident management team.

    Answer: B. The development of security policies.

    Explanation: Security policies indicate the intent of the management. Based on these policies, the security architecture and various procedures are designed.

4. Which of the following factors primarily drives information security governance?

    A. Technology requirements.

    B. Compliance requirements.

    C. The business strategy.

    D. Financial constraints.

    Answer: C. The business strategy.

    Explanation: Information security governance should support the business strategy. Security must be aligned with business objectives. The other options are not a primary driver of information security governance.

5. Which of the following is the responsibility of the information security governance steering committee?

    A. To manage the information security team.

    B. To design content for security training.

    C. To prioritize the information security projects.

    D. To provide access to critical systems.

    Answer: C. To prioritize the information security projects.

    Explanation: One of the important responsibilities of a steering committee is to discuss, approve, and prioritize information security projects and to ensure that they are aligned with the goals and objectives of the enterprise.

6. Which of the following is the first step of information security governance?

    A. To design security procedures and guidelines.

    B. To develop a security baseline.

    C. To define the security strategy.

    D. To develop security policies.

    Answer: C. To define the security strategy.

    Explanation: The first step is to adopt the security strategy. The next step is to develop security policies based on this strategy. The step after this is to develop security procedures and guidelines based on the security policies.

7. Which of the following is the most important factor for an information security governance program?

   A. To align with the organization's business strategy.

   B. To be derived from a globally accepted risk management framework.

   C. To be able to address regulatory compliance.

   D. To promote a risk-aware culture.

   Answer: A. To align with the organization's business strategy.

   Explanation. The most important objective of an information security governance program is to ensure that the information security strategy is in alignment with the strategic goals and objectives of the enterprise. The other options are secondary factors.

8. Which of the following is effective governance best indicated by?

   A. An approved security architecture.

   B. A certification from an international body.

   C. Frequent audits.

   D. An established risk management program.

   Answer: D. An established risk management program.

   Explanation: An effective and efficient risk management program is a key element of effective governance. The other options are not as significant as an established risk management program.

9. Which of the following is the effectiveness of governance best ensured by?

   A. The use of a bottom-up approach.

   B. Initiatives by the IT department.

   C. A compliance-oriented approach.

   D. The use of a top-down approach.

   Answer: D. The use of a top-down approach.

   Explanation: In a top-down approach, policies, procedures, and goals are set by senior management, and as a result, the policies and procedures are directly aligned with the business objectives. A bottom-up approach may not directly address management priorities. Initiatives by the IT department and a compliance-oriented approach are not as significant as the use of a top-down approach.

10. What is the prime responsibility of the information security manager in the implementation of security governance?

A. To design and develop the security strategy.

B. To allocate a budget for the security strategy.

C. To review and approve the security strategy.

D. To train the end users.

Answer: A. To design and develop the security strategy.

Explanation: The prime responsibility of the information security manager is to develop the security strategy based on the business objectives in coordination with the business process owner. The review and approval of the security strategy is the responsibility of the steering committee and senior management. The security manager is not directly required to train the end users. The budget allocation is the responsibility of senior management.

11. What is the most important factor when developing information security governance?

A. To comply with industry benchmarks.

B. To comply with the security budget.

C. To obtain a consensus from the business functions.

D. To align with organizational goals.

Answer: D. To align with organizational goals.

Explanation: The objective of the security governance is to support the objectives of the business. The most important factor is to align with organizational objectives and goals. The other options are secondary factors.

12. What is the prime objective of GRC:

A. To synchronize and align the organization's assurance functions.

B. To address the requirements of the information security policy.

C. To address the requirements of regulations.

D. To design low-cost a security strategy.

Answer: A. To synchronize and align the organization's assurance functions.

Explanation: The concept of GRC is an effort to synchronize and align the assurance activities across the organization for greater efficiency and effectiveness. The other options can be considered secondary objectives.

13. What organizational areas are the main focus for GRC?

    A. Marketing and risk management.

    B. IT, finance, and legal.

    C. Risk and audit.

    D. Compliance and information security.

    Answer: B. IT, finance, and legal.

    Explanation: Though a GRC program can be applied in any function of the organization, it is mostly focused on IT, finance, and legal areas. Financial GRC focuses on effective risk management and compliance for finance processes. IT GRC focuses on IT processes. Legal GRC focuses on the overall enterprise-level regulatory compliance. GRC is majorly focused on IT, finance, and legal processes to ensure that regulatory requirements are adhered to and risks are appropriately addressed.

14. What is the most effective way to build an information security governance program?

    A. To align the requirements of the business with an information security framework.

    B. To understand the objectives of the business units.

    C. To address regulatory requirements.

    D. To arrange security training for all managers.

    Answer: B. To understand the objectives of the business units.

    Explanation: The information security governance program will not be effective if it is not able to address the requirements of the business units. The objective of the business units can be best understood by reviewing their processes and functions. Option *A* is not correct, as security requirements should be aligned with the business and not the other way round. Options *C* and *D* are not as significant as option *B*.

15. What is the main objective of information security governance?

    A. To ensure the adequate protection of information assets.

    B. To provide assurance to the management about information security.

    C. To support complex IT infrastructure.

    D. To optimize the security strategy to support the business objectives.

Answer: D. To optimize the security strategy to support the business objectives.

Explanation: The objective of security governance is to set the direction to ensure that the business objectives are achieved. Unless the information security strategy is aligned with the business objectives, the other options will not offer any value.

16. The security manager noticed inconsistencies in the system configuration. What is the most likely reason for this?

    A. Documented procedures are not available.

    B. Ineffective governance.

    C. Inadequate training.

    D. Inappropriate standards.

    Answer: B. Ineffective governance.

    Explanation: Governance is the process of oversight to ensure the availability of effective and efficient processes. A lack of procedures, training, and standards is a sign of ineffective governance.

17. What is an information security framework best described as?

    A. A framework that provides detailed processes and methods.

    B. A framework that provides required outputs.

    C. A framework that provides structure and guidance.

    D. A framework that provides programming inputs.

    Answer: C. A framework that provides structure and guidance.

    Explanation: A framework is a structure intended to support the processes and methods. They provide outlines and basic structure rather than detailed processes and methods. Frameworks are generally not intended to provide programming inputs.

18. What is the main reason for integrating information security governance into business activities?

    A. To allow the optimum utilization of security resources.

    B. To standardize the processes.

    C. To support operational processes.

    D. To address operational risks.

    Answer: D. To address operational risks.

Explanation: The main objective of integrating the security aspect in business processes is to address operational risks. The other options may be considered secondary benefits.

19. Which of the following is the most important attribute of an effective information security governance framework?

    A. A well-defined organizational structure with necessary resources and defined responsibilities.

    B. The availability of the organization's policies and guidelines.

    C. The business objectives support the information security strategy.

    D. Security guidelines supporting regulatory requirements.

    Answer: A. A well-defined organizational structure with necessary resources and defined responsibilities.

    Explanation: The most important attribute is a well-defined organizational structure that minimizes any conflicts of interest. This ensures better governance. Options *B* and *D* are important aspects, but option *A* is more critical. Option *C* is not correct, as the security strategy supports the business objectives, and not the other way round.

20. What is the most effective method to use to develop an information security program?

    A. A standard.

    B. A framework.

    C. A process.

    D. A model.

    Answer: B. A framework.

    Explanation: A framework is the most suitable method for developing an information security program as they are more flexible in adoption. Some of the common frameworks include ISO 27001 and COBIT. Standards, processes, and models are not as flexible as frameworks.

Understanding governance, risk management, and compliance

GRC is a term used to align and integrate the processes of governance, risk management, and compliance. GRC emphasizes that governance should be in place for effective risk management and the enforcement of compliance.

Governance, risk management, and compliance are three related aspects that help to achieve the organization's objectives. GRC aims to lay down operations for more effective organizational processes and avoiding wasteful overlaps. Each of these three disciplines impacts the organizational technologies, people, processes, and information. If governance, risk management, and compliance activities are handled independently of each other, it may result in a considerable amount of duplication and a waste of resources. The integration of these three functions helps to streamline the assurance activities of an organization by addressing the overlapping and duplicated GRC activities.

Though a GRC program can be applied in any function of the organization, it is mostly focused on the financial, IT, and legal areas.

Financial GRC focuses on effective risk management and compliance for finance processes. **IT GRC** focuses on information technology processes. **Legal GRC** focuses on the overall enterprise-level regulatory compliance.

GRC is an ever-evolving concept, and a security manager should understand the current state of GRC in their organization and determine how to ensure its continuous improvement.

Key aspects from the CISM exam perspective

The following are some of the key aspects from a CISM exam perspective:

Question	Possible answer
What is the main objective of implementing GRC procedures?	• To improve risk management processes by integrating various assurance-related activities. • To synchronize and align an organization's assurance functions.
What organizational areas are the main focus of GRC?	IT, finance, and legal.

Table 1.2 – Key aspects from the CISM exam perspective

Questions

1. Which of the following is the main objective of implementing GRC procedures?

    A. To minimize the governance cost.

    B. To improve risk management.

    C. To synchronize security initiatives.

    D. To ensure regulatory compliance.

    Answer: B. To improve risk management.

    Explanation: GRC is implemented by integrating interrelated control activities across the organization for improving risk management activities. The other options are secondary objectives.

2. What is the prime objective of GRC?

    A. To synchronize and align the organization's assurance functions.

    B. To address the requirements of the information security policy.

    C. To address the requirements of regulations.

    D. To design a low-cost security strategy.

    Answer: A. To synchronize and align the organization's assurance functions.

    Explanation: The concept of GRC is an effort to synchronize and align the assurance activities across the organization for greater efficiency and effectiveness. The other options can be considered secondary objectives.

Discovering the maturity model

CISM aspirants are expected to understand the basic details of a **maturity model**. A maturity model is a tool that helps the organization to assess the current effectiveness of a process and to determine what capabilities they need to improve their performance.

Capability maturity models (**CMMs**) are useful to determine the maturity level of governance processes. The following list defines the different maturity levels of an organization:

*   **Level 0: Incomplete**: On this level, the process is not implemented or does not achieve its intended purpose.

*   **Level 1: Performed**: On this level, the process can achieve its intended purpose.

*   **Level 2: Managed**: On this level, the process can achieve its intended purpose. Also, the process is appropriately planned, monitored, and controlled.

- **Level 3: Established**: Apart from the Level 2 process, there is a well-defined, documented, and established process to manage the process.

- **Level 4: Predictable**: On this level, the process is predictable and operates within defined parameters and limits to achieve its intended purpose.

- **Level 5: Optimized**: This is the level at which the process is continuously improved to meet the current as well as projected goals.

The CMM indicates a scale of *0* to *5* based on process maturity level, and it is the most common method applied by organizations to measure their existing state and then to determine the desired one.

Maturity models identify the gaps between the current state of the governance process and the desired state to help the organization to determine the necessary remediation steps for improvement. A maturity model requires continuous improvement in the governance framework. It requires continuous evaluation, monitoring, and improvement to move towards the desired state from the current state.

Key aspects from the CISM exam perspective

The following are some of the key aspects from an exam perspective:

Question	Possible answer
Which models are used to determine the extent and level of processes?	• The maturity model • Process performance and capability models
What is the best way to determine the continuous improvement of the risk management process?	The adoption of the maturity model.

Table 1.3 – Key aspects from the CISM exam perspective

Questions

1. What is the most important factor for the development of a maturity model-based information security governance framework?

    A. Continuous evaluation, monitoring, and improvement.

    B. The return on technology investment.

    C. Continuous risk mitigation.

    D. Continuous **key risk indicator** (**KRI**) monitoring.

Answer: A. Continuous evaluation, monitoring, and improvement.

Explanation: The maturity model requires continuous improvement in the governance framework. It requires continuous evaluation, monitoring, and improvement to move towards the desired state from the current state. The other options are not as significant as option *A*.

2.   What best indicates the level of information security governance?

A. A defined maturity model.

B. The size of the security team.

C. The availability of policies and procedures.

D. The number of security incidents.

Answer: A. A defined maturity model.

Explanation: A defined maturity model will be the best indicator to determine the level of security governance. The maturity model indicates the maturity of the governance processes on a scale of *0* to *5*, where *Level 0* indicates incomplete processes, and *Level 5* indicates optimized processes. The other options may not be as useful as the maturity model in determining the level of security.

3.   What is the most effective indicator of the level of security governance?

A. The annual loss expectancy.

B. The maturity level.

C. A risk assessment.

D. An external audit.

Answer: B. The maturity level.

Explanation: A defined maturity model will be the best indicator to determine the level of security governance. The maturity model indicates the maturity of the governance processes on a scale of *0* to *5*, where *Level 0* indicates incomplete processes, and *Level 5* indicates optimized processes. The other options may not be as useful as the maturity model in determining the level of security.

Getting to know the information security roles and responsibilities

It is very important to ensure that security-related *roles* and *responsibilities* are clearly defined, documented, and communicated throughout the organization. Each employee of the organization should be aware of their respective roles and responsibilities. Clearly defined roles also facilitate effective access rights management, as access is provided based on the respective job functions and job profiles of employees – that is, on a *need-to-know* basis only.

One of the simplest ways of defining roles and responsibilities in a business or organization is to form a matrix known as a **RACI chart**. This stands for **responsible, accountable, consulted**, and **informed**.

This chart indicates who is *responsible* for a particular function, who is *accountable* with regard to the function, who should be *consulted* about the function, and who should be *informed* about the particular function. Clearly defined RACI charts make the information security program more effective.

Let's look at the definitions of RACI in more detail:

- **Responsible**: This is the person who is required to execute a particular job function.
- **Accountable**: This is the person who is required to supervise a job function.
- **Consulted**: This is the person who gives suggestions and recommendations for executing a job function.
- **Informed**: This is the person who should be kept updated about the progress of the job function.

In the next section, I will take you through the various roles that are integral to information security.

Board of directors

The role of board members in information security is of utmost importance. Board members need to be aware of security-related **KRIs** that can impact the business objectives. The intent and objectives of information security governance must be communicated from the board level down.

The current status of key security risks should be tabled and discussed at board meetings. This helps the board to determine the effectiveness of the current security governance.

Another essential reason for the board of directors to be involved in security governance is **liability**. Most of the organization obtains specific insurance to make good on the financial liability of the organization in the event of a security incident. This type of insurance requires those bound by it to exercise due care in the discharge of their duties. Any negligence from the board in addressing the information security risk may make the insurance void.

Senior management

The role of **senior management** is to ensure that the intent and requirements of the board are implemented in an effective and efficient manner. Senior management is required to provide ongoing support to information security projects in terms of budgets, resources, and other infrastructure. In some instances, there may be disagreement between IT and security. In such cases, senior management can take a balanced view after considering performance, cost, and security. The role of senior management is to map and align the security objectives with the overall business objectives.

Business process owners

The role of a **business process owner** is to own the security-related risks impacting their business processes. They need to ensure that information security activities are aligned and support their respective business objectives. They need to monitor the effectiveness of security measures on an ongoing basis.

Steering committee

A **steering committee** comprises the senior management of an organization. The role of a steering committee is as follows:

- To ensure that security programs support the business objectives
- To evaluate and prioritize the security programs
- To evaluate emerging risk, security practices, and compliance-related issues

The roles, responsibilities, and scope of a steering committee should be clearly defined.

Chief information security officer

The **chief information security officer (CISO)** is a senior-level officer who has been entrusted with making security-related decisions and is responsible for implementing security programs. The CISO should be an executive-level officer directly reporting to the **chief executive officer (CEO)**. The role of the CISO is fundamentally a regulatory role, whereas the role of the CIO is to generally focus on IT performance.

Chief operating officer

The **chief operating officer (COO)** is the head of operational activities in the organization. Operational processes are reviewed and approved by the COO. The COO has a thorough knowledge of the business operations and objectives. The COO is most likely the sponsor for the implementation of security projects as they have a strong influence across the organization. **Sponsoring** means supporting the project financially or through products or services. Although the CISO should provide security advice and recommendations, the sponsor should be the COO for effective *ground-level* implementation.

Data custodian

The **data custodian** is a staff member who is entrusted with the safe custody of data. The data custodian is different from the **data owner**, though in some cases, both data custodian and data owner may be the same individual. A data custodian is responsible for managing the data on behalf of the data owner in terms of data backup, ensuring data integrity, and providing access to data for different individuals through the approval of the data owner. From a security perspective, a data custodian is responsible for ensuring that appropriate security measures are implemented and are consistent with organizational policy.

Communication channel

A well-defined **communication channel** is of utmost importance in the management of information security. A mature organization has dedicated systems to manage risk-related communication. This should be a two-way system, wherein management can reach all the employees and at the same time employees can reach a designated risk official to report identified risks. This will help in the timely reporting of events as well as to disseminate the security information. In the absence of an appropriate communication channel, the identification of events may be delayed.

Indicators of a security culture

The following list consists of some of the indicators of a successful security culture:

- The involvement of the information security department in business projects.
- The end users are aware of the identification and reporting of the incidents.
- There is an appropriate budget for information security programs.
- The employees are aware of their roles and responsibilities with regard to information security.

Understanding the roles and responsibilities as covered in this section will help the security manager to implement an effective security strategy.

Key aspects from the CISM exam perspective

The following are some of the key aspects from the CISM exam perspective:

Question	Possible answer
What is the best course of action when there is disagreement on security aspects between the IT team and the security team?	To refer the matter to senior management along with any necessary recommendations.
What is the immediate benefit of well-defined roles and responsibilities?	Better accountability.
Who has the ultimate responsibility for legal and regulatory requirements?	The board of directors and senior management.
What is the best way to prioritize information security projects?	Security projects should be assessed and prioritized based on their impact on the organization.
Who has the responsibility to enforce the access rights of employees?	The data custodian/security administrations.
What is the most important factor on which data retention policy is based?	The business requirements.
What is the prime responsibility of an information security manager?	To manage the risks to information assets.
Which models are used to determine the extent and level of processes?	<ul><li>The maturity model</li><li>The process performance and capability model</li></ul>

Question	Possible answer
What is the major concern if database administrators have access to **data base administrator** (**DBA**)-related logs?	The unauthorized modification of logs by the database administrator.
What is the main objective of integrating security-related roles and responsibilities?	To address the security gaps that exist between assurance functions.
What is the role of the information owner with regard to the data classification policy?	To determine the level of classification for their respective data.
What is the role of the information security manager with regard to the data classification policy?	To define and ratify the data classification process.
What is the best way to ensure that responsibilities are carried out?	Assign accountability.
Who is responsible for complying with the organization's security policies and standards?	• All organizational units • Every employee

Table 1.4 – Key aspects from the CISM exam perspective

Questions

1. The process of mapping job descriptions to relevant data access rights will help in adherence to which of the following security principles?

    A. The principle of accountability.

    B. The principle of proportionality.

    C. The principle of integration.

    D. The principle of the code of ethics.

    Answer: B. The principle of proportionality.

    Explanation: The principle of proportionality requires that the access should be proportionate to the criticality of the assets and access should be provided on a need-to-know basis. The principle of accountability is important for the mapping of job descriptions; however, people with access to data may not always be accountable. Options *C* and *D* are not directly relevant to mapping job descriptions.

2. The data custodian is primarily responsible for which of the following?

    A. Approving access to the data.

    B. The classification of assets.

    C. Enhancing the value of data.

    D. Ensuring all security measures are in accordance with organizational policy.

    Answer: D. Ensuring all security measures are in accordance with organizational policy.

    Explanation: The data custodian is responsible for ensuring that appropriate security measures are implemented and are consistent with organizational policy. The other options are not the responsibility of the data custodian.

3. In the case of a disagreement between the IT team and security team on a security aspect, the security manager should do which of the following?

    A. Refer the matter to an external third party for resolution.

    B. Request senior management to discontinue the relevant project immediately.

    C. Ask the IT team to accept the risk.

    D. Refer the matter to senior management along with any necessary recommendations.

    Answer: D. Refer the matter to senior management along with any necessary recommendations.

    Explanation: The best option for a security manager in this case is to highlight the issue to senior management. Senior management will be in the best position to take a decision after considering business as well security aspects.

4. Which of the following is an immediate benefit of having well-defined roles and responsibilities from an information security perspective?

    A. The adherence to security policies throughout the organization.

    B. Well-structured process flows.

    C. The implementation of **segregation of duties (SoD)**.

    D. Better accountability.

    Answer: D. Better accountability.

Explanation: Having clearly set out roles and responsibilities ensures better accountability, as individuals are aware of their key performance area and expected outcomes. The other options may be indirect benefits, but the only direct benefit is better accountability.

5.   What is the prime role of an information security manager in a data classification process?

A. To define and ratify the data classification process.

B. To map all data to different classification levels.

C. To provide data security, as per the classification.

D. To confirm that data is properly classified.

Answer: A. To define and ratify the data classification process.

Explanation: The primary role of an information security manager is to define the structure of data classification. They need to ensure that the data classification policy is consistent with the organization's risk appetite. The mapping of data as per the classification is the responsibility of the data owner. Providing security is the responsibility of the data custodian. Confirming proper classification may be the role of the information security manager or the information security auditor.

6.   Which of the following is the area of most concern for the information security manager?

A. That there are vacant positions in the information security department.

B. That the information security policy is approved by senior management.

C. That the steering committee only meets on a quarterly basis.

D. That security projects are reviewed and approved by the data center manager.

Answer: D. That security projects are reviewed and approved by the data center manager.

Explanation: Security projects should be approved by the steering committee consisting of senior management. The data center manager may not be in a position to ensure the alignment of security projects with the overall enterprise objectives. This will have an adverse impact on security governance. The approval of the security policy by senior management indicates good governance. Vacant positions are not a major concern. The steering committee meeting on a quarterly basis is also not an issue.

7. An information security manager should have a thorough understanding of business operations with a prime objective of which of the following?

A. Supporting organizational objectives.

B. Ensuring regulatory compliance.

C. Concentrating on high-risk areas.

D. Evaluating business threats.

Answer: A. Supporting organizational objectives.

Explanation: The main objective of the security manager having a thorough understanding of the business operations is to support the organization's objectives. The other options are specific actions to support the business objectives.

8. In a big multi-national organization, the best approach to identify security events is to do which of the following?

A. Conduct frequent audits of the business processes.

B. Deploy a firewall and **intrusion detection system (IDS)**.

C. Develop communication channels across the organization.

D. Conduct vulnerability assessments of new systems.

Answer: C. Develop communication channels across the organization.

Explanation: The best approach is to develop communication channels that will help in the timely reporting of events as well as to disseminate security information. The other options are good practices; however, without an appropriate communication channel, the identification of events may be delayed.

9. Legal and regulatory liability is the responsibility of which of the following?

A. The chief information security officer.

B. The head of legal.

C. The board of directors and senior management.

D. The steering committee.

Answer: C. The board of directors and senior management.

Explanation: The ultimate responsibility for compliance with legal and regulatory requirements is with the board of directors and senior management. The CISO, head of legal, and steering committee implement the directive of the board and senior management, but they are not individually liable for the failure of security.

10. What is the best way to gain support from senior management for information security projects?

   A. Lower the information security budget.

   B. Conduct a risk assessment.

   C. Highlight industry best practices.

   D. Design an information security policy.

   Answer: B. Conduct a risk assessment.

   Explanation: The best way to gain the support of senior management is to conduct a risk assessment and present it to management in the form of an impact analysis. A risk assessment will help management to understand areas of concern. The other options may be considered secondary factors.

11. Prioritization of information security projects should be best conducted based on which of the following?

   A. The turnaround time of the project.

   B. The impact on the organization's objectives.

   C. The budget of the security project.

   D. The resource requirements for the project.

   Answer: B. The impact on the organization's objectives.

   Explanation: Security projects should be assessed and prioritized based on their impact on the organization. The other options are secondary factors.

12. Who is responsible for enforcing the access rights of employees?

   A. The process owner.

   B. The data owner.

   C. The steering committee.

   D. The security administrators.

   Answer: D. The security administrators.

   Explanation: The security administrators are custodians of the data and they need to ensure that data is in safe custody. They are responsible for enforcing and implementing security measures in accordance with the information security policy. The data owner and process owner are responsible for classifying the data and approving access rights. However, they do not enforce and implement the security controls. The steering committee is not responsible for enforcement.

13. Who is responsible for information classification?

    A. The data administrator.

    B. The information security manager.

    C. The information system auditor.

    D. The data owner.

    Answer: D. The data owner.

    Explanation: The data owner has responsibility for the classification of their data in accordance with the organization's data classification policy. The data administrator is required to implement security controls as per the security policy. The security manager and system auditor oversee the data classification and handling process to ensure conformance to the policy.

14. What is the data retention policy primarily based on?

    A. Industry practices.

    B. Business requirements.

    C. Regulatory requirements.

    D. Storage requirements.

    Answer: B. Business requirements.

    Explanation: The primary basis for defining the data retention period is the business requirements. Business requirements will consider any legal and regulatory aspects. If its data is not retained as per business needs, it may have a negative impact on the business objectives.

15. What is the most important security aspect for a multi-national organization?

    A. The local security programs should comply with the corporate data privacy policy.

    B. The local security program should comply with the data privacy policy of the location where the data is collected.

    C. The local security program should comply with the data privacy policy of the country where the headquarters are located.

    D. Local security program should comply with industry best practices.

    Answer: B. The local security program should comply with the data privacy policy of the location where the data is collected.

Explanation: Data privacy laws are country-specific. It is very important to ensure adherence to local laws. The organization's privacy policy may not be able to address all the local laws and requirements. The organization's data privacy policy cannot supersede the local laws.

16. Ultimate accountability for the protection of sensitive data is with which of the following?

    A. The security administrators.

    B. The steering committee.

    C. The board of directors.

    D. The security manager.

    Answer: C. The board of directors.

    Explanation: The board of directors has the ultimate accountability for information security. The other options such as the security administrators, steering committee, and security managers are responsible for implementing, enforcing, and monitoring security controls as per the directive of the board.

17. The most likely authority to sponsor the implementation of new security infrastructure for business processes is which of the following?

    A. The CISO.

    B. The COO.

    C. The head of legal.

    D. The data protection officer.

    Answer: B. The COO.

    Explanation: The chief operating officer is the head of operational activities in the organization. Operational processes are reviewed and approved by the COO. The COO has the most thorough knowledge of the business operations and objectives. The COO is most likely the sponsor for the implementation of security projects as they have a strong influence across the organization. Sponsoring means supporting the project financially or through products or services. Although the CISO should provide security advice and recommendations, the sponsor should be the COO for effective ground-level implementation.

18. Who should determine the requirements for access to data?

    A. The security officer.

    B. The data protection officer.

    C. The compliance officer.

    D. The business owner.

    Answer: D. The business owner.

    Explanation: The business owner needs to ensure that their data is appropriately protected, and access is provided on a need-to-know basis only. The security officer, data protection officer, and compliance officer can advise on security aspects, but they do not have final responsibility.

19. The responsibility for establishing information security controls in an application resides with which of the following?

    A. The information security steering committee.

    B. The data owner.

    C. The system auditor.

    D. The system owner.

    Answer: B. The data owner.

    Explanation: The data owner is responsible for determining the level of security controls for the data, as well as for the application that stores the data. The system owner is generally responsible for platforms rather than applications or data. The system auditor is responsible for evaluating the security controls. The steering committee consists of senior-level officials and is responsible for aligning the security strategy with the business objectives.

20. The information security manager observes that not enough details are documented in the recovery plan and this may prevent meeting the recovery time objective. Which of the following compensates for the lack of details in the recovery plan and ensures that the recovery time objective is met?

    A. Establishing more than one operation center.

    B. Delegating authority for the recovery execution.

    C. Outsourcing the recovery process.

    D. Taking incremental backups of the database.

    Answer: B. Delegating authority for recovery execution.

Explanation: During an incident, considerable time is taken up in escalation procedures, as decisions need to be made at each management level. The delegation of authority for the recovery execution makes the recovery process faster and more effective. However, the scope of the recovery delegation must be assessed beforehand and appropriately documented. Having multiple operation centers is too expensive to implement. Outsourcing is not a feasible option. Incremental backups do facilitate faster backups; however, they generally increase the time needed to restore the data.

21. The effectiveness of SoD is best ensured by which of the following?

    A. Implementing strong password rules.

    B. Making available a security awareness poster on the intranet.

    C. Frequent information security training.

    D. Reviewing access privileges when an operator's role changes.

    Answer: D. Reviewing access privileges when an operator's role changes.

    Explanation: In the absence of access privilege reviews, there is the risk that a single staff member can acquire excess operational capabilities. This will defeat the objective of SoD. In order to maintain the effectiveness of SoD, it is important to review access privileges more frequently and more specifically when an operator's role changes.

22. What is the prime responsibility of an information security manager?

    A. To manage the risk to information assets.

    B. To implement the security configuration for IT assets.

    C. To conduct disaster recovery testing.

    D. To close identified vulnerabilities.

    Answer: A. To manage the risk to information assets.

    Explanation: The prime responsibility of an information security manager is to evaluate and manage the information security risk by involving risk owners. Implementing the security configuration is the responsibility of the asset owner. Disaster recovery testing should be conducted by the process owner, and the closing of vulnerabilities is the responsibility of the asset owner.

23. To determine the extent of sound processes, the maturity model is used. Another approach is to use which of the following?

    A. The Monte Carlo method.

    B. Process performance and capabilities.

    C. Vulnerability assessments.

    D. Risk analysis.

    Answer: B. Process performance and capabilities.

    Explanation: Process performance and capabilities provide a detailed perspective of the maturity levels, just like the maturity model. The other options will not help to determine the level of maturity of the process. The Monte Carlo method is a risk assessment method that uses simulations.

24. Information system access should be primarily authorized by which of the following?

    A. The information owner.

    B. The system auditor.

    C. The CISO.

    D. The system administrator.

    Answer: A. The information owner.

    Explanation: The information owner is ultimately responsible for the protection of their data. The information owner is the best person to know the criticality of the data and who should have access to the data. Therefore, information system access should be primarily authorized by the information owner.

25. The information security manager observed that the incident log is stored on a production database server. Which of the following is a major concern?

    A. The unavailability of log details if the server crashes.

    B. The unauthorized modification of logs by the database administrator.

    C. Log capturing makes the transaction process slow.

    D. Critical information may not be captured in the log files.

    Answer: B. The unauthorized modification of logs by the database administrator.

Explanation: The database administrator will have access to logs if they are stored in the database server. The database administrator can modify or delete the log entries. This is a major cause of concern. Backup of the logs will address the issue of server crashes. Log capturing may not always impact transaction processing. If critical information is not captured in logs, it is a design failure and has nothing to do with log entries stored in the production database. The database administrator should not have access to logs related to the database.

26. Appointing a CISO indicates which of the following?

    A. The organization wants to enhance the role of senior management.

    B. The organization is committed to its responsibility for information security.

    C. The board of directors wants to pass on their accountability.

    D. The organization wants to improve its technology architecture.

    Answer: B. The organization is committed to its responsibility for information security.

    Explanation: Appointing a CISO indicates that the organization wants to have a clear line of responsibility for information security. Information security is one of the focus areas for the organization. Having a CISO does not impact the role of senior management. Even if the CISO is appointed, accountability lies with the board of directors. The CISO is generally not accountable for technology projects.

27. The main objective of integrating security-related roles and responsibilities is which of the following?

    A. To address the security gaps that exist between assurance functions.

    B. To address the unavailability of manpower.

    C. To address the gap in business continuity and disaster recovery.

    D. To address the complications in system development processes.

    Answer: A. To address the security gaps that exist between assurance functions.

    Explanation: Whenever there are shared responsibilities for information security, gaps tend to exist. Integrating the roles and responsibilities is the best way to address these gaps and ensure consistent risk management. The other options are secondary factors.

28. Which of the following is the best compensating control when the same employee is responsible for updating servers, maintaining the access control, and reviewing the logs?

    A. To verify that only approved changes are made.

    B. To conduct penetration tests.

    C. To conduct risk assessments.

    D. To conduct reviews of log files by the manager.

    Answer: A. To verify that only approved changes are made.

    Explanation: In the absence of SoD, the best compensatory control is to ensure that only approved changes are made by the employee. This verification can either be done for all cases or on a sample basis depending on the risk involved. The review of logs by the manager may not be meaningful as an employee can manipulate the logs and hide activities from the supervisor. Penetration tests and risk assessments may not be able to detect the unauthorized activities.

29. What is the responsibility of the information owner when complying with the information classification scheme?

    A. To implement security measures to protect their data.

    B. To determine the level of classification for their data.

    C. To arrange backups of their data.

    D. To delegate the processes of information classification to the system administrator.

    Answer: B. To determine the level of classification for their data.

    Explanation: The information owner is required to determine the level of classification for their respective data. Based on its classification, the system administrator implements the required security measures and data backups. The information owner may delegate the process of classification to some other responsible employee but not to the system administrator.

30. The effectiveness of the organization's security measures is the final responsibility of which of the following?

    A. The security administrator.

    B. The CISO.

    C. Senior management.

    D. The information security auditor.

    Answer: C. Senior management.

    Explanation: Senior management has the final responsibility for the effectiveness of the organization's security measures. Although the authority to implement, monitor, and evaluate the security measures is delegated to the security administrator, CISO, and the information security auditor, the responsibility cannot be delegated. The final responsibility rests with senior management.

31. What is the best way to ensure that responsibilities are carried out?

    A. Signed non-disclosure agreements.

    B. Heavy penalties for non-compliance.

    C. Assigned accountability.

    D. Documented policies.

    Answer: C. Assigned accountability.

    Explanation: If accountability is properly assigned and made known to the individuals, individuals will be more proactive and concerned about their responsibilities, and this will ensure that duties are properly carried out.

32. Who is responsible for complying with the organization's security policies and standards?

    A. The CISO.

    B. Senior management.

    C. The compliance officer.

    D. All organizational units.

    Answer: D. All organizational units.

    Explanation: Every employee is required to comply with security policies and standards, as applicable to their performance areas. Though CISO and senior management monitor the level of compliance, all organizational units should adhere to policies and standards.

33. Continuous improvement of the risk management process is most likely ensured by which of the following?

    A. The regular review of implemented security controls.

    B. Implementing an information classification policy.

    C. The adoption of a maturity model.

    D. Regular audits of risk management processes.

    Answer: C. The adoption of a maturity model.

    Explanation: A maturity model like the CMM can be used to determine the maturity level of the risk management process from *Level 0* (that is, initial) to *Level 5* (that is, optimized). The organization can know where it falls and can gradually move towards higher levels and thus improve its risk management process. The other options are secondary factors.

34. Information security is the responsibility of which of the following?

    A. All personnel.

    B. IT personnel.

    C. Security personnel.

    D. Operational personnel.

    Answer: A. All personnel.

    Explanation: It is the responsibility of all personnel to adhere to the security requirements of the organization.

35. Who should security policies be finally approved by?

    A. Operation managers.

    B. The CISO.

    C. Senior management.

    D. The **chief technical officer (CTO)**

    Answer: C. Senior management.

    Explanation: Senior management is in the best position to understand the key business objectives and how they should be protected by way of policies and procedures. Other officials (for example, the operation manager, CISO, and CTO) may provide necessary inputs, but final approval should be provided by senior management.

36. Confidentiality of information can be best ensured by which of the following?

    A. Implementing an information classification policy.

    B. Implementing SoD.

    C. Implementing the principle of least privilege.

    D. Implementing information security audits.

    Answer: C. Implementing the principle of least privilege.

    Explanation: The most effective method to protect the confidentiality of information assets is to follow the principle of least privilege. The principle of least privilege ensures that access is provided only on a need-to-know basis and it should be restricted for all other users. The other options are good measures; however, in the absence of the principle of least privilege, they may not be effective.

Finding out about the governance of third-party relationships

In today's world, most organizations are heavily reliant on a **third party** to achieve business objectives. The primary reason to obtain the services of a third party is to avail yourself of expert services in a cost-effective manner. These third parties can be in the form of a **service provider**, **trading partners**, **group companies**, or others.

These third parties are connected to the systems of the organization and have access to the data and other resources of the organization. To protect the organization, it is very important for an information security manager to assess the risk of such third-party relationships and ensure relevant controls are in place.

Policies and requirements of information security should be developed before the creation of any third-party relationship.

Also, the security manager should understand the following challenges of third-party relationships:

- The cultural differences between an organization and the service provider.
- Technology incompatibilities.
- The business continuity arrangements of the service provider may not have aligned to the requirements of the organization.
- Differences in **incident management processes**.
- Differences in **disaster recovery capabilities**.

Effective governance is highly dependent on the culture of the organization. Let's discuss this in more detail in our next topic.

The culture of an organization

The culture of an organization and its service provider is the most important factor that determines the implementation of an *information security program*. The culture of the organization influences *risk appetite*, that is, the willingness to take risks. This will have a significant influence on the design and implementation of the information security program. A culture that favors taking risks will have a different implementation approach to a culture that is risk-averse.

Cultural differences and their impact on data security are generally not considered during security reviews. Different cultures have different perspectives on what information is considered sensitive and how it should be handled. This cultural practice may not be consistent with an organization's requirements.

Compliance with laws and regulations

An information security manager should be cautious about adherence to laws and regulations. Laws and regulations should be addressed to the extent that they impact the organization.

The process should be in place to scan all the new regulations and determine the applicability of regulations to the organization.

The information security manager is required to determine the processes and activities that may be impacted and whether existing controls are adequate to address the new regulations. If not, then further controls should be implemented to address the new regulations.

Departments affected by the new regulations are in the best position to determine the impact of new regulatory requirements on their processes and the best way to address them.

The information security manager is required to assess the impact of privacy law on business processes. The prime focus of privacy law is to protect the identifiable personal data held by an organization.

Key aspects from the CISM exam perspective

The following are some of the key aspects from the CISM exam perspective:

Question	Possible answer
Who should determine the control processes for any new regulatory requirements?	The affected department (they are in the best position to determine the impact of new regulatory requirements on their processes and the best way to address the same).
What is the first step of an information security manager who noticed a new regulation impacting one of the organizations' processes?	• To determine the processes and activities that may be impacted • To assess whether existing controls meet the regulation
What is the major focus of privacy law?	To protect identifiable personal data.
Which factors have the greatest impact on the security strategy?	Organizational goals and objectives.

Table 1.5 – Key aspects from the CISM exam perspective

Questions

1. What should be the first step of the information security manager when an organization plans to implement a **bring your own device (BYOD)** policy for mobile devices?

    A. To ask management to stop the BYOD policy implementation, stating the associated risk.

    B. To prepare a business case for the implementation of BYOD controls.

    C. To make the end users aware of BYOD risks.

    D. To determine the information security strategy for BYOD.

    Answer: D. To determine the information security strategy for BYOD.

    Explanation: The first step for the information security manager is to determine a strategy to protect the organization from the risks of BYOD. Option *A* is not feasible, as the role of the security manager is to facilitate business processes by mitigating the risk. Options *B* and *C* will be based on the security strategy.

2.   The factor that influences the design and implementation of the information security program the most is which of the following?

A. Types of vulnerabilities.

B. The culture of the organization.

C. The business objectives.

D. The complexity of the business.

Answer: B. The culture of the organization.

Explanation: The culture of the organization influences the risk appetite which in turn has a significant influence on the design and implementation of the information security program. The business objective is important to prioritize the risk treatment. But the culture of the organization will have a major influence on the design and implementation of the security program. A pro-risk culture will have a different implementation approach to a risk-averse culture.

3.   Which of the following will have the biggest influence while planning for business record retention?

A. Potential changes in storage capacity.

B. Potential changes in regulatory requirements.

C. Potential changes in the business strategy.

D. Potential changes in the application systems and media.

Answer: D. Potential changes in the application systems and media.

Explanation: The type and nature of the application systems and media and their capability to read and interpret different types of data formats is the most important factor for planning record retention. New application systems may not be able to read and interpret data generated by earlier applications. This is a major risk.

4.   New regulatory requirements impacting information security will mostly come from which of the following?

A. The chief legal officer.

B. The chief audit officer.

C. Affected departments.

D. Senior management.

Answer: C. Affected departments.

Explanation: Departments affected by the new regulations are most likely to raise the requirements. They are in the best position to determine the impact of new regulatory requirements on their processes and the best way to address them.

5. Due to changes in the business strategy, certain information now no longer supports the purpose of the business. What should be done with this information?

A. It should be analyzed under the retention policy.

B. It should have restricted access.

C. It should be frequently backed up.

D. It should be evaluated by a business impact analysis.

Answer: A. It should be analyzed under the retention policy.

Explanation: From an information security perspective, such data should be analyzed under the retention policy, and then it should be determined whether the data is required to be maintained for business or regulatory reasons. If the data is no longer required, it should be removed in a secure manner. The other options are not sensible for data if it is of no use.

6. Primarily, the requirements of an information security program are based on which of the following?

A. The IT policy.

B. The desired outcomes.

C. The management perceptions.

D. The security strategy.

Answer: B. The desired outcomes.

Explanation: The desired outcomes should dictate the input requirements of an information security program. It is the responsibility of the security manager to ensure that the program is implemented in such a way that it achieves the desired outcome. The security strategy should also be based on the desired outcomes of the information security program.

7. The first step of an information security manager who noticed a new regulation impacting one of the organizations' processes should be which of the following?

A. To pass on responsibility to the process owner for compliance.

B. To survey the industry practices.

C. To assess whether existing controls meet the regulation.

D. To update the IT security policy.

Answer: C. To assess whether existing controls meet the regulation.

Explanation: The first step is to determine whether existing controls are adequate to address the new regulation. If existing controls are adequate, the need to perform other options is not required.

8. Privacy laws are mainly focused on which of the following?

A. Big data analytics.

B. Corporate data.

C. Identity theft.

D. Identifiable personal data.

Answer: D. Identifiable personal data.

Explanation: The prime focus of privacy law is to protect identifiable personal data. Identity theft is one of the ways of misusing personal data. There can also be other consequences. If analytics are done on identifiable personal data, it could impact privacy only if this violates regulatory provisions.

9. The information security manager noticed a regulation that impacts the handling of sensitive data. They should first do which of the following?

A. Determine the processes and activities that may be impacted.

B. Present a risk treatment option to senior management.

C. Determine the cost of control.

D. Discuss the possible consequences with the process owner.

Answer: A. Determine the processes and activities that may be impacted.

Explanation: The very first step is to determine the processes and activities that may be impacted. Based on that, the security manager can do a risk assessment and determine the level of impact. The other options are subsequent steps.

10. The most important factor to consider while developing a control policy is which of the following?

    A. Protecting data.

    B. Protecting life.

    C. Protecting the business's reputation.

    D. Protecting the business objectives.

    Answer: B. Protecting life.

    Explanation: The most important consideration is to protect human life. For example, carbon dioxide fire extinguishers should be restricted for areas where employees are working. Also, electric door access should be set to fail open in case of fire. The other options are secondary factors.

11. The information security manager should address laws and regulations in which way?

    A. To the extent they impact the organization.

    B. To meet the certification standards.

    C. To address the requirements of policies.

    D. To reduce the cost of compliance.

    Answer: A. To the extent they impact the organization.

    Explanation: Laws and regulations should be addressed to the extent they impact the organization, irrespective of whether they are required for certification standards or the requirements of policies.

12. Which of the following is the most important consideration in the retention of business records?

    A. Strategic objectives

    B. Regulatory and legal requirements.

    C. Storage capacity.

    D. The level of controls implemented.

    Answer: B. Regulatory and legal requirements.

Explanation: Record retention should be primarily based on two factors: business requirements and legal requirements. If a record is required to be maintained for two years as per business requirements, and three years as per legal requirements, it should be maintained for three years. Organizations generally design their business requirements after considering the relevant laws and regulations.

13. What is the most important consideration for organizations involved in cross-border transactions?

    A. The capability of the IT architecture.

    B. The evolving data protection regulations.

    C. The cost of network bandwidth.

    D. The incident management process.

    Answer: B. The evolving data protection regulations.

    Explanation: Privacy laws vary from country to country and organizations must comply with the applicable laws from each country where their data is collected, processed, or stored. The other options are secondary factors.

14. What should be the next step for the board of directors when noticing new regulations impacting some of the organization's processes?

    A. Instruct the information security department for specific controls.

    B. Evaluate various solutions to address the new regulations.

    C. Require management to report on compliance.

    D. Evaluate the cost of implementing new controls.

    Answer: C. Require management to report on compliance.

    Explanation: The board of directors has oversight responsibilities, and they should monitor compliance. The board would not be directly involved in evaluating various alternatives and the cost of implementation. Also, the board will not directly instruct the information security department.

15. Which of the following factors is the most difficult to estimate?

    A. Vulnerabilities in the system.

    B. Legal and regulatory requirements.

    C. Compliance timelines.

    D. The threat landscape.

    Answer: D. The threat landscape.

Explanation: A *threat* is something that *exploits* a vulnerability. Threat factors are not in the control of the organization. Examples of threat factors are hackers, fires, earthquakes, changes in the regulatory environment, and more. All of these factors are difficult to estimate and control. Other options are not as difficult to estimate as the threat landscape.

16. Which of the following is the risk that is likely to be most ignored during an onsite inspection of an offshore service provider?

    A. Cultural differences.

    B. Security controls.

    C. The network security.

    D. The documented IT policy.

    Answer: A. Cultural differences.

    Explanation: Cultural differences and their impact on data security are generally not considered during security reviews. Different cultures have different perspectives on what information is considered sensitive and how it should be handled. This cultural practice may not be consistent with the organization's requirements.

17. What does an organization's risk appetite mostly depend on?

    A. The threat landscape.

    B. The size of the information security team.

    C. The security strategy.

    D. The organization's culture.

    Answer: D. The organization's culture.

    Explanation: The culture of the organization determines the risk appetite of the organization. Pro-risk organizations generally tend to have more of a risk appetite as compared to risk-averse organizations. Other options do not directly impact the risk appetite.

18. What factor has the greatest impact on the security strategy?

    A. IT technology.

    B. System vulnerabilities.

    C. Network bandwidth.

    D. Organizational goals.

Answer: D. Organizational goals.

Explanation: The prime objective of a security strategy is to facilitate and support organizational goals. The other options are secondary factors.

19. What is the most important consideration for designing a security policy for a multi-national organization operating in different countries?

    A. The cost of implementation.

    B. The level of security awareness of the employees.

    C. The culture of the different countries.

    D. The capability of the security tools.

    Answer: C. The culture of the different countries.

    Explanation: Culture plays an important role for designing security policies. Different countries have different cultures and these impact their local legal requirements. The organization needs to ensure that the local laws of all the countries are appropriately addressed. Other options are not as significant as the local culture.

20. What should the next step be for the information security manager when noticing new regulations impacting some of the organization's processes?

    A. To identify whether the current controls are adequate.

    B. To update the audit department about the new regulations.

    C. To present a business case to senior management.

    D. To implement the requirements of new regulations.

    Answer: A. To identify whether the current controls are adequate.

    Explanation: The first step is to analyze and identify whether current controls are adequate. If current practice already adheres to the regulations, then there is no need to implement further controls.

21. What is the most important factor that determines the acceptable level of organizational standards?

    A. The current level of vulnerability.

    B. The risk appetite of the organization.

    C. IT policies and processes.

    D. The documented strategy.

    Answer: B. The risk appetite of the organization.

Explanation: The risk appetite is the level of willingness of the organization to take risks. It sets the boundary of acceptable risks. This would determine the acceptable limit for the organizational standards. The other options do not directly impact the acceptable level of organizational standards.

22. What is the most important factor for promoting a positive information security culture?

    A. Monitoring by an audit committee.

    B. High budgets for security initiatives.

    C. Collaboration across business lines.

    D. Frequent information security audits.

    Answer: C. Collaboration across business lines.

    Explanation: Collaboration across business lines is of utmost importance to promote a positive information security culture. This will ensure collective efforts toward common security goals. The other options are not as significant as collaboration across business lines.

Obtaining commitment from senior management

For the effective implementation of security governance, support and commitment from **senior management** is the most important prerequisite. A lack of high-level sponsorship will have an adverse impact on the effectiveness of security projects.

It is very important for the information security manager to gain support from senior management. The most effective way to gain this is to ensure that the security program continues to be aligned with and supports the business objectives. This is critical in gaining management support. Senior management is more concerned with the achievement of business objectives and will be keen to address all the risks impacting them.

Obtaining commitment from senior management is very important to ensure appropriate investment in information security, as we'll cover in the next section.

Information security investment

Investment should be able to provide value to the business. The primary driver for investment in an information security project is **value analysis** and a sound **business case**. To obtain approval for an information security budget, the budget should primarily include a **cost-benefit analysis**. Senior management is more interested in the benefit that is derived from the budget.

For example, as a security manager, if you request a budget of $5,000 for security investment, the senior management may not be convinced. But if you also project annualized savings of $10,000 against an investment of $5,000, the senior management may be more willing to invest.

Strategic alignment

Information security activities are said to have a **strategic alignment** when it supports the requirements of key business stakeholders. Information security should support the achievement of organizational objectives by minimizing business disruptions. The most effective way to enhance the senior management's commitment toward information security is to conduct a periodic review of the alignment between security and business goals. A discussion with key business stakeholders will give a correct picture of the alignment of security programs with business objectives.

A survey of the organization's management is the best way to determine whether the security programs support business objectives. Achieving strategic alignment means business process owners and managers believe that information security is effectively supporting their goals. If business management is not confident in the security programs, the information security manager should redesign the processes to provide value to the business.

Another aspect of determining the strategic alignment is to review the business **balanced scorecard**. A business scorecard contains important metrics from a business perspective. It will help to determine the alignment of the security goals with the business goals.

Key aspects from the CISM exam perspective

The following are some of the key aspects from the CISM exam perspective:

Question	Possible answer
What is the most important factor to be included in a budget note when obtaining approval from management?	Cost-benefit analysis.
What is the best way to gain support from senior management for security projects?	To explain to management the impact of security risks on key business objectives.
What is the primary driver for investment in information security projects?	Value analysis and a sound business case.

Table 1.6 – Key aspects from the CISM exam perspective

Questions

1. To obtain approval for information security budgets, what should a budget primarily include?

    A. A cost-benefit analysis.

    B. Industry benchmarks.

    C. The total cost of ownership.

    D. All the resources required by business units.

    Answer: A. A cost-benefit analysis.

    Explanation: Senior management is more interested in the overall business benefit derived from the security budget. The other options are important considerations when evaluating and approving budgets, but the most important factor is the cost-benefit analysis.

2. What should senior management do to support information security?

    A. Evaluate the latest security products.

    B. Conduct risk assessments

    C. Approve policy statements and funding.

    D. Mandate information security audits.

    Answer: C. Approve policy statements and funding.

Explanation: Policy statements contain the intent and direction of the management. Senior management should approve policy statements and provide sufficient budgets to achieve the organization's information security objectives. The management may be involved in evaluating products and risk assessment and mandating information security audits, but their primary role is to provide direction, oversight, and governance.

3. When are information security activities are said to have strategic alignment?

    A. When they support the requirements of key business stakeholders.

    B. When they support the requirements of the IT team.

    C. When they support the requirements of globally accepted standards

    D. When they provide reliable and cost-effective services.

    Answer: A. When they support the requirements of key business stakeholders.

    Explanation: Information security should support the achievement of organizational objectives by minimizing business disruptions. When information security supports the requirements of key business units, there is alignment. The IT department is one of the stakeholders. The other options are secondary factors.

4. What is the best way to gain support from senior management?

    A. To provide examples of security breaches in other organizations.

    B. To provide details of technical risks applicable to the organization.

    C. To showcase industry best practices.

    D. To explain the impact of security risks on key business objectives.

    Answer: D. To explain the impact of security risks on key business objectives.

    Explanation: Senior management is more concerned about the achievement of business objectives and will be keen to address all the risks impacting these. The other options will not be as effective as mapping security risks to key business objectives.

5. How can support from senior management be obtained for implementing a new project?

    A. Conducting risk assessments.

    B. Explaining regulatory requirements.

    C. Developing a business case.

    D. Selecting the latest technology.

Answer: C. Developing a business case.

Explanation: The business case contains the need and justification for the project. It will be the most important document to gain support from senior management. The other options will not be as effective as the business case.

6. What is the most effective way to enhance the commitment from senior management toward information security?

    A. To have security policies approved by the CEO.

    B. To conduct frequent security awareness training.

    C. To conduct periodic reviews of the alignment between security and business goals.

    D. To conduct periodic information security audits

    Answer: C. To conduct periodic reviews of the alignment between security and business goals.

    Explanation: The most effective way to enhance the commitment from senior management toward information security is to ensure that the security program continues to be aligned with and support the business objectives. This is critical to management support. The other options will not have as much of an effect on management as ensuring alignment with the business goals.

7. What is the most effective way to justify the information security budget?

    A. To consider the number of security breaches.

    B. To consider the expected annual loss.

    C. To consider a cost-benefit analysis.

    D. To consider industry benchmarks.

    Answer: C. To consider a cost-benefit analysis.

    Explanation: The most effective way to justify the budget is to consider a cost-benefit analysis. Other options may be considered when conducting a cost-benefit analysis.

8. What best indicates commitment from senior management toward security programs?

    A. Their involvement in the asset risk assessment.

    B. Their review and approval of the risk management methodology.

C. Their review and approval of residual risks.

D. Their review and approval of inherent risks.

Answer: B. Their review and approval of the risk management methodology.

Explanation: The involvement of senior management in the review of the risk management methodology is the best indicator that management support and are committed to effective information security. The other options do show some level of management support and commitment, but not as much as option *B*.

9. What is the most effective justification to gain support from senior management for security investment?

A. The reduction in the security budget.

B. The adherence to regulatory requirements.

C. The protection of information assets.

D. The enhanced business value.

Answer: D. The enhanced business value.

Explanation: The objective of security investments is to increase the business value by addressing instances of business disruptions, thereby reducing losses and improving productivity. The protection of information assets is one of the elements of enhanced business value.

10. Who is most likely to sponsor the security steering committee?

A. The chief audit officer.

B. The information security manager.

C. The chief operating officer.

D. The head of legal.

Answer: C. The chief operating officer.

Explanation: The steering committee should be sponsored by an authority who is well versed in the business objectives and strategy. The COO has the most knowledge of the business operations and objectives. The COO is in the best position to align the security strategy with the business objectives.

11. What is the best driver for investment in information security projects?

    A. An information security audit report.

    B. Value analysis.

    C. The business environment.

    D. Penetration test reports.

    Answer: B. Value analysis.

    Explanation: Investment in security should be able to provide value to the business. The primary driver for investment in information security projects is value analysis and a sound business case. The other options are secondary factors.

12. What is the most important prerequisite for implementing the information security program?

    A. Senior management commitment.

    B. A documented framework.

    C. A documented policy.

    D. Frequent security awareness training.

    Answer: A. Senior management commitment.

    Explanation: The support and commitment from senior management is the most important prerequisite. Without that, the other options may not add value to the information security program.

13. Who is the best person to approve the information security governance plan?

    A. The system auditor.

    B. The security manager.

    C. The steering committee.

    D. The system administrator.

    Answer: C. The steering committee.

    Explanation: The steering committee consists of senior officials from different departments. They are well versed in the business objectives and strategy. They can ensure that the security governance is aligned with the business strategy and objectives.

14. What is the best method to change an organization's security culture?

    A. Stringent penalties for non-compliance.

    B. Obtaining strong management support.

    C. Implement strong security controls.

    D. Conducting frequent system audits.

    Answer: B. Obtaining strong management support.

    Explanation: The intention and support from senior management is of utmost importance in changing an organization's security culture. In the absence of support from management, the other options will not add value.

15. Which of the following will have the most adverse impact on the effective implementation of security governance?

    A. A complex organizational environment.

    B. A limited budget for information security.

    C. Improper business priorities.

    D. A lack of high-level sponsorship.

    Answer: D. A lack of high-level sponsorship.

    Explanation: A lack of high-level sponsorship means a lack of commitment and support from senior management. Support from senior management is a prerequisite for effective security governance. With high-level sponsorship, budget constraints and business priorities can be set right.

16. What is the best method to measure the strategic alignment of an information security program?

    A. To survey the business stakeholders.

    B. To conduct frequent audits.

    C. To analyze incident trends.

    D. To evaluate the business case.

    Answer: A. To survey the business stakeholders.

Explanation: Discussion with key business stakeholders will give a correct picture about the alignment of security programs to support business objectives. Incident trends will help us to understand the effectiveness of security programs but not directly about their alignment. A business case is prepared at the time of initiation of the project and a discussion with the business owner will help us to understand whether alignment, as indicated in the business case, is being adhered to.

17. What is the most important factor that affects the successful implementation of the information security program?

    A. Support from senior management.

    B. The level of the security budget.

    C. The team size of the security team.

    D. Regular information system audits.

    Answer: A. Support from senior management.

    Explanation: The most important factor that affects the successful implementation of an organization's information security program is the support and commitment from senior management. The other options are secondary factors. Without appropriate support, it will be difficult to achieve the desired objective of a security program.

18. What is the most effective method for achieving strategic alignment?

    A. Periodically surveying the management.

    B. Employing an industry-accepted governance framework.

    C. Conducting frequent audits.

    D. Developing enterprise risk management processes.

    Answer: A. Periodically surveying the management.

    Explanation: A survey of the management is the best way to determine whether security supports the business objectives. Achieving strategic alignment means the business process owners and managers believe that information security is effectively supporting their goals. If business management is not confident in security programs, the information security manager should redesign the process to provide value to the business. The other options do not directly indicate the strategic alignment.

19. What is the objective of aligning information security governance with corporate governance?

    A. To ensure that the security team understands the business objectives.

    B. To comply with regulations.

    C. To maximize the cost-effectiveness of the control.

    D. To reduce the number of rules required for governance.

    Answer: C. To maximize the cost-effectiveness of the control.

    Explanation: The alignment ensures that assurance functions are integrated to maximize the cost-effectiveness. A lack of alignment can result in potentially duplicate or contradictory controls, which negatively impacts cost-effectiveness. The others are secondary factors.

20. What is the best method for addressing the concerns of senior management about the effectiveness of the existing information security program?

    A. Redesign the program based on industry-recognized standards.

    B. Analyze the cost-benefit of the existing program.

    C. Discuss with senior management to understand their concerns.

    D. Show an approved business case to senior management.

    Answer: C. Discuss with senior management to understand their concerns.

    Explanation: The best method to address the concerns of senior management is to first discuss their concerns to better understand them. Following this, the security program can be redesigned to be more valuable to senior management.

21. What is the most effective method for obtaining a commitment from senior management for the implementation of the security program?

    A. Discuss industry best practices with senior management.

    B. Discuss various risk scenarios with the process owners.

    C. Discuss a cost-benefit analysis with senior management.

    D. Discuss the relationship between the security program and the business goals.

    Answer: D. Discuss the relationship between the security program and the business goals.

    Explanation: Senior management is keen to protect and achieve the business goals and objectives. If they see value in the project in terms of business support, there will not be any reluctance. The other options can be secondary factors.

22. What is the most effective method for obtaining a commitment from senior management for the implementation of the security program?

    A. Demonstrate the success of industry peers.

    B. Demonstrate the potential loss and other negative impacts due to lack of support.

    C. Demonstrate regulatory requirements related to security.

    D. Demonstrate support for the desired outcome.

    Answer: D. Demonstrate support for the desired outcome.

    Explanation: Demonstrating the support for the desired outcome is the best approach. This can be done by demonstrating improvement in performance metrics related to business objectives. Senior management is keen to protect and achieve the business goals and objectives. The other options are secondary factors.

23. What factor has the most influence on the success of an information security strategy?

    A. Its approval from the chief information officer.

    B. Its alignment with the IT plan.

    C. Its alignment with the goals set by the board of directors.

    D. If it is measured by key performance indicators.

    Answer: C. Its alignment with the goals set by the board of directors.

    Explanation: The security strategy is said to be successful if it supports the achievement of goals set up by the board of directors. The other options do not directly influence whether the security program is successful.

Introducing the business case and the feasibility study

A **business case** is a justification for a proposed project. The business case is prepared to justify the effort and investment in a proposed project. It captures the reasoning for initiating a project or task. Generally, the business case is the precursor to the start of the project.

The business case is a key element in decision-making for any project. The proposed **returns on investments (ROIs)**, along with any other expected benefits, are the most important consideration for decision-making in any new project.

The first step of developing a business case is to define the need and justification of the problem.

Feasibility analysis

A **feasibility study** is an analysis that takes various factors into account, including economic, technical, and legal factors, to ascertain the likelihood of completing the project successfully.

The feasibility study should consider how the project will impact the organization in terms of risks, costs, and benefits. It helps to assess whether a solution is practical and achievable within the established budgets and schedule requirements.

Key aspects from the CISM exam perspective

The following are some of the key aspects from the CISM exam perspective:

Question	Possible answer
What is the objective of a business case?	To justify the implementation of a new project.
What is the first step in the development of a business case?	<ul><li>To define the issues to be addressed</li><li>To define the need for the project</li></ul>
On what basis is a business case primarily developed?	Feasibility and value proposition.

Table 1.7 – Key aspects from the CISM exam perspective

Questions

1. What should a business case primarily include?

    A. An appropriate justification.

    B. Results of a gap analysis.

    C. Legal requirements.

    D. Expected annual loss.

    Answer: A. An appropriate justification.

    Explanation: The objective of a business case is to justify the implementation of a new project. Its justification can be either the results of a gap analysis, legal requirements, the expected annual loss, or any other reason.

2. What is the first step of developing a business case?

    A. To determine the budget.

    B. To determine the vendor.

    C. To define the need.

    D. To determine the cost-efficiency.

    Answer: C. To define the need.

    Explanation: Without defining the need for the new project, the other options of the business case cannot be evaluated and determined. The first step of developing a business case is to define the need and the justification of the project.

3. For implementing a new project, support from senior management can be obtained by which of the following?

    A. Conducting a risk assessment.

    B. Explaining regulatory requirements.

    C. Developing a business case.

    D. Selecting the latest technology.

    Answer: C. Developing a business case.

    Explanation: The business case contains the need and justification for the project. It will be the most important document to gain support from senior management. The other options will not be as effective as the business case.

4. What are the main criteria for selecting a security technology?

    A. The technology can mitigate the risk.

    B. The technology is widely accepted in industry.

    C. It is the latest available technology.

    D. The technology provides benefits in comparison to its costs.

    Answer: D. The technology provides benefits in comparison to its costs.

    Explanation: The technology should provide benefits by mitigating risks and at the same time should be cost-efficient. The technology should be effective as well as efficient. If the technology is not cost-effective, then it will not be meaningful, even if it mitigates the risk.

5. Which of the following is the lowest concern for information security managers?

    A. Technical requirements.

    B. Regulatory requirements.

    C. Privacy requirements.

    D. Business requirements.

    Answer: A. Technical requirements.

    Explanation: Business requirements are the most important aspect for an information security manager, followed by privacy and other regulatory requirements. The other options (regulatory requirements, business requirements, and privacy requirements) are more important for a security manager as compared to technical requirements.

6. What is the most effective report while proposing the implementation of a new security solution?

    A. A vendor evaluation report.

    B. A risk analysis report.

    C. A business case.

    D. A budget utilization report.

    Answer: C. A business case.

    Explanation: A business case contains the need and justification of the proposed project. It helps to illustrate the costs and benefits of the project. The other options can be considered as part of the information required in the business case.

7. What is the biggest challenge in preparing the business case for obtaining approval from senior management for new security projects?

    A. To make the senior management understand the technical aspects of security.

    B. To demonstrate values and benefits.

    C. To present various risk scenarios.

    D. To provide comparative data of the industry.

    Answer: B. To demonstrate values and benefits.

    Explanation: It is very important and challenging to include the values and benefits in a business case in such a way as to convince the senior management. Technical aspects are generally not covered in a business case. Risk scenarios and comparative data is used to demonstrate values and benefits.

8. What is the best way to obtain support from senior management for information security initiatives?

    A. Develop and present a business case.

    B. Present various risk scenarios.

    C. Demonstrate the financial benefit of the project.

    D. Align the security initiative to the organization's goals.

    Answer: A. Develop and present a business case.

    Explanation: All the options are important, but a significant aspect is developing and presenting a business case to demonstrate that the security initiative is aligned to the organization's goal and provides value to the organization. A business case includes all of the other options.

9. Which of the following is the first step for the development of a business case?

    A. To conduct an industry survey.

    B. To work out the ROI.

    C. To evaluate cost-effective alternatives.

    D. To define the issues to be addressed.

    Answer: D. To define the issues to be addressed.

    Explanation: The first step for the development of a business case is to understand the issues that need to be addressed. Without clear requirements being defined, the other options may not add value.

10. What is a business case primarily based on?

    A. Various risk scenarios.

    B. The predicted ROI.

    C. Organizational objectives.

    D. The feasibility and value proposition.

    Answer: D. The feasibility and value proposition.

    Explanation: The most important basis for developing a business case is the feasibility and value proposition. It helps to determine whether a project should be implemented. The feasibility and value proposition indicates whether the project will be able to address risk with effective ROIs and whether it will help to achieve organizational objectives.

11. What is the best way to address the reluctance of the senior management in providing a budget for new security initiatives?

    A. To develop and present a business case.

    B. To develop various risk scenarios.

    C. To let the user management take the initiative.

    D. To organize security awareness training for the senior management.

    Answer: A. To develop and present a business case.

    Explanation: A business case is the best way to present the link between a new security project and organization's business objectives. Senior management is keen to protect and achieve the business objectives. If they see value in the project in terms of business support, there will not be any reluctance. Risk scenarios should be considered as a part of the business case. The other options will not be effective to address their concerns.

12. The information security manager is evaluating two technologies to address a particular risk and is required to select one for implementation. What is the best approach for the security manager with a limited budget to choose between the two technologies?

    A. A risk assessment.

    B. A business impact analysis.

    C. An ROI prediction.

    D. A cost-benefit analysis.

    Answer: D. A cost-benefit analysis.

    Explanation: A cost-benefit analysis will be the best approach to inform a decision. Cost-benefit analyses indicate the cost of implementing the control and its expected benefits. The cost of a control should not exceed the benefit to be derived from it. A risk assessment is a step prior to the evaluation and implementation of a control. In security parlance, ROI is difficult to calculate, as returns are in terms of safety and security.

13. How is an information security program best justified?

    A. An impact analysis.

    B. A detailed business case.

    C. Industry benchmarks

    D. Acceptance by users.

Answer: B. A detailed business case.

Explanation: A business case is the justification for the implementation of the program. It contains a rationale for making an investment. It indicates the cost of the project and its expected benefits. The other options by themselves are not sufficient to justify the information security program. User acceptance may not always be reliable for a security program, as security and performance often clash.

14. What factor is most likely to persuade the management of the approval of a new information security budget?

    A. A detailed risk assessment.

    B. Risk treatment options.

    C. A well-developed business case.

    D. Calculating the future value of a current budget

    Answer: C. A well-developed business case.

    Explanation: A business case is the justification for the implementation of the security program. It contains a rationale for making an investment. It indicates the cost of the project and its expected benefits. The other options by themselves are not sufficient to justify the information security budget.

15. Which of the following is the most important thing to consider in the development of a business case?

    A. Various risk scenarios.

    B. Industry benchmarks.

    C. Implementation benefits.

    D. Affordability.

    Answer: C. Implementation benefits.

    Explanation: A business case is the justification for the implementation of the security program. It contains a rationale for making an investment. It indicates the cost of the project and its expected benefits. The other options by themselves are not sufficient to justify the information security budget.

Understanding information security governance metrics

A **metric** is a measurement of a process to determine how well the process is performing. Security-related metrics indicate how well the controls can mitigate the risks. For example, a **system uptime metric** helps us to understand whether a system is available to the user as per requirements.

The objective of metrics

On the basis of effective metrics, an organization evaluates and measures the achievement and performance of various processes and controls. The main objective of a metric is to help the management in decision-making. A metric should be able to provide relevant information to the recipient so that informed decisions can be made.

Technical metrics vis-à-vis governance-level metrics

Technical metrics help us to understand the functioning of technical controls such as IDS, firewalls, antivirus software, and more. They are useful for tactical operational management. However, these metrics have little value from a governance standpoint.

Management is more concerned about the overall security posture of the organization. Full audits and comprehensive risk assessments are a few of the activities that help the management to understand security from a governance perspective.

Characteristics of effective metrics

Good metrics should be **SMART**. That is, **specific, measurable, attainable, relevant,** and **timely**. Let's look at those in more detail:

- **Specific**: The metric should be specific, clear, and concise.
- **Measurable**: The metric should be measurable so that it can be compared over a period.
- **Attainable**: The metric should be realistic and achievable.
- **Relevant**: The metric should be linked to specific risks or controls.
- **Timely**: The metric should be able to be monitored on a timely basis.

Key aspects from the CISM exam perspective

The following are some of the key aspects from the CISM exam perspective:

Question	Possible answer
What is the prime objective of a metric?	Decision making (on the basis of effective metrics, organizations evaluate and measure the achievements and performance of various processes and controls. Effective metrics are primarily used for security-related decision making).

Table 1.8 – Key aspects from the CISM exam perspective

Questions

1. What should information security decisions be based on primarily?

    A. Market research.

    B. Predicative analysis.

    C. Industry standards.

    D. Effective metrics.

    Answer: D. Effective metrics.

    Explanation: Based on effective metrics, organizations evaluate and measure the achievements and performance of various processes and controls. Effective metrics are primarily used for security-related decision making. The other options are secondary factors.

2. Which of the following is considered to have the most important strategic value?

    A. A privileged access management process.

    B. Trends in incident occurrence.

    C. System downtime analysis.

    D. Results of penetration tests.

    Answer: B. Trends in incident occurrence.

    Explanation: Trends in incidents will be more valuable from a strategic perspective as they will indicate whether a security program is heading in the right direction or not. The other options are more of an operational metric.

3. What is the most important metric that indicates the organizational risk?

    A. The expected annual loss.

    B. The number of security incidents.

    C. The number of unplanned business interruptions.

    D. The number of open vulnerabilities.

    Answer: C. The number of unplanned business interruptions.

    Explanation: The number of unplanned business interruptions is the best indication to evaluate organizational risk by determining how much business may be lost due to interruptions. Annual loss expectancy is based on projections and does not indicate actual value. Security incidents and open vulnerabilities do not reveal impact.

4. What is the best method to determine the level of alignment of the security objectives with the business objectives?

    A. Interview the security manager.

    B. Review the capability maturity model.

    C. Review the risk assessment report.

    D. Review the business balanced scorecard.

    Answer: D. Review the business balanced scorecard.

    Explanation: Reviewing the business balanced scorecard will help to determine the alignment of the security goals with the business goals. The business scorecard contains important metrics from the business perspective. The other options do not address the alignment directly.

5. What is the most essential attribute for a metric?

    A. Metrics should be easy to implement.

    B. Metrics should be meaningful to the process owner.

    C. Metrics should be qualitative.

    D. Metrics should be able to support regulatory requirements.

    Answer: B. Metrics should be meaningful to the process owner.

Explanation: Metrics are a measurement used to evaluate and monitor a particular process. Metrics are most effective when they are meaningful to the person receiving the information. The process owner should be able to take appropriate action based on the metrics. Metrics can be either quantifiable or qualitative based on the nature of the process. Options *A* and *D* are important, but more significant is the ability of metrics to convey meaning.

6. What is the most important attribute of a **key risk indicator (KRI)**?

    A. A KRI should be flexible and adaptable.

    B. A KRI should be arrived at by consistent methodologies and practices.

    C. A KRI should be easy to understand.

    D. A KRI should be convenient for the process owner to use.

    Answer: B. A KRI should be arrived at by consistent methodologies and practices.

    Explanation: A KRI will be effective only if it is arrived at by consistent methodologies and practices. In the absence of this, the KRI will be meaningless as it cannot be compared over different periods of time and hence it may not be able to indicate actual risk. Other options are good attributes but do not provide a consistent approach to determine deviation over the period.

7. What is the best indicator to determine the effectiveness of the security strategy?

    A. The strategy helps to improve the risk appetite of the organization.

    B. The strategy helps to implement countermeasures for all the threats.

    C. The strategy helps to minimize the annual losses.

    D. The strategy helps to achieve the control objective.

    Answer: D. The strategy helps to achieve the control objective.

    Explanation: The control objectives are developed to achieve the acceptable level of risk. The strategy is effective if the control objectives are met. The other options may be part of the control objectives, but the effectiveness of the security strategy is best measured by evaluating the extent to which the overall control objectives are met.

8. The information security manager has been asked to implement a particular security standard. Which of the following is the most effective to monitor this?

    A. The key success factor.

    B. The key objective indicator.

    C. The key performance indicator.

    D. The key goal indicator.

    Answer: C. The key performance indicator.

    Explanation: The key performance indicator measures how well a process is performing compared to its expectations. The key success factor determines the most important aspects or issues to achieve the goal. The key objective indicator and key goal indicator define the objective set by the organization.

Summary

In this chapter, you have learned about the importance of assurance functions, that is, governance, risk, and compliance, and how their integration is key to effective and efficient information security management. You have also understood how organizations can use the maturity model to improve their processes. We discussed the importance of the commitment of senior management toward the security aspects of an organization.

Reading this chapter will have helped the CISM aspirant to get an overview of information security governance.

In our next topic, we will discuss the practical aspects of information security governance.

2
Practical Aspects of Information Security Governance

In this chapter, we will discuss practical aspects of information security governance and understand how governance impacts the success of security projects. You will learn about different aspects of what a *security strategy* is. You will also understand the role of an information security manager in supporting business objectives.

The following topics will be covered in this chapter:

- Information security strategy and plan
- Information security program
- Enterprise information security architecture
- Organization structure
- Record retention
- Awareness and education

Let's understand each one of these topics in detail.

Information security strategy and plan

An **information security strategy** is a set of actions to achieve the security objectives. The strategy includes what should be done, how it should be done, and when it should be done in order to achieve the security objectives.

The strategy is basically a road map of specific actions required to achieve the objective. Based on the strategy, long- and short-term plans are finalized.

The prime objective of any security strategy is to support the business's objectives. An information security strategy should be aligned with a particular business's objectives. The first step for an *information security manager* in creating a plan is to understand and evaluate the business strategy. This is essential to align the information security strategy and plan with business strategy.

A **strategic plan** should include the desired state of information security. A strategy is considered to be effective if *control objectives* are met. The final responsibility for the appropriate protection of an organization's information falls to the board of directors. The involvement of board members in information security initiatives indicates good governance. The company directors can be protected from liability if the board has exercised due diligence. Many laws and regulations make the board responsible in the event of data breaches. Even cyber security insurance policies often require the board to exercise due diligence as a prerequisite for insurance coverage.

The **Chief Information Security Officer (CISO)** is primarily responsible for the design and development of the information security strategy in accordance with the security policy.

Information security policies

Policies take the form of a high-level document containing the intent and direction of management. Security policies are developed based on the security strategy. Security policies indicate the intent of the management. Based on the security policy, various procedures and architecture are designed.

Any changes in the management's intent should also be appropriately addressed in the policy.

It is also important to ensure compliance with the requirements at regular intervals. Self-assessment is the best way to determine the readiness of, and then remediate, non-compliant items. This will help the organization to prepare for regulatory review.

Key aspects from the CISM exam perspective

The following are some of the key aspects of this topic from the perspective of the exam:

Question	Possible Answer
What is the first step in developing an information security plan?	To evaluate and understand business strategy.
What is the main objective of designing an information security strategy?	To support the business objectives.
What is the first step in developing an information security management program?	To ascertain the need and justification for creating the program.
What is the best way to address the conflicting requirements of a multinational organization's security policy with local regulations?	The best way in such a situation is to establish a local version of the policy that is aligned with local laws and regulations.
What is the conflict between security controls and business requirements?	<ul><li>The objective of security controls is to support the business objectives and requirements.</li><li>Security controls should not restrict the ability of users to perform their jobs.</li><li>When a security control is not supporting business needs, it is termed as a conflict between security controls and business requirements.</li></ul>
The objective of information security can be best described as what?	The requirements of the desired state (that is, what is required to achieve the desired state).
What is value delivery in information security?	Value delivery means designing a process that gives the maximum benefit to the organization. It indicates the high utilization of available resources for the benefit of the organization.
What is the road map for information security implementation primarily based on?	The security strategy.
On what basis are intangible assets best valued?	The ability of the assets to generate revenue.

Table 2.1 – Key aspects from the CISM exam perspective

Practice questions

1. The first step in developing an information security plan is which of the following?

    A. To conduct a vulnerability assessment

    B. To evaluate the current business strategy

    C. To perform an information system audit

    D. To evaluate the risk culture of the organization

    Answer: B. To evaluate the current business strategy

    Explanation: The first step for an information security manager is to understand and evaluate the current strategy. This is essential to align the information security plan with the business strategy. The other options here are subsequent steps.

2. The most important factor to be included in the information security strategic plan is which of the following?

    A. Information security manpower requirements

    B. Information security tools and technique requirements

    C. Information security mission statement

    D. Desired future state of information security

    Answer: D. Desired future state of information security

    Explanation: The strategic plan should include the desired state of information security. This is the most important factor. The desired state will impact options A and B. The mission statement is a high-level statement that may not indicate the detailed desired state for information security.

3. The main objective of designing an information security strategy is which of the following?

    A. To monitor performance

    B. To support the business objectives

    C. To enhance the responsibility of the security manager

    D. To comply with legal requirements

    Answer: B. To support the business objectives

    Explanation: The prime objective of any security strategy is to support the business objective. The information security strategy should be aligned with business objectives. The other options are secondary objectives.

4. The most important factor for the development of a security strategy is which of the following?

    A. To understand the key business objectives

    B. To provide training to the information security team

    C. To provide sufficient resources for information security

    D. To develop a risk-aware culture

    Answer: A. To understand the key business objectives

    Explanation: Understanding the key business objectives is the most critical factor to align the security strategy with the business strategy. The security strategy should support the business objectives. The other options are secondary factors.

5. The most important factor to be included in an information security strategy is which of the following?

    A. Details of key business controls

    B. Security objective and process

    C. Budget for a specific security tool

    D. Details of network security control

    Answer: B. Security objective and process

    Explanation: The security strategy consists of desired security objectives supported by processes, methods, and relevant tools and techniques. The other options here are not as significant as security objectives and process.

6. The best way to address the conflicting requirements of a multinational organization's security policy with local regulations is which of the following?

    A. To give priority to policy requirements over local laws

    B. To follow local laws only

    C. To establish a local version of the organization's policy

    D. To discontinue service in conflicting jurisdictions

    Answer: C. To establish a local version of the organization's policy

    Explanation: The best way in such a situation is to establish a local version of the policy that is aligned with local laws and regulations. The other options are not sensible.

7.   7. The best way to prepare for a regulatory audit is which of the following?

   A. To nominate a security administrator as the regulatory liaison

   B. To conduct self-assessments using regulatory guidelines and reports

   C. To discuss previous years' regulatory reports with the process owner

   D. To ensure all regulatory inquiries are approved by the legal department

   Answer: B. To conduct self-assessment using regulatory guidelines and reports

   Explanation: Self-assessment is the best way to determine the readiness of, and then remediate, non-compliant items. This will help the organization to prepare for regulatory review. The other options are not as effective as option B.

8.   Who is responsible for the enforcement of the information security policy?

   A. IS steering committee

   B. **Chief Technical Officer (CTO)**

   C. CISO

   D. Chief Compliance Officer

   Answer: C. CISO

   Explanation: Generally, the CISO is responsible for enforcing the information security policy. The steering committee monitors the enforcement process but is not responsible for enforcement. The steering committee ensures that the security policy is aligned with business objectives. The CTO and Chief Compliance Officer may to some extent be involved in the enforcement of the policy, but are not directly responsible for it.

9.   The most important role for a CISO is which of the following?

   A. Design and develop an information security strategy.

   B. Conduct **business continuity planning (BCP)** testing.

   C. Approve system accesses.

   D. Deploy patch releases.

   Answer: A. Design and develop an information security strategy.

   Explanation: The CISO is primarily responsible for designing and developing the information security strategy. The other functions listed here are normally carried out by IT and operational staff.

10. The timeline for the implementation of information security strategic plan should be which of the following?

A. In accordance with the IT strategic plan

B. In accordance with changes in technology

C. One to five years

D. Aligned with the business strategy

Answer: D. Aligned with the business strategy

Explanation: The timeline for the information security strategic plan should be designed in accordance and aligned with the business strategy. The other options here should be secondary considerations. The business strategy and requirements should be the primary consideration.

11. Commitment and support from senior management with respect to information security can be best addressed by which of the following?

A. Emphasizing the organizational risk

B. Emphasizing the requirements of global security standards

c. Emphasizing the industry benchmarks

D. Emphasizing the responsibility of the organization

Answer: A. Emphasizing the organizational risk

Explanation: Emphasizing organizational risk and its impact on the business objectives is the best way to gain commitment and support from senior management. The other options here are secondary factors.

12. The prime objective of developing an information security strategy is which of the following?

A. To manage the risk impacting business objectives

B. To mitigate the risk level to zero

C. To transfer risk to insurers

D. To develop a risk-aware culture

Answer: A. To manage the risk impacting business objectives

Explanation: The prime objective of the security strategy is to manage and reduce the risk impacting the business objectives. It is not feasible to mitigate risk levels to zero. The transfer of risk and the development of a risk-aware culture are other aspects of managing risk.

13. Immediately after implementing access control for the internet, employees started complaining of being unable to perform business functions on internet sites. This is an example of which of the following?

A. Conflict between security controls and business requirements

B. Stringent security controls

C. Mandatory access controls

D. Discretionary access controls

Answer: A. Conflict between security controls and business requirements

Explanation: This is an example of a conflict between security controls and business requirements where the security controls are not supporting business needs. These controls should not restrict the ability of users to perform their jobs.

14. Which of the following should be the first action while developing an information security strategy?

A. To identify the assets

B. To perform a risk analysis

C. To define the scope of the strategy program

D. To determine critical business processes

Answer: C. To define the scope of the strategy program.

Explanation: The first step should be to define the scope of the strategy program. The other options are subsequent steps to be performed.

15. The most important objective of the information security strategy is which of the following?

A. To minimize the risk to an acceptable level

B. To support the business objectives and goals of the enterprise

C. To ensure the optimum utilization of security resources

D. To maximize the return on security investments

Answer: B. To support the business objectives and goals of the enterprise

Explanation: The most important objective of the information security strategy is that it should support the objective of the organization. The other options are secondary objectives.

16. The most critical factor for designing an information security strategy is which of the following?

    A. Defined objectives

    B. Defined time frame

    c. Defined framework

    D. Defined policies

    Answer: A. Defined objectives

    Explanation: Defined objectives are the most important element, as without objectives, a strategy to achieve the objectives cannot be developed. Policies are developed after the development of the strategy. The time frame and framework are not as important as defined objectives.

17. In an information security steering committee, there is no representation from user management. Which of the following is the main risk as a result of this?

    A. Functional requirements may not be adequately addressed.

    B. Inadequate user training.

    C. Inadequate budget allocation.

    D. The information security strategy may not be aligned with business requirements.

    Answer: D. The information security strategy may not be aligned with business requirements.

    Explanation: The information security steering committee monitors and controls the security strategy. In the absence of input from user management, the strategy may not support the business requirements. This is the major risk from the lack of user management representation. The other options are not as significant as the strategy not supporting the business requirements. User training and budget allocation are not normally under the purview of the steering committee.

18. Which of the following is the best approach for an information security manager when there is a disagreement between them and the business manager on security aspects of a new process?

    A. To accept the decision of the business manager as they are the owner of the process

    B. To mandate the decision of the security manager

C. To review the risk assessment with senior management for final consideration

D. To prepare a new risk assessment to address the disagreement

Answer: C. To review the risk assessment with senior management for final consideration

Explanation: Senior management will be in the best position to evaluate the impact of risks on business requirements. They will be able to make any trade-offs required between security and business processes. The other options will not address the issue.

19. The connection between business objectives and security should be demonstrated by which of the following?

A. Indirect linkages

B. Mapping to standardized controls

C. Interconnected constraints

D. Direct traceability

Answer: D. Direct traceability

Explanation: Direct traceability is the best way to ensure that business and security objectives are connected and that security is adding value to the business objectives. The other options are not as good as traceable connections.

20. Accountability for information categorization and protective measures reside with which of the following?

A. Security administrator

B. Senior management

C. System administrator

D. End user

Answer: B. Senior management

Explanation: Overall accountability resides with senior management though they may delegate responsibility to different functions. The security administrator and system administrator support the security objectives of senior management.

21. The most important consideration while developing an information security strategy is which of the following?

    A. Availability of information security resources

    B. Adherence to laws and regulations

    C. Effectiveness in mitigating risk

    D. Budget allocation for information security

    Answer: C. Effectiveness in mitigating risk

    Explanation: The most important factor is the effectiveness of the information security strategy to address the risk impacting the business objectives. The other options are secondary factors. Even a considerable budget will be meaningless if the security strategy is not effective in mitigating the risk.

22. The objective of the information security strategy can be best described as which of the following?

    A. Requirements of the desired state

    B. Attributes of the current state

    C. Key business process

    D. Control objective for loss expectations

    Answer: A. Requirements of the desired state

    Explanation: The objective of the security strategy can be best described as what is required to achieve the desired state. It is not restricted to only key processes or loss expectations.

23. The most important factor for developing risk management strategies is which of the following?

    A. Industry-adopted risk assessment framework

    B. Business objectives and risk appetite

    C. Technology architecture

    D. Geographical spread of business units

    Answer: B. Business objectives and risk appetite

    Explanation: The risk management strategy should support and be aligned with the business objectives and risk appetite of the organization. The other options are not as significant as the business objectives and risk appetite.

24. "Systems thinking" in reference to information security indicates which of the following?

    A. The perspective of artificial intelligence

    B. The perspective of the whole being greater than the sum of its individual parts

    C. The perspective of supporting the business objective

    D. The perspective of governing the entire organization

    Answer: B. The perspective of the whole being greater than the sum of its individual parts

    Explanation: "Systems thinking" in reference to information security indicates the perspective that the system is greater than the sum of its individual parts.

25. An information security manager is asked to develop a cost-effective information security strategy. What is the most important step?

    A. To identity information assets

    B. To conduct a valuation of information assets

    C. To determine the objective of the security strategy

    D. To classify assets as per risk assessment

    Answer: C. To determine the objective of the security strategy

    Explanation: Determining the objectives of the security strategy is a must before any other steps are taken as all other steps are developed on the basis of the security strategy. The other options are important but not as significant as determining the objective of the security strategy.

26. Which of the following is considered to have the most important strategic value?

    A. Privileged access management processes

    B. Trends in incident occurrence

    C. System downtime analysis

    D. Results of penetration tests

    Answer: B. Trends in incident occurrence

    Explanation: Trends in incident occurrence are more valuable from the strategic perspective as they indicate whether the security program is heading in the right direction or not. The other options are more operational metrics.

27. The information security manager is considered to have achieved value delivery at which of the following points?

A. When resource utilization is high

B. When budget requirements are low

C. When the lowest cost vendors have been appointed

D. When staff costs are reduced

Answer: A. When resource utilization is high

Explanation: Value delivery means designing a process that gives the maximum benefit to the organization. It suggests a high utilization of available resources for the benefit of the organization. The other options by themselves do not indicate value delivery.

28. The most important factor in the development of an information security strategy is which of the following?

A. IT architecture

B. Governance framework

C. Current state of security and future objectives

D. Support from senior management

Answer: C. Current state of security and future objectives

Explanation: It is very important to understand the current state of security and the desired future state or objective. In the absence of clearly defined objectives, it will not be possible to develop the strategy. The other options are important but not as significant as the other objectives.

29. While developing the security strategy, the security manager should be most concerned about which of the following?

A. Whether the strategy supports the business objective

B. Whether the strategy ensures the optimum utilization of available resources

c. Whether the strategy ensures compliance with regulatory requirements

D. Whether the strategy minimizes the budget requirements

Answer: A. Whether the strategy supports the business objective

Explanation: The most important objective of the security strategy is to support the business requirements and goals. The strategy should support the business objective. The other options are secondary objectives.

30. What is the main objective of the information security strategy?

    A. To determine the security goals and plan to achieve them

    B. To determine the configuration of the security controls

    C. To determine the acceptable usage of information assets

    D. To determine the budget of the information security program

    Answer: A. To determine the security goals and plan to achieve them

    Explanation: The main objective of the strategy is to set out the goals of the information security program and create a plan to achieve those goals. The budget is linked to the security objectives. A strategy is a high-level management intent and does not generally include the implementation aspects mentioned in options B and C.

31. A road map for information security implementation is primarily based on which of the following?

    A. IT architecture

    B. IT policy

    C. Security strategy

    D. Regulatory requirements

    Answer: C. Security strategy

    Explanation: The security strategy is the guiding force for the implementation of the security program. The road map detailing the security implementation (that is, procedure, resources, timelines, and so on) is developed based on the strategy. The other options may be input factors for designing the strategy. However, once the strategy has been developed, it is considered as the overall guiding principles for the implementation of the security program.

32. Intangible assets should be best valued based on which of the following?

    A. Acquisition cost

    B. Replacement cost

    C. Ability to generate revenue

    D. Risk analysis

Answer: C. Ability to generate revenue

Explanation: Valuation should be done based on the ability of the asset to generate revenue for the organization. In the absence of the availability of assets, the organization will lose much of that revenue acquisition, and the replacement cost of the asset may be more or less than its actual ability to generate revenue.

33. Which of the following is the main reason for a change in policy?

    A. Changes in regulation

    B. Changes in the security baseline

    C. Changes in management intent and direction

    D. Changes in organization culture

    Answer: C. Changes in management intent and direction

    Explanation: The policy reflects the intent and direction of management. Any changes in management intent should also be appropriately addressed in the policy. Changes in regulation and the security baseline should be addressed in procedures, guidelines, and standards. Changes in culture may or may not impact the policy, however the management intent is more significant here.

34. The most important result of an information security strategy is which of the following?

    A. Mature policies and procedures

    B. Ensuring that residual risk is within an acceptable level

    C. Mature vulnerability assessment procedures

    D. Alignment of controls to international standards

    Answer: B. Ensuring that residual risk is within an acceptable level

    Explanation: Residual risk is the risk that remains after the controls are implemented. One of the objectives of a security strategy is to ensure that residual risks are well within an acceptable limit. This gives comfort to management. The other options are not as significant as keeping residual risk within an acceptable level.

35. The best indicator to determine the effectiveness of a security strategy is which of the following?

    A. The strategy helps to improve the risk appetite of the organization.

    B. The strategy helps to implement countermeasures for all the threats.

C. The strategy helps to minimize the annual losses.

D. The strategy helps to achieve the control objective.

Answer: D. The strategy helps to achieve the control objective.

Explanation: Control objectives are developed to achieve an acceptable level of risk. The strategy is considered to be effective if the control objectives are met. The other options may be part of the control objectives, but effectiveness is best measured by evaluating the extent to which the overall control objectives are met.

36. The primary reason for the board of directors to be involved in information security initiatives is which of the following?

A. Concerns regarding IT architecture

B. Concerns regarding the organization's liability

C. Concerns regarding compliance

D. Concerns regarding the implementation of policy

Answer: B. Concerns regarding the organization's liability

Explanation: The involvement of board members in information security initiatives indicates good governance. Directors can be protected from liability if the board has exercised due diligence. Many laws and regulations make the board responsible in the event of data breaches. Even cyber security insurance policies require the board to exercise due diligence as a prerequisite for insurance coverage. The board is not required to involve themselves in routine compliance and policy implementation processes.

37. The information security manager has been asked to implement a particular security standard. Which of the following is most effective to monitor this?

A. Key success factor

B. Key objective indicator

C. Key performance indicator

D. Key goal indicator

Answer: C. Key performance indicator

Explanation: A key performance indicator is a measure to determine how well a process is performing compared to expectations. Key success factors determine the most important aspects or issues in achieving a goal. The key objective indicator and key goal indicator define the objective set by the organization.

38. The best indicator to determine the level of alignment of the security objectives with the business objectives is which of the following?

    A. Interview with security manager

    B. Review of the capability maturity model

    C. Review of the risk assessment report

    D. Review of the business' balanced scorecard

    Answer: D. Review of the business' balanced scorecard

    Explanation: A review of the business' balanced scorecard will help to determine the alignment of security goals with business goals. The balanced scorecard contains important metrics from the business perspective. The other options do not address the alignment of security and business goals directly.

39. The best way to align the security goals with the business goals is which of the following?

    A. Functional goals should support security goals.

    B. Business goals and security goals should support each other.

    C. Security goals should be derived from business goals.

    D. Business goals and security goals should be independent of each other.

    Answer: C. Security goals should be derived from business goals.

    Explanation: Security goals should be developed based on overall business objectives. The security strategy should support the business goals and objectives.

40. The security baseline of a mature organization is most likely defined as which of the following?

    A. Availability of policies

    B. Availability of IT architecture

    C. Control objectives being met

    D. Adherence to regulatory requirements

    Answer: C. Control objectives being met

    Explanation: A baseline is a basic standard with which to comply. In a mature organization, it is expected that control objectives of security should be met. The other options may be part of the control objectives, but whatever the objectives defined, they should be met in a mature organization.

41. Which of the following is the area of most concern for a security manager of an organization that operates in multiple countries?

    A. Difficulty in implementing a standardized security program

    B. Difficulty in monitoring the security posture over wide geographical distance

    C. Difficulty in developing customized security awareness programs

    D. Difficulty in monitoring compliance with laws and regulations

    Answer: D. Difficulty in monitoring compliance with laws and regulations

    Explanation: The area of most concern is compliance with laws and regulations. Security managers need to ensure that appropriate care is taken to meet local laws. Local laws vary from country to country and sometimes may conflict with the global security requirements of the organization. Non-compliance with laws and regulations may have major impacts on business processes. The other options are not as significant as monitoring compliance with laws and regulations.

42. Which of the following is considered the most significant key risk indicator?

    A. Abnormal deviations from normal employee attrition rates

    B. High counts of virus quarantined by anti-virus software

    C. High counts of packets filtered by a firewall

    D. Low numbers of information security officers on the staff

    Answer: A. Abnormal deviations from normal employee attrition rates

    Explanation: A sudden increase in employee attrition rates can indicate suspicious activity that requires the attention of the security manager. For example, if a large number of developers are leaving the organization, it may indicate that a competitor is trying to obtain the organization's development plan. High counts of virus and filtered packets may indicate a change in the threat environment, but there is no direct impact as these are controlled through the use of antivirus software or firewalls. A low number of security officers on the staff does not necessarily indicate a risk.

43. The most important aspect from the perspective of senior management in an information security strategy is which of the following?

    A. Details of technology

    B. Details of compliance requirements

    C. Business priorities

    D. Details of procedural aspects

Answer: C. Business priorities

Explanation: Management will be more interested to understand how the security strategy is supporting the business objectives; whether their top-level goals and objectives are supported by security. The other options are not relevant at the strategic level.

44. The best method to develop an effective data protection strategy is which of the following?

    A. To conduct a vulnerability assessment

    B. To design a tailored methodology based on exposure

    C. To obtain an insurance policy for data losses

    D. To implement industry best practices

    Answer: B. To design a tailored methodology based on exposure

    Explanation: The classification of data in accordance with its value and exposure, followed by the development of a strategy for each class, is the best method to create an effective data protection strategy. This will address the risk of under as well as overprotection of the data. Vulnerability assessments do not consider threats and other factors that impact the risk treatment. Insurance policies and industry practices may be considered based on risk and classification of data.

Information security program

A **program** can be defined as a set of activities implemented in a structured way to achieve a common objective. A **security program** includes various activities such as implementing controls, conducting awareness campaigns, and monitoring and reporting on controls.

The **security strategy** is the guiding force for the implementation of the security program. The road map detailing the security implementation (that is, the procedure, resources, timelines, and so on) is developed based on the strategy. Based on a developed strategy, various implementation activities can be aligned and integrated to achieve the security objectives in a more effective and efficient manner.

The information security program should be aligned with the business objectives of the organization. The effectiveness of the information security program is determined based on its ability to address the impact of risk on the business objectives.

Key aspects from the CISM exam perspective

The following are some of the key aspects of this topic from an exam perspective:

Question	Possible Answer
Define *program*.	A program can be defined as a set of activities implemented in a structured way to achieve a common objective.
What is the first step in developing an information security management program?	To ascertain the need and justification for creating the program.
What is the road map for the implementation of information security primarily based on?	Security strategy.

Table 2.2 – Key aspects from the CISM exam perspective

Practice questions

1. What is the first step in developing an information security management program?

    A. To ascertain key business risks

    B. To ascertain the need for creating the program

    C. To appoint the information security program manager

    D. To ascertain the sufficiency of existing controls

    Answer: B. To ascertain the need for creating the program

    Explanation: The first step is to justify the need for the program by conducting a cost benefit analysis. Once the need for the program is established, the other options here can be acted upon.

2. Which of the following should be the first step to implement a new security monitoring solution?

    A. To evaluate various alternatives available for the solution

    B. To determine the budget for the new solution

    C. To evaluate and determine the correlation of the solution with the business objectives

    D. To develop a team for the implementation

Answer: C. To evaluate and determine the correlation of the solution with the business objectives

Explanation: The first step should be to assess and determine whether the proposed solution is aligned with the business objectives and requirements. Once this is established, the other options here can be followed.

3. An information security program is created primarily to do which of the following?

   A. Develop an information security strategy.

   B. Establish a business continuity plan.

   C. Ensure the optimum utilization of security resources.

   D. Mitigate the impact of risks on the business.

   Answer: D Mitigate the impact of risks on the business.

   Explanation: The most important objective of an information security program is to reduce the impact of risks on the business objectives. The other options are secondary factors.

4. The most important factor to develop a security strategy before implementing the security program is which of the following?

   A. To reduce the cost of implementation

   B. To align and integrate development activities

   C. To obtain support from management

   D. To adhere with international requirements

   Answer: B. To align and integrate development activities

   Explanation: The strategy is the roadmap to achieve the objectives. Based on a developed strategy, various implementation activities can be aligned and integrated to achieve the security objectives in a more effective and efficient manner. The other options may be secondary factors.

5. The most likely reason for a sudden increase in the number of security events is which of the following?

   A. Greater exploitation of vulnerabilities

   B. An increase in the number of threat actors

   C. Failure of detection controls

   D. Absence of an information system audit

Answer: A. Greater exploitation of vulnerabilities

Explanation: A threat by itself cannot harm the organization unless and until it finds some vulnerability in the system to exploit. Detection controls will not be able to prevent the event in any case. The absence of a system audit is an unlikely explanation for the increased number of security events.

6. The primary objective of an information security program is which of the following?

   A. To protect information assets in accordance with the business strategy and objectives

   B. To standardize the operational risk management process

   C. To protect the confidentiality of information

   D. To develop the information security policy

   Answer: A. To protect information assets in accordance with the business strategy and objectives

   Explanation: The primary objective of an information security program is to align the security implementation with the business strategy and objectives. The information security program is not limited only to operational risks. The security program should consider the confidentiality, integrity, and availability of assets. A security policy is developed as a part of the security program to achieve the protection of information assets.

7. The combination of management, administrative, and technical control is important for effective information security because of which of the following?

   A. Organizations cannot completely depend on technical controls to address faulty processes.

   B. Technical controls are too expensive to manage.

   C. Monitoring and reporting the effectiveness of technical controls is difficult.

   D. Implementing the right technical control is an iterative process.

   Answer: A. Organizations cannot completely depend on technical controls to address faulty processes.

   Explanation: A structured and resilient process in addition to the technical control is the most effective method to manage and address risks. An appropriate combination of management, administrative, and technical controls is the best way to address risk in the most effective and efficient manner.

8. The best way to learn and improve after a security incident is which of the following?

   A. To improve the integration of business and security processes

   B. To increase information security budgets

   C. To set up a separate compliance monitoring department

   D. To acquire high-end technical controls

   Answer: A. To improve the integration of business and security processes

   Explanation: The integration of security governance and overall governance is the best way to ensure that key business processes are well protected. The other options are actionable that may arise due to the close integration of business and security processes.

Enterprise information security architecture

An **enterprise architecture** (**EA**) is a blueprint that defines the structure and operation of the organization. It describes how different elements such as processes, systems, data, employees, and other infrastructure are integrated to achieve the current and future objectives of the organization.

The **security architecture** is a subset of the overall EA. The objective of the security architecture is to improve the security posture of the organization. The security architecture clearly defines what processes a business performs and how those processes are executed and secured.

The first step for a security manager implementing the security strategy is to understand and evaluate the IT architecture and portfolio. Once they have a fair idea of the IT architecture, they can determine the security strategy.

Challenges in designing security architectures

While designing the security architecture, it is important for a security manager to understand the possible challenges. This will help them to address the challenges in an effective and efficient manner.

The following are some of the challenges of designing a security architecture:

- It is not easy to design a security architecture. Most instances of this kind of project are expensive and time consuming.
- A lack of competent security architects results in more effort required to build a reliable security architecture.
- The potential benefits of a well-designed security architecture cannot be directly quantified and hence gaining support from management can be very difficult.

Benefits of security architectures

A security architecture provides detailed information on how a business operates and what security controls are required. This helps the security manager to determine the processes and systems where efforts toward security should be focused.

Key aspects from the CISM exam perspective

The following is one of the key aspects of this topic from an exam perspective:

Question	Possible Answer
The information security architecture should be aligned with what?	Business goals and objectives.

Table 2.3 – Key aspects from the CISM exam perspective

Practice questions

1. The information security architecture is best aligned with which of the following?

    A. International security standards

    B. Business goals and objectives

    C. IT architecture

    D. Industry standards

    Answer: B. Business goals and objectives

    Explanation: The security architecture should primarily be aligned with business goals and objectives. The other options are secondary considerations.

2. An information security manager has been entrusted to create the information security strategy for the organization. Their first step should be which of the following?

    A. To understand the IT architecture and portfolio

    B. To determine the security baseline

    C. To document the information security policy

    D. To conduct an IT risk assessment

    Answer: A. To understand the IT architecture and portfolio

Explanation: The first step of the security manager is to understand and evaluate the IT architecture and portfolio. Once they have a fair idea about the IT architecture, they can then determine the security strategy. The other options can follow once the security strategy has been defined.

Organizational structure

The development of a security strategy is highly influenced by the **organizational structure**. Organizational structure means the roles and responsibilities of different individuals, the reporting hierarchy, whether the organization functions in a centralized or decentralized way, and so on. A flexible and evolving organizational structure is more open to the adoption of a security strategy as opposed to a more constrained organizational structure.

The independence of the **security function** is the most important factor to be considered while evaluating organizational functions. This can be assessed through the reporting structure of the security function.

Board of directors

The ultimate responsibility for the appropriate protection of an organization's information falls to the **board of directors**. The involvement of board members in information security initiatives indicates good governance. The company directors can be protected from liability if the board has exercised due diligence. Many laws and regulations make the board responsible in the event of data breaches. Even cyber security insurance policies require the board to exercise due diligence as a prerequisite for insurance coverage.

Security steering committee

The **security steering committee** is generally composed of senior management from different business units. The security steering committee is best placed to determine the level of acceptable risk for the organization. The security steering committee monitors and controls the security strategy. They also ensure that the security policy is aligned with business objectives.

Reporting of the security function

In the past, the security function in most organizations reported to the **CIO**. However, it has since been observed that the CIO is primarily concerned with IT performance and costs, with security as a secondary objective. Whenever there was a conflict between performance and security, security was generally ignored.

However, with increased awareness and more experience, the responsibility for security is now entrusted to senior-level functionaries directly reporting to the COO, CEO, or the board of directors. This ensures the independence of the security function.

Organizations' security functions can work in either a **centralized** or **decentralized** way, as we will touch on in the next section.

Centralized vis-à-vis decentralized security functioning

In a centralized process, information security activities are handled from a central location, usually the head office of the organization. In a decentralized process, the implementation and monitoring of security activities are delegated to local offices of the organization.

The following table shows the differentiation between centralized and decentralized processes:

Centralized process	Decentralized process
More consistency in security processes.	Comparatively less consistency.
Optimum utilization of information security resources.	Comparatively greater resource requirements.
Comparatively less alignment with the requirements of decentralized units.	Better alignment with decentralized unit requirements.
A centralized process will generally take more time to process requests due to the larger gap between the information security department and the end user.	Faster turnaround of requests compared to centralized processes.

Table 2.4 – Centralized and decentralized processes

Centralization of information security management results in greater uniformity and easier monitoring of the process. This in turn will advance better adherence to security policies.

Key aspects from the CISM exam perspective

The following is one of the key aspects of this topic from an exam perspective:

Question	Possible Answer
Which approach (that is, top-down or bottom-up) is more effective for governance?	In a top-down approach, policies, procedures, and goals are set by senior management and hence policies and procedures are directly aligned with business objectives. A bottom-up approach may not directly address management priorities. The effectiveness of governance is best ensured by a top-down approach.

Table 2.5 – Key aspects from the CISM exam perspective

Practice questions

1. Which of the following is a characteristic of a decentralized information security process?

    A. Consistency in information security processes

    B. Better compliance with policy

    C. Better alignment with decentralized unit requirements

    D. Optimum utilization of information security resources

    Answer: C. Better alignment with decentralized unit requirements

    Explanation: In a decentralized environment, more emphasis is placed on the needs and requirements of business units. Options A and D are more relevant for centralized processes. Decentralized processes may not always ensure compliance with policy.

2. Which of the following is a characteristic of a centralized information security management process?

    A. Processes are costlier to manage compared to decentralized processes.

    B. Better adherence to policy compared to decentralized processes.

C. Better alignment with business unit requirements compared to decentralized processes.

D. Faster turnaround of requests compared to decentralized processes.

Answer: B. Better adherence to policy as compared to decentralized processes.

Explanation: The centralization of information security management will result in greater uniformity and easier monitoring of processes. This in turn will help achieve better adherence to security policies. Decentralized processes are generally more expensive to manage, but will be more aligned with business unit requirements. Centralized processes will generally have a slower turnaround for requests due to a larger gap between the information security department and the end user.

3. Ultimate responsibility for the protection of an organization's information lies with which of the following?

A. System administrator

B. CISO

C. CIO

D. Board of directors

Answer: D. Board of directors

Explanation: Ultimate responsibility for the appropriate protection of an organization's information lies with the board of directors. The other options here support the board in this role.

4. Who should determine the acceptable level of information security risk?

A. Legal department

B. CISO

C. Audit department

D. Steering committee

Answer: D. Steering committee

Explanation: Senior management members who are on the steering committee are best placed to determine the level of acceptable risk for the organization.

Record retention

The information security manager should ensure that an adequate **record retention** policy is in place and that this is followed throughout the organization. A record retention policy will specify what types of data and documents are required to be preserved, and what should be destroyed. It will also specify the number of years for which that data is required to be preserved.

Record retention should primarily be based on the following two factors:

- **Business requirements**
- **Legal requirements**

If a record is required to be maintained for 2 years as per the business requirements, and for 3 years from a legal perspective, then it should be maintained for 3 years. Organizations generally design their business requirement after considering the relevant laws and regulations.

Electronic discovery

Electronic discovery (**e-discovery**) is the process of the identification, collection, and submission of electronic records in a lawsuit or investigation. The best way to ensure the availability of electronic records is to implement comprehensive retention policies. A retention policy dictates the terms for storing, backing up, and accessing the records.

Key aspects from the CISM exam perspective

The following are some of the key aspects of this topic from an exam perspective:

Question	Possible Answer
What is e-discovery?	E-discovery is the process of identifying, collecting, and submitting electronic records in a lawsuit or investigation.
What are the factors on which record retention is based?	- Business requirements - Legal requirements (If both options are available, then preference should be given to business requirements as it is generally assumed that business requirements already include consideration of legal requirements.)

Table 2.6 – Key aspects from the CISM exam perspective

Practice questions

1. The most effective way to minimize the impact of e-discovery in the event of litigation is which of the following?

   A. Keep backups of sensitive data.

   B. Limit access to sensitive data.

   C. Not storing sensitive data.

   D. Implement comprehensive retention policies.

   Answer: D. Implement comprehensive retention policies.

   Explanation: E-discovery is the process of identifying, collecting, and submitting electronic records in a lawsuit or investigation. The best way to ensure the availability of electronic records is to implement comprehensive retention policies. A retention policy will dictate the terms of storage and backup of, and access to, the records.

2. Which of the following has the most influence while planning business record retention?

   A. Potential changes in storage capacity

   B. Potential changes in regulatory requirements

   C. Potential changes in business strategy

   D. Potential changes in application systems and media

   Answer: D. Potential changes in application systems and media

   Explanation: The type and nature of application systems and media and their capability to read and interpret different data formats is the most important factor in planning record retention. New application systems may not be able to read and interpret data generated by earlier applications. This is a major risk.

3. Which of the following is the most important consideration in business record retention?

   A. Strategic objectives

   B. Regulatory and legal requirements

   C. Storage capacity

   D. Level of controls implemented

   Answer: B. Regulatory and legal requirements

Explanation: Record retention should be primarily based on two factors: business requirements and legal requirements. If a record is required to be maintained for 2 years per the business requirements, and 3 years from the legal perspective, then it should be maintained for 3 years. Organizations generally design their business requirements after considering the relevant laws and regulations.

Awareness and education

End users are one of the most important elements for consideration in the overall security strategy. **Training**, **education**, and **awareness** are of extreme importance to ensure that policies, standards, and procedures are appropriately followed.

Increasing the effectiveness of security training

The most effective way to increase the effectiveness of security training is to customize the training to the target audience and to address the systems and procedures applicable to that particular group. For example, system developers need to undergo an enhanced level of training covering aspects of security related to coding, while data entry operators should be trained on the aspects of security related to their functions.

Key aspects from the CISM exam perspective

The following is one of the key aspects of this topic from an exam perspective:

Question	Possible Answer
What is the best method to increase the effectiveness of security training?	Customized training for the target audience.

Table 2.7 – Key aspects from the CISM exam perspective

Summary

In this chapter, we discussed various aspects of security strategies, the impact of organizational structure on security, record retention procedures, and other aspects of security. We learned how centralized and decentralized security functions impact the overall security posture of the organization. We also looked at how to increase the effectiveness of security training. This will help CISM aspirants understand different aspects of organizational structure.

In our next chapter, we will discuss important aspects of risk management activities.

Section 2: Information Risk Management

This part is about the management of risk and implementing effective controls. It covers 30% of the CISM certification exam.

This section contains the following chapters:

- *Chapter 3, Overview of Information Risk Management*
- *Chapter 4, Practical Aspects of Information Risk Management*
- *Chapter 5, Procedural Aspects of Information Risk Management*

3
Overview of Information Risk Management

In this chapter, we will provide an overview of **information risk management** and understand risk management tools and techniques, along with other important concepts from the perspective of the **CISM** exam. This chapter will help CISM candidates understand the different aspects of implementing risk management strategies.

The following topics will be covered in this chapter:

- Risk management overview
- Risk management strategy
- Implementing risk management
- Risk assessment and analysis methodologies
- Risk assessment

Let's look at each of these topics in detail.

Risk management overview

The prime objective of a risk management process is to achieve an optimum balance between maximizing business opportunities and minimizing vulnerabilities and threats. To achieve this objective, the information security manager should have a thorough understanding of the nature and extent of the risks that an organization may encounter. A mature organization has a dedicated **enterprise risk management (ERM)** group to monitor and control such risks.

The first step in developing a risk management program is to establish the context and purpose of the program. Management support can be gained only if the program has an appropriate context and purpose.

Risk management must operate at multiple levels, including strategic as well as operational. The effectiveness of risk management depends on how well risk management is integrated into an organization's culture and the extent to which risk management becomes everyone's responsibility.

Phases of risk management

The overall risk management program includes the following four phases:

1. **Step 1: Risk identification**: In risk identification, various risks impacting the business objectives are identified by way of risk scenarios. In risk identification, the threat landscape and vulnerabilities are identified.

2. **Step 2: Risk analysis**: In risk analysis, the impact and the level of the risk are determined (that is, high, medium, or low). Risk analysis helps determine the exposure to the business and to plan for remediation.

3. **Step 3: Risk evaluation**: In risk evaluation, it is determined whether the risk is within an acceptable range or whether it should be mitigated. Thus, based on risk evaluation, risk responses are decided.

4. **Step 4: Risk response**: Risk response can be in the form of risk mitigation, risk acceptance, risk avoidance, or risk transfer.

A security manager should also understand the outcome of the risk management program, which is detailed in the next section.

The outcome of the risk management program

The most important outcome of an effective risk management program is to reduce the incident that's impacting the business objectives. This can be done by addressing the threat and reducing the vulnerabilities and their exposure. The **risk management program** supports the organization's ability to operate effectively and efficiently.

Key aspects from the CISM exam's perspective

The following are some of the key aspects from an exam perspective:

Question	Possible Answer
What is the first step in developing a risk management program?	To establish the context and purpose of the program.
What is the main objective of risk evaluation?	In risk evaluation, it is determined whether the risk is within an acceptable range or whether it should be mitigated. Thus, based on risk evaluation, risk responses are decided.
What is the main objective of risk response?	To control the level of impact.
What is the main objective of risk analysis?	To determine the level of exposure/impact.

Table 3.1 – Key aspects from the CISM exam perspective

Questions

1. The first step in developing a risk management program is to establish what?

    A. Management support

    B. A security policy and procedure

    C. An oversight committee

    D. The context and purpose of the program

    Answer: D. The context and purpose of the program.

    Explanation: The first step is to establish the context and purpose of the program. Management support can only be gained if the program has an appropriate context and purpose. The security policy and oversight committee are subsequent steps.

2.   What is the main objective of risk evaluation?

A. It provides a basis for selecting risk response.

B. It ensures that all the controls are effective.

C. It provides an assessment of the risk management program.

D. It ensures that risks are categorized appropriately.

Answer: A. It provides a basis for selecting risk response.

Explanation: In risk evaluation, it is determined whether a risk is within an acceptable range or whether it should be mitigated. Thus, based on risk evaluation, risk responses are decided.

3.   What is the main objective of risk response?

A. To decrease the cost of control

B. To decrease the level of vulnerability

C. To decrease the level of threat

D. To decrease the level of impact

Answer: D. To decrease the level of impact.

Explanation: The most important objective of risk response is to treat the risk in such a way that the impact of the risk is within an acceptable level. Lowering the vulnerability or addressing the threat is one of the approaches to controlling the impact of risk. The objective of risk response is not to decrease the cost of control.

4.   What is the main objective of risk analysis?

A. To justify the security budget

B. To prioritize the assets to be protected

C. To determine the residual risk

D. To assess the level of exposure and plan for remediation

Answer: D. To assess the level of exposure and plan for remediation.

Explanation: In risk analysis, the impact and level of the risk are determined (that is, high, medium, or low). Risk analysis helps determine the exposure and planning for remediation. Prioritizing assets is the indirect benefit of risk analysis but not the main objective.

Risk management strategy

First, let's understand what a *strategy* is. A strategy is a plan that helps us achieve the objective. In this sense, a **risk management strategy** is a plan for achieving the risk management objective. The ultimate objective of any risk management program is to support the business objective by mitigating the risk to an acceptable level. Thus, the main objective of the risk management strategy is to support the business objective.

The risk management strategy should be aligned with the overall governance strategy. It should be consistent and integrated with the overall governance strategy.

Risk capacity, appetite, and tolerance

The first step of learning about risk management is understanding the following three important terms:

- **Risk capacity**
- **Risk tolerance**
- **Risk appetite**

Let's understand the difference between risk capacity, risk appetite, and risk tolerance, as follows:

- **Risk capacity**: This is the maximum risk an organization can afford to take.
- **Risk tolerance**: This is made up of two things: that the risk tolerance levels are acceptable deviations from risk appetite, and that they are always lower than the risk capacity.
- **Risk appetite**: This is the amount of risk that an organization is willing to take.

Now that you have an idea of what these terms are, let's dive into an example.

Example

Mr. A's total savings are *$1,000*. He wants to invest in equities to earn some income. Since he is risk-averse, he decides to only invest up to *$700*. If the markets are good, he is willing to invest a further *$50*. Let's derive the risk capacity, risk appetite, and risk tolerance for this example, as follows:

- **Risk capacity**: Total amount available; that is, $1,000
- **Risk appetite**: His willingness to take risks; that is, $700
- **Risk tolerance**: The acceptance deviation from risk appetite; that is, $750

The following diagram demonstrates the relationship between risk capacity, risk tolerance, and risk appetite:

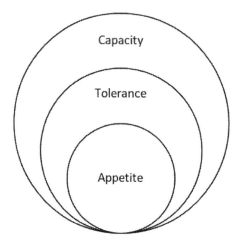

Figure 3.1 – Risk appetite/tolerance/capacity

We can infer the following from this diagram:

- Risk capacity is always greater compared to tolerance and appetite.

- Tolerance can either be equal to, or greater than, appetite. Risk tolerance levels are acceptable deviations from risk appetite.

- Risk acceptance should generally be within the risk appetite of the organization. In no case should it exceed the risk capacity.

Another important aspect for a security manager is to understand in terms of risk communication, which we will discuss in the next section.

Risk communication

The **communication** of risk management activities is key to effectively implementing a risk management strategy. Communication should involve all the relevant stakeholders. Communication channels should have the ability to provide interaction both ways; that is, management can communicate to end users and end users should also be able to pass on information related to risks to management.

Risk awareness

Having an **awareness** of risk management programs improves the risk culture of the organization. Awareness is a key element that impacts the behavior of end users. Through an **awareness program**, each member of the organization can help identify vulnerabilities, suspicious activities, and other abnormal behavior patterns. This helps with responding faster to an attack or incident and thus minimizing the impact.

Tailored awareness program

An effective **awareness program** should be tailored to the needs of the individual groups. Specific awareness content, as applicable to respective job functions, enhances the effectiveness of awareness training. For example, a developer can be made aware of the secure coding practices, whereas the end user may be made aware of the risk of phishing emails.

While developing an awareness program, the following aspects need to be considered:

- The awareness program should be capable of highlighting the relevant risk.
- The awareness program should be able to highlight the impact if risks are not controlled.
- The awareness program should not openly discuss open vulnerabilities or the details of an ongoing investigation.
- The awareness program should periodically change messages and communication channels so that it's more effective.

Training effectiveness

It is equally important to determine the effectiveness of awareness training at periodic intervals. Metrics can be in the form of security quizzes, phishing attack simulations, blind penetration tests, and so on.

Awareness training for senior management

Senior management should be frequently reminded that they are the ones who own the risk and are responsible for implementing the relevant controls. The highlights for senior management should be regulatory requirements, the impact on business objectives, and the liability of the organization. Senior management plays an important role in adopting a risk-aware culture in the organization.

Key aspects from the CISM exam's perspective

The following are some of the key aspects from an exam perspective:

Question	Possible Answer
What is the main objective of the risk management program?	To reduce risk to an acceptable level.

Table 3.2 – Key aspects from the CISM exam perspective

Questions

1. What is the most effective strategy for risk management?

    A. To achieve a balance between risk and business goals

    B. To reduce the risk to an acceptable level

    C. To develop policy statements

    D. To document all unmitigated risks

    Answer: B. To reduce the risk to an acceptable level.

    Explanation: The most effective strategy for risk management is to reduce the risk to an acceptable level. This will help the organization manage risk as per their risk appetite. It may not always be practical to achieve a balance between risk and business goals. Developing a policy statement and documentation of the risks is not as significant as reducing the risk to an acceptable level.

2. Risk assessment is always subjective. The best way to improve the accuracy of the assessment is to do what?

    A. Provide training to the assessor

    B. Use a standardized assessment framework

    C. Ensure the independence of the assessor

    D. Use a different framework

    Answer: A. Provide training to the assessor.

    Explanation: The best way to reduce the subjectivity of the risk assessment is to provide frequent training to the risk assessor. This improves the accuracy of assessment. Without appropriate training, other options may not be effective.

3. What is the main objective of the risk management program?

    A. To reduce the inherent risk

    B. To eliminate all the risk

    C. To establish effective control

    D. To achieve acceptable risk

    Answer: D. To achieve acceptable risk.

    Explanation: The main objective of a risk management program is to ensure that risk is within a level acceptable to management. If an inherent risk is already within the acceptable level, there is no need to further reduce the same. It is not practical and feasible to eliminate all risks. The ultimate objective of establishing effective control is to ensure that risks are within an acceptable level.

4. What is the most effective way to ensure the overall effectiveness of the risk management program?

    A. The program is convenient to implement.

    B. The program is adopted from industry standards.

    C. The program is monitored by senior management.

    D. The program is supported by all members of the organization.

    Answer: D. The program is supported by all members of the organization.

    Explanation: For effective risk management, the most important criterion is that the program should be supported by all members of the organization. All staff members should be able to understand their roles and responsibilities concerning risk management. The other options are secondary criteria.

5. The objective of the risk management program is to reduce the risk to what?

    A. Nil

    B. An acceptable level

    C. An acceptable percentage of revenue

    D. Eliminate all the hazards

    Answer: B. An acceptable level.

    Explanation: The objective of a risk management program is to reduce the risk to an acceptable level for management. Reducing the risk to zero is not possible.

6. The information security team noted that management has not mitigated the risk, even though the risk exceeds the risk appetite. What is the most likely reason for this?

    A. Controls have already been applied.

    B. Controls are expensive.

    C. The risk is within the risk tolerance level.

    D. The probability of it occurring is very low.

    Answer: C. The risk is within the risk tolerance level.

    Explanation: Risk tolerance is an acceptable level of deviation from risk appetite. Generally, risk tolerance is slightly higher than risk appetite. Other options are not the main factor for ignoring risk.

7. For effective risk management, it should be applied to what?

    A. All organizational processes

    B. Processes identified by a risk assessment

    C. Processes whose risk appetite is low

    D. Processes that can have a potential impact

    Answer: A. All organizational processes.

    Explanation: Risk management should be applied to all the processes of the organization. Whether a risk level is acceptable can only be determined when the risk is known.

8. What is the best way to support the business objectives through risk management?

    A. The risk assessment is to be performed by asset owners.

    B. Timely updates of the risk register.

    C. Monitoring by the steering committee.

    D. Risk activities are embedded in business processes.

    Answer: D. Risk activities are embedded in business processes.

    Explanation: The main objective of a risk management process is that risk is identified and mitigated promptly. This can be best done by embedding risk activities into all business processes. The other options are not as significant for embedding risk management activities into business processes.

Implementing risk management

Implementing a risk management program is one of the important aspects for ensuring effective and efficient **governance, risk management, and compliance (GRC)**. The security manager should identify the existing risk management activities and try to integrate these activities to utilize resources. Integrating risk management activities helps prevent efforts from being duplicated and minimizes the gaps in assurance functions.

Risk management process

Implementing a risk management program in a structured way helps you achieve maximum efficiency and effectiveness with minimum effort. It is recommended to implement the program as per the following sequence:

1. Determine the scope and boundaries of the program.

2. Determine the assets and processes that need to be protected.

3. Conduct a risk assessment by identifying the risks, analyzing the level of risk based on the impact, and evaluating whether the risk meets the criteria for acceptance.

4. Determine the risk treatment options for risks that are above the acceptable level. Risk treatment can be in any of the following forms:

   A. Mitigating the risk by implementing additional controls.

   B. Accepting the risk (generally, this option is selected when the impact is low and the cost of treatment exceeds the impact).

   C. Avoid the risk (generally, this option is selected when the feasibility study or business case does not indicate positive results).

   D. Transfer the risk to third parties such as insurance companies (generally, this option is selected for a low probability risk that has a high impact, such as natural disasters).

   An appropriate risk treatment method helps achieve the control objective efficiently.

5. Determine the acceptability of the residual risk (that is, any risks remaining after treatment) by management.

6. Monitor the risk continuously and develop an appropriate procedure to report the results of risk monitoring to management.

During all these steps, it is equally important to share relevant information about risk management activities with concerned stakeholders. Having an effective communication process improves the whole risk management process.

Effective risk management requires participation, support, and acceptance by the relevant members of the organization, starting with senior management. Employees must understand their responsibilities and be able to perform their required roles.

Risk controls are measures and are considered to be sufficient when the residual risk is less than or equal to an acceptable risk.

Integrating risk management in business processes

For effective risk management, the risk management processes must be integrated with the **business processes**. The best way to implement this is to conduct workflow analysis, understand the process vulnerabilities, and build the relevant controls within the process.

Prioritization of risk response

It may not be feasible for the organization to address all the risks. In such cases, the risk should be prioritized based on its criticality. High-level risks should be addressed first. Prioritizing the treatment options will be most effective if they're based on the likelihood of compromise and their impact on the business.

Defining a risk management framework

A framework is a structure or outline that supports the implementation of any program. Frameworks are flexible structures that any organization can adopt as per their environment and requirements. Many standards and guidelines on best practices are available for effectively managing IT risk, such as the following:

- **COBIT**
- **ISO 31000** on **Enterprise Risk Management**
- **ISO 27001** on the **Information Security Management System**

Generally, all these frameworks/standards have the following requirements:

- The documented policy that defines the objective of the program must be available.
- The documented roles and responsibilities for implementing the program must be available.
- Commitment from senior management to review the program frequently.
- Procedure documents must be available.
- Adequate records to satisfy an independent audit must be available.

By defining the risk management framework, the basic parameters for managing the risk are established. Basic parameters include criteria for acceptable risk, the objective of the controls, and processes to monitor the effectiveness of these controls. A framework helps achieve the following objectives:

- Having a common understanding of organizational objectives.

- Developing a set of criteria for measuring risk.

- Developing a structured process for identifying risk and assessing the level of risk.

- Integrating different assurance functions.

Defining the external and internal environment

While designing the risk management program, the requirements of the stakeholders should be considered. Stakeholders can be either external or internal. External context includes laws and regulations, social and cultural conditions, risk from competitors, financial and political environment, and so on. It also includes considering threats and opportunities that have been generated by external sources.

The internal context includes the management requirements, the organization's structure, culture, goals, and objectives, and the organization's strengths and weaknesses.

Determining the risk management context

Context means the scope and applicability of risk management activities. Context defines the environment in which risk management will operate. A security manager needs to understand the risk management context. Context is generally determined by the culture of the organization in terms of risk averseness or risk aggressiveness.

Gap analysis

Gap analysis is the process of determining the gap between the existing level of the risk management process compared to the desired state. Based on the desired state, control objectives are defined. The objective of gap analysis is to identify whether control objectives can be achieved through the risk management process.

Periodically determining the gap between the actual controls and their objectives should be routine practice. Gap analysis is generally done by determining the effectiveness of controls through control testing. If a gap is identified, then the controls may need to be modified or redesigned to improve their effectiveness.

Cost-benefit analysis

The most important factor when selecting controls is the cost-benefit balance. Implemented controls should be effective (that is, able to address the risk) as well as efficient (providing the most benefit compared to cost incurred).

Cost-benefit analysis is performed to ensure that the cost of a control does not exceed its benefit and that the best control is implemented for the given cost. Cost-benefit analysis helps justify the implementation of a specific control measure.

Other kinds of organizational support

Organizations can rely on the services of external service providers to understand the current threat landscape and to identify industry-level best practices. These services help leverage the expertise of service providers and improve the security posture of the organization. Some of the most widely used services are as follows:

- Organizations such as ISACA, NIST, ISC, and SANs, which often publish best practices and other industry-wide data that can be used to determine and evaluate the security program.

- Many organizations sponsor security-related roundtables to discuss topics of common interest. This helps accumulate the knowledge base from experts in the industry.

- Various organizations sponsor research and studies related to security-related aspects.

- Many institutes are involved in training related to security aspects such as vulnerability assessment, penetration testing, secure coding, and end user awareness.

- Many organizations release a list of current vulnerabilities impacting specific technology. This can be either a free service or a subscription-based service. External vulnerability sources are the most cost-effective way of identifying new vendor vulnerabilities.

Information security is an ever-evolving subject and security managers should keep themselves updated by using these sources.

Key aspects from the CISM exam's perspective

The following are some of the key aspects from an exam perspective:

Question	Possible Answer
What is the prime objective of an acceptable usage policy?	To reduce the risk of data leakage.
What is the most cost-effective way of identifying new vulnerabilities for third-party products?	Subscriptions to organizations publishing vulnerabilities. External vulnerability sources are the most cost-effective way of identifying new vendor vulnerabilities.
In which phase of system development should risk assessment should be initiated?	Feasibility phase (risk should be addressed as early as possible in the development cycle).
Which factor is the most influential while selecting controls?	Cost-benefit balance.
What is the objective of cost-benefit analysis?	Cost-benefit analysis is performed to ensure that the cost of a control does not exceed its benefit and that the best control is implemented for the given cost.
Taking insurance is an example of which risk treatment option?	Risk transfer.
What is the prime objective of gap analysis?	To measure the current state vis-à-vis the desired state.
What is the most effective way to mitigate the risk of phishing?	User awareness.
What is the prime objective of the risk management program?	To reduce risk to an acceptable level.
What is the most effective way to treat risks such as natural disasters, which have a low probability and a high impact level?	Risk transfer.
What is the most effective way to address insider threats to confidential information?	Implementing role-based access controls.
What are the components of risk treatment (risk response)?	<ul><li>Risk mitigation</li><li>Risk acceptance</li><li>Risk avoidance</li><li>Risk transfer</li></ul>

Question	Possible Answer
What are the essential elements of the risk?	• Probability (likelihood) • Impact (consequences)
What is the objective of segmenting sensitive data?	To reduce the exposure of sensitive data. (Reducing exposure reduces the likelihood of a vulnerability being exploited.)
What is the objective of the indemnity clause?	To reduce the financial impact on the organization. The indemnity clause helps an organization to claim financial loss from the service provider in case loss is suffered due to what the service provider does. Indemnification clauses can transfer operational risk and financial impacts, but the legal responsibility of the consequences of compromise generally remains with the original organization.
Which analysis is used to determine the priority of actions in a BCP?	Business impact analysis.
Under which circumstances will management not want to mitigate the risk, even if the level of risk is above the risk appetite?	The risk falls within the risk tolerance level. (Risk tolerance levels are acceptable deviations from risk appetite.)
What is the best way to determine the sufficiency of risk control measures?	To determine whether the residual risk is less than or equal to the acceptable level.
The acceptable level of residual risk is determined by what?	Management discretion.
What is the main objective of risk response?	To control the impact.
Prioritizing risk response is based on what?	The likelihood of compromise and the impact on the business.

Table 3.3 – Key aspects from the CISM exam perspective

Questions

1. What is the most effective way to address the risk of data leakage?

    A. Availability of backup procedures

    B. Availability of data integrity checks

    C. Availability of acceptable usage policy

    D. Availability of the incident management process

    Answer: C. Availability of acceptable usage policy.

    Explanation: An acceptable usage policy is a document stipulating constraints and practices that a user must agree on to use organizational resources. Many organizations require employees to sign an acceptable use policy before access is granted. Other options may not directly impact data leakages.

2. What is the best way to identify new vendor vulnerability cost-effectively?

    A. External vulnerability reporting sources

    B. Network scanning software

    C. Periodic vulnerability assessment

    D. Implementing honeypots

    Answer: A. External vulnerability reporting sources.

    Explanation: Many agencies publish new vulnerabilities and provide recommendations to address the vulnerabilities. This is the most cost-effective way to understand new vulnerabilities. Other options may not be as cost-effective as external vulnerability sources.

3. What is the SDLC phase in which risk assessment should first be conducted?

    A. Implementation

    B. Testing

    C. Programming

    D. Feasibility

    Answer: D. Feasibility.

    Explanation: Risk assessment should commence at the earliest phase of SDLC; that is, the feasibility phase. The feasibility study should include risk assessment so that the cost of controls can be determined at the beginning.

4. What is the most important factor for implementing controls and countermeasures?

    A. Reducing IT risk

    B. Cost-benefit balance

    C. Resource utilization

    D. Count of assets protected

    Answer: B. Cost-benefit balance.

    Explanation: Selecting controls and countermeasures primarily depends on cost-benefit analysis. The others are secondary factors.

5. Which area is the data owner responsible for risk mitigation?

    A. Operating system security

    B. User entitlements

    C. Network security

    D. Intrusion detection

    Answer: B. User entitlements.

    Explanation: The data owner is accountable for ensuring that access to their data is provided based on user entitlement and on a need-to-know basis. The other options are the responsibility of the security team.

6. Taking out insurance is an example of what?

    A. Risk avoidance

    B. Risk acceptance

    C. Risk transfer

    D. Risk mitigation

    Answer: C. Risk transfer.

    Explanation: Taking out insurance is an example of risk transfer. In risk transfer, the risk is shared with partners or transferred via insurance coverage, a contractual agreement, or other means. Natural disasters have a very low probability but a high impact. A response to such risks should be risk transfer.

7. The mitigating control should be decided by who?

    A. Senior manager

    B. Business manager

    C. Audit manager

    D. Security manager

    Answer: B. Business manager.

    Explanation: The business manager will be in the best position to decide on any particular control based on the risk assessment as they are aware of the risks that are relevant to their processes. The senior manager should provide appropriate funding for the control. The audit and security managers support the business manager by reviewing and monitoring the effectiveness of the control.

8. What is the prime objective of a gap analysis?

    A. To evaluate the business impact

    B. To design a balanced score card

    C. To determine the overall cost of control

    D. To measure the current state versus the desired future state

    Answer: D. To measure the current state versus the desired future state.

    Explanation: The objective of a gap analysis is to identify the gap between the current level of control versus the desired level of control. This gap is also known as control deficiencies. Risk practitioners analyze the desired state of the risk management requirements of the organization and then determine the current condition of the risk management affairs. This helps them identify the gaps. They should recommend that the gaps are closed.

9. Which risk of a new application should be assessed first?

    A. Feasibility

    B. Design

    C. Development

    D. Testing

    Answer: A. Feasibility.

    Explanation: It is always advisable to identify and address the risk at the early stage of new system development. The risk of the new system may challenge the feasibility of the system's development.

10. What is the most effective way to select a control when there is a budget constraint?

   A. A business impact analysis

   B. A risk analysis

   C. A cost-benefit analysis

   D. A vulnerability analysis

   Answer: C. A cost-benefit analysis.

   Explanation: The objective of a cost-benefit analysis is to determine the benefits compared to the cost of the project. If the benefit that's realized from the control is less than the cost of implementing the control, then it does not justify implementing it. Selecting a control is primarily based on a cost-benefit analysis.

11. An organization started operating in a country where identity theft is widespread. What is the best course of action for the organization?

   A. Set up monitoring techniques to detect and react to fraud.

   B. Make the customer liable for fraud.

   C. Make the customer aware of the possibility of fraud.

   D. Outsource the process to a well-established service provider.

   Answer: A. Set up monitoring techniques to detect and react to fraud.

   Explanation: The best course of action for the organization in this situation is to set up monitoring techniques to detect and react to potential frauds. It is not possible to make customers liable for the fraud. Making customers aware of fraud is a good option but not as effective as setting up monitoring techniques. For outsourcing the process, a business case needs to be reviewed so that decisions can be made. However, the most effective method would be setting up monitoring techniques to detect and react to fraud.

12. What is the first step in establishing a data leakage program?

   A. Create user awareness training

   B. Develop an information classification program

   C. Design network control

   D. Develop physical control

   Answer: B. Develop an information classification program.

   Explanation: The first step is to develop a classification program. Based on that, critical data can be identified. The other options are subsequent steps.

13. What is the most effective way to mitigate a phishing attack?

    A. Create user awareness training.

    B. Email encryption.

    C. Develop two-factor authentication.

    D. Develop physical control.

    Answer: A. Create user awareness training.

    Explanation: Phishing is an attack where employees are contacted via email by someone posing as a legitimate institution to lure individuals into providing sensitive data such as personally identifiable information, banking and credit card details, and passwords. The best way to combat this attack is by providing frequent user awareness.

14. What is the next step after identifying residual risk?

    A. Transferring risk to an insurance company

    B. Transferring risk to a third-party service provider

    C. Determining that residual risk is acceptable

    D. Accepting the residual risk

    Answer: C. Determining that residual risk is acceptable.

    Explanation: Once the residual risk has been determined, the next step is to validate whether the residual risk is acceptable. If the risk is within the risk appetite, it can be accepted. Otherwise, further controls are to be implemented to reduce the same.

15. What is the best response to a risk scenario with low probability and high impact, such as a natural disaster?

    A. Risk avoidance

    B. Risk acceptance

    C. Risk transfer

    D. Risk mitigation

    Answer: C. Risk transfer.

    Explanation: Taking out insurance is an example of risk transfer. In risk transfer, the risk is shared with partners or transferred via insurance coverage, a contractual agreement, or other means. Natural disasters have a very low probability but a high impact. A response to such a risk should be risk transfer.

16. What is the most important factor in determining an acceptable level of IT risk?

    A. Organizational requirements

    B. Security requirements

    C. International standards

    D. Audit requirements

    Answer: A. Organizational requirements.

    Explanation: The acceptable level of risk is determined by the overall organizational requirements. Other options may not directly determine an acceptable level of IT risk.

17. What is the best way to mitigate the liability risks that arise due to breaches in privacy laws?

    A. To mitigate the impact by purchasing insurance

    B. To implement an application-level firewall

    C. To conduct a business impact analysis

    D. To implement an intrusion prevention system

    Answer: A. To mitigate the impact by purchasing insurance.

    Explanation: The best way is to purchase insurance to compensate for the financial liability. Privacy laws aim to protect the privacy of the customer and generally mandate heavy penalties for data breach incidents. Breaches can still happen, even after implementing technical controls, so the best way is to purchase insurance.

18. What is the outcome of a successful risk management program?

    A. The organization can quantify the risk.

    B. The organization can eliminate the inherent risk.

    C. The organization can minimize the residual risk.

    D. The organization can monitor control risk.

    Answer: C. The organization can minimize the residual risk.

    Explanation: The prime objective of any risk management program is that residual risk is minimized and is within the risk appetite of the organization. It is not practical and feasible to eliminate inherent risk. The quantification of risk and the monitoring thereof is a good indicator, but something more significant is minimizing the residual risk.

19. What is the best way to protect confidential information from insider threats?

    A. Role-based access control

    B. Capturing transaction logs

    C. Developing a privacy policy

    D. Defense-in-depth

    Answer: A. Role-based access control.

    Explanation: The best way is to provide access to confidential information on a need-to-know basis, which can be done through role-based access control. Defense-in-depth is generally for external threats. Capturing transaction logs is a detective control.

20. Risk acceptance is one of the components of which of the following?

    A. Risk reporting

    B. Risk treatment

    C. Risk monitoring

    D. Risk assessment

    Answer: B. Risk treatment.

    Explanation: Risk treatment consists of four options: risk acceptance, risk avoidance, risk mitigation, and risk transfer.

21. A security manager has determined the likelihood of a risk event. What should be assessed next to determine the level of risk?

    A. Magnitude of impact

    B. Tolerance for the risk

    C. Appetite for the risk

    D. Asset book value

    Answer: A. Magnitude of impact.

    Explanation: To determine the risk level, two things are required: the probability (likelihood) of the event and the impact of the event. The risk is a combination of probability and impact. Once the likelihood has been determined, the next step is to assess the magnitude of the impact. Once the level of risk has been determined, it is compared against risk appetite and risk tolerance.

22. What is the most important aspect of risk?

    A. Threat and impact

    B. Likelihood and consequences

    C. Impact and insurance

    D. Sensitivity and threat

    Answer: B. Likelihood and consequences.

    Explanation: To determine the risk level, two things are required: the probability of the event and the impact of the event. Risk is a combination of probability (likelihood) and impact (consequences).

23. What is the prime objective of segmenting a critical database?

    A. To reduce the threat

    B. To reduce the sensitivity

    C. To reduce the criticality

    D. To reduce the exposure

    Answer: D. To reduce the exposure.

    Explanation: Segmenting the data helps reduce exposure as more controls are implemented for segmented critical databases. Segmentation by itself does not reduce threats, sensitivity, or criticality.

24. What is the main objective of implementing security aspects during the first stage of the project life cycle?

    A. To minimize the cost of security

    B. To determine project feasibility

    C. To obtain budget approval

    D. To classify the project

    Answer: B. To determine project feasibility.

    Explanation: Information security requirements may directly impact the feasibility of the project. The cost of security must be considered while calculating business cases and feasibility studies. Sometimes, the cost of security may exceed the benefit that's expected from the project, so you may not be able to implement the project.

25. What is the main objective of including an indemnity clause in a service-level agreement?

    A. To decrease the probability of the incident

    B. To limit the impact on the organization

    C. To comply with regulatory requirements

    D. To improve performance

    Answer: B. To limit the impact on the organization.

    Explanation: The objective of the indemnity clause is to compensate or recover from any losses due to a breach of the agreement. It helps reduce the financial impact on the organization. An indemnity clause may not always be a regulatory requirement. Merely by incorporating an indemnity clause, probability cannot be reduced, and performance improvement cannot be ensured.

26. The information security manager has noted that due to slow biometric responses and a large number of employees, a substantial amount of time is wasted in gaining access to buildings. This has also increased instances of piggybacking. What should the security manager do?

    A. Replace the biometric system with a better response time

    B. Escalate the issue to management

    C. Discontinue the use of the biometric access system

    D. Ensure strict enforcement

    Answer: B. Escalate the issue to management.

    Explanation: Management will be the best position for addressing such kinds of issues where security requirements are adversely impacting the business.

27. In a BCP, prioritizing an action is primarily dependent on what?

    A. A business impact analysis

    B. A risk analysis

    C. A threat analysis

    D. A vulnerability assessment

    Answer: A. A business impact analysis.

    Explanation: A business impact analysis helps determine the critical processes/assets of the organization. These critical processes/assets should be recovered on priority.

28. What is the most effective way to determine the existing level of risk?

    A. A vulnerability analysis

    B. A threat analysis

    C. An impact analysis

    D. A security review

    Answer: D. A security review.

    Explanation: A security review is conducted to determine the current state of the security posture of the organization. Vulnerability and threat analyses will help determine the level of vulnerability and threat, but without knowing about the existing security arrangement, existing risks cannot be determined. An impact analysis is more effective for determining the potential impact of a loss event.

29. What are the results of the risk management process used for?

    A. Changing business objectives

    B. Updating audit charters

    C. Making security policy decisions

    D. Updating SDLC processes

    Answer: C. Making security policy decisions.

    Explanation: The risk management process helps highlight the risks that can impact the business processes. It helps make security policy decisions address the highlighted risks. The risk management process is used to support the business objectives and not change them. The audit charter highlights the roles and responsibilities of the audit department and is not directly impacted by the risk management process.

30. What is the best way to determine the most critical factor among confidentiality, integrity, and availability?

    A. Based on the threats that can be applied to each factor

    B. Confidentiality should always be given preference

    C. Based on the risks that can be applied to each factor

D. All three factors should be treated equally

Answer: C. Based on the risks that can be applied to each factor.

Explanation: The most important factors are considered based on the risks that can be applied to them. For example, if an automatic door fails, the organization can opt for fail open (the door should remain open) or fail closed (the door should remain closed). In the case of fail open, confidentiality and integrity may be compromised, while in the case of fail closed, availability may be compromised. In such a situation, risks must be determined for each element and a call needs to be given. Considering only the threat elements will not serve this purpose as both the threat and its impact (that is, the overall risk) need to be considered.

31. What area is of most concern for a security manager concerning a homogeneous network?

    A. Risk of reliability

    B. Single point of failure

    C. Slow network performance

    D. Aggregated risk

    Answer: D. Aggregated risk.

    Explanation: A homogenous network is a computer network comprised of similar configurations and protocols. This allows for common threats for all the devices, so a major concern is that all the devices are being impacted by a single threat. The other options are not directly impacted by homogeneous networks.

32. The recommendation to implement information system controls such as antivirus software is an example of what?

    A. Risk acceptance

    B. Risk mitigation

    C. Risk transfer

    D. Risk avoidance

    Answer: B. Risk mitigation.

    Explanation: Risk mitigation is the act of implementing security controls to reduce the impact of risk and bringing the risk level down to an acceptable level.

33. What is the best risk treatment method?

    A. A method that eliminates risks completely

    B. A method that is least costly

    C. A method that addresses the control objective

    D. A method that reduces the risk as much as possible

    Answer: C. A method that addresses the control objective.

    Explanation: The control objective is met when risk is mitigated effectively and efficiently. The best risk treatment should be both effective (that is, it should be able to address the risk) and efficient (that is, the cost of treatment should be optimal).

34. What is the prime objective of a cost-benefit analysis before control is implemented?

    A. It helps us adhere to a budget.

    B. It is a mandatory requirement by senior management.

    C. Conducting industry benchmarks.

    D. Ensuring that costs are justified by the reduction in risk.

    Answer: D. Ensuring that costs are justified by the reduction in risk.

    Explanation: The main objective of a cost-benefit analysis is to ensure that the cost of the project does not exceed the benefit expected from the project. The cost should be justified by an appropriate reduction in the risk.

35. What is the most effective way to mitigate the critical vulnerabilities identified during a recent security test?:

    A. All the vulnerabilities should be addressed immediately.

    B. Mitigation should be based on threat, impact, and cost considerations.

    C. Mitigation should be based on the available security budget.

    D. Compensating controls must be implemented for major vulnerabilities.

    Answer: B. Mitigation should be based on threat, impact, and cost considerations.

    Explanation: Mitigation must consider the level of risk and the cost of various treatment options. High-risk vulnerabilities should be addressed based on priorities. Low-risk vulnerabilities may not be addressed immediately. Resources should be utilized first to address any high-risk vulnerabilities.

36. What is the most effective way to address the risk of the acquisition of new IT resources?

    A. Acceptance of the risk by the IT manager.

    B. To obtain approval of compliance before acquiring the new system.

    C. To obtain approval from the senior manager before acquiring the new system.

    D. Implement the appropriate procurement process.

    Answer: D. Implement the appropriate procurement process.

    Explanation: The most important aspect is to implement a structured process that will help identify the risks that may be introduced by the new system. Options A, B, and C can be made part of a structured process.

37. When should a risk assessment be performed in an SDLC life cycle?

    A. Only before starting development

    B. During the system deployment stage

    C. During the feasibility stage

    D. At each stage of the SDLC life cycle

    Answer: D. At each stage of the SDLC life cycle.

    Explanation: Risk management should be performed at each stage of the SDLC life cycle. This will help in identifying risks early as they can occur during any stage.

38. The enterprise's current risk appetite can be best quantitatively indicated by which of the following?

    A. A count of the incidents and subsequent mitigation efforts

    B. Layers of implemented controls

    C. Level of security requirements in policy and standards

    D. Ratio of cost to insurance coverage for business interruption protection

    Answer: D. Ratio of cost to insurance coverage for business interruption protection.

    Explanation: The best quantification is to derive the cost of business interruption and the level of insurance that's been taken to protect against such losses. For example, let's say that the cost of business disruption is $100,000 and that the insurance covers up to $80,000. Here, the risk appetite of the organization can be considered $20,000. Other options will only provide a rough estimate of the risk appetite.

39. What is the most effective way to manage a security program with low funding?

    A. Remove security services that address low risk.

    B. Accept all the remaining risks.

    C. Use third-party service providers to manage low-risk activities.

    D. Eliminate monitoring and reporting activities.

    Answer: C. Use third-party service providers to manage low-risk activities.

    Explanation: The best option is to use the services of a third party that has expertise in information security. This will result in cost reductions and ensure that the security requirements are adhered to. Other options are not feasible and practicable and increase security risks.

40. When is the control level said to be appropriate?

    A. The risk acceptable level is less than the total risk level.

    B. The residual risk level is less than the risk acceptable level.

    C. The residual risk level is more than the risk acceptable level.

    D. The annual risk expectancy is more than the risk acceptable level.

    Answer: B. The residual risk level is less than the risk acceptable level.

    Explanation: Controls are said to be effective when the residual risk is less than the risk acceptance level. The residual risk is the risk that remains once the controls have been implemented. An acceptable level of risk is the willingness of the management to take risks.

41. What is the most important factor for risk-based information security programs?

    A. Prioritization

    B. Threat

    C. Standardization

    D. Budget

    Answer: A. Prioritization.

    Explanation: Prioritization helps determine the importance of assets/processes that need to be addressed first. Prioritization is done based on risk level. The highest risks are addressed first on a priority basis. Threats are not sufficient as we need to consider the vulnerability as well as impact.

42. An organization has two servers having similar content, but only if the server is hardened. What is the most plausible reason for this?

    A. The second server is only a backup server.

    B. The second server supports non-critical functions.

    C. The second server has been placed where there is no exposure.

    D. The second server is monitored continuously.

    Answer: C. The second server has been placed where there is no exposure.

    Explanation: If the second server is placed where there is no exposure, then there is no chance of compromise and hence hardening may not be required. For other options, such as having a second server in a backup server, it supports non-critical functions, or it is monitored continuously, while the risk remains the same as it contains the identical content, so it should be given the same level of protection as the first server.

43. What is the most effective risk treatment where the probability of the event occurring is very low but the impact can be very high?

    A. Accept the high cost of controlling such an event.

    B. Install the detective control.

    C. Avoid the risk.

    D. Transfer the risk to a third party.

    Answer: D. Transfer the risk to a third party.

    Explanation: The best risk response in such a scenario (low probability and high impact) is to transfer the risk to a third party. Insurance for natural calamities is one such example. This will help the organization compensate itself for financial losses.

44. What is the first course of action when integrating risk management practices into business processes?

    A. A workflow analysis

    B. A threat analysis

    C. A hierarchy analysis

    D. A business impact analysis

    Answer: A. A workflow analysis.

    Explanation: A workflow analysis is the process of understanding the workflow and helps determine the risk and build relevant controls. The other steps follow this step.

45. An indemnification clause in a service agreement does what?

    A. Addresses the legal as well as the financial liability of the organization

    B. Makes it preferable to purchasing insurance

    C. Addresses the reputational risk of the organization

    D. Addresses the financial liability but leaves legal and reputational risk generally unchanged

    Answer: D. Addresses the financial liability but leaves legal and reputational risk generally unchanged.

    Explanation: The objective of an indemnity clause is to compensate the organization for any financial loss due to what the service provider has done. However, it does not reduce the legal or reputation risk for the organization.

46. Reducing exposure will result in what?

    A. A reduction in impacts, if compromised

    B. A reduction in vulnerabilities

    C. A reduction in the likelihood of being exploited

    D. A reduction in the time needed to recover

    Answer: C. A reduction in the likelihood of being exploited.

    Explanation: Reducing exposure means keeping the information assets away from public reach. For example, a sensitive database is not connected through the public internet. This reduction in exposure will reduce the likelihood of being exploited. However, this will not automatically reduce other vulnerabilities. Also, it will not reduce the impact in case the database is compromised.

47. Residual risk is best determined by what?

    A. Management discretion

    B. Legal requirements

    C. Level of security budget

    D. Audit findings

    Answer: A. Management discretion.

    Explanation: Residual risk means the risk that management is willing to accept. It is an acceptable level of risk for management. Residual risk is ultimately subject to management discretion.

48. Prioritization of risk is based on what?

    A. Asset value

    B. Frequency and impact

    C. Legal requirements

    D. Frequency and scope

    Answer: B. Frequency and impact.

    Explanation: Risk is a product of probability and impact. Frequency (that is, probability) and impact can help determine the actual level of risk. Both terms are equally important when determining the level of risk. Each risk is determined based on its frequency (that is, probability), and impact and high-level risks are prioritized and addressed first. The other options are not as important as frequency and impact.

49. What is the best indicator of a quantifiable acceptable level of risk?

    A. Interviewing senior management

    B. Ratio of security budget to total budget

    C. Ratio of insurance coverage to the total cost of business interruption

    D. Determining the count of an incident impacting the organization

    Answer: C. Ratio of insurance coverage to the total cost of business interruption.

    Explanation: The objective here is to determine the acceptable level of risk by management. The best quantification is to derive the cost of business interruption and the level of insurance taken to protect against such losses. For example, the cost of business disruption is $100,000 and the insurance covers up to $80,000. Here, the risk appetite of the organization can be considered $20,000. The other options will only provide a rough estimation of the risk appetite.

50. What is the most important outcome of a risk management program?

    A. Continuous monitoring of vulnerabilities

    B. Continuous monitoring of threats

    C. Determining the implementation of control objectives

    D. Decreasing the number of incidents impacting the organization

    Answer: D. Decreasing the number of incidents impacting the organization.

    Explanation: The most important objective of a risk management program is to reduce the number of incidents that harm the objective of the organization. The other options are specific and actionable to achieve the outcome of addressing the adverse incidents.

51. Effectively protecting information assets strongly supports which of the following?

    A. Data workflow

    B. Data classification policy

    C. Security culture

    D. Business-oriented risk policy

    Answer: D. Business-oriented risk policy.

    Explanation: A risk policy that is aligned with business objectives helps in achieving an organization's objectives. A business-oriented risk policy is strongly supported by effectively managing information assets. The other options do not directly impact the effectiveness or efficiency of information assets.

52. What is the most effective option for addressing the defined threat?

    A. Implementing a deterrent control

    B. Reducing the exposure

    C. Implementing a compensating control

    D. Implementing an administrative control

    Answer: B. Reducing the exposure.

    Explanation: If a threat is already known, then the best way is to reduce its exposure. This reduces the probability of the risk being exploited. The other options are not as effective as reducing the exposure itself.

53. What is the best way to address the excessive exposure of sensitive databases?

    A. Implement an incident response procedure.

    B. Reduce the attack surface.

    C. Compartmentalize the sensitive database.

    D. Implement a deterrent control.

    Answer: B. Reduce the attack surface.

    Explanation: The attack surface is where you have various entry points where an attack can happen. The attack surface determines the level of exposure. By decreasing the attack surface, the level of exposure decreases. The attack surface can be reduced by limiting entry points, ports, and protocols and disabling unused services. The other options are not as effective at reducing the attack surface.

54. What is the best way to measure the effectiveness of risk management?

    A. The number of incidents not detected by the security team

    B. The number of security audits

    C. The number of vulnerabilities not mitigated by the security team

    D. The number of security incidents causing significant financial loss or business disruptions

    Answer: D. The number of security incidents causing significant financial loss or business disruptions.

    Explanation: The main objective of risk management is to reduce the number of security incidents that can cause a significant financial loss or business disruption. If such incidents are high, then the effectiveness of risk management is questionable. The other options are not as significant as security incidents.

55. What is the most likely reason for management choosing to mitigate risk, even though it is within the risk tolerance level?

    A. A mandate from the board of directors to address all the risks.

    B. Management does not want to accept the risk.

    C. Addressing the risk is very cost-effective.

    D. Management may have concerns that the impact is underestimated.

    Answer: D. Management may have concerns that the impact is underestimated.

    Explanation: The most likely reason is that management may have doubts about the estimation of the level of risk. In such cases, management may choose to mitigate the risk, even though it is within the risk tolerance level. It is less likely that the board will require all the risks to be mitigated. This is not practical or feasible. Also, management generally accepts the risk if the risk is within the risk appetite. It makes no sense to address a risk that is within the risk appetite, even though treatment is cost-effective.

56. What is the most likely reason for the security manager to not be concerned about an identified major threat?

    A. The vulnerability is compartmentalized.

    B. The availability of the incident response procedure.

C. The availability of the compensating control.

D. The threat hasn't been exploited so far.

Answer: A. The vulnerability is compartmentalized.

Explanation: Compartmentalization means separating sensitive information assets in such a way that there is reduced or no exposure. If compartmentalization of the vulnerability results in no exposure, then there is no risk. The availability of an incident response procedure and compensating controls are not as effective as compartmentalization is a preventive control. Even if no exploits occurred in the past, threats can materialize at any time, so the appropriate safeguards should be in place.

57. Prioritizing risk treatment is primarily based on what?

A. Identified threats and vulnerabilities

B. Likelihood of compromise and the subsequent impact

C. Cost of risk treatment

D. Level of exposure of the asset

Answer: B. Likelihood of compromise and the subsequent impact.

Explanation: Risk is a product of probability and impact. Probability (that is, likelihood) and impact can help determine the actual level of risk. Both terms are equally important for determining the level of risk. Each risk is determined based on its probability (that is, likelihood) and impact and then high-level risks are prioritized and addressed first. The other options are not as important as likelihood and impact.

58. What area is a major concern when arranging for disaster recovery in a reciprocal agreement?

A. Variation in the processes in both the organizations

B. Variation in the BCP testing procedure in both organizations

C. Variation in the infrastructure and capacity in both organizations

D. Variation in the security policy and procedure in both organizations

Answer: C. Variation in the infrastructure and capacity in both organizations

Explanation: In a reciprocal agreement, two organizations that have similar capabilities and processing capacities agree to provide support to one another in case of an emergency. If both organizations have different infrastructure and capacities, then they may not be able to support the other organization in the case of a disaster. Recovery becomes difficult in such cases. This is the area of major concern for a reciprocal agreement. The other options will not have a major impact on the recovery aspect.

Risk assessment and analysis methodologies

Different **methodologies** are available for assessing the risk. An organization should use a methodology that best fits its requirements. The method should have the ability to achieve the goals and objectives of the organization to identify the relevant risk. One such risk assessment methodology is COBIT 5.

Risk assessment is an important process for identifying significant risks and cost-effective controls to address the identified risks.

Phases of risk assessment

Generally, a risk assessment process follows three phases:

1. **Risk identification**: In this phase, significant business risks are identified. Risk identification is generally conducted by risk scenarios. A risk scenario is a visualization of a possible event that can have some adverse impact on the business objective. Organizations use risk scenarios to imagine what could go wrong and create hurdles for achieving the business objectives.

2. **Risk analysis**: Risk analysis is where you rank a risk based on its impact on business processes. The impact can be either quantifiable in dollar terms or can be qualitative, such as high risk, medium risk, or low risk. Both the probability of the event and the impact on the business are considered to determine the level of risk.

   A risk with a high level is ranked higher and given priority to address the same. More resources are allocated to high-risk areas.

   Risk analysis results help prioritize risk responses and allocate resources.

3. **Risk evaluation**: Risk evaluation is the process of comparing the result of risk analysis against the acceptable level of risk. If the level of risk is more than the acceptable risk, then risk treatment is required to bring down the level of risk.

Let's understand each of these by looking at a practical example of each:

- Risk identification: The risk of a machine malfunctioning due to heavy rain.

- Risk analysis: In this phase, the level of risk is determined. Let's say that a machine costs $100,000 and that the probability of heavy rain is 50%. In that case, the risk level is $50,000 (that is, $100,000 * 50%).

- Risk evaluation: In this phase, we will compare the risk level with the level acceptable to management. Let's say, that the acceptable level is only $20,000, so the current risk of $50,000 exceeds the acceptable level of risk. In such cases, risk treatment is required to bring the risk level down. The organization may choose to take out insurance worth $30,000 so that the net risk remains as $20,000.

Risk assessment

As we discussed in the previous section, risk assessment includes the following three components:

- **Risk identification**

- **Risk analysis** (to determine the level of risk; that is, whether the risk is high, medium, or low)

- **Risk evaluation** (to determine whether the risk is acceptable or whether risk treatment is required)

Asset identification

The first and most important step in a risk assessment process is to identify and list all the information assets and determine their value based on criticality or sensitivity. In the absence of a detailed asset inventory, you may miss out on protecting some significant assets. Assets can be in the form of people, processes, system and network components, databases, or any other factor that can have an impact on business processes. Assets aren't only tangible assets but intangible assets such as the reputation of the organization.

Asset valuation

Once all the assets have been identified, the next step is to determine their valuation. This is very important to avoid underprotecting or overprotecting the asset. The efforts required to protect an asset should be justified by its criticality. It does not make sense to spend $100 to protect a $10 asset.

The security manager should be careful while valuing the assets. In some situations, valuation should not be based only on the actual cost or replacement cost but based on the impact it will have on the business if such an asset is not available.

Let's understand this with an example. A server that costs $1,000 is hosting data that supports the project, which is worth $20,000. If this server is not available, then the full project will be adversely impacted. In this case, the value of the server is considered to be $20,000, even though the cost of the server is $1,000.

This is also known as **opportunity cost**. Opportunity cost reflects the cost of the organization/business loss that results from the unavailability of an asset.

Aggregated and cascading risk

The security manager should consider the impact of the **aggregated risk** and the **cascading risk** while designing the overall control environment.

Aggregated risk

Aggregated risk means having a significant impact caused by a large number of minor vulnerabilities. Such minor vulnerabilities individually do not have a major impact but when all these vulnerabilities are exploited at the same time, they can cause a huge impact.

The goal of risk aggregation is to identify the significant overall risk from a single threat vector. Let's understand this with an example. To protect a critical database, the organization has implemented multiple controls. Even if one control fails, the other controls can compensate for the same. However, when a threat exploits all the controls together, it can have a significant adverse impact.

Cascading risk

Cascading risk is where one failure leads to a chain reaction of failures. This is more relevant when IT and operations have close dependencies. The security manager should consider the impact of one activity failing on other dependent systems.

Identifying risk

Risk management begins with **risk identification**. Risk identification is the process of identifying and listing the risks in the risk register.

The primary objective of the risk identification process is to recognize the threats, vulnerabilities, assets, and controls of the organization. Risk practitioners can use the following sources to identify the risk:

- Review past audit reports.

- Review incident reports.

- Review public media articles and press releases.

- Through systematic approaches such as vulnerability assessment, penetration testing, reviewing BCP and DRP documents, conducting interviews with senior management and process owners, scenario analysis, and more.

All the identified risks should be captured in the risk register, along with details such as description, category, probability, impact, and risk owner. Maintaining the risk register process starts with the risk identification process.

Risk identification process

The following steps are part of the risk identification process:

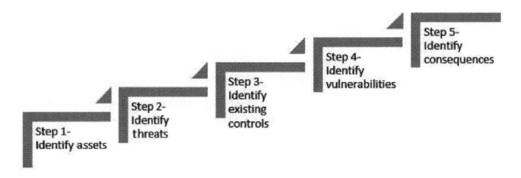

Figure 3.2 – Risk identification process

A security manager should understand the risk identification process. Generally, this process begins with identifying the critical assets. A security manager should be aware of all the assets that need to be protected. Once the threats have been identified, assets should be determined, followed by the existing control and vulnerabilities being identified, and the consequences being determined.

Conducting interviews

The following are some of the good practices for using interview techniques to identify risk:

- Risk practitioners should ensure that the staff who are being interviewed have sufficient authority and knowledge about the process.

- Risk practitioners should study the business process in advance of the interview. This will help in smoothly conducting interviews. It also means that risk practitioners can concentrate on areas of concern.

- Interview questions should be prepared in advance and shared with the interviewee so that they come prepared and bring any supporting documentation, reports, or data that may be necessary.

- Risk practitioners should obtain and review relevant documentation such as SOPs, reports, and other notes that support the statement of the interviewee.

- Risk practitioners should encourage interviewees to be open about various risk scenarios.

Information can be gathered through the **Delphi** technique, which will be covered in the next section.

Delphi technique

Many organizations resort to using the Delphi technique, in which polling or information gathering is done either anonymously or privately between the interviewer and interviewee.

Threats and vulnerabilities

CISM aspirants should be able to establish the difference between **threat** and **vulnerability**. Vulnerability means weakness in the system. A threat is a factor that attempts to exploit the vulnerability. For example, when antivirus software is not updated, it is a vulnerability. The hacker who attempts to exploit the vulnerability (un-updated antivirus) is a threat. The objective of an internal control is to reduce the vulnerability; that is, its weakness. The internal control cannot directly control the threat.

Advanced persistent threat

An **advanced persistent threat** (**APT**) is a type of cyberattack that's performed on a computer network where the attacker gains and maintains unauthorized access to the targeted network and remains undetected for a significant period. During the time between infection and remediation, the hacker will often monitor, intercept, and relay information and sensitive data.

The term's definition was traditionally associated with nation-state sponsorship, but over the last few years, we have seen multiple examples of non-nation state groups conducting large-scale targeted attacks for specific goals.

Risk, likelihood, and impact

Let's understand some of the widely accepted definitions of *risk*, as shown in the following table:

Source	Risk defined as	Key words
ERM-COSO	Potential events that may impact the entity.	Probability/impact
Oxford Dictionary	The probability of something happening, multiplied by the resulting cost or benefit if it does.	Probability/cost/benefit
Business Dictionary	The probability or threat of damage, injury, liability, loss, or any other negative occurrence that is caused by external or internal vulnerabilities and that may be avoided through preventive action.	Probability/damage
ISO 31000	The effect uncertainty has on the objectives.	Uncertainty/effect
Dictionary	A situation involving exposure to danger.	Exposure
ISO/IEC 73	A combination of an event and its consequences.	Event/consequences

Table 3.4 – Definitions of risk

From a CISM exam perspective, you don't need to worry about any of the definitions in this table. As you can see, almost every definition speaks directly or indirectly about two terms: **probability** and **impact**. In its simplest form, the risk is the product of probability and impact. In other words, we can say the following:

- *Risk = Probability * Impact*
- *Risk = P * I*

The following diagram illustrates this:

Figure 3.3 – Risk

> **Note**
> Probability is also known as likelihood, possibility, and chances.

Both terms are equally important while determining risk. Let's understand this with an example. The probability of a product being damaged is very high – let's say 1. However, that product hardly costs anything and the impact is nil, which is zero, even if the product is damaged. So, the risk of rain will be *Risk = P * I*. In other words, *Risk = 1 * 0 = 0*.

Risk register

All the identified risks should be captured in the risk register, along with details such as its description, category, probability, impact, risk owner, and other details. Maintaining the **risk register** process starts with the risk identification process.

The risk register is the inventory of all the existing risks of the organization. The best way to understand any kind of risk is to review the risk register. This includes details of all the risks, along with the relevant control activities. The most effective use of a risk register is to facilitate a thorough review of all the risks periodically.

Risk analysis

Risk analysis is where you rank a risk based on its impact on business processes. The risk with the highest impact is ranked higher and given priority to address the same. More resources are allocated to high-risk areas.

The risk analysis results help prioritize the risk responses and how resources are allocated.

Risk analysis is the process of ranking various risks so that areas of high risk can be prioritized and be treated. Risk can be measured and ranked by using any of the following methods:

- **Quantitative risk assessment**
- **Qualitative risk assessment**
- **Semi-quantitative risk assessment**

One factor that influences what technique is selected is the availability of accurate data for the risk assessment. When a data source is accurate and reliable, an organization will prefer quantitative risk assessment as it will give risk value in numeric terms, such as monetary values. Monetary value is easy to evaluate to determine the risk response.

In the next section, we will look at each method in detail.

Quantitative risk assessment

In quantitative risk assessment, the risk is measured based on numerical values. This helps with a cost-benefit analysis as the risk, in monetary terms, can easily be compared to the cost of various risk responses. In quantitative risk assessment, various statistical methods are used to derive the risk.

Risk is quantified as per the following formula: Risk = Probability * Impact.

CISM aspirants should always remember that risk is quantified by a combination of probability and impact. Let's understand this with the help of an example.

The probability of equipment being damaged that costs $1,000 is 0. Here, the probability is zero and the impact is $1,000. The risk is probability * impact; that is, P * I. In this case, the risk is 1000*0; that is, 0. If some other asset's probability is 0.5 and the asset costs $100, then the risk will be $50 (0.5 * 100). The risk of the equipment costing $100 is more than the risk of the equipment costing $1,000. This is because probability plays an important role in quantifying risk.

Challenges in implementing quantitative risk assessment

A major challenge when conducting a quantitative risk assessment is the availability of reliable data. To quantify a risk, accurate details of the probability and impact are required.

Determining the probability or frequency of the occurrence of a threat is a challenging aspect. Mostly, the probability can be found based on historical data. However, it is very difficult to ascertain the probability of natural events such as hurricanes, earthquakes, and tsunamis.

Quantitative risk assessment is not feasible for events where the probability or impact cannot be quantified or expressed in numerical terms.

Thus, a quantitative risk assessment does the following:

- Makes use of statistical methods to derive risk
- Makes use of likelihood and impact
- Helps derive a financial impact

Qualitative risk assessment

In a qualitative risk assessment, risks are measured based on qualitative parameters such as high, medium, and low or on a scale of 1 to 5.

Qualitative assessment is considered more subjective compared to quantitative assessment.

Few risks cannot be calculated in numeric terms. Qualitative assessment is useful in such scenarios.

Qualitative risk assessment is more relevant for examining new and emerging threats and **advanced persistent threats** (**APTs**). The qualitative risk analysis method involves conducting interviews with various stakeholders. There are some techniques such as the Delphi method wherein information can be gathered by way of anonymous questionnaires.

Semi-quantitative risk assessment

Here are some facts about this type of risk assessment:

- A semi-quantitative risk assessment is the combination of qualitative and quantitative risk assessment. It is a hybrid approach that considers the input of the qualitative approach combined with a numerical scale to determine the impact of a quantitative risk assessment.

- In a semi-quantitative analysis, the descriptive rankings are associated with a numeric scale.

- For example, the qualitative measure of "high" may be given a quantitative weight of 5, "medium" may be given 3, and "low" may be given 1.

- Such methods are frequently used when it is not possible to use a quantitative method or reduce subjectivity in qualitative methods.

- Risk practitioners should ensure that a standardized process and scale are used throughout the organization for semi-quantitative risk assessment. Also, risk owners should not mistake the origins of these values as coming from purely objective sources.

The best method for risk analysis

A risk practitioner should always prefer a quantitative approach. The quantitative approach helps with a cost-benefit analysis as the risk, in monetary terms, can easily be compared to the cost of various risk responses. However, a major challenge in conducting a quantitative risk analysis is the availability of accurate data. In the absence of proper data or when data accuracy is questionable, a qualitative analysis is preferable.

Annual loss expectancy

Annual loss expectancy is a calculation that helps you determine the expected monetary loss for an asset due to a particular risk over a single year.

The annualized loss expectancy is the product of the annual rate of occurrence and the single loss expectancy. It is mathematically expressed as SLE * ARO. For example, a particular risk event can have an impact of $1,000 every time it occurs. $1,000 is the **single loss expectancy** (**SLE**). Now it is expected that this particular risk event will materialize 5 times a year. 5 is the **annual rate of occurrence** (**ARO**). So, in this case, the annual loss expectancy is $5,000.

Value at Risk (VaR)

Value at Risk (**VaR**) is a statistical computation based on historical data to arrive at probability. VaR is mostly used in the financial sector to determine the risk of an investment. However, although primarily being used by a financial organization, it can be applied to the information security domain also. The following are some of the characteristics of VaR:

- VaR is a quantitative approach to evaluating risk.
- VaR is used to determine the maximum probable loss over a certain period.
- VaR calculations are typically complex and time-consuming.

OCTAVE

Operationally critical threat asset and vulnerability evaluation (**OCTAVE**) is a risk assessment approach with the following characteristics:

- In this approach, critical assets are identified first.
- The next step is to focus risk analysis activities on identified critical assets.
- It considers the relationship between critical assets and threats and the vulnerabilities that can be applied to critical assets.
- It evaluates the risk in terms of operational aspects; that is, the impact on business operations due to the risk of these critical assets.
- It creates a protection strategy for risk mitigation to safeguard the critical assets of the organization.

Other risk analysis methods

A consistent risk analysis technique should be used whenever the goal is to produce results that can be compared over time. Each approach has certain advantages and possible weaknesses, and the risk practitioner should choose a technique that's appropriate for the circumstances of the assessment.

The following are some of the most common approaches:

- **Bayesian analysis**

  - This is a method of statistical inference that uses prior distribution data to determine the probability of a result.

  - This technique relies on the prior distribution data to be accurate to be effective and produce accurate results.

- **Bow tie analysis**

  - A bow tie analysis is a simple process for identifying areas of concern.
  - It makes the analysis more effective by linking possible causes, controls, and consequences.
  - The cause of the event is depicted in the middle of the diagram (the "knot" of the bow tie). In this diagram, threats are placed on the left, whereas consequences are placed on the right.

The following diagram shows the flow of a bow tie analysis:

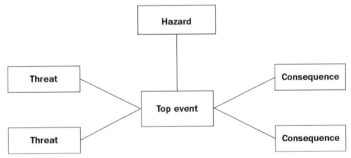

Figure 3.4 – Bow tie analysis

- **Delphi method**:

  - In the Delphi method, opinions from experts are obtained using two or more rounds of questionnaires.

  - After each round of questioning, the results are summarized and communicated to the experts by a facilitator.

- This collaborative technique is often used to build a consensus among experts.

- In the Delphi technique, polling or information gathering is done either anonymously or privately between the interviewer and interviewee.

- **Event tree analysis**:

  - In an event tree analysis, an event is analyzed to examine possible outcomes.

  - An event tree analysis is a forward-looking model for assessing the probability of different events resulting in possible outcomes.

- **Fault tree analysis**:

  - In a fault tree analysis, an event is identified and then possible means for the event are determined.

  - Results are displayed in a logical tree diagram and attempts are made to reduce or eliminate potential causes of the event.

- **Markov analysis**:

  - A Markov analysis is a method that's used to forecast the value of a variable whose predicted value is influenced only by its current state.

  - The Markov model assumes that future events are independent of past events.

  - A Markov analysis is often used to predict behaviors and decisions within large groups of people.

  - A Markov analysis is used to analyze systems that can exist in multiple states.

- **Monte Carlo analysis**:

  - Monte Carlo analysis is a risk management technique that is used for conducting a quantitative analysis of risks.

  - This technique is used to analyze the impact of risks on your project.

  - Monte Carlo methods, or Monte Carlo experiments, are a broad class of computational algorithms that rely on repeated random sampling to obtain numerical results.

Evaluating risk

In the risk evaluation phase, the level of each risk is compared against the acceptable risk criteria. If the risk is within an acceptable level, then the risk is accepted as-is. If the risk exceeds the acceptable level, then treatment will be some form of mitigation.

Risk ranking

A risk with high impact is ranked higher and given priority to address the same. More resources are allocated to high-risk areas. Ranking each risk based on impact and likelihood is critical in determining the risk mitigation strategy. Ranking the risk helps the organization determine its priority.

Risk ownership and accountability

The following are some of the important aspects concerning risk ownership and accountability:

- For successful risk management, each risk should have assigned ownership and accountability.
- Risk should be owned by a senior official who has the necessary authority and experience to select the appropriate risk response based on analyses and guidance provided by the risk practitioner.
- Risk owners should also own associated controls and ensure the effectiveness and adequacy of the controls.
- Risk should be assigned to an individual employee rather than as a group or a department. Allocating accountability to the department as a whole will circumvent ownership.
- The accountability for risk management lies with senior management and the board.
- Risk ownership is best established by mapping risk to specific business process owners.
- The details of the risk owner should be documented in the risk register.
- The results of the risk monitoring process should be discussed and communicated with the risk owner. This is because they own the risk and are accountable for maintaining the risk within acceptable levels.

Risk treatment options

The following are the four options for responding to risk:

1. **Risk avoidance**:

   - In this approach, projects or activities that cause the risk are avoided.
   - Risk avoidance is the last choice when no other response is adequate.
   - For example, declining a project when business cases show a high risk of failure.

2. **Risk mitigation**:

    - In this approach, efforts are made to reduce the probability or impact of the risk event by designing the appropriate controls.

    - The objective of risk mitigation is to reduce the risk to an acceptable level.

3. **Risk sharing/transferring**:

    - In this approach, the risk is shared with partners or transferred via insurance coverage, contractual agreement, or other means.

    - Natural disasters have a very low probability but a high impact. The response to such a risk should be risk transfer.

4. **Risk acceptance**:

    - In this approach, the risk is accepted as per the risk appetite of the organization.

    - Risk is accepted where the cost of controlling the risk is more than the cost of the risk event.

    - For example, for a few non-critical systems, the cost of anti-malware installation is more than the anticipated cost of damage due to malware attacks. In such cases, the organization generally accepts the risk as-is.

    - In risk acceptance, no steps are taken to reduce the risk.

    - However, organizations need to be careful while accepting the risk. If the risk is accepted while the correct level of risk isn't known, it may result in a higher level of liabilities.

Understanding inherent risk and residual risk

Let's understand this with the help of an example. Let's say you have purchased a machine for $100,000 that is placed in an earthquake-sensitive zone. Any damage to the machine will cost you $100,000. To safeguard against this loss, you take out insurance worth $80,000 for the machine. Now, if anything happens to your machine, the insurance company will reimburse you up to $80,000. Your final loss will only be $20,000.

In this case, your risk before taking out insurance is $100,000. This risk is known as the **inherent risk**; that is, the gross risk or risk before implementing any control.

The risk after taking out insurance is only $20,000. This risk is known as the **residual risk**; that is, the net risk or risk after implementing any control.

Inherent risk

This is the risk that an activity would pose if no controls or other mitigating factors were in place (the gross risk or risk before controls). It is the susceptibility of a business or process to make an error that is material in nature, assuming there were no internal controls.

The inherent risk depends on the number of users and business areas. The higher the number of users and business processes, the higher the level of inherent risk.

Residual risk

This is the risk that remains after controls are considered (the net risk or risk after controls). *Residual Risk = Inherent Risk - Controls.*

For a successful risk management program, residual risk should be within the risk appetite. When the residual risk is within the risk appetite, it is an acceptable risk level.

The primary objective of a risk management program is to ensure that residual risk is within levels acceptable to management. If the residual risk is within the risk appetite of the organization, it determines its compliance with the risk appetite. Achieving acceptable risk indicates that the residual risk is minimized and within control.

Security baseline

The **security baseline** is the minimum security requirement across the organization. The baseline may be different based on asset classification. For highly classified assets, the baseline will be more stringent. For example, for low classified assets, the baseline can be single-factor authentication, though the baseline will increase to two-factor authentication for highly classified assets.

Baseline security should form part of the control objective. The baseline should be reviewed at regular intervals to ensure that it is aligned with the organization's overall objectives.

Key aspects from the CISM exam's perspective

The following are some of the key aspects from an exam perspective:

Question	Possible Answer
Who will be in the best position to perform risk analysis for a business process?	The process owner.
At what interval should a risk assessment typically be conducted?	Annually, or whenever there is a significant change.
What is the objective of network vulnerability assessment?	To identify misconfigurations and missing updates.
Why it is very important to conduct a risk assessment continuously?	Because the risk environment is changing constantly.
In which scenario is policy exception generally allowed?	When the risk is justified by the benefit.
Which risk analysis (quantitative/qualitative) is most appropriate to derive percentage estimates?	Quantitative risk analysis.
Valuation of an asset in a business impact analysis should be based on what?	Opportunity cost (the opportunity cost reflects the cost to the organization/ business loss resulting from the unavailability of an asset).
Risk is a combination of probability and impact. Which requires the greatest amount of speculation?	Probability (likelihood).
Which of the following is the *BEST* resolution when a security standard conflicts with a business objective?	To perform a risk analysis and decide based on cost and benefit for allowing exceptions to the standard.
What is the best way to assess the aggregate risk of multiple minor vulnerabilities linked together?	To conduct a penetration test. (A penetration test can determine the aggregate risk of linked vulnerabilities by exploiting them sequentially.)
Who should be the primary driver when implementing new regulatory changes?	The business process owner.
What is the main objective of performing a penetration test?	To identify weaknesses in network and server security.
What is the output of a risk assessment?	A list of risks that impact the organization.

Question	Possible Answer
What is the most important aspect of a vulnerability scanning tool?	Regular signature updates.
What is the objective of risk aggregation?	• To identify significant overall risk from a single threat vector. • To identify significant overall risk from multiple minor vulnerabilities linked to each other.
What is the objective of integrating different assurance functions?	To achieve cost-effective risk mitigation across the organization.
What is the main advantage of performing a risk assessment consistently?	It provides trends in the evolving risk profile.

Table 3.5 – Key aspects from the CISM exam perspective

Questions

1. A risk analysis for a business process can be best conducted by which of the following?

   A. Audit team

   B. Legal team

   C. Business process owner

   D. External consultant

   Answer: C. Business process owner.

   Explanation: The business process owner is in the best position to conduct the risk analysis for their respective processes. They have detailed knowledge of the risks and controls that can be applied to their processes.

2. When should a risk assessment for a project be performed?

   A. At the initial stage of the project

   B. Continuously

   C. Before implementing the project

   D. When there is a change in the process

   Answer: B. Continuously.

   Explanation: The effectiveness of risk assessment increases if the assessment is done continuously. This will help the organization address the emerging risks and other significant changes in the business environment. It must be noted that risk assessment is not a one-time activity.

3. What is the main objective of a risk management program?

    A. To eliminate all the risks

    B. To support management's due diligence process

    C. To comply with regulatory requirements

    D. To improve the investment portfolio

    Answer: B. To support management's due diligence process.

    Explanation: It is the responsibility of management to conduct due diligence for organization processes. The risk management program supports this objective. The main objective when conducting risk management is that it is an important part of management's due diligence.

4. The frequency for a risk assessment should be done when?

    A. Annually for each process

    B. As per the risk management budget

    C. Every 6 months for critical business processes

    D. Annually or whenever there is a significant change

    Answer: D. Annually or whenever there is a significant change.

    Explanation: The risk environment is changing constantly. The most effective risk assessment frequency is annual or whenever there is a significant change. This will help to assess risk at a reasonable timeframe and provides flexibility for assessing the risk when there is a significant change.

5. A risk analysis includes assessing what?

    A. Probability and visibility

    B. Likelihood and impact

    C. Impact and appetite

    D. Appetite and tolerance

    Answer: B. Likelihood and impact.

    Explanation: Risk is a combination of two components: probability (likelihood) and impact. Both components are essential for analyzing risk. Hence, likelihood and impact are the primary elements that are determined in a risk analysis.

6.   What is the main objective of a network vulnerability assessment?

A. To identify deviation from a secure coding policy

B. To identify malware and spyware

C. To identify weaknesses in the security design

D. To identify misconfigurations and missing updates

Answer: D. To identify misconfigurations and missing updates.

Explanation: The objective of a network vulnerability assessment is to identify common misconfigurations.

7.   What is the prime objective of conducting a risk assessment continuously?

A. For optimum utilization of the security budget

B. To comply with the security policy

C. To address a constantly changing risk environment

D. For optimum utilization of security resources

Answer: C. To address a constantly changing risk environment.

Explanation: Changes in the risk environment introduce new threats and vulnerabilities to the organization. To address this risk, assessments should be conducted continuously. Other options are not prime objectives for conducting a risk assessment.

8.   Which of the following is used to identify deficiencies in the system?

A. Performance metrics

B. A business impact analysis

C. A security gap analysis

D. Incident management procedure

Answer: B. A business impact analysis.

Explanation: The objective of a security gap analysis is to identify any deficiencies in the control environment against the desired state of control.

9.   What are the main criteria for approving a policy exception?

A. Project deadlines.

B. The risk is justified by the benefits.

C. High cost of policy compliance.

D. Inconvenience to the users.

Answer: B. The risk is justified by the benefits.

Explanation: Generally, policy exceptions are approved where the impact of non-compliance is less than the benefits of taking the risk.

10. The security manager has observed that the organization is using FTP access, which can be exploited. Which of the following is used to determine the necessity for remedial action?

    A. To conduct a penetration test

    B. To conduct a security baseline review

    C. To conduct a risk assessment

    D. To conduct a business impact analysis

    Answer: C. To conduct a risk assessment.

    Explanation: A risk assessment helps determine the impact of the vulnerability. Based on that impact, the necessary remedial measures can be decided. The other options will not help determine the impact of the vulnerability.

11. What is the main objective when using risk assessment techniques?

    A. To justify the selection of risk mitigation strategies

    B. To maximize the return on investment

    C. To comply with regulations

    D. To provide better documentation

    Answer: A. To justify the selection of risk mitigation strategies.

    Explanation: Risk assessment will help you determine the impact of the vulnerability, on which basis the necessary remedial measures can be decided. It helps justify the selection of risk mitigation strategies.

12. What is the prime objective of a risk management program?

    A. To remove all inherent risk

    B. To maintain residual risk at an acceptable level

C. To comply with regulatory requirements

D. To remove all control risk

Answer: B. To maintain residual risk at an acceptable level.

Explanation: The objective of a risk management program is to ensure that the risks that apply to the organization are brought down to an acceptable level by implementing various mitigation strategies. It is not possible to eliminate all inherent risks or control risks.

13. What is the most important element of risk assessment?

A. Protecting all the assets

B. Benchmarking the process with other organizations

C. Evaluating both monetary value and the likelihood of loss

D. Evaluating past threats

Answer: C. Evaluating both monetary value and the likelihood of loss.

Explanation: Risk is a combination of two components: probability (likelihood) and impact. Both components are essential for analyzing risk. Hence, likelihood and impact are the primary elements that are determined in a risk analysis.

14. The security manager has noted that a new regulatory requirement applies to the organization. What should be the next course of action?

A. To take approval from the information security committee to implement the new requirement

B. To perform a gap analysis

C. To implement control

D. To evaluate budget availability

Answer: B. To perform a gap analysis.

Explanation: The first step is to perform a gap analysis to determine whether the organization already complies or whether some action is required for the compliance. Based on the gap analysis, further action can be decided.

15. What is the main reason for repeating risk assessment at regular intervals?

A. To address constantly changing business threats

B. To rectify errors of earlier assessments

C. To apply different methodologies

D. To improve security awareness

Answer: A. To address constantly changing business threats.

Explanation: The business environment changes constantly and hence new threats emerge. Risk assessments should be repeated at regular intervals because business threats are constantly changing.

16. The security manager has noted that a new privacy requirement has been enacted. What should be the next course of action to determine the potential impact of the privacy law on the organization?

A. To develop a roadmap for the implementation to achieve compliance with the privacy law

B. To determine systems and processes that contain privacy components

C. To stop business processes until compliance is achieved

D. To determine the action that will be taken by other organizations

Answer: B. To determine systems and processes that contain privacy components.

Explanation: The best course of action is to determine systems and processes that may have an impact due to new privacy laws. The other options may be implemented as subsequent steps.

17. Quantitative risk assessment is best used to assess which of the following?

A. Reputational risk arising due to data leakage

B. Risk of an electrical power outage for a business process

C. Risk of a defaced website

D. Risk of high staff turnover

Answer: B. Risk of an electrical power outage for a business process.

Explanation: Impact due to loss of power can be more easily measurable and quantifiable compared to the other options.

18. The most important element of a quantitative risk analysis is that the result does what?

    A. Includes customer perceptions

    B. Contains percentage estimates

    C. Lacks specific details

    D. Is subjective

    Answer: B. Contains percentage estimates.

    Explanation: Results derived from a quantitative risk analysis are measurable. Percentage estimates are a characteristic of a quantitative risk analysis. The other options are general characteristics of a qualitative risk analysis.

19. What is the most important aspect of an effective risk management program?

    A. High-security budget

    B. Defined security baseline

    C. Being able to detect new risks

    D. Documented risk reporting process

    Answer: C. Being able to detect new risks.

    Explanation: Though all these options are very important for effective risk management, if the program can't identify new risks, other procedures will only be useful for a limited period.

20. The valuation of assets in a business impact analysis is based on which of the following?

    A. Cost of acquisition

    B. Cost of replacement

    C. Opportunity cost

    D. Cost to recreate

    Answer: C. Opportunity cost.

    Explanation: For business impact analysis purposes, valuation should be based on the opportunity lost due to the unavailability of the assets. This is known as opportunity cost.

21. What is the best way to estimate the potential loss?

    A. Determine the productivity ratio

    B. Determine the impact of data leakage

    C. Determine the value of the information or asset

    D. Determine the probability of it occurring

    Answer: C. Determine the value of the information or asset.

    Explanation: The best way to estimate the potential loss is to determine the value of the information assets. Value can be in the form of productivity loss, the impact of data leakage, or opportunity costs due to the unavailability of the assets.

22. What is the risk register best used for?

    A. Identifying emerging risks

    B. Identifying risk owners

    C. Reviewing all IT-related risks periodically

    D. Recording annualized loss due to incidents

    Answer: C. Reviewing all IT-related risks periodically.

    Explanation: The risk register contains details about all the identified risks. The main objective of the risk register is to facilitate a thorough review of all the risks periodically. The other options are secondary factors.

23. Which of the following components of a risk assessment will require the highest amount of speculation?

    A. Consequences

    B. Exposure

    C. Vulnerability

    D. Likelihood

    Answer: D. Likelihood.

    Explanation: Likelihood is the most difficult to estimate. It will require the highest amount of speculation. The other options can be determined within a range.

24. The security manager has received a request from a business unit to implement a new technology that is against the information security standards. What should be the next course of action for the information security manager?

    A. Reject the request.

    B. Modify the standard to allow the new technology.

    C. Conduct a risk assessment to quantify the risk.

    D. Engage experts to identify the better technology.

    Answer: C. Conduct a risk assessment to quantify the risk.

    Explanation: The first course of action for a risk manager is to conduct a risk assessment and determine the level of risk. Policy exceptions are generally allowed where benefits from the project outweigh the perceived risks. The other options can be meaningful, but only if the security manager is aware of the level of risk.

25. The security manager has received a request from the IT function to not update the business impact analysis for a new application as there is no change in the business process. What should be the next course of action for the security manager?

    A. Verify the decision of the business unit after a risk analysis.

    B. Reject the request.

    C. Instruct IT to modify the business impact analysis after a post-implementation review of the new application.

    D. Recommend an audit review.

    Answer: A. Verify the decision of the business unit after a risk analysis.

    Explanation: The best course of action in this scenario is to conduct a risk analysis and determine the impact that the new application will have on the business impact analysis. If there is no impact, then there is no need to update the business impact analysis.

26. What is the best way to address the conflict of security requirements with a business objective?

    A. To change the security requirements

    B. To change the business objective

    C. To conduct a risk analysis

    D. To accept the risk

    Answer: C. To conduct a risk analysis.

Explanation: The first course of action for a risk manager is to conduct a risk assessment and determine the level of risk. Policy exceptions are generally allowed where benefits from the project outweigh the perceived risks. The other options can be meaningful, but only if the security manager is aware of the level of risk. A business objective could be changed to accommodate a security requirement.

27. An aggregate risk of linked vulnerabilities can be assessed by which of the following?

    A. System audits

    B. Penetration tests

    C. Auditing the codes

    D. A vulnerability analysis

    Answer: B. Penetration tests.

    Explanation: Aggregated risk means a significant impact caused by a large number of minor vulnerabilities. Such minor vulnerabilities individually do not have a major impact, but when all these vulnerabilities are exploited at the same time, they can have a huge impact. The goal of risk aggregation is to identify the significant overall risk from a single threat vector. Penetration testing is the best way to assess the aggregate risk by exploiting them sequentially. This gives you a good measurement and prioritization of the risk. Penetration testing can give the risk a new perspective and can prioritize it based on the result of a sequence of security problems.

28. What is the most important factor when reviewing the migration of IT operations to an offshore location?

    A. Reviewing new regulations

    B. Modifying operating processes

    C. Reviewing budget adherence

    D. Performing a risk assessment

    Answer: D. Performing a risk assessment.

    Explanation: Risk assessment will help the organization determine new risks introduced by migrating IT operations to an offshore location. The new risk may inform you of non-adherence to regulations, overspending, or some operational aspects.

29. The security manager has noted a security breach at another organization that has employed similar technology. What should be the next course of action for the security manager?

    A. Evaluate the likelihood of incidents from the reported cause.

    B. Stop using the already breached technology.

    C. Assure senior management about the security posture.

    D. Remind staff that the organization is not affected by security breaches.

    Answer: A. Evaluate the likelihood of incidents from the reported cause.

    Explanation: The first course of action for a security manager is to evaluate the likelihood of the incident from the reported cause. Once the likelihood has been determined, other suitable actions can be taken.

30. What is the main objective of including threat and vulnerability assessment in a change management process?

    A. To reduce the requirement for periodic full risk assessments

    B. To ensure that the risk assessment is cost-effective

    C. To ensure that changes are approved by the information security team

    D. To ensure legal compliance

    Answer: A. To reduce the requirement for periodic full risk assessments.

    Explanation: Threat and vulnerability assessment during change management helps identify vulnerabilities in the initial stages. The same can be addressed without us having to wait until a full risk assessment has been performed. This keeps the risk assessment current without the need to complete a full reassessment.

31. What is the objective of calculating Value at Risk?

    A. To evaluate the risk by applying a qualitative approach

    B. To determine the maximum possible loss over a certain period

    C. To evaluate risk but only for the financial organization

    D. To expedite the assessment process

    Answer: B. To determine the maximum possible loss over a certain period.

    Explanation: Value at Risk is a statistical computation based on historical data to arrive at a probability. Value at Risk is mostly used in the financial sector to determine the risk of an investment. However, since it is primarily used by the financial organization, it can be applied to the information security domain as well.

32. Which process can help address the risk at various life cycle phases?

    A. The change management process

    B. The patch management process

    C. The configuration management process

    D. The problem management process

    Answer: A. The change management process.

    Explanation: The change management process can be best used to address risk in the various life cycles of the system. All these changes should go through the risk management process. This helps identify and address the new risks at the earliest possible time. Change management addresses a broader range of risks. The other options are not directly relevant to the life cycle stages.

33. What is the main objective of a vulnerability assessment?

    A. To eliminate all the risks to the business

    B. To adhere to the security policy

    C. To assure management

    D. To monitor the efficiency of the security team

    Answer: C. To assure management.

    Explanation: Vulnerability assessment helps identify all the existing vulnerabilities and plans to address the same. This gives comfort to management that the risks to business objectives are actively being monitored and controlled. It is not possible to eliminate all the risks. Vulnerability assessment is not primarily conducted to adhere to the security policy or to monitor the efficiency of the security team.

34. A project for implementing new regulatory requirements should be primarily driven by which of the following?

    A. The audit department

    B. The system analyst

    C. The business process owners

    D. The legal department

    Answer: C. The business process owners.

Explanation: The business process owners will be in the best position to drive the project for implementing regulatory requirements. They have a thorough understanding of their processes and the impact of regulatory requirements on their processes. The other options do support the business process owner when implementing the project but primarily, the project should be driven by the business process owner.

35. A security manager is conducting a qualitative risk analysis. What is the best way to get the most reliable result?

    A. Estimate the productivity losses

    B. Determine the possible scenarios, along with their threats and impacts

    C. Determine the value of assets

    D. Conduct a vulnerability analysis

    Answer: B. Determine the possible scenarios, along with their threats and impacts.

    Explanation: For a qualitative risk analysis, the best way is to list all possible threats and impact scenarios. This will facilitate an informed risk management decision. The other options are generally used for quantifying risk.

36. Which is the most important aspect of the effective risk management of IT activities?

    A. Risk management activities should be treated as different processes.

    B. Risk management activities should be controlled by the IT department.

    C. Risk management activities should be integrated within business processes.

    D. Risk management activities are communicated to all staff.

    Answer: C. Risk management activities should be integrated within business processes.

    Explanation: Integrating risk management activities within business processes is a more effective way to enhance risk management. Risk management should not be treated as a separate activity.

37. What is the most important element of a business impact analysis?

    A. Downtime tolerance

    B. Security budget

C. The BCP testing process

D. The crisis management procedure

Answer: A. Downtime tolerance.

Explanation: A business impact analysis is a process that determines the critical processes of the organization and decides on the recovery strategy during a disaster. The key criterion for determining the severity of service disruption is the period for which the system will remain down. The higher the system downtime, the higher the severity of the disruption. The other options are not directly related to the business impact analysis.

38. The security manager has determined the objective of the review. Their next step is to determine what?

    A. Limitations

    B. Approach

    C. Scope

    D. Report structure

    Answer: C. Scope.

    Explanation: Once the objective has been finalized, the next step is to determine the scope. The limitations and the approach must be defined after the scope. The report's structure is the last step.

39. The security manager has noted that there is a considerable delay between identifying a vulnerability and applying a patch. What should be the first course of action to address the risk during this period?

    A. Apply compensating controls for vulnerable systems.

    B. Discontinue the service of vulnerable systems.

    C. Communicate the weakness to end users.

    D. Update the signature of the antivirus system.

    Answer: A. Apply compensating controls for vulnerable systems.

    Explanation: The best course of action is to apply compensating control until the time patch is installed. This will help address the risk. Updating signatures for antivirus does not address the zero-day vulnerability.

40. The security manager has noted that not all employees comply with the access control policy for the data center. To address this issue, the security manager should do what?

    A. Determine the risk of non-compliance

    B. Arrange security awareness training

    C. Report the same to senior management

    D. Impose a heavy penalty for non-compliance

    Answer: A. Determine the risk of non-compliance.

    Explanation: The most important aspect for a security manager is knowing the level of risk for this non-compliance. The risk may be very high or may be negligible. Based on the level of risk, a further course of action needs to be determined.

41. What is the main objective when conducting a penetration test?

    A. Determining weaknesses in the network and server security

    B. Determining improvements in the incident management procedure

    C. Determining the capabilities of threat vectors

    D. Determining the strength of the security team

    Answer: A. Determining weaknesses in the network and server security.

    Explanation: The objective of a penetration test is to identify weaknesses in the network and server security. Based on the results of the penetration test, these weaknesses that have been identified are addressed to improve the security posture of the organization.

42. Risk assessment produces output in the form of what?

    A. A list of implemented controls

    B. A list of applicable threats

    C. A list of possible impacts

    D. A list of risks that may impact the organization

    Answer: D. A list of risks that may impact the organization.

    Explanation: Risk assessment helps derive a list of all the applicable risks that may impact the organization.

43. Which of the following is used to determine the level of effort required to improve risk management processes?

    A. A workflow analysis

    B. Program evaluation and review technique

    C. A gap analysis

    D. Return on investment

    Answer: C. A gap analysis.

    Explanation: The objective of a gap analysis is to identify the gap between the current level of control versus the desired level of control. A gap analysis is used to improve the maturity level of risk management processes. A workflow analysis is used to understand the current level of the risk management process, but it does not provide support for improvement opportunities. **Program evaluation and review technique** (**PERT**) is used to determine project timelines.

44. The security manager is implementing a **bring your own device** (**BYOD**) program. What should their first step be?

    A. To allow or reject access to devices, as per their approval status

    B. To perform a comprehensive assessment process before approving the devices

    C. To report compliance with the BYOD policy to senior management

    D. To install a mobile device management system in each of the approved devices

    Answer: B. To perform a comprehensive assessment process before approving the devices.

    Explanation: The first step is to develop a comprehensive assessment process, based on which approval should be granted to devices. The other options are subsequent steps.

45. The security manager noted that different criteria are used by different departments for measuring risk. To improve this situation, the security manager should recommend which of the following?

    A. Applying standard risk measurement criteria throughout the organization

    B. Introducing a common risk appetite across the organization

C. Mandating the quantification of each risk

D. Getting the results of the risk assessment reviewed by the head of the department

Answer: A. Applying standard risk measurement criteria throughout the organization.

Explanation: The best way to address this situation is to apply a standard risk measurement criterion for all the departments throughout the organization. This will help in arriving at a standard risk level where each risk can be compared to others to prioritize the risk response. The other options will not help address this issue directly.

46. What is the most important aspect to be included in a BYOD policy?

A. Requirement to return the device to the organization

B. Requirements to protect the sensitive information on the device

C. Restrictions on installing third-party applications

D. Requirement to seize the application during a forensic investigation

Answer: B. Requirements to protect the sensitive information on the device.

Explanation: The most important aspect is to ensure that users understand various requirements for protecting sensitive data on the device. Generally, personal devices are not returned to the organization. The other options are not as important for protecting data.

47. How should regulatory compliance requirements be dealt with?

A. As a zero deviation area

B. As a risk management area of focus

C. As operational issues

D. Just another risk

Answer: D. Just another risk.

Explanation: It should be dealt with just like any other risk. Like every other risk, regulatory risk should be addressed while considering its impact on business processes. Priority should be given based on feasibility, possible impacts, and the cost of compliance.

48. What is the most effective way to address regulatory risk?

   A. Regulatory risk should be treated like any other risk.

   B. Regulatory risk should be treated as a zero deviation area.

   C. Regulatory risk should be complied with mandatorily.

   D. Regulatory risk should be transferred by taking out insurance.

   Answer: A. Regulatory risk should be treated like any other risk.

   Explanation: Regulatory risk should be treated just like any other risk. Like every other risk, regulatory risk should be addressed while considering its impact on business processes. Priority should be given based on feasibility, possible impacts, and the cost of compliance.

49. The security manager should be most concerned about what while evaluating a vulnerability scanning tool?

   A. The ability of a tool to perform multiple functions

   B. Regular signature updates of the scanning tool

   C. Its user-friendly graphical user interface

   D. Ability to delete viruses

   Answer: B. Regular signature updates of the scanning tool.

   Explanation: The most important aspect of a scanning tool is to update it with new signatures to address the new and emerging risks. A vulnerability scanner doesn't need to delete viruses. Multiple functions and GUIs are good to have features but regular updates are extremely important.

50. Risk management should be considered as an ongoing activity because of which reason?

   A. Processes are prone to errors.

   B. Technology gets updated.

   C. The environment changes.

   D. The policy gets updated.

   Answer: C. The environment changes.

   Explanation: Existing controls may not be relevant for addressing new and emerging risks due to changes in the environment. As a result, effective risk management should be applied on an ongoing basis.

51. The security manager has noted that a web-based service is gaining popularity in the market. What should the security manager do first?

    A. Conduct an annual vulnerability assessment.

    B. Obtain third-party liability insurance.

    C. Perform a business impact analysis.

    D. Arrange a real-time failover capability.

    Answer: C. Perform a business impact analysis.

    Explanation: The first thing a security manager should do is determine the level of risk of the non-availability of the service. This can be done by performing a business impact analysis. The other options can be considered based on the results of the business impact analysis.

52. What is the best way to treat vulnerabilities?

    A. All identified vulnerabilities should be treated, even though there is no threat.

    B. Identified vulnerabilities should be prioritized based on the number of threats.

    C. Identified vulnerabilities should be prioritized based on the effectiveness of control.

    D. Identified vulnerabilities should be evaluated for threat, impact, and the cost of mitigation.

    Answer: D. The vulnerability identified should be evaluated for threat, impact, and the cost of mitigation.

    Explanation: To prioritize and decide on how to treat a vulnerability, it should be evaluated based on the threat, impact, and the cost of mitigation. All three factors should be considered.

53. What is the most cost-effective way to test the security of a legacy application?

    A. To determine the security weaknesses of similar applications

    B. To use debugging software to identify code errors

    C. To determine system functionality by using reverse engineering

    D. To conduct a vulnerability assessment to detect the application's weaknesses

    Answer: D. To conduct a vulnerability assessment to detect the application's weaknesses.

    Explanation: The most cost-effective way to test the security of a legacy application is to conduct a vulnerability assessment.

54. What is the objective of risk aggregation?

    A. To merge all homogenous types of processes to reduce the overall risk

    B. To increase the risk appetite of the organization

    C. To simplify the risk reporting process

    D. To identify the significant overall risk of a single threat

    Answer: D. To identify the significant overall risk of a single threat.

    Explanation: The goal of risk aggregation is to identify the significant overall risk from a single threat vector. An aggregated risk has a significant impact that's caused by a large number of minor vulnerabilities. Such minor vulnerabilities individually do not have a major impact, but when all these vulnerabilities are exploited at the same time, they can have a huge impact.

55. What is the best way to achieve cost-effective risk mitigation activities throughout the organization?

    A. Decentralized risk management

    B. Continuous risk assessments

    C. Assurance process integration

    D. Having a standard risk appetite across the organization

    Answer: C. Assurance process integration.

    Explanation: Integrating the activities of various assurance functions helps ensure that there are no overlapping activities or gaps in risk management activities. It is the most cost-effective method as duplicate efforts are streamlined. decentralization of risk management functions increases the cost of risk management. The other options do not directly impact the cost-effectiveness of risk management functions.

56. What is the most essential element for conducting a risk assessment?

    A. Consequences

    B. Likelihood

    C. Vulnerability

    D. Budget

    Answer: A. Consequences.

    Explanation: If there is no impact or consequences of the exploitation, then there is no risk. Risk analysis, risk evaluation, and risk treatment are primarily based on the impact of the risk.

57. The security manager has received a request to overwrite the data stored on a magnetic tape due to limited storage availability. The security manager should refer to which policy?

    A. Data classification policy

    B. Data retention policy

    C. Data access policy

    D. Data protection policy

    Answer: B. Data retention policy.

    Explanation: The data retention policy defines the minimum period of data retention. Overwriting any data may impact the data retention policy.

58. What is the most essential element when considering the extent of protection requirements?

    A. Exposure

    B. Threat

    C. Vulnerability

    D. Probability

    Answer: A. Exposure.

    Explanation: The level of exposure of the data affects the threat, vulnerability, probability, and impact of the data. It is the most important aspect when considering the extent of the level of protection.

59. Legal and regulatory requirements should be prioritized based on what?

    A. The level of penalty action

    B. Probability and consequences

    C. The level of the director's liability

    D. The discretion of the compliance manager

    Answer: B. Probability and consequences.

    Explanation: Risk can be determined based on probability and consequences. They will help derive the level of risk for non-compliance. Hence, both probability and consequences should be used to prioritize requirements.

60. As per good practices, when should a full risk reassessment be performed?

    A. In case of material control failure

    B. In case of a residual risk above the acceptable risk level

    C. In case a new patch is installed

    D. In case of emergency changes being implemented

    Answer: A. In case of material control failure.

    Explanation: Failure of material control indicates that control was not designed and monitored properly. It indicates the requirement for a full reassessment of risk. All the other options do not require a full reassessment.

61. In which of the following circumstances is high-risk tolerance useful?

    A. When the risk appetite is high

    B. When the uncertainty of a risk is high

    C. When the impact of a risk is high

    D. When the inherent risk is high

    Answer: B. When the uncertainty of a risk is high.

    Explanation: Risk tolerance is the acceptable deviation from risk appetite. For example, the risk appetite of an organization is $100 and their risk tolerance is $125. In this case, the organization is comfortable even if the risk level reaches $125. High-risk tolerance means a wider gap between risk appetite and risk tolerance. This will be more helpful when there is high uncertainty regarding the level of risk.

62. What is the main objective of conducting a risk assessment consistently?

    A. To lower the cost of risk assessments

    B. To adhere to the security budget

    C. To comply with the security policy

    D. To determine trends in the evolving risk profile

    Answer: D. To determine trends in the evolving risk profile.

    Explanation: Consistency in the risk assessment process helps determine trends over a certain period. If the risk assessment process is not consistent, then the results of the risk assessment cannot be compared to earlier results.

Summary

In this chapter, we discussed the important aspects of risk management. We learned about different risk identification and risk assessment methods. We also understood various risk treatment options. This will help security managers identify the risks in their organization, access the level of risk, and determine the appropriate treatment options.

In the next chapter, we are going to cover the practical aspects of **risk management**.

4
Practical Aspects of Information Risk Management

In this chapter, we will discuss the practical aspects of information risk management. We will learn about risk management tools and techniques and other important concepts from the perspective of the CISM exam.

The following topics will be covered in this chapter:

- Information asset classification
- Asset valuation
- Operational risk management
- Outsourcing and third-party service providers
- Risk management integration with the process life cycle

Let's understand the preceding topics in detail.

Information asset classification

Information asset classification means classifying assets based on their criticality to the business. An asset can be classified as confidential data, private data, or public data. This classification helps the organization provide the appropriate level of protection to the assets. More resources should be utilized to protect confidential data compared to public data.

Benefits of classification

The following are the objectives/benefits of information classification:

- Classification helps reduce the risk of assets being under-protected. Assets are protected in proportion to their criticality.
- Classification helps reduce the cost of assets being overprotected.

In the next section, we'll understand the steps involved in classification.

Understanding the steps involved in classification

CISM aspirants should understand the following steps to successfully implement an information classification program:

1. The first step is to create an inventory of all the information assets of the organization.
2. The next step is to establish ownership for each information asset. Identifying the asset owner is an essential prerequisite for implementing a classification policy. In the absence of an owner, the true value of the asset cannot be determined.
3. The next step is to arrive at the value of the assets that need protection.
4. The next step is to classify the information assets based on their valuation. Classification can be in the form of high-value data, medium-value data, and low-value data, or can be in form of confidential data, sensitive data, private data, and public data. The classification should be kept simple considering the different degrees of the criticality of the assets.
5. Each asset should be labeled according to its classification.
6. Implement the level of protection according to the level of classification. Confidential data should be highly protected, whereas public data may not require any protection.

Success factors for effective classification

The following are some of the important factors for an effective classification program:

- The data owner and data custodian need to have knowledge and awareness of the information classification policy of the organization. This ensures proper classification of data, as per organizational requirements.

- Accountability for the maintenance of proper security controls over information assets should reside with the data owner/system owner.

- Information classification must take the following requirements into account:

  - Legal/regulatory/contractual

  - Confidential

  - Integrity

  - Availability

- Information classification is primarily based on inputs from the data owner. Business managers (data owners) will have a thorough knowledge of the business impact due to the non-availability of their systems, data, or other assets.

  Security managers need to ensure that the requirements of the data owners are properly identified and appropriately addressed in the information classification policy.

On a lighter note, the following figure depicts awareness of the classification policy:

Figure 4.1 – Classification policy

Security managers need to ensure that the classification policy is made available to all users. The content of the classification policy should be part of the security awareness program. Without user awareness of the classification requirements, the policy will not be implemented in its true essence.

Criticality, sensitivity, and impact assessment

The primary basis for determining the classification of information assets is the criticality and sensitivity of the assets in achieving the business objectives. An impact assessment is used to determine the criticality and sensitivity of the assets.

Business dependency assessment

Many organizations may find it difficult to implement comprehensive classification due to resources or other constraints. In such cases, they can classify their resources based on a business dependency assessment. In this approach, critical business functions are identified, and all the assets of critical functions are given high priority for protection.

Risk analysis

A risk analysis is the process of determining the level of risk. The risk level can be quantified in terms of dollars or can be expressed as a qualitative indicator such as high risk, medium risk, or low risk.

The results of the risk analysis help the security manager determine the efforts that would be required to address a particular risk. More resources may be required to mitigate high-risk areas, whereas fewer resources may be required to mitigate low-risk areas.

Business interruptions

The objective of the classification policy is to ensure that the appropriate level of protection is applied for each class of information. However, it should not interrupt the business processes. Data should be made available to authorized users. A classification policy should not create unnecessary hurdles for normal business processes, as depicted in the following figure:

Figure 4.2 – Classification policy

Security managers need to ensure that the classification policy does not impact the availability of the data to authorized individuals.

Key aspects from the CISM exam's perspective

The following are some of the key aspects from an exam perspective:

Question	Possible Answer
What is the main advantage of asset classification?	It determines the appropriate level of protection to the asset. (Classification helps reduce the risk of under-protecting assets and, at the same time, reduces the cost of overprotecting assets.) Controls are commensurate with the impact.
The prime responsibility to determine the level of information classification resides with who?	Owner/business manager.
Which policy defines the level of protection to be provided for each category of data based on the business value?	Data classification policies.

Question	Possible Answer
What should be the prime basis for determining the classification of information assets?	Criticality and sensitivity.
What should be the prime basis for determining the criticality and sensitivity of information assets?	Impact assessment.
What is the most important factor for achieving proportionality when protecting information assets?	Asset classification.

Table 4.1 – Key aspects from the CISM exam's perspective

Questions

1. The security manager is implementing asset classification. Which of the following is the first step to be taken?

    A. Assess the risk.

    B. Asset classification.

    C. Asset valuation.

    D. Implement controls.

    Answer: C. Asset valuation.

    Explanation: Among all the options provided, the first step is to value the assets. Based on this valuation, the asset can be classified, its risk can be assessed, and various controls can be implemented.

2. Which of the following should have ownership of sensitive financial data that is used only by the finance department?

    A. Finance department

    B. System administrator

    C. Head of IT

    D. Head of the finance department

Answer: D. Head of the finance department.

Explanation: Ownership should be assigned to an individual who has enough authority in the department. To the best extent possible, ownership should be assigned to a department or group as individual accountability cannot be established. The head of IT and system administrators will not be in a position to determine the usage and importance of data and relevant security concerns.

3. What is the most important factor while designing the information classification policy?

   A. Benchmark with competitors

   B. Availability of the technology

   C. Number of staff

   D. Requirements of the data owners

   Answer: D. Requirements of the data owners.

   Explanation: It is very important to consider the requirements of the data owner while defining the information classification policy. The data owner may have specific requirements to address the risk related to their data. The other options do not directly impact the design of the classification policy.

4. Who is mainly responsible for the classification level of the information asset?

   A. Data custodian

   B. Data administrator

   C. Data user

   D. Data owner

   Answer: D. Data owner.

   Explanation: The data owner has the prime responsibility of determining the appropriate level of classification as they are the ones who own the risk related to their data.

5. The extent of a resource's utilization for mitigating risk is determined by which of the following?

    A. Risk analysis results

    B. Audit observations

    C. Vulnerability assessment

    D. Security budget

    Answer: A. Risk analysis results.

    Explanation: Risk analysis is the process of determining the level of risk. The risk level can either be quantified in dollar terms or can be expressed as a qualitative indicator such as high risk, medium risk, or low risk. The results of a risk analysis help the security manager determine the efforts required to address a particular risk. More resources may be required to mitigate high-risk areas, whereas fewer resources may be required to mitigate low-risk areas.

6. What is the main prerequisite when implementing an information classification?

    A. Defining roles and responsibilities

    B. Conducting a risk assessment

    C. Identifying data owners

    D. Documenting a data destruction policy

    Answer: C. Identifying data owners.

    Explanation: Identifying the asset owner is an essential prerequisite when implementing a classification policy. In the absence of an owner, the true value of the asset cannot be determined. The other options are not prerequisites for implementing classification policy.

7. What is the objective of asset classification?

    A. It helps determine critical business objectives.

    B. It helps determine the amount of insurance coverage.

    C. It helps determine the appropriate level of protection for the asset.

    D. It helps benchmark against the processes of the peer organization.

Answer: C. It helps determine the appropriate level of protection for the asset.

Explanation: Information asset classification means classifying assets based on their criticality to the business. An asset can be classified as confidential data, private data, or public data. This classification helps the organization provide the appropriate level of protection to the assets. More resources should be utilized to protect confidential data compared to public data.

8. What is the main advantage of conducting an information asset classification?

    A. To align security requirements with business objectives

    B. To determine controls commensurate with the impact

    C. To establish access rights

    D. To determine asset ownership

    Answer: B. To determine controls commensurate with the impact.

    Explanation: Information asset classification means classifying assets based on their criticality to the business. It determines the appropriate level of protection to the asset; that is, controls are commensurate with the impact. Classification helps reduce the risk of under-protection of assets and, at the same time, it reduces the cost of overprotecting assets.

9. An organization has developed a software code that gives it a competitive edge. Which of the following policies will govern the protection level of the code?

    A. Usage acceptable policy

    B. Data classification policy

    C. Access control policy

    D. IS training policy

    Answer: B. Data classification policy.

    Explanation: Data classification means classifying data based on its criticality to the business. An asset can be classified as confidential data, private data, or public data. This classification helps the organization provide the appropriate level of protection to the assets. More resources should be utilized for protecting confidential data compared to public data.

10. The responsibility for classifying information rests with whom?

    A. Top management

    B. Security manager

    C. Data owner

    D. Data administrator

    Answer: C. Data owner.

    Explanation: The responsibility for maintaining proper security controls over information assets should reside with the data owner. The ultimate responsibility resides with the senior management. The security manager and data administrator support the data owner with classifying and providing the appropriate controls.

11. What is the main cause of data classification regarding criticality and sensitivity?

    A. Determining the owner for each set of data

    B. Determining the appropriate level of access control

    C. Calculating the RoI for each information asset

    D. Deciding on the information security budget

    Answer: B. Determining the appropriate level of access control.

    Explanation: Information asset classification means classifying the assets based on their criticality to the business. An asset can be classified as confidential data, private data, or public data. This classification helps the organization provide the appropriate level of protection to the assets. More resources should be utilized for protecting confidential data compared to public data.

12. For a publicly traded organization, the security manager is expected to accord the lowest protection to what?

    A. The business strategy plan

    B. The customer's personally identifiable information

    C. The personal information of key employees

    D. Published financial results

    Answer: D. Published financial results.

    Explanation: Information asset classification means classifying assets based on criticality to the business. An asset can be classified as confidential data, private data, or public data. This classification helps the organization provide the appropriate level of protection to the assets. Published financial results are considered as public data and hence require the lowest level of protection.

13. The criticality and sensitivity of information assets are primarily based on which of the following?

    A. Penetration tests

    B. Vulnerability tests

    C. Annualized expected loss

    D. Impact assessment

    Answer: D. Impact assessment.

    Explanation: The primary reason for determining the classification of information assets is the criticality and sensitivity of the assets in achieving the business objectives. An impact assessment is used to determine the criticality and sensitivity of the assets.

14. Information assets should be classified by which of the following?

    A. Data administrator

    B. Top management

    C. Security manager

    D. Data manager

    Answer: D. Data manager.

    Explanation: Information classification is primarily based on inputs from the data owner. Business managers (data owners) will have thorough knowledge and understanding of an asset's impact on overall business processes. They are in the best position to determine the value of the information assets.

15. Which of the following is the most important factor when determining the appropriate protection level of an information asset?

    A. The acquisition cost of the asset

    B. The level of vulnerabilities reported in the asset

    C. The level of exposure of the asset

    D. The criticality of the business function supported by the asset

    Answer: D. The criticality of the business function supported by the asset.

    Explanation: Assets can be classified and protected based on a business dependency assessment. In this approach, critical business functions are identified, and all the assets of critical functions are given high priority for protection.

16. A data classification level is mainly decided based on which of the following?

    A. Criticality and sensitivity

    B. Probability and consequences

    C. Cost of asset acquisition

    D. Threat factors

    Answer: A. Criticality and sensitivity.

    Explanation: The main reason for determining the classification of information assets is the criticality and sensitivity of the assets in achieving the business objectives. An impact assessment is used to determine the criticality and sensitivity of the assets.

17. Which of the following is a prerequisite to classifying an asset?

    A. Vulnerability analysis

    B. Impact assessment

    C. Control assessment

    D. Security test

    Answer: B. Impact assessment.

    Explanation: The main reason for determining the classification of information assets is the criticality and sensitivity of the assets in achieving the business objectives. An impact assessment is performed to determine the criticality and sensitivity of the assets.

18. What is the most important factor for an information classification scheme?

    A. It should consider the impact of a security breach.

    B. It should adhere to the security budget.

    C. It should be designed by the information security manager.

    D. It should be based on the vulnerability assessment.

    Answer: A. It should consider the impact of a security breach.

    Explanation: Classification should be based on the impact assessment; that is, potential impact due to asset loss. Classification should be performed by the asset owner rather than the security manager. Vulnerability should not be the basis of classification; instead, the potential impact due to loss of the asset is the basis.

19. What is the most important factor for an information classification scheme?

    A. Vulnerability

    B. Threat

    C. Potential impact

    D. Acquisition cost

    Answer: C. Potential impact.

    Explanation: Classification should be based on the impact's assessment; that is, the potential impact due to asset loss.

20. A client has requested staff to share some information with them. What should be the staff's first course of action?

    A. Obtain a non-disclosure agreement from the client.

    B. Determine the information classification level of the requested information.

    C. Encrypt the requested information.

    D. Transmit the requested information through a secure channel.

    Answer: B. Determine the information classification level of the requested information.

    Explanation: The first step is to determine the classification level of the requested information. If information is classified as confidential, then such information should not be made available to any unauthorized user. Other steps are subsequent actions.

21. What is the most important factor when determining the appropriate levels of asset protection?

    A. The vulnerability assessment of the asset

    B. The feasibility study report

    C. The classification of the asset

    D. The valuation of the asset

    Answer: C. The classification of the asset.

    Explanation: Information asset classification means classifying assets based on their criticality to the business. An asset can be classified as confidential data, private data, or public data. This classification helps the organization provide the appropriate level of protection to the assets. More resources should be utilized for protecting confidential data compared to public data.

22. Asset classification helps determine which of the following?

   A. The vulnerability of the asset

   B. The impact of a compromise

   C. The value of the asset

   D. The annual loss expectancy

   Answer: B. The impact of a compromise.

   Explanation: Information asset classification means classifying assets based on their criticality to the business. More critical assets can have an impact from a compromise, whereas less critical assets have less impact.

23. What is the main reason for asset classification?

   A. To maximize the utilization of resources

   B. To adhere to the IS policy

   C. To determine IT capabilities

   D. To determine the protection level

   Answer: D. To determine the protection level.

   Explanation: Information asset classification means classifying assets based on their criticality to the business. An asset can be classified as confidential data, private data, or public data. This classification helps the organization provide the appropriate level of protection to the assets. More resources should be utilized to protect confidential data compared to public data.

24. What is the most important factor in determining the classification of data?

   A. An assessment of the impact by the data owner

   B. The requirements of information security policy

   C. The existing level of protection

   D. An assessment of the impact by the security manager

   Answer: A. An assessment of the impact by the data owner.

Explanation: Data classification means classifying data based on its criticality to the business. Data classification is primarily based on inputs from the data owner. Business managers (data owners) will have a thorough knowledge and understanding of the asset's impact on overall business processes. They are in the best position to determine the value of the information assets. The requirement of an IS policy is generally applicable once the assets have been classified. The protection level is determined based on the classification and not the other way round, as indicated in option C.

25. What is the most important factor when achieving proportionality to protect information assets?

    A. Classification of assets

    B. Vulnerability assessment

    C. Change management

    D. Security architecture

    Answer: A. Classification of assets.

    Explanation: Information asset classification means classifying assets based on their criticality to the business. The assets are then protected in proportion to their criticality. An asset can be classified as confidential data, private data, or public data. This classification helps the organization provide the appropriate level of protection to the assets. More resources should be utilized to protect confidential data compared to public data.

26. An asset is generally classified based on which of the following?

    A. Business value

    B. Cost of acquisition

    C. Replacement cost

    D. Current market value

    Answer: A. Business value.

    Explanation: An asset is generally classified based on business value; that is, the impact on the business if the asset is compromised. From a risk management perspective, an asset is generally valued based on the business value and not only based on simple acquisition or replacement costs. Business value is measured in terms of revenue loss or other potential impacts when an asset is compromised. For example, software is acquired for $1,000 and it generates a revenue of $5,000 in a single day. So, the business value will be $5,000 per day and not merely the cost of acquisition.

Asset valuation

Asset valuation provides a cost representation of what the organization stands to lose in the event of a major compromise. From the perspective of risk management, an asset is generally valued based on the business value and not only based on a simple acquisition or replacement cost. Business value is measured in terms of revenue loss or other potential impacts when an asset is compromised.

Determining the criticality of assets

The best way to determine the criticality of the asset is by performing a **business impact analysis (BIA)**. A BIA determines the critical business assets by analyzing the impact of the unavailability of an asset on business objectives. In the case of a disaster, the identified critical assets are recovered and restored based on priority to minimize the damage.

To determine the business impact, two independent cost factors are to be considered. The first one is the downtime cost. Examples of downtime costs include a drop in sales, the cost of idle resources, interest costs, and so on. Another element of cost concerns alternative collective measures, such as activating a **business continuity plan (BCP)** and other recovery costs.

Once the business impact is available for each asset, it is important to prioritize the assets that need to be given the topmost level of protection. This criticality analysis should be performed in coordination with IT and business users.

A BIA is the best tool for determining the priority of restoration for applications. **Recovery time objectives (RTOs)** are primarily based on the BIA.

Key aspects from the CISM exam's perspective

The following are some of the key aspects from an exam perspective:

Question	Possible Answer
What is the first step in performing information risk analysis?	Prepare the asset inventory
What is the best tool for determining the priority of restoration for applications?	BIA
On what basis are RTOs primarily based?	BIA

Table 4.2 – Key aspects from the CISM exam's perspective

Questions

1. To determine the impact of a disaster, an asset should be valued based on which of the following?

   A. Cost of acquisition

   B. Net present value

   C. Cost of an identical asset

   D. Replacement cost

   Answer: D. Replacement cost.

   Explanation: An asset should be valued at the replacement cost as this is the cost to replace the asset if the same is damaged or destroyed. The replacement cost will give a realistic impact assessment. The other options will not be true indicators of an impact assessment.

2. When conducting an information risk analysis, what is the first step you should perform?

   A. Conduct a valuation of the asset.

   B. Establish the ownership of the assets.

   C. Create an inventory of the assets.

   D. Classify the assets.

   Answer: C. Create an inventory of the assets.

   Explanation: The first step is to create an inventory of all the information assets of the organization. Once the inventory is available, ownership is established and the asset is valued. Based on this valuation, the assets are classified.

3. An incident was reported for the loss of a mobile device containing unencrypted data. The security manager should be most concerned about which of the following?

   A. The insurance coverage of the mobile device

   B. Their awareness regarding handling mobile devices

   C. The potential impact of the data loss

   D. The replacement cost of mobile devices

   Answer: C. The potential impact of the data loss.

   Explanation: Organizations can suffer a huge impact if data loss is critical and sensitive from a business perspective. If PII data is leaked, the organization is liable for legal consequences. The other options are not as critical.

4.   The value of information assets can be best determined by which of the following?

A. Business managers

B. The system administrator

C. The security manager

D. Top management

Answer: A. Business managers.

Explanation: Valuation is done based on an impact assessment. Business managers are in the best position to understand the impact an asset has on a business. The other people (including top management) will not have detailed knowledge of each process and its impact on the business.

5.   What is the most important factor when conducting a risk assessment?

A. Support for management regarding a risk assessment

B. The documented process for calculating annual loss expectations

C. The availability of the assets list and their appropriate valuation

D. Understanding the attack motives of threats

Answer: C. The availability of the assets list and their appropriate valuation.

Explanation: Identifying all the available assets is the first step in risk assessment. If the identification process is not followed properly, some assets may not be protected. Valuation is performed to understand the criticality and sensitivity of the assets that need protection. Support from management, annual loss expectations, and threat motives are important, but risk assessment would be meaningless without asset inventory and valuation.

6.   The security manager wants to determine the impact of losing network connectivity for 8 to 10 hours. Which of the following is the most important aspect?

A. Service provider charges per hour

B. Quantum of data transmitted per hour

C. Aggregate RoI for all affected business users

D. Overall financial losses incurred by the affected business units

Answer: D. Overall financial losses incurred by the affected business units.

Explanation: Impact can be considered as the overall financial losses incurred by the affected business units. The impact is not only restricted to service provider charges or the quantum of data transmitted. RoI is not based on connectivity and would not be useful in calculating the impact.

7. What is the first step in performing a risk assessment?

A. Identifying business assets

B. Identifying existing controls

C. Identifying asset vulnerabilities

D. Conducting a business impact analysis

Answer: A. Identifying business assets.

Explanation: The first step is to create a list of all assets. This will ensure that no assets are missed while conducting a risk assessment. The other options are subsequent steps.

8. What is the greatest challenge in using annual loss expectancy to predict losses?

A. Dependency on subjective information.

B. It's a time-consuming process.

C. Complexity in terms of the calculation.

D. High cost.

Answer: A. Dependency on subjective information.

Explanation: Lacking accurate information is always a challenge when calculating annual loss expectancy. It is calculated based on assumptions. The other options are comparatively less significant.

9. What is the most important aspect when evaluating an information asset?

A. Potential financial loss

B. Replacement cost

C. Insurance cost

D. Legal requirements

Answer: A. Potential financial loss.

Explanation: Assets should be valued based on potential financial loss due to the unavailability of the assets. The other options are not key considerations.

10. An asset's value can be best judged through which of the following?

    A. A vulnerability assessment

    B. Audit findings

    C. Certification

    D. Classification

    Answer: D. Classification.

    Explanation: Information asset classification means classifying assets based on their criticality to the business. If it is classified as confidential, this means that the asset has a high value to the organization.

11. The impact of a major compromise can be best determined by which of the following?

    A. A vulnerability assessment

    B. Asset valuation

    C. Audit findings

    D. An architectural analysis

    Answer: B. Asset valuation.

    Explanation: Asset valuation indicates the cost impact that the organization may lose in the event of a major compromise. The other options will not be able to provide direct cost representations.

12. A business impact analysis involves which of the following?

    A. Identifying vulnerabilities

    B. Identifying threats

    C. Designing incident notification procedures

    D. Listing critical business resources

    Answer: D. Listing critical business resources.

    Explanation: A business impact analysis determines the critical business assets by analyzing the impact of the unavailability of an asset on business objectives. In the case of a disaster, identified critical assets are recovered and restored on priority to minimize the damage. Threats and vulnerabilities are identified in a risk assessment. The incident notification procedure is part of the business continuity and disaster recovery plan.

13. Which area is of the most concern while prioritizing risk management activities?

    A. Having an incomplete list of information assets

    B. Having an incomplete threat assessment

    C. Having an incomplete vulnerability assessment

    D. Having an inaccurate valuation of information assets

    Answer: D. Having an inaccurate valuation of information assets.

    Explanation: This question is about prioritization. Prioritization is based on the valuation of the assets. High-value assets are given priority for risk treatment. An inaccurate valuation may impact prioritization. An incomplete list may also impact prioritization as some assets may be missed altogether. However, generally, an organization will adopt a procedure to identify at least all the critical assets, so worrying about having an incomplete list is not as major as an inaccurate valuation.

14. You should perform a business impact analysis to decide on which of the following?

    A. The cost of the acquisition

    B. The restoration priority

    C. The yearly rate of loss expectation

    D. The residual risk

    Answer: B. The restoration priority.

    Explanation: A BIA is the best way to determine the criticality of the asset. A BIA determines the critical business assets by analyzing the impact of unavailability of the asset on business objectives. In the case of a disaster, the identified critical assets are recovered and restored to minimize the damage.

15. The RTO is derived from which of the following?

    A. Risk assessment

    B. Gap analysis

    C. BCP testing

    D. Business impact analysis

    Answer: D. Business impact analysis.

    Explanation: The RTO determines the time within which the system should be restored. The RTO is derived from the business impact analysis. The BIA helps determine the critical systems of the organization and the impact due to system downtime.

Operational risk management

Operational risk means risk related to the processes and systems that can interrupt the business's operations. Managing operational risk is one of the key roles of the information security manager. Some of the key aspects that an information security manager must understand regarding operational risks are as follows:

- **Recovery time objective (RTO)**
- **Recovery point objective (RPO)**
- **Service delivery objective (SDO)**
- **Maximum tolerable outage (MTO)**
- **Allowable interruption window (AIW)**

Let's discuss each of these in detail.

Recovery time objective (RTO)

The RTO is a measure of the user's tolerance to system downtime. In other words, the RTO is the extent of acceptable system downtime. For example, an RTO of 2 hours indicates that an organization will not be overly impacted if its system is down for up to 2 hours.

Recovery Point Objective (RPO)

The RPO is a measure of the user's tolerance to data loss. In other words, the RPO is the extent of acceptable data loss. For example, an RPO of 2 hours indicates that an organization will not be overly impacted if it loses data for up to 2 hours.

Difference between RTO and RPO

Let's understand the difference between the RTO and RPO with the following table:

RTO	RPO
RTO is acceptable system downtime.	RPO is acceptable data loss.

Table 4.3 – Difference between the RTO and RPO

So, remember, the RTO (that is, time) is for system downtime, whereas the RPO (that is, point) is for data loss.

Let's understand the differences with the aid of some practical examples:

- **Example 1**: An organization can accept data loss for up to 4 hours. However, it cannot afford to have any downtime.

  Solution: RTO – 0 hours; RPO – 4 hours.

- **Example 2**: An organization takes a data backup twice daily; that is, at noon and then at midnight. What is the RPO?

  Solution: Here, a data backup is done every 12 hours, so the maximum data loss is 12 hours. Hence, the RPO is 12 hours.

- **Example 3**: An organization takes a data backup three times a day. The first backup is at 8 A.M., the second at 4 P.M., and the third at 12 A.M. What is the RPO?

  Solution: Here, a data backup is done every 8 hours, so the maximum data loss is 8 hours. Hence, the RPO is 8 hours.

- **Example 4**: Following an incident, the systems at the primary site went down at 3 P.M. and the systems then resumed from the alternate site at 6 P.M., as per the defined RTO. What is the RTO?

  Solution: The system was down for 3 hours, so the RTO is 3 hours.

- **Example 5**: Identify the RTO and RPO in an instance where the BCP of an organization requires zero data loss (that is, no data should be lost) and processing should be resumed in 36 hours.

  Solution: Here, the organization is accepting a system downtime of up to 36 hours, so the RTO is 36 hours. However, the organization cannot afford to have any data loss, so the RPO is 0 hours:

  - RTO – 36 hours

  - RPO – 0 hours

RTO and RPO for critical systems

The RTO indicates a user's tolerance for system downtime. Similarly, the RPO indicates a user's tolerance to data loss. In the case of critical systems and critical data, an organization cannot afford to have much downtime or data loss. Hence, in the case of critical systems, generally, the RTO and RPO are zero, or near zero. A low RTO indicates that a system should be resumed at the earliest possible juncture. A low RPO indicates that data loss should be at a minimum.

To put it in another way, if the RTO and RPO are low (that is, zero or near zero), then systems and data will be critical for the organization.

RTO and RPO and maintenance costs

A low RTO indicates that systems are critical and need to be resumed as soon as possible. To achieve this objective, organizations need to invest heavily in redundancy. A hot site is ideal where the RTO is lower. This will be a costly affair.

On the other hand, if the RTO is high, this indicates that systems are not that critical and that an organization can afford downtime to some extent. An organization doesn't need to invest in redundancy for systems with a high RTO. A cold site is ideal where the RTO is higher.

A low RPO indicates that data is critical, and it should not be lost. That is, in a case where the RPO is 0, the security manager needs to ensure that there should not be any data loss. They should invest heavily in data backup management. Data mirroring or data synchronization is an ideal technique where the RPO is zero or very low. Hence, for a low RPO, data maintenance costs will be higher compared to a high RPO. Thus, if the RTO and RPO are low (that is, zero or near zero), then the cost of maintaining the environment is high.

RTO, RPO, and disaster tolerance

Disaster tolerance indicates the tolerance level of the organization to accept the non-availability of IT facilities. A low RTO/RPO indicates that disaster tolerance is low; that is, the organization cannot tolerate system downtime. A high RTO/RPO indicates that disaster tolerance is high; that is, the organization can tolerate system downtime up to a certain level.

RTO, RPO, and BIA

The RTO and RPO are primarily based on the BIA. The BIA helps determine the critical systems and processes of the organization. The RTO and RPO of critical systems and processes are low compared to non-critical systems and processes. For example, online banking systems have almost zero RTO and RPO. A bank cannot afford to lose even a single transaction.

Service delivery objective (SDO)

The SDO is the level of service and operational capability to be maintained from an alternate site. The SDO is directly related to business needs and is the level of service to be attained during disaster recovery. This is influenced by business requirements.

Maximum tolerable outage (MTO)

The MTO is the maximum amount of time that an organization can operate from an alternate site. Various factors affect the MTO, such as location availability, resource availability, raw material availability, or electric power availability at alternate sites, among other constraints.

Allowable interruption window (AIW)

The AIW is the maximum amount of time for which the normal operations of the organization can be down. After this point, the organization starts facing major financial difficulties that threaten its existence. The MTO should be as long as the AIW to minimize the risk to the organization.

Questions

1. The RTO is derived from which of the following?

    A. Risk assessment

    B. Gap analysis

    C. BCP testing

    D. Business impact analysis

    Answer: D. Business impact analysis.

    Explanation: The RTO determines the time within which the system should be restored. The RTO is derived from the business impact analysis. The BIA helps determine the critical systems of the organization and their impact due to system downtime.

Outsourcing and third-party service providers

Outsourcing services to a third-party vendor is a widely accepted practice in today's world for two major reasons. The first is the tremendous savings in cost, while the other is to avail the services of experts in the field.

CISM aspirants should be aware of the following important terms concerning outsourcing:

- **Insourced**: Activities performed by the organization's staff
- **Outsourced**: Activities performed by the vendor's staff
- **Hybrid**: Activities performed jointly by staff from both the organization and the vendor

- **Onsite**: Staff working onsite in the IT department

- **Offsite**: Staff working from remote locations in the same geographical area

- **Offshore**: Staff working from remote locations in different geographical areas

Evaluation criteria for outsourcing

CISM aspirants should understand the evaluation criteria for outsourcing any function. Certain functions cannot be outsourced, as depicted in the following figure:

Figure 4.3 – Outsourcing

The following functions should not be outsourced:

- The core functions of the organization

- Roles that require specific expertise, procedures, and key resources that cannot be replicated externally or anywhere else

- Functions that cannot be outsourced due to contractual or regulatory constraints

Functions can be outsourced if the following applies:

- Functions can be carried out by another party to the same level of quality or better, at the same price or lower, without increasing the risk.

- The organization has sufficient experience in managing third parties working on its behalf.

Steps for outsourcing

The following steps will help you determine whether outsourcing will enable the company to achieve its desired goal while considering the costs and risks involved:

1. **Define the function to be outsourced**: The organization should define and determine the functions that need to be outsourced. This step should also include risk assessment for outsourcing a particular function.

2. **Define a service-level agreement (SLA)**: Defining a SLA is a very important aspect of outsourcing. SLAs should be approved by the legal, risk management, and compliance teams.

3. **Determine the cost**: Here, you need to determine the cost of outsourcing.

4. **Conduct due diligence**: Due diligence includes verifying the profile of the service provider, their market credibility, financial stability, capability to serve on a long-term basis, and other relevant details.

5. **Confirm the contractual or regulatory requirements for outsourcing**: It is also of the utmost importance to determine any regulatory and contractual requirements when outsourcing any activity.

Once the contract has been signed, the security manager should ensure that continuous vendor monitoring processes and metrics are developed and implemented. This control will help identify and address the areas of concern.

Outsourcing – risk reduction options

The security manager should be involved in the third-party management process from the beginning of the selection process, which is when the business is defining what it needs. This will ensure that all security requirements are considered at the initial phase itself to reduce the outsourcing risks. The following are important aspects for reducing the risks related to outsourcing:

*   A requirement for achievable output should be included in the SLA.
*   The use of an escrow arrangement for software assets.
*   The use of multiple suppliers helps lower the risk of dependence.
*   Periodic reviews of performance.
*   Building a cross-functional contract management team.
*   Setting up appropriate controls for any anticipated contingencies.

Provisions for outsourcing contracts

SLAs will serve as monitoring tools for the outsourcing process. They should contain, at the very least, the following clauses:

- Requirements for achievable output

- **Confidentiality, Integrity, and Availability** (**CIA**) requirements for resources/ systems/data

- Confidentiality agreements to protect both parties

- A right-to-audit clause

- Business continuity and disaster recovery provisions

- Intellectual property rights

The role of the security manager in monitoring outsourced activities

The following are some of the important functions of the security manager in monitoring outsourced activities:

- Reviewing contracts at the service level at periodic intervals

- Reviewing documented procedures and outcomes of the outsourcer's quality assurance programs

- Performing periodic checks to ensure that the processes and procedures comply with the organization's quality standards

Service-level agreement

The most important contractual element when contracting with an outsourcer to provide service is the **service-level agreement** (**SLA**). The SLA defines the level of the service that's expected from a service provider. Apart from operational parameters, it also includes security-related clauses, such as adherence to security requirements, a penalty clause, an indemnity clause, and the rights to the audit clause.

The security manager can enforce security requirements, but only if the contract mandates compliance with the information security policy. SLAs ensure that the service provider is contractually obliged to comply with the requirements of the service receiver. This protects both organizations.

Right to audit clause

A right to audit clause in the contract is essential to ensure contract compliance. The absence of a *right to audit* clause would prevent the organization from determining the security arrangement of the service provider. The organization would not have any assurance about contractual and legal compliance from the service provider.

A periodic audit is the most effective method to ensure that the service provider is complying with the security requirements of the service receiver. An SLA should include clauses concerning the right to audit the system and the processes of the service provider. The service provider may not allow the service receiver to audit them directly. In such cases, there should be a way to assess compliance by an independent auditor. If such provisioning is not included in the agreement, then the service receiver has no way of ensuring compliance or proper handling of their data.

Impact of privacy laws on outsourcing

Privacy is the right of the individual to demand the utmost care of their personal information that has been shared with any organization or individual. Individuals can demand that the use of their information should be appropriate, legal, and for a specific purpose for which information is obtained. Non-compliance to privacy requirements may lead to legal consequences.

Security managers need to ensure that applicable privacy laws are adhered to before sharing personally identifiable data with a third-party service provider.

Sub-contracting/fourth party

Sub-contracting is a term that's used where the service provider also outsources the process to another entity. The same has been explained in a lighter note in the following figure:

Figure 4.4 – Outsourcing

An SLA should specifically restrict the sub-contracting to a fourth party. In case it is allowed, considering the business requirement, the security manager should consider the risk of subcontracting. In the case of subcontracting, service receivers generally do not have control over the fourth party. The subcontracting process has to be thoroughly reviewed when the process involves sharing critical data.

Compliance responsibility

The service receiver retains the responsibility for ensuring compliance with regulatory requirements. The service receiver is deemed to be the owner of the data and responsible for the safe custody of the data. If the service provider fails to safeguard the data, then the authority will generally hold the service receiver responsible for non-compliance and take appropriate action, including penalties.

Key aspects from the CISM exam's perspective

The following are some of the key aspects from the exam's perspective:

Question	Possible Answer
What is the primary objective of outsourcing?	To obtain the services of expert firms and to save on costs.
What is the primary concern when outsourcing to an offshore location?	Privacy laws and regulatory requirements.
What is the primary function of IT management when a service has been outsourced?	To monitor the outsourcing provider's performance.
What is the best way to determine whether the terms of the contract are adhered to according to the SLA?	Independent audit.
What is the primary requirement for developing software from the vendor?	Escrow arrangement for source code.
What is the primary risk of subcontracting?	The requirement to protect information may be compromised.
What is the most important contractual element when contracting with a service provider?	Service-level agreement.
What is the best way to ensure the ongoing security of outsourced IT services?	To conduct regular security audits and reviews of the third-party provider.

Question	Possible Answer
What is the most important reason for a security manager reviewing the contract?	To help ensure the appropriate controls are included.
At what point should information security become involved in the vendor management process?	At the beginning stage, when requirements are being established.
What should be the next step of the security manager once the contract with the service provider is entered?	Establishing the processes and metrics for monitoring the service provider.
What should be the first step when deciding to allow access to a new external party?	Conducting a risk assessment.
To address the resolution of an operational issue, what is the most important aspect to be included in the service-level agreement?	Defined responsibilities.
What is the most effective way to ensure that no backdoor codes are implemented when an application is developed by a third party?	Conducting security code reviews for the entire application.

Table 4.4 – Key aspects from the CISM exam's perspective

Questions

1. The information security manager is reviewing the outsourcing arrangement. Which of the following is the most critical contractual element?

    A. Penalty clause

    B. Indemnity clause

    C. Service-level agreement

    D. Right to terminate clause

    Answer: C. Service-level agreement.

    Explanation: An SLA defines the level of service expected from a vendor and it also includes other options such as the penalty clause, indemnity clause, and right to terminate.

2. The information security policy of the organization requires independent assessment for all third parties associated with the organization. The security manager should ensure what is included in the contract?

    A. A right to audit clause

    B. An indemnity clause

    C. A requirement for a firewall

    D. A requirement for an exclusive security manager

    Answer: A. A right to audit clause.

    Explanation: To conduct an independent assessment of the service provider, the right to audit clause must be included in the contract. In the absence of the right to audit clause, the service provider may not be allowed to audit their processes. The other options depend on the nature of service outsources and should be evaluated during the audit.

3. What is the most important aspect a security manager should consider while entering an agreement with a third-party service provider?

    A. The outsourcing arrangement should be within the approved budget.

    B. The availability of the business continuity arrangement.

    C. The service provider is contractually obliged to follow all the relevant security requirements.

    D. Obtaining industry references for the service provider.

    Answer: C. The service provider is contractually obliged to follow all the relevant security requirements.

    Explanation: In the absence of contractual liability, the security manager will not be able to ensure compliance with the security requirements of the service provider. Contractual obligations help both parties with the contract. Adhering to the budget and obtaining an industry reference is the responsibility of the business unit, not the security manager. The availability of the business continuity arrangement is a secondary aspect.

4. The ongoing security arrangement of a third-party service provider can be best ensured by which of the following?

    A. Conducting a continuous security awareness program for employees of the third-party service provider

    B. Conducting regular security reviews of the third-party service providers

C. Increasing the contract rate every year

D. Including security requirements in the service contract

Answer: B. Conducting regular security reviews of the third-party service providers.

Explanation: Frequent audits and security reviews of the third-party service provider is the best way to ensure appropriate security arrangements on an ongoing basis. Including security requirements in the service contract is important, but it does not help to ensure ongoing effectiveness. Security training and increasing contract rate are secondary aspects.

5. Which of the following is best to be included in the service-level agreement to ensure that the confidentiality requirement is complied with by the third-party service provider?

A. Access control matrix

B. Security budget

C. Authentication mechanism

D. Encryption strength

Answer: A. Access control matrix.

Explanation: The required level of access control matrix is to be included in the service-level agreement to ensure the confidentiality of the data. The other options are generally not included in an SLA.

6. What is the most important aspect a security manager should consider while entering into an agreement with a third-party service provider?

A. The contract rate is approved by the security steering committee.

B. The contract should include a confidentiality clause.

C. The contract should mandate that the service provider complies with the security requirements of the organization.

D. The contract should mandate that the service provider conducts regular security audits.

Answer: C. The contract should mandate that the service provider complies with the security requirements of the organization.

Explanation: The security manager can only enforce security requirements if the contract mandates compliance with the information security policy. The confidentiality clause and security audit should be part of the security requirements. The contract rate is required to be approved by business management and not by the steering committee.

7. A third-party service provider handles sensitive customer data. The security manager is most likely to be interested in which of the following?

    A. The security arrangement for stored and transmitted sensitive data

    B. Adherence to the industry benchmark

    C. The implementation of security technologies

    D. Adherence to operational processes

    Answer: A. The security arrangement for stored and transmitted sensitive data.

    Explanation: As the third party is involved in handling sensitive customer data, the primary consideration for the security manager is to determine the security arrangement for storing and transmitting sensitive data. The other options are secondary aspects.

8. An organization shares critical data with the third-party service provider for processing. What should the security manager primarily ensure regarding the data classification requirements of the organization?

    A. They are aligned with the requirements of the third-party service provider.

    B. They are communicated to the third-party provider.

    C. They are included in the training module.

    D. They are included in the contract.

    Answer: D. They are included in the contract.

    Explanation: The most effective method is to ensure that the requirements are included in the contract. This will help enforce the requirements. The other options are secondary aspects.

9. What is the best way to ensure that outsourced service providers comply with the organization's information security policy?

    A. To obtain periodic reports from the service provider

    B. To conduct periodic meetings with the manager of the service provider

    C. To conduct periodic audit reviews of the service provider

    D. To include performance parameters in the service-level agreement

    Answer: C. To conduct periodic audit reviews of the service provider.

    Explanation: The best control to monitor the services of third-party service providers is to conduct periodic audit reviews of the given service provider. The other options will not be as effective as conducting an audit. An audit will help determine the level of actual compliance with the security requirements.

10. Before executing the contract, the information security manager should do what?

    A. Ensure that the operational issues are clearly defined

    B. Ensure that the contract rate is within the approved budget

    C. Ensure that the appropriate controls are included

    D. Ensure that the right to audit clause is included

    Answer: C. Ensure that the appropriate controls are included.

    Explanation: The role of the security manager is to ensure that the appropriate controls are included in the contract. In the absence of a well-defined contractual agreement, an organization cannot enforce the necessary security requirements. The right to audit is one of the controls to be included in the contract. Operational issues and the contract rate are not within the purview of the security manager.

11. The organization is unable to convince one of its major trading partners to comply with its security requirements. What is the best course of action for the security manager?

    A. Ask the trading partner to sign a legal agreement to own all liabilities for any breach.

    B. Revoke all the connections and access rights of the trading partner.

    C. Implement a firewall to restrict network traffic from that location.

    D. Continue periodic reminders to comply with security requirements.

    Answer: C. Implement a firewall to restrict network traffic from that location.

    Explanation: The best way to continue the business relationship and, at the same time, address the risk is to set up firewall rules restricting the network traffic from trading with a partner.

12. What is the most important factor before outsourcing customer relationship management to a third-party service provider?

    A. Conduct a background check of the employees of the service providers.

    B. Conduct a risk assessment to determine the required controls.

    C. Conduct a security assessment to determine the security vulnerabilities.

    D. Conduct an audit of the third-party service provider to determine their controls.

    Answer: B. Conduct a risk assessment to determine the required controls.

Explanation: The most important step is to conduct a risk assessment to identify the risks and determine the required controls. Performing a background check of the employees of the service provider is the responsibility of the service provider. Auditing and security assessments are subsequent steps of the risk assessment.

13. From a security perspective, which of the following is the most important aspect that needs to be negotiated with a third-party service provider?

    A. The right to conduct an independent security review

    B. The right to carry out a background verification on the third party's employees

    C. The right to encrypt the data transmission between the organization and the service provider

    D. The right to conduct a joint risk assessment of the system

    Answer: A. The right to conduct an independent security review.

    Explanation: The most important aspect is the right to conduct an independent security review of the third-party service provider. This will help the organization determine the security posture of the service provider. The other options are secondary aspects.

14. The information security manager should be involved in outsourcing the arrangement at which point?

    A. At the time of contract negotiation

    B. As and when business units require assistance

    C. When the requirements are being established

    D. Only when there is a security incident

    Answer: C. When the requirements are being established.

    Explanation: It is important to get the information security manager involved from the beginning, when the requirements are being established. Security requirements should be considered at the time of bids and other negotiations with third parties.

15. The organization has provided access to its system to a supplier to remotely access important business data. What is the most effective way to ensure that the supplier does not improperly access or modify the database?

    A. Limit user access rights.

    B. Implement two-factor authentication.

C. Implement biometric access control.

D. Conduct user awareness training.

Answer: A. Limit user access rights.

Explanation: The most effective method is to limit access to the extent required for the user to perform their job. User authentication by way of two-factor authentication and biometric controls is important, but once access is granted, the user should have only specific rights.

16. From a security perspective, what is the most important aspect of outsourcing a critical process to a third-party service provider?

A. Compliance with international standards

B. Implementing two-factor authentication

C. The availability of an alternative processing site

D. Adherence to the organization's information security requirements

Answer: D. Adherence to the organization's information security requirements.

Explanation: The most important aspect is to ensure compliance with the organization's information security requirements. Authentication and alternate processing sites will be already included in the organization's security requirements. Compliance with international standards is a secondary aspect.

17. A request for proposal (RFP) when selecting a third-party service provider is to be issued when?

A. Before the project's feasibility stage

B. Post finalization of the service provider

C. Before developing a project budget

D. Before the business case stage

Answer: C. Before developing a project budget.

Explanation: An RFP is the process of requesting technical details and the cost of the proposed project. The budget is generally finalized based on the proposal from service providers. Project feasibility and business case are initial steps to decide whether the project should be implemented.

18. What should be the next step on the part of the information security manager once the contract has been entered into with a third-party service provider for IT support services?

    A. To establish the process for monitoring the service provider

    B. To define the roles and responsibilities of the service provider

    C. To finalize the contract rate

    D. To get the service provider to sign a non-disclosure agreement

    Answer: A. To establish the process for monitoring the service provider.

    Explanation: After entering into the contract, the next step will be to ensure that continuous service provider monitoring is established. This will help the information security manager control and monitor the activities of the service providers. At this point, irregularities, if any, can be addressed immediately. All the other options are actions that occur before entering the contract.

19. When sensitive data is stored at a third-party location, the security manager will require which of the following?

    A. Assurances that the third party will comply with the requirements of the contract

    B. A background check of the employee of the third party

    C. Frequent security training for all third-party employees

    D. That the security policy is reviewed periodically

    Answer: A. Assurances that the third party will comply with the requirements of the contract.

    Explanation: The service provider is required to assure compliance with the requirements of the contract. One of the best ways to provide assurance is by using independent security audit reports. Awareness training and background checks may be one of the requirements of the contract. Reviewing the contracts and policies is important, but it does not assure compliance.

20. What area is of the most concern for a security manager when payroll processes are outsourced to a third-party service provider?

    A. Whether a cost-benefit analysis has been conducted

    B. Whether privacy requirements have been complied with

C. Whether secure data transfer has been ensured

D. Whether a background reference has been obtained for the service provider

Answer: B. Whether privacy requirements have been complied with.

Explanation: Privacy is the right of the individual to demand the utmost care of their personal information while it's being shared with any organization or individual. Individuals can demand that the use of their information should be appropriate, legal, and for a specific purpose for which information is obtained. Non-compliance with privacy requirements may lead to legal consequences. The other options are secondary aspects.

21. What area is of most concern for a security manager when an organization is storing sensitive data in a third-party cloud service provider?

A. High cost of maintenance

B. Unavailability of proper training for end users

C. Unavailability of a service due to a network failure

D. The possibility to disclose sensitive data in transit or storage

Answer: D. The possibility to disclose sensitive data in transit or storage.

Explanation: The primary area of concern is disclosing sensitive data, which may lead to regulatory, financial, and reputational loss. Generally, cloud storage is cost-effective. The unavailability of proper training and network problems are secondary aspects.

22. An organization is planning to provide access to a third-party service provider. Which of the following should be the first step?

A. Deciding on the terms of access

B. A risk assessment

C. Determining the level of exposure

D. Conducting due diligence of the third party

Answer: B. A risk assessment

Explanation: The first step is to conduct a risk assessment to determine the level of risk involved in providing access to a third-party service provider. The other options are covered in the risk assessment process.

23. Which of the following is the most important clause to be included in an SLA for outsourcing an IT support service?

    A. A clause for staff background checks

    B. A clause concerning the right to audit

    C. A clause for a non-disclosure agreement

    D. A clause for staff training

    Answer: B. A clause for the right to audit.

    Explanation: The absence of a "right to audit" clause would prevent the organization from determining the security arrangement of the service provider. The organization would not have any assurance about contractual and legal compliance from the service provider. The other options are not as significant as the right to audit clause.

24. What is the most important area for an information security manager when selecting a third-party service provider for a critical business function?

    A. Whether the service provider agrees with the penalty for non-compliance

    B. Whether the service provider has alternate site processing

    C. Whether the contract rate is within the approved budget

    D. Whether the service provider meets the organization's security requirements on an ongoing and verifiable basis

    Answer: D. Whether the service provider meets the organization's security requirements on an ongoing and verifiable basis.

    Explanation: From a security perspective, the most important consideration is the service provider's capability to meet the organization's security requirements. The other options are secondary aspects.

25. What is the most difficult factor to determine while conducting a security review of an offshore service provider?

    A. Technological capability

    B. Incompatible culture

    C. Network controls

    D. Adequate procedures

    Answer: B. Incompatible culture

Explanation: It is very difficult to determine the culture of other organizations. The incompatible culture of a third-party service provider proves to be a high risk to the organization. Employees with different cultures often have different perspectives on data privacy. Sometimes, the perspectives of the employees may not be consistent with the organization's requirements. Employees in different cultures may have different perspectives on what information is considered as sensitive or confidential and how such information is handled.

The other areas can be evaluated and determined during a security review.

26. An organization has renewed an agreement with a third-party service provider every year for the last 5 years without changing any agreement clauses. However, recently, complaints are being received concerning security lapses on the part of the service providers. Which of the following actions is the *FIRST* one that the information security manager should take in this situation?

    A. Ensure that the security requirements included in the service agreement meet current business requirements.

    B. Determine whether the service provider complies with the service agreement.

    C. Impose a heavy penalty for non-compliance with the service agreement.

    D. Automate the compliance monitoring process.

    Answer: A. Ensure that the security requirements included in the service agreement meet current business requirements.

    Explanation: The first step is to ensure that the current business and security requirements are included in the service agreement. As the service agreement has not been significantly revised in 4 years, the third-party service provider may not be aware of the current requirements of the organization. If the requirements are not included in the service agreement, even compliance with the service agreement, heavy penalties, and automatic monitoring will not be meaningful.

27. When addressing the resolution of an operational issue, what is the most important aspect to be included in the service-level agreement?

    A. Escalation matrix

    B. Documented process

    C. Court of jurisdiction

    D. Defined responsibilities

    Answer: D. Defined responsibilities.

Explanation: It is easy to assign the ownership and accountability of an operational issue if roles and responsibilities are properly defined in the service-level agreement. If you have any concerns, it is important to identify responsibility ownership. This will help you determine the next action to be taken for the follow-up. The other options are secondary aspects.

28. What is the most important area for an information security manager when selecting a cloud service provider?

    A. Whether the service-level agreement provides a guarantee of continuous application availability

    B. Whether the service provider's security architecture meets the organization's requirements

    C. Whether the contract rate is within an approved budget

    D. Whether the service provider has alternate site processing

    Answer: B. Whether the service provider's security architecture meets the organization's requirements

    Explanation: From a security perspective, the most important consideration is the service provider's capability to meet the organization's security requirements. The security manager is generally not concerned with the contract rate. Application availability and alternate site processing will already be included in the organization's security requirements.

29. An application has been developed by a third-party service provider. What is the most effective way to ensure that no backdoor codes are implemented?

    A. Monitoring the network traffic

    B. Conducting penetration testing

    C. Conducting an internal audit

    D. Conducting a security code review for the entire application

    Answer: D. Conducting a security code review for the entire application.

    Explanation: The best security measure when a third party is engaged in application development is to conduct a security code review for the entire application. This allows you to detect all the malware, including backdoors.

Risk management integration with the process life cycle

The security manager should understand that risk management activities are not one-time events. Risk management is a continuous process. For effective risk management, activities related to risk management should be integrated with the process life cycle.

System development life cycle

The security manager should be aware of the following **system development life cycle (SDLC)** phases:

Phase	Description
Phase 1: Initiation/ Feasibility	· The objective, purpose, and scope of the system are discussed, finalized, and documented. · In this phase, the system design is finalized and approved. Internal controls should be incorporated during the initial design stage. · During the feasibility phase (planning or initiation), the process for change management should be defined. It is very important to prevent scope creep.
Phase 2: Development/ Acquisition	In this phase, alternatives are evaluated, and the system is developed or acquired from a third party.
Phase 3: Implementation	In this phase, the system is tested, and migration activities are carried out.
Phase 4: Operations/ Maintenance	In this phase, regular updates and maintenance are carried out for the upkeep of the system.
Phase 5: Disposal	In this phase, obsolete systems are discarded by moving, archiving, discarding, or destroying information and sanitizing the hardware and software.

Table 4.5 – Phases of the SDLC

The security manager should be involved in all the preceding phases of the SDLC and the security requirements should be integrated into all SDLC phases. Performing risk assessments at each stage of the SDLC is the most cost-effective way to address any flaws early.

The following aspects need to be addressed during the risk assessment of the project:

- What level of confidentiality is required for the system?
- What level of availability is required for the system?
- What impact do any laws or regulations have on the project (for example, privacy laws)?
- What are the architectural and technological risks?
- What secure information systems will be used in the development process?
- What security training will be put in place for the developers and staff members?

The best way to implement risk management processes continuously is to develop a structured change management procedure.

Key aspects from the CISM exam's perspective

The following are some of the key aspects from the exam's perspective:

Question	Possible Answer
What is the most effective approach to ensure the continued effectiveness of information security controls?	Effective life cycle management
What is the best way to address risk at various life cycle stages?	Using a structured change management procedure

Table 4.6 – Key aspects from the CISM exam's perspective

Questions

1. What process best supports addressing the risk at various life cycle phases?

    A. Change management

    B. Patch management

    C. Release management

    D. Configuration management

    Answer: A. Change management.

Explanation: A change management process includes approval, testing, scheduling, and rollback arrangements. Changes at various life cycle stages should be appropriately controlled through a structured change management process. The other options do not relate to complete life cycle stages.

2. What is the best way to ensure the continued effectiveness of controls?

    A. To increase the security budget

    B. To ensure strategic alignment

    C. To ensure effective life cycle management

    D. To ensure frequent benchmarking

    Answer: C. To ensure effective life cycle management

    Explanation: If controls are managed throughout the life cycle, it will reduce the scope of the degradation of controls and ensure control effectiveness throughout the life cycle.

Summary

In this chapter, we discussed the practical aspects of risk management. This chapter will help you classify various assets and manage the operational risk of the organization. This chapter will also help you integrate risk management into an asset's life cycle.

In the next chapter, we will discuss the procedural aspects of information risk management.

5
Procedural Aspects of Information Risk Management

In this chapter, we will discuss the procedural aspects of information risk management and understand the risk management tools and techniques and other important concepts from the perspective of the CISM exam.

The following topics will be covered in this chapter:

- Change management
- Patch management
- Security baseline control
- Risk monitoring and communication
- Security awareness training and education
- Documentation

Let's look at each one of the preceding topics in detail.

Change management

A change management process is used to change hardware, install software, and configure various network devices. A change management process includes approval, testing, scheduling, and rollback arrangements.

Any changes to a system or process are likely to introduce new vulnerabilities and hence it is very important for the security manager to identify and address new risks.

The objective of change management

The main objective of the change management process is to support the processing and traceability of changes to a system. The change management process ensures that any modification to or updating of the system is carried out in a controlled manner.

Approval from the system owner

The security manager should also consider a structured change management process. While implementing a change, all relevant personnel should be kept informed and specific approval should be obtained from the relevant information asset owners.

Regression testing

Regression testing is a part of change management. The objective of regression testing is to prevent the introduction of new security exposures when making modifications. Thus, change management is the best way to ensure that modifications made to systems do not introduce new security exposures. System users will be in the best position to conduct the user acceptance testing and determine whether any new vulnerabilities have been raised during the change management process.

Involvement of the security team

For effective change management, it is important that the security team should be apprised of every major change. It is recommended to include representation from the security team on the change control board. This will ensure that security aspects are considered for any change.

Preventive control

Change management is considered to be a preventive control as it requires all change requests to pass through formal approval, documentation, and testing by a supervisory process.

Key aspects from a CISM exam perspective

The following are some of the key aspects from an exam perspective:

Question	Possible answer
What is the prime objective of change management?	To ensure that only authorized changes are carried out. To ensure that modifications made to the system do not introduce new security exposures.
What is the best way to reduce the risk arising from modification of the system?	Change management process.
Change management is considered to be (preventive/detective/corrective) control.	Preventive control.

Table 5.1 – Key aspects from the CISM exam perspective

Questions

1. What is the best method to determine whether all patch updates have gone through the proper change control process?

    A. Verify the change control request and trace it to the patch logs

    B. Verify whether the last patch is properly documented

    C. Verify the patch logs and trace them to the change control request

    D. Verify whether the last change control request is properly documented

    Answer: C. Verify the patch logs and trace them to the change control request

    Explanation: The most effective method to ensure that all patch updates went through the change management process is to start with the patch logs and select a few samples and then verify whether change control requests are available for these sample patch updates. When the starting point is taken as the change request and then tracing it back to the patch logs, this will not be able to determine whether all patches went through the change control process.

2. What is the most effective method to ensure that modifications made to software do not introduce new security exposures?

    A. Load testing

    B. Patch management

    C. Change management

    D. Security baseline

Answer: C. Change management

Explanation: Change management is the process of requesting, planning, implementing, testing, and evaluating changes to a system. Regression testing is a part of change management. The objective of regression testing is to prevent the introduction of new security exposures when making modifications. Thus, change management is the best way to ensure that modifications made to systems do not introduce new security exposures.

3. What is the most effective way to prevent weakness being introduced into the existing system?

    A. Anti-malware

    B. Patch management

    C. Change management

    D. Firewall

    Answer: C. Change management

    Explanation: Change management is the process of requesting, planning, implementing, testing, and evaluating changes to a system. Regression testing is a part of change management. The objective of regression testing is to prevent the introduction of new security exposures when making modifications. Thus, change management is the best way to ensure that modifications made to systems do not introduce new security exposures.

4. Who will be in the best position to determine that a new vulnerability has not been introduced during the change management process?

    A. Internal auditor

    B. System user

    C. System administrator

    D. Data security manager

    Answer: B. System user

    Explanation: Change management is the best way to ensure that modifications made to systems do not introduce new security exposures. System users will be in the best position to conduct the user acceptance testing and determine whether any new vulnerabilities have been introduced during the change management process.

5. What is the most effective method to evaluate the security risk while modifying applications?

    A. Incident management process

    B. Problem handling process

    C. Change control process

    D. System benchmarking

    Answer: C. Change control process

    Explanation: Change control process is the best way to ensure that modifications made to systems do not introduce new security exposures. System users will be in the best position to conduct the user acceptance testing and determine whether any new vulnerabilities have been introduced during the change management process.

6. What is the most important aspect of a change management process?

    A. The change management process should be handled by the information security team.

    B. The change management process should be monitored by the steering committee.

    C. The change management process should be part of release and configuration management.

    D. The change management process should include the mandatory involvement of the information security department.

    Answer: D. The change management process should include the mandatory involvement of the information security department.

    Explanation: For effective change management, it is important that the security team should be apprised every major change. It is recommended to include representation from the security team on the change control board. This will ensure that security aspects are considered for any change. It is not required that change management should be handled by the information security team; just having a representation is enough. Monitoring of the change management process may not be the responsibility of the steering committee. Change management should be a separate function from release and configuration management.

7. Which type of control is a change management process?

    A. Compensating control

    B. Corrective control

    C. Preventive control

D. Deterrent control

Answer: C. Preventive control

Explanation: Change management is considered to be preventive control as it requires all change requests to pass through formal approval, documentation, and testing by a supervisory process. An effective change management process can prevent and detect unauthorized changes. The primary objective of a change management process is not compensating or corrective or deterrent control.

8. For an emergency change, which of the following steps can be bypassed?

A. Detailed documentation

B. Impact analysis

C. Scheduling

D. Authorization

Answer: C. Scheduling

Explanation: Scheduling in change management is the process of planning the implementation at a particular time that will cause the least disturbance to business processing. However, for an emergency change, maintaining the schedule may not be possible. The other options – documentation, impact analysis, and authorization – are an integral part of change management and for an emergency change may be performed post implementation.

9. What is production risk primarily addressed by?

A. Audit management

B. Release management

C. Change management

D. Configuration management

Answer: C. Change management

Explanation: A major risk related to production is continuity of operations. This can be best addressed by a structured change management process. Change management is a structured process of change request, approval, planning, implementation, and testing. The main objective of a change management process is to support the processing and traceability of changes to a system. Change management ensures that any changes or updates are processed in a controlled manner.

10. Why it is important to get approval from the security manager to implement any major change?

    A. To ensure that changes comply with business objectives

    B. To ensure that any risk from the proposed change is managed

    C. To ensure that rollback arrangements are incorporated

    D. To ensure adherence to budget

    Answer: B. To ensure that any risk from the proposed change is managed

    Explanation: Any major change may introduce new risks to the system. The security manager is required to ensure that the new change does not have an adverse impact on the security environment. The other options are not the primary reason.

11. Disruptions to the production system can be most effectively prevented by which of the following?

    A. Structured patch management process

    B. Structured security baseline

    C. Structured anti-malware system

    D. Structured change management system

    Answer: D. Structured change management system

    Explanation: A change management process includes approval, testing, scheduling, and rollback arrangements. Any changes to a system or process is likely to introduce new vulnerabilities and hence it is very important for the security manager to identify and address new risks. Changes that are not properly reviewed can disrupt the production systems. The other options – patch management, baseline management, and anti-malware management – should also be implemented through a proper change management process.

12. An organization's change management process includes threat and vulnerability assessment. What is the primary reason for this?

    A. To reduce the requirement for periodic full risk assessments

    B. To reduce the expenses of risk management activities

    C. To change the policy to address new risks

    D. To adhere to legal requirements

Answer: A. To reduce the requirement for periodic full risk assessments

Explanation: Threat and vulnerability assessment during change helps to identify the proposed changes at the early stage. This helps to keep the risk assessment updated and current, which eventually reduces the requirement for complete full assessment. The other options are not the primary objective. A policy is a high-level statement and is generally not impacted by new risk.

13. What is an area of major concern with respect to the security risk for an organization having multiple locations?

    A. System operational guidelines are not monitored.

    B. Poor change management procedures.

    C. Outsourcing of application development.

    D. Poor capacity management procedure.

    Answer: B. Poor change management procedures.

    Explanation: Lack of an effective change management process can have significant risk for disruption of systems and procedures. The other options are not as significant as poor change management process. Guidelines are generally not mandatory. Outsourcing activities can be controlled and monitored. Poor capacity management may not impact security risk.

Patch management

Patch management is the process of updating operating systems and other software to correct an error or enhance performance.

A well-defined and structured patch management process helps to address the new vulnerabilities related to operating systems. Timely updating of patches helps to secure operating systems and applications.

Patches are generally applied to operating systems, applications, and network software. Patches will help to fix the vulnerability in the system.

Patches should be applied through a structured change management process that includes approval, testing, user acceptance testing, and proper documentation. Testing a patch prior to implementation is one of the most important aspects, as deploying an untested patch may cause the system to fail. Also, appropriate rollback procedures should be in place in case of unexpected failure.

Key aspects from a CISM exam perspective

The following are some of the key aspects from an exam perspective:

Question	Possible answer
What is the best way to ensure that newly identified security weaknesses in an operating system are mitigated in a timely fashion?	Patch management.
What is the first step when an organization receives a patch for updating?	To validate the authenticity of the patch.
What is the correct frequency for patch updating?	Whenever important security patches are released. However, the patch should be tested first.

Table 5.2 – Key aspects from the CISM exam perspective

Questions

1. What is the most effective way for timely mitigation of a newly identified vulnerability in an operating system?

   A. Patch management

   B. Internal audit

   C. Change management

   D. Security baseline

   Answer: A. Patch management

   Explanation: Patch management is the process of applying updates to operating systems and other software. These patches are often necessary to correct errors in the software. A well-defined and structured patch management process helps to address the new vulnerabilities related to operating systems. Timely updating of patches helps to secure operating systems and applications.

2. What is the best method to determine whether all patch updates have gone through a proper change control process?

   A. Verify the change control request and trace it to the patch logs

   B. Verify whether the last patch is properly documented

C. Verify the patch logs and trace them to the change control request

D. Verify whether the last change control request is properly documented

Answer: C. Verify the patch logs and trace them to the change control request

Explanation: To determine whether all patches passed through the change control process, it is necessary to use the patch logs as a starting point and then verify whether change control requests are available for these patch updates. When the starting point is taken as the change request and then tracing it back to the patch logs, this will not be able to determine whether all patches went through the change control process.

3. What is an area of major concern for an **enterprise resource planning (ERP)** system?

    A. User logs are not reviewed at regular intervals.

    B. Only a single switch is used for routing network traffic.

    C. Operating system security patches are not applied.

    D. Vendor default ERP setting is not changed.

    Answer: C. Operating system security patches are not applied.

    Explanation: Patch management is the process of applying updates to operating systems and other software. These patches are often necessary to correct errors in the software. If patches are not applied as and when released, then it is an area of serious concern. The other options are not as significant as patch updating.

4. What is the most important factor to be considered while implementing a patch management procedure?

    A. Testing the patch prior to deployment

    B. Technical ability of the responsible team

    C. Automated procedure for deployment

    D. Adherence to patch management budget

    Answer: A. Testing of the patch prior to deployment

    Explanation: Patches should be applied through a structured change management process that includes approval, testing, user acceptance testing, and proper documentation. The testing of a patch prior to implementation is one of the most important aspects, as deploying an untested patch may cause the system to fail. Also, appropriate rollback procedures should be in place in case of unexpected failure.

5. What is the first step when a system starts creating issues immediately after deploying a patch?

    A. Assess the problem and institute rollback procedures, if required.

    B. Switch off the network till the problem is corrected.

    C. Remove the patches from the systems.

    D. Raise a ticket with the vendor about the problem.

    Answer: Assess the problem and institute rollback procedures, if required.

    Explanation: Patches should be applied through a structured change management process that includes approval, testing, user acceptance testing, and proper documentation. The testing of a patch prior to implementation is one of the most important aspects, as deploying an untested patch may cause the system to fail. Also, appropriate rollback procedures should be in place in case of unexpected failure. The other options are secondary steps once the problem has been assessed.

6. An organization has received a patch by email to be applied on an emergency basis. What should be the first step?

    A. The patch should be downloaded to an isolated machine.

    B. The patch should be applied immediately.

    C. The patch should be validated to ensure its authenticity.

    D. The patch should be encrypted to prevent tampering.

    Answer: C. The patch should be validated to ensure its authenticity.

    Explanation: The first step is to validate the authenticity of the patch before taking any further action. If the patch is not from an authenticated source, it may be a malicious file.

7. When should new patches for an operating system be updated?

    A. When new applications are rolled out

    B. At the end of every month

    C. At the time of hardware maintenance

    D. As and when critical security patches are released

    Answer: D. As and when critical security patches are released

    Explanation: Patches should be applied as and when new patches are released. However, the patch management process should include an appropriate process of testing and approval.

Security baseline controls

Baseline means basic requirements. A security baseline means a minimum basic requirement for security. The objective of implementing a security baseline throughout the organization is to ensure that controls are consistently implemented as per acceptable risk levels. The level of the baseline is set as per asset classification. For example, for critical applications it is mandatory too have at least two-factor authentication whereas for non-critical applications it is mandatory to have at least one-factor authentication. In other words, the baseline for critical applications is two-factor authentication whereas the baseline for non-critical applications is one-factor authentication.

Benefits of a security baseline

The following are the benefits of a security baseline:

- It helps to standardize the basic security requirements throughout the organization.
- A baseline provides a point of reference against which improvement can be measured.
- It helps to establish uniform system hardening for similar types of systems.

Developing a security baseline

The security manager can refer to the following sources for developing a security baseline:

- Different frameworks for security controls such as NIST, COBIT, ISO, and so on
- Legal and regulatory requirements impacting the organization
- Industry-specific requirements

The preceding references will provide a good source of information for developing a baseline. However, the security manager should consider the needs and priorities of the organization.

Key aspects from a CISM exam perspective

The following are some of the key aspects from an exam perspective:

Question	Possible answer
What is the best way to define the minimum requirement for security?	Security baseline.
What is the best way to ensure uniform security arrangements across the organization?	Security baseline.
What is the importance of an information security baseline?	It mandates the minimum acceptable security to be implemented.

Table 5.3 – Key aspects from the CISM exam perspective

Questions

1. What is the primary advantage of an information security baseline?

   A. It helps to identify sensitive information assets.

   B. It helps to design a security policy for the enterprise.

   C. It helps to define the minimum acceptable security across the organization.

   D. It helps to design system controls.

   Answer: C. It helps to define the minimum acceptable security across the organization.

   Explanation: Baseline means basic requirements. A security baseline means the minimum basic requirement for security. The objective of implementing a security baseline throughout the organization is to ensure that controls are consistently implemented as per acceptable risk levels.

2. What is the most effective way to make sure that each application is compliant with information security requirements?

   A. To conduct a vulnerability assessment

   B. To implement a security baseline

   C. To use vendor-provided settings

   D. To conduct frequent user awareness training

   Answer: B. To implement a security baseline

Explanation: A security baseline means the minimum basic requirement for security. The objective of implementing a security baseline throughout the organization is to ensure that controls are consistently implemented as per acceptable risk levels. The other options will not directly address compliance with information security policy. Frequent user awareness training will not necessarily ensure that compliance is followed.

3. What is the primary use of a security baseline?

    A. To secure critical assets

    B. To establish uniform system hardening

    C. To prioritize risk treatment

    D. To develop an information security policy

    Answer: B. To establish uniform system hardening

    Explanation: The objective of implementing a security baseline throughout the organization is to ensure that controls are consistently implemented as per acceptable risk levels. A baseline helps to establish a uniform and consistent security standard throughout the organization.

4. What is the most effective way to determine the minimum requirements for an application security setting?

    A. Guidelines

    B. Policy

    C. Baseline

    D. Procedures

    Answer: C. Baseline

    Explanation: A baseline means basic requirements. A security baseline means the minimum basic requirement for security. The objective of implementing a security baseline throughout the organization is to ensure that controls are consistently implemented as per acceptable risk levels. Procedures determine the detailed process but do not include configuration requirements. Guidelines are not mandatory in nature. Policy is high-level management intention but does not include details about configuration requirements.

5. What is the most effective method to handle regulatory and legal requirements in a multinational organization having operations in different countries?

    A. To prepare a list of aggregate requirements and mandate it for all the locations

B. To prepare baseline requirements for all locations and add supplementary standards as per local requirements

C. To let each location decide on their own requirements

D. To let all locations agree on a standard set of requirements

Answer: B. To prepare baseline requirements for all locations and add supplementary standards as per local requirements

Explanation: The most effective and efficient way is to determine a baseline standard and then add additional requirements as per local requirements. Mandating all locations to follow all the requirements will place an undue burden and may also result in contradictory requirements. Letting each location decide on their own requirements may cause some of the corporate-level compliance to fail. Hence, deciding a baseline is a must.

6.   What is the primary objective of a security baseline?

A. To improve the network bandwidth

B. To establish uniform system hardening

C. To improve the security budget

D. To comply with privacy laws

Answer: B. To establish uniform system hardening

Explanation: A security baseline means a minimum basic security requirement for a specific group of applications. It helps to establish a uniform security standard. The others are secondary aspects.

Risk monitoring and communication

Risk monitoring and communication is one of the important elements of the risk management process. Risk monitoring is an ongoing process that helps to ensure continuous control effectiveness. There should be a structured communication channel for employees to report risk to management and at the same time management should provide relevant risk-related information to the concerned employees.

Risk reporting

The results of risk monitoring should be presented to the management at regular intervals. The results should be meaningful to the recipient and should be presented in a simple form without the use of too many technical terms. Red, amber, and green reporting helps management understand the risk posture of the organization.

Risk analysis should also include the potential impact as this will help to determine the extent of risk mitigation measures.

Key risk indicators

A risk indicator is a measure used by an organization to determine the level of current risk for an activity. This helps the organization to monitor the risk level and receive an alert when a risk level approaches an unacceptable level.

Thus, the objective of key risk indicators is to flag the exception as and when it occurs. This provides an opportunity for the organization to respond to the risk before damage is done. Examples of key risk indicators are as follows:

- Number of pieces of unauthorized software detected in audit
- Hours of system downtime
- Number of systems without antivirus

Let's take the example of system downtime. Risk indicators can be set as follows:

Description	Risk indicator
System downtime less than 5 hours	Acceptable
System downtime between 5 and 10 hours	Close monitoring
System downtime more than 10 hours	Unacceptable

Table 5.4 – System downtime

Reporting significant changes in risk

As business processes and technology change, the risk environment also gets changed with new types of threats. No systems can be considered as secured perpetually. This indicates that risk assessment should be done at regular intervals to address the emerging risks. The main benefit of performing a risk assessment on a consistent basis is that it helps to understand the trends in the risk profile. Risk should be reassessed periodically because risk changes over time.

The prime objective of periodically analyzing the gap between existing controls and the control objectives is to address the change in exposure. A change in exposure or business environment may require implementing additional controls.

Reporting a change in risk profile to management is the responsibility of the security manager. The security manager should present to management a status of updated risk profile of the organization at regular intervals. Management should also be updated about significant events or incidents impacting the organization.

Key aspects from a CISM exam perspective

The following are some of the key aspects from an exam perspective:

Question	Possible answer
What is the objective of periodically analyzing the gap between controls and the control objectives?	To address changes in exposure (changes in exposure or business environment may require additional controls).
What is the primary goal of a risk management program?	To support the achievement of business objectives.
Why should risk be assessed periodically?	Risk should be reassessed periodically because risk changes over time.

Table 5.5 – Key aspects from the CISM exam perspective

Questions

1. What is the most important reason to include potential impact in a risk analysis?

    A. Potential impact helps to determine risk treatment options

    B. Potential impact indicates the cost of the assets

    C. Potential impact affects the extent of mitigation

    D. Potential impact helps to determine the probability of the occurrence of a risk event

    Answer: C. Potential impact affects the extent of mitigation

    Explanation: Potential impact helps the management to determine the extent of mitigation. If the impact is on the higher side, management may allow more budget for mitigation efforts. Potential impact does not directly relate to risk treatment options. Potential impact can be more than the cost of assets as it may include the cost of recovery, business downtime, and other costs. Potential impact is in no way useful in determining the probability.

2. The best way to identify a new threat is to first do what?

    A. Conduct frequent reviews of risk factors

    B. Develop different security risk scenarios

    C. Understand business objectives and the flow and classification of information

    D. Review post-incident reports prepared by IT

    Answer: C. To understand business objectives and the flow and classification of information

    Explanation: The most important factor to determine a new threat is to first understand the business objectives and the flow and classification of information. To determine the threat knowledge of business processes is of utmost importance. The other options can be subsequent steps.

3. What is an area of major concern for the use of cloud services?

    A. Increase in cost

    B. Difficulty in identification of the source of a business transaction

    C. Increase in risk scenarios

    D. Increased chance of being hit by attackers

    Answer: C. Increase in risk scenarios

    Explanation: The use of cloud services introduces new risk scenarios as dependency will be on the third-party cloud service provider. This new risk has to be included in the risk profile of the organization. A cloud service is generally considered to be a cost-effective resource. The source of a business transaction is not impacted by a cloud service. Cloud service providers generally have more stringent security controls to prevent attacks.

4. What is an area of major concern for the use of mobile devices?

    A. High network connectivity issues

    B. High cost of battery recharge

    C. Unstructured operating system standardization

    D. Mobile devices can be easily lost or stolen

    Answer: D. Mobile devices can be easily lost or stolen

Explanation: Because of their small size and easy mobility, mobile devices are subject to a high risk of being lost or stolen. This results in unauthorized disclosure of sensitive data in the mobile devices. The other options are not significant security concerns.

5. The security manager received a request to approve an exception to the security standard for a proposed system change. What should be the first course of action for the security manager?

    A. To calculate the risk

    B. To mandate the security standard

    C. To suggest a new design for the system change

    D. To implement new controls

    Answer: A. To calculate the risk

    Explanation: The first course of action for a security manager is to calculate the risk of exception and on the basis of that take a call for approval. If the potential benefit from the exception is more than the potential loss of the risk, an exception may be granted.

6. The security manager noted exceptions with a set of standards that result in significant risk. What should be the first course of action for the security manager?

    A. Update the standard to approve the exceptions.

    B. Design new guidelines to address the risk.

    C. Advise management of the risk and potential impact.

    D. Benchmark standards with industry practices.

    Answer: C. Advise management of the risk and potential impact.

    Explanation: The best course of action for the security manager is to discuss with management the risk and potential impact of non-compliance. Management is in the best position to address the conflict between security requirements and business requirements. An exception can be approved if management considers the potential benefit of the exception more significant as compared to the perceived risk. Designing new guidelines and benchmarking of standards are not relevant options.

7. The security policy of an organization mandates the encryption of data that is sent to external parties. However, a regulatory body insists unencrypted data is shared with them. What should the security manager do?

    A. Train the employee of the regulatory body in the encryption process.

    B. Send the data with encryption to the regulatory body.

    C. Define an exception process for sending the data without encryption.

    D. Tell the regulator that unencrypted data will not be shared.

    Answer: C. Define an exception process for sending the data without encryption.

    Explanation: In the given situation, the best course of action is to work out an exception process to send the data without encryption. The security manager should work out another secured way of communication and other compensating controls for the protection of unencrypted data.

8. When should residual risk be determined?

    A. When determining the results of implementation of controls

    B. At the time of classification of assets

    C. At the time of identification of new risk

    D. At the time of valuation of assets

    Answer: A. When determining the results of implementation of controls

    Explanation: Residual risk means the remaining risk after controls are implemented. Residual risk is compared to the acceptable risk level to determine whether controls are effective. If residual risk is higher than acceptable risk then more control is required. Classification of assets is based on asset value. Residual risk is not relevant at the time of identification of risk or at the time of valuation of assets.

9. What are the results of risk analysis best used for?

    A. Preparation of business impact analysis

    B. Preparation of a list of action items to mitigate the risk

    C. Assigning the risk to the process owner

    D. Quantification of overall risk

    Answer: B. Preparation of a list of action items to mitigate the risk

Explanation: Risk analysis results give a list of the most critical risks that need to be addressed on a priority basis. The other options are not directly impacted by the results of risk analysis.

10. The security manager received a request to approve an exception to security standards for a proposed system change. What should be the best course of action for the security manager?

    A. To understand the risk due to non-compliance and recommend alternative controls

    B. To reject the approval and insist on compliance with security policy

    C. To update the security policy and allow for the exception

    D. To provide training to the business manager on the importance of security compliance

    Answer: A. To understand the risk due to non-compliance and recommend alternative controls

    Explanation: The best course of action for the security manager is to evaluate the risk due to non-compliance. If the potential benefit from the exception is more than the potential loss of the risk, an exception may be granted along with some alternative controls.

11. The effectiveness of a risk assessment can be best measured by what?

    A. Resource utilization and cost of risk assessment

    B. Sensitivity of new risks discovered

    C. Collective impact of identified risks

    D. Percentage of incidents from unknown risks

    Answer: D. Percentage of incidents from unknown risks

    Explanation: An incident from an unidentified risk indicates the effectiveness of risk assessment. A low percentage indicates that almost all the sources of risks have been identified whereas a high percentage indicates that risk assessment was not able to identify a major source of risks. The other options do not directly indicate the effectiveness of risk assessment.

12. The security manager notes that risk management activities are inconsistent throughout the organization. What should be their first course of action?

    A. Escalate the issue to senior management.

    B. Review compliance with standards and policy.

C. Create a stringent penalty for non-compliance.

D. Ensure stringent enforcement.

Answer: B. Review compliance with standards.

Explanation: The first area of action is to review compliance with standards and policy. If risk management procedures are in accordance with standards and policy and also risk management procedures are inadequate and inconsistent then it indicates that standards and policy are not properly drafted. Policy and standards need to be reviewed to determine whether they are adequate. The other options will not be meaningful if policy and standards are inconsistent and inadequate.

13. The continuous monitoring tool has flagged a non-compliance. What should be the first course of action by the security manager?

    A. To validate the non-compliance

    B. To report non-compliance to senior management

    C. To include non-compliance in the risk register

    D. To compare the non-compliance with the **key risk indicator** (**KRI**) threshold

    Answer: A. To validate the non-compliance

    Explanation: The first step for the security manager is to validate the non-compliance to rule out any false positives. The other options are subsequent actions.

14. An organization uses electronic swipe cards for physical access. The security manager has requested access to physical access data. What is the primary cause for asking for this data?

    A. To ensure that employees are attending the office on time

    B. To determine the correctness of wage payment

    C. For comparing logical access and physical access for deviations

    D. For determining the operating effectiveness of the physical access control system

    Answer: C. For comparing logical access and physical access for deviations

    Explanation: The security manager is more concerned with loopholes in physical and logical access controls. By comparing physical access records with logical access records, the security manager can identify areas such as tailgating, password sharing, and other form of compromise. The other options are comparatively less significant.

15. The risk of disruption due to **distributed denial of service (DDoS)** is regarded as what?

    A. Aggregate risk

    B. Systemic risk

    C. Residual risk

    D. Operational risk

    Answer: D. Operational risk

    Explanation: Operational risk is risk related to failed processes and systems due to either internal or external events. The objective of a DDoS attack is to bring down a system by flooding it with excessive traffic. Aggregate risk is defined as the overall impact from a single threat vector. Systemic risk is the risk of the collapse of an entire system. Residual risk refers to the risk that remains after controls are implemented.

16. What is the most effective way to address an insider security threat?

    A. Penetration testing

    B. Network address translation

    C. Background checks for prospective employees

    D. Security awareness program

    Answer: C. Background checks for prospective employees

    Explanation: A background check helps to determine the integrity of new employees. Security awareness will not necessarily guarantee that the employee will behave with honesty. Penetration testing and **network address translation (NAT)** will be more effective to address external attacks.

17. How should legal and regulatory requirements be considered?

    A. As per the security policy

    B. As per business decisions

    C. As per budget availability

    D. As mandatory compliance

    Answer: B. As per business decisions

Explanation: Compliance with legal and regulatory requirements should be considered on the basis of business decisions. Business decisions are based on cost benefit analyses. Legal and regulatory requirements should be considered like any other requirements for risk assessment and decision making. Sometimes the cost of compliance is much more than the expected benefit; in such cases, management need to take a business call.

18. What is the area of most concern for a security manager reviewing parameters for the acquisition of a new system?

    A. The functionality of the new system may not support business processes

    B. Existing staff may not able to provide ongoing support for the new system

    C. The new system may affect the security or operation of another system

    D. The time required to install and implement new system

    Answer: C. The new system may affect the security or operation of another system

    Explanation: The area of most concern for a security manager is the impact of the new system on security aspects and the operation of other systems. Functionality, support staff, and time of installation are the responsibility of the business and IT departments.

19. The security manager has been advised by an enforcement agency that their organization is the target of a group of hackers. What should be the first step for the security manager?

    A. Conduct a detailed review of the organization's exposure to the attack

    B. Conduct awareness training for all staff members

    C. Immediately inform top management about the elevated risk

    D. Consult experts to improve the security posture of the organization

    Answer: C. Immediately inform top management about the elevated risk

    Explanation: In this scenario, the first step is to advise management about the elevated risk. In consultation with management, subsequent actions can be taken.

20. What is the primary objective of periodic analysis of the gap between controls and control objectives?

    A. To reduce the count of audit findings

    B. To address change in exposure

    C. To utilize the security budget

D. To comply with regulatory requirements

Answer: B. To address change in exposure

Explanation: Periodic analysis of the gap will help to determine the ongoing effectiveness of the controls. Any exposure highlighted during gap analysis should be addressed immediately. The other options are not the prime objective.

21. What is the primary objective of a risk management program?

    A. To protect IT assets

    B. To implement preventive controls

    C. To achieve stated objectives

    D. To ensure availability of IT systems

    Answer: C. To achieve stated objectives

    Explanation: The primary goal of a risk management program is to achieve the stated objective. The stated objective can be in the form of protection of assets, availability of systems, or implementation of preventive controls.

22. Which of the following vulnerabilities allows attackers access to data through a web application?

    A. Validation checks missing in data input fields

    B. Password history rule not implemented

    C. Application logs not monitored at frequent intervals

    D. Two-factor authentication not implemented.

    Answer: A. Validation checks missing in data input fields

    Explanation: In the absence of validation checks in data input fields, attackers are able to exploit other weaknesses in the system. For example, through SQL injection attacks, hackers can illegally retrieve application data. The other options may make applications vulnerable, but these can be countered in other ways.

23. What is the best way to understand the evolving nature of attacks?

    A. To place a honeypot

    B. A rogue access point

    C. Industry tracking groups

    D. Penetration test

Answer: C. Industry tracking groups

Explanation: Industry tracking groups provide insights into the nature of attacks at the industry level and the global level. They are engaged in different surveys and closely monitor the attack types. Their publications can be either free or subscription based and provide a detailed overview of current scenarios. A honeypot is used to trap the attacker and to understand the attack methods. However, not all hackers will fall into honeypot traps. A rogue access point is a trap set up by hackers to lure legitimate users to get connected to it. A penetration test is more to do with assessing the security posture of the organization and will not be able to identify the evolving nature of an attack.

24. How should previously accepted risk be addressed?

    A. It should be reassessed on a periodic basis as risk changes over time.

    B. It does not need to be assessed again in the future.

    C. It should be removed from the risk register.

    D. It should be mitigated on the next assessment.

    Answer: A. It should be reassessed on a periodic basis as risk changes over time.

    Explanation: Risk changes over time and hence even if a risk was accepted previously, it should be again assessed on a periodic basis to determine the current impact of the risk.

25. The security manager noted an incident though none of the controls failed. What is the most likely cause of failure?

    A. Inadequate risk analysis

    B. Absence of a control

    C. New type of attack

    D. Operational error

    Answer: B. Absence of a control

    Explanation: An incident can happen due to either failure of a control or absence of a control. Inadequate risk analysis may be one of the reasons for the absence of a control. A new attack or operational error can have an impact only if there is no control or a control has failed.

26. What is the best metric to determine the effectiveness of a control monitoring program?

A. Count of the key controls that are being monitored

B. Time gap between detection and initiating corrective action

C. Cost of the control monitoring program

D. Time gap between occurrence of incident and detection

Answer: D. Time gap between occurrence of incident and detection

Explanation: The level of impact of an incident depends on the time gap between occurrence of incident and its detection. Early identification of incidents helps to reduce the damage. The other options are important; however, they are not as significant as early detection of incidents.

27. An organization decides to not to comply with a recent set of regulations. What is the most likely reason for this decision?

A. The regulations will increase the complexity of business processes.

B. The regulations are difficult to interpret.

C. The cost of implementation is much higher than the risk of non-compliance.

D. There are frequent changes in regulations.

Answer: C. The cost of implementation is much higher than the risk of non-compliance.

Explanation: An organization may decide to accept the risk of non-compliance if the cost of implementation is much higher than the risk of non-compliance. The other options are the major factors for deciding not to comply.

Security awareness training and education

Security awareness training is the most important element of an information security program. In the absence of a structured and well-defined security awareness training program, the security program will not be providing the desired results. It is not possible to address the security risks only through technical security measures. It is important to address behavioral aspects of the employees through continuous awareness and education. Compliance with the requirements of the information security policy can be best ensured by education and improving the awareness of the employees. On a lighter note, the following illustration is for the security manager who believes that security awareness training is not required as long as controls are automated:

Figure 5.1 – Human weakness

The security manager should consider the following aspects of security awareness training and education:

- The most effective way to increase the effectiveness of the training is to customize the training as per the target audience and to address the systems and procedures applicable to that particular group. For example, a system developer needs to undergo an enhanced level of training that covers secure coding aspects while data entry operators should be trained on security aspects related to their functions.

- To address common user security concerns, a security awareness program should concentrate on password selection, acceptable use of information resources, social engineering attacks, email safety, web browser safety, and so on.

- For a new joiner, a security awareness program should be part of their orientation program. It must be ensured that a user has been trained on acceptable usage of information resources before any system or data access is provided. Security awareness training and education is a continuous activity, and it should start from the point of joining the organization.

- The following are some of the common mechanisms for raising security awareness:

  - Classroom-based security awareness and training program

  - Email-based security tips

  - Circulating security policies and procedures

  - Obtaining non-disclosure statements from users

  - Awareness through different media such as intranet, newsletters, posters, login banners, and so on

  - Documented security-related job descriptions

  - Incentive for reporting suspicious events

  - Security-related simulation exercises

- The security manager should design some quantitative evaluation criteria to determine the effectiveness of security training and user comprehension, for example, a quiz or other type of assessment. One such metric is the number of incidents reported. Incident reporting indicates the awareness level of staff. An increase in incident reporting indicates that the staff are paying more attention to security.

- Security awareness training and education plays an important role in changing the organization's culture toward security consciousness. However, the security manager should understand that this is a gradual process and employees should be trained at frequent intervals.

- A security program should be launched through a top-down approach. A top-down approach means commitment for the success of security awareness should start from senior management. Support from senior management will provide enough resources for the success of the program.

- The security manager can obtain support from influential people within the organization to promote security awareness. Influential people in the organization means employees with substantial authority and who have great interest in promoting the security culture. They act as ambassadors for the security culture within their department and can bring significant change in an organization's security culture.

Key aspects from a CISM exam perspective

The following are some of the key aspects from an exam perspective:

Question	Possible answer
What is the most important success factor to design an effective IT security awareness program?	Customization of content as per target audience
What is the most effective method to change an organization's culture to one that is more security conscious?	Security awareness campaigns
When should security awareness training be provided to new employees?	Before they have access to systems or data
What is the primary objective of security awareness?	To influence employee behavior toward security consciousness To decrease the number of security incidents
For which group of employees is ethics training primarily organized?	Employees involved in monitoring user activities

Table 5.6 – Key aspects from the CISM exam perspective

Questions

1. What is the prime responsibility of a human resources department for information security?

    A. To allot a budget for information security

    B. To support in the recruitment of the best technicians

    C. To conduct periodic risk assessment

    D. To conduct security awareness training for employees

    Answer: D. To conduct security awareness training for employees

    Explanation: Human resources should primarily support the creation of awareness about the information security requirements of the organization. Recruitment is a secondary factor. Budget allocation and risk assessment may not be the responsibility of human resources.

2. What is the best way to improve the effectiveness of a security training program?

    A. To customize the content of the program as per the target audience

    B. More emphasis on the technical aspects of security

C. Mandatory training of all senior management

D. Use of industry-recognized training programs

Answer: A. To customize the content of the program as per the target audience

Explanation: The most effective way to increase the effectiveness of the training is to customize the training as per the target audience and to address the systems and procedures applicable to that particular group. For example, a system developer needs to undergo an enhanced level of training that covers secure coding aspects, while data entry operators should be trained on security aspects related to their functions. The other options are secondary aspects.

3. What is the most effective way to improve an organization's culture in terms of security consciousness?

A. Documented security policies and procedures

B. Periodic audit of security posture

C. Steering committee

D. Security awareness campaigns

Answer: D. Security awareness campaigns

Explanation: Frequent security awareness campaigns is the best way to improve the organization's culture. The other options are secondary aspects.

4. What should a security awareness program primarily focus on?

A. Number of open incidents

B. Details of ongoing investigations

C. What employees should or should not do in the context of their job responsibilities

D. Cost-benefit analysis for establishing various controls

Answer: C. What employees should or should not do in the context of their job responsibilities

Explanation: An awareness program will be more relevant if it is customized to include dos and don'ts within the context of the job responsibilities of employees. A security awareness program should focus on employee behavior and its impact on the security posture of the organization. The other options are secondary aspects.

5. What is the most effective method to make the end user aware of their security responsibilities at regular intervals?

    A. Logon banners displayed at every logon

    B. Frequent security-related email messages

    C. Making the security policy available on the organization's intranet

    D. Periodic audit of end user behavior

    Answer: A. Logon banners displayed at every logon

    Explanation: The most effective method is to create awareness through the use of logon banners. A security message will be displayed every time the user logs on and the user will be required to read and agree to the message before access is granted. This will help to enforce the security requirements throughout the organization. The other options are not as effective as logon banners.

6. When is the best time to provide security awareness training to a new employee?

    A. As and when the employee asks for training

    B. Once the user becomes comfortable with the process

    C. Before access to data is provided

    D. When a substantial number of new joiners are available

    Answer: C. Before access to data is provided

    Explanation: Security awareness training should be completed before a new joiner is given access to data. They should be aware of the secured data handling process.

7. What is the main objective of a security awareness program?

    A. To comply with regulatory requirements

    B. To influence employee behavior

    C. To adhere to the security budget

    D. To comply with the requirements of standards

    Answer: B. To influence employee behavior

    Explanation: Through frequent awareness programs, efforts are made to influence the behavior of employees from a security aspect. This helps the employee to take security-conscious decisions and actions.

8. How can the effectiveness of a security awareness program best be measured?

    A. Decrease in security violation reports

    B. Some quantitative evaluation to ensure user comprehension

    C. Amount spent on security training

    D. Fewer helpdesk requests

    Answer: B. Some quantitative evaluation to ensure user comprehension

    Explanation: The security manager should design some quantitative evaluation criteria to determine the understanding level of the user, for example, a quiz or other type of assessment. It should be measurable. The other options are secondary aspects.

9. An organization is in the process of selecting a consultant to conduct the maturity assessment of its risk management program. What is the most important element for the selection of a consultant?

    A. Methodology to be used in the assessment

    B. Experience of the consultant

    C. Reference from industry

    D. Fees of the consultant

    Answer: A. Methodology to be used in the assessment

    Explanation: Methodology helps to understand the process and formulae for the assessment. This is the most important element for selection of the consultant. The other options, though important, are not as significant as the assessment methodology.

10. What is the best method to improve the effectiveness of a security awareness program?

    A. Sufficient security budget

    B. Number of employees covered

    C. Top-down approach

    D. Expertise level of trainers

    Answer: C. Top-down approach

    Explanation: A top-down approach means commitment for the success of security awareness can be seen from senior management level. Support from senior management will provide enough resources for the success of the program. The other options, though important, are not the primary success factor.

11. How can the security awareness of employees best be provided in a cost-effective manner?

    A. Incentivize the employee's actions

    B. User education and training

    C. Heavy penalty for non-compliance

    D. Setting up a helpdesk service

    Answer: B. User education and training

    Explanation: Periodic education and training is the most cost-effective method to improve the security awareness of employees. The other options will not be effective in the absence of user education and training.

12. Who is responsible for the deployment of security awareness and training materials for intended users?

    A. Internal audit department

    B. Business manager

    C. Human resources department

    D. Information security department

    Answer: D. Information security department

    Explanation: An information security program is generally managed by the information security department. Security awareness and training is part of an information security program.

13. What is the fundamental component of any information security program?

    A. Encryption technology

    B. Stringent access control

    C. Security awareness training

    D. Automated access provisioning

    Answer: C. Security awareness training

    Explanation: In the absence of structured security awareness training, other components of program may not be effective.

14. What does a security awareness program for new staff having general operational duties generally include?

    A. Discussion on the constraints of various security frameworks

    B. Discussion on how to construct a strong password

    C. Discussion on operating system vulnerabilities

    D. Discussion on vulnerability assessment results

    Answer: B. Discussion on how to construct a strong password

    Explanation: To improve the effectiveness of awareness training, modules should be customized as per the job function of the audience. Employees engaged in general operational duties are expected to create strong passwords for their authentication. They are not required to have a thorough understanding of the other options.

15. What is the most effective method to improve security awareness among employees?

    A. To discuss industry-wide incident statistics

    B. To discuss different attack methods

    C. To implement a heavy penalty for non-compliance

    D. To continually reinforce the security policy

    Answer: D. To continually reinforce the security policy

    Explanation: The most effective method is to continuously reinforce the security policy and management expectations of the behavior of the employees. The other options will not be as effective as continuous training about security policy.

16. What is the most effective method to improve the effectiveness of an information security program?

    A. To increase the information security budget

    B. To obtain the service of security training from specialized external experts

    C. To conduct role-specific awareness training

    D. To conduct general online security awareness training for all staff

    Answer: C. To conduct role-specific awareness training

Explanation: The most effective way to increase the effectiveness of the training is to customize the training as per the target audience and to address the systems and procedures applicable to that particular group. For example, a system developer needs to undergo an enhanced level of training that covers secured coding aspects while data entry operators should be trained on security aspects related to their functions.

17. What is the prime objective of a security awareness training program?

    A. To decrease the likelihood of an information security incident

    B. To adhere to the security budget

    C. To comply with regulations

    D. To encourage compliance with policy

    Answer: A. To decrease the likelihood of an information security incident

    Explanation: The prime objective of security training is to influence the behavior and attitude of employees and thereby reduce the likelihood of an information security incident. Although compliance with the information security policy is important, the objective of security training is to influence the cultural and behavioral elements of information security. The other options are secondary factors.

18. What is the prime objective of an information security awareness and training program?

    A. To comply with security policy

    B. To obtain support from senior management

    C. To establish a culture that is favorable to security

    D. To define roles and responsibilities with respect to security

    Answer: C. To establish a culture that is favorable to security

    Explanation: Structured and well-defined security awareness training will help to build a favorable environment for secure business processes. The other options are secondary factors.

19. What is most effective way to authenticate a call received from an employee of another branch through **voice over internet protocol** (**VoIP**) who is asking for a customer information?

    A. Ask for the name and designation of the caller

    B. Make a call to the branch number listed in the office phone directory

C. Ask some business questions and, if they are found to be genuine, provide the relevant information

D. Ask the caller to pass the phone to their superior to validate the caller

Answer: B. Make a call to the branch number listed in the office phone directory

Explanation: The best way to authenticate the caller is to make a call to the branch number listed in the office phone directory. However, the recipient should not use a phone number or email address provided by the caller. Once the call has been verified, the information may be provided to the caller. The other options will not be as effective as making a call using the listed number.

20. The most important reason why security awareness training is to be imparted at regular intervals is to address a change in what?

A. Security budget

B. Information technology

C. Compliance requirement

D. Threats and vulnerabilities

Answer: D. Threats and vulnerabilities

Explanation: Security awareness training should be a continuous process as threats and vulnerabilities changes over time. Regular refresher training is an important part of security awareness. Changes in technology and compliance requirements are covered in changes in threats and vulnerabilities.

21. Who is ethics training primarily meant for?

A. Employees engaged in monitoring activities

B. Employees engaged in designing training modules

C. Employees engaged in accessing user access

D. Employees engaged in managing the risk of the organization

Answer: A. Employees engaged in monitoring activities

Explanation: Ethics training is important for all employees, but primarily it is useful for employees engaged in monitoring activities as they have access to sensitive corporate and personal information. Ethics training includes guidance on appropriate legal behavior to reduce corporate liability and awareness about data privacy and ethical behavior.

22. Which of the following is influenced by an effective information security awareness program?

    A. Inherent risk

    B. Residual risk

    C. Acceptable risk

    D. Business objectives

    Answer: B. Residual risk

    Explanation: Residual risk means risk that remains after controls are implemented. The awareness program objective is to improve the controls and reduce the vulnerability and thereby reduce the residual risk. The other options are not primarily influenced by a security awareness program.

23. What is the most effective way to promote the security culture?

    A. Promote the advantages of the security culture through influential people

    B. Increase the security budget

    C. Mandate online security training for each employee

    D. Upload the security policy to the organization's intranet

    Answer: A. Promote the advantages of the security culture through influential people

    Explanation: Influential people in the organization means employees with substantial authority and who have greater interest in promoting the security culture. They act as ambassadors for the security culture within their departments and can bring significant changes in an organization's security culture. The other options will not be as effective as option A.

Documentation

Structured documentation regarding risk management policies, standards, registers, and other relevant documents is of utmost importance for the effective management of risk. The need and process for documentation should be defined in the risk management policy, strategy, and program. Generally, the following aspects of risk management processes should be documented:

- **Risk register**: A risk register should include details such as the following:

  - Source and nature of risk

  - Risk owner

  - Risk ranking and severity

  - Risk score

  - Details about existing controls and additional recommendations

- **Asset inventory**: An asset inventory should include details such as the following:

  - Description of assets

  - Asset owner

  - Asset classification

- **Risk mitigation and action plan**: This should include details such as the following:

  - Mitigation plan

  - Responsibility for mitigation

  - Timelines for mitigation

- **Results of risk monitoring**: These should include the following:

  - Monitoring process

  - Results of the monitoring process, such as audit reports and security review reports

  - Closure status of recommendations

All the documents should include appropriate version control, classification level, document owner and approver, revision date, and number.

The process of documentation is not easily adopted by end users; as depicted in the following image, the security manager needs to gradually develop a culture for it:

Figure 5.2 – Documentation

Generally, documentation is considered to be an additional burden by the employees. Security managers need to highlight the benefits of the right documentation.

Summary

In this chapter, we discussed the procedural aspects of risk management. This chapter will help the CISM candidate to incorporate change management and patch management procedures in a structured way. This chapter will also help the CISM candidate to develop a security baseline for the organization.

In our next chapter, we will give an overview of information security program development and management.

Section 3: Information Security Program Development Management

This part provides an overview of the different frameworks for IS program development management. It covers 27% of the CISM certification exam.

This section contains the following chapters:

- *Chapter 6, Overview of Information Security Program Development Management*
- *Chapter 7, Information Security Infrastructure and Architecture*
- *Chapter 8, Practical Aspects of Information Security Program Development Management*
- *Chapter 9, Information Security Monitoring Tools and Techniques*

6
Overview of Information Security Program Development Management

In this chapter, we will discuss information security program development management and look at the methods, tools, and techniques for developing an information security program. The main objective of information security program development is to achieve the objectives of information security in an effective and efficient manner. Program development includes the process of planning, implementing, testing, monitoring, and controlling the activities related to information security. A structured security program will help an organization manage its security initiatives in an effective manner.

The following topics will be covered in this chapter:

- Information security program management overview
- Information security program objectives
- Information security framework components
- Defining an information security program road map
- Information security policies standards, and procedures
- Security budget
- Security program management and administrative activities
- Privacy laws

Let's look at each one of the preceding topics in detail.

Information security program management overview

An information security program covers all the activities and processes that collectively provide security services to an organization. Some of the common activities of security programs include the design, development, and implementation of security-related controls throughout the organization. Controls can be in the form of simple policies and processes or an advanced technological structure. Depending upon the size and nature of the organization, the security program can be managed by either a single individual or an exclusive team headed by a **chief information security officer (CISO)**.

A security manager is expected to have a thorough knowledge of information technology as it helps to understand how changes in the technical environment affect the security posture. An information security manager is required to evaluate the risk of technology and determine relevant controls to safeguard the IT resources.

Apart from technical skills, a security manager is expected to have a thorough understanding of business processes and objectives. A security manager should ensure that the objectives of the security program are aligned with business objectives. Security objectives should have the consensus of business management. Security objectives are an important element of a security program and without security objectives, it will not be possible to define metrics and monitor the progress of the program. The main goal of a security program is to implement the strategy and achieve the defined program.

Outcomes of an information security program

Security programs should have the following outcomes to support the business objectives.

Strategic alignment

A security program should be designed in such a way that it provides strategic alignment with business requirements. Alignment should take into account business processes, culture, governance, existing technology, and the structure of the organization. Strategic alignment can best be achieved through a security strategy committee that is composed of senior representatives of all the relevant business units.

A security manager is required to have a thorough understanding of business processes and regular interaction with business owners to gain an understanding of their requirements. Strategic alignment also requires the submission of key aspects of the security program to senior management at regular intervals.

Risk management

Security programs should be able to manage the risk applicable to the business objectives. For effective risk management, a security manager should be aware of threats, vulnerabilities, and the risk profile of the organization. Risk must be managed to a level acceptable to senior management.

Value delivery

A security program should provide value to the organization. For value delivery, security should be managed effectively and efficiently. Security investment should be managed to provide maximum value to the organization.

Resource management

A security manager should be able to utilize resources – that is, staff, finance, technology, and the knowledge bank – efficiently and effectively. If there is resource constraint, protection efforts should be prioritized to support areas of greatest needs and benefits. These efforts will provide the basis for good resource management.

Performance management

A security manager should develop processes to monitor the performance of the security program. Metrics should be developed to determine the performance. Performance metrics should be submitted to senior management at regular intervals.

Assurance process integration

A security manager should be aware of various assurance functions to align security activities with the activities of other assurance functions. Assurance functions generally include physical security, risk management, quality control, audit, legal, HR, IT, business continuity, and so on.

The starting point of a security program

Most of the framework starts with conducting a risk assessment and establishing the objectives of control. An information security program is established to close the gap between the existing state of controls (as identified by a risk assessment) and the desired state (that is, control objectives).

Information security charter

A charter is the formal grant of authority or rights. An information security charter states that the organization formally recognizes the information security department. In the absence of a charter, it will be difficult for the information security department to operate within the environment. A charter defines the scope, responsibility, and authority of the information security function.

A charter can act as the foundation to provide guidance to the governance of information security.

Support from senior management

Support from senior management is considered the biggest challenge for every security manager. Investment in security does not provide any tangible benefits and calculating **return on investment (ROI)** is not as simple as ROI for any other business investment. On a lighter note, most security managers face the challenge depicted in the following diagram:

"Your security proposal seems good. Let us make it more interesting by not allotting additional budget, no support staff, and a strict deadline. At last, this will give you the chance to impress everyone"

Figure 6.1 – Senior management support

A security manager should consider the following aspects when seeking support and budget from senior management:

- The security strategy should be aligned with the business objectives and goals.
- The security manager should obtain consensus from other business units when designing a security strategy.
- To the extent possible, the benefits of the proposed project should be quantified in the business case.

Thus, the best way to obtain support from senior management is to let them know how information security is supporting the business objectives.

Defense in depth

Defense in depth (**DiD**) is an arrangement wherein multiple layers of controls are implemented to protect the information resources. Its intent is to provide redundancy in case one control fails. The first layer of defense in depth is to prevent the event from occurring, that is, implementing preventive controls such as authentication. The second layer is containment, that is, to isolate and minimize the impact. The third layer is reaction, that is, incident response procedures, and the next layer is the recovery and restoration procedure, that is, backup arrangements.

Key aspects from a CISM exam perspective

The following are some of the key aspects from an exam perspective:

Question	Possible answer
What is the most important reason why an information security manager needs to have an understanding of information technology?	To understand the risk of technology and its contribution to the security objectives
What is the most common starting point for the development of an information security program?	A risk assessment and control objectives

Table 6.1 – Key aspects from the CISM exam perspective

Questions

1. An organization has recently been impacted by a major security incident. Learning from this incident can be best utilized by the security manager doing which of the following?

   A. Improving the integration of business and information security processes

   B. Increasing the information security budget

   C. Improving the industry benchmarking process

   D. Obtaining better technical controls

   Answer: A. Improving the integration of business and information security processes

   Explanation: The most important challenge for a security manager is to obtain support from senior management and other business units to change the business processes to include the security aspect. As an incident has already occurred, business units will be open to supporting security processes. In the absence of close integration of business and security processes, other options will not be effective.

2. Why should an information security manager have a thorough understanding of information technology?

   A. To ensure that the latest and most feasible technology is being used

   B. To understand the risk of technology and its contribution to the security objectives

   C. To provide consultation on the deployment of information technology

   D. To improve the relationship between information security and business units

Answer: B. To understand the risk of technology and its contribution to the security objectives

Explanation: An information security manager is required to evaluate the risk of technology and determine relevant controls to safeguard the IT resources. The other options are secondary aspects.

3. The requirements for information security resources are identified in which of the following?

   A. Risk assessment

   B. Architecture

   C. Strategy

   D. Guidelines

   Answer: C. Strategy

   Explanation: An information security strategy is a set of actions to achieve the security objectives. The strategy includes what should be done, how it should be done, and when it should be done to achieve the security objectives. The strategy also includes details of the resources necessary to implement the program.

4. What is generally the starting point for an information security framework?

   A. Development of an information security policy

   B. Remediation of internal audit findings

   C. A risk assessment and control objectives

   D. Allocating a security budget

   Answer: C. A risk assessment and control objectives

   Explanation: Most of the framework starts with conducting a risk assessment and establishing the objectives of control. Once the objectives are established, the information security policy is developed and a security budget is allotted. An internal audit is not relevant.

5. What is the most important aspect to be considered at the time of establishing an information security program?

   A. To understand the existing culture within the organization

   B. To understand the existing control system of the organization

C. To understand the overall risk exposure of the organization

D. To determine the availability of security resources in the organization

Answer: C. To understand the overall risk exposure of the organization

Explanation: It is of utmost importance that the security manager is aware of the overall risk exposure of the organization. The other options – that is, culture, control system, and resource constraints – will be evaluated as a part of risk exposure.

6. The involvement of senior management in the information security program will first determine what?

A. The charter

B. The security strategy

C. The budget

D. The security procedure

Answer: A. The charter

Explanation: A charter is a formal grant of authority or rights. An information security charter states that the organization formally recognizes the information security department. In the absence of a charter, it will be difficult for the information security department to operate within the environment. All of the other choices follow the charter.

7. What is the first layer of a defense in depth strategy?

A. Containment

B. Prevention

C. Reaction

D. Recovery

Answer: B. Prevention

Explanation: DiD is an arrangement wherein multiple layers of controls are implemented to protect the information resources. Its intent is to provide redundancy in case one control fails. The first layer of defense in depth is to prevent the event from occurring, that is, implementing preventive controls such as authentication. The second layer is containment, that is, to isolate and minimize the impact. The third layer is reaction, that is, incident response procedures, and the next layer is the recovery and restoration procedure, that is, backup arrangements.

8. Which of the following is the first layer for defense in depth?

    A. Isolation

    B. Authentication

    C. Incident procedures

    D. Recovery procedures

    Answer: B. Authentication

    Explanation: Defense in depth is an arrangement wherein multiple layers of controls are implemented to protect the information resources. Its intent is to provide redundancy in case one control fails. The first layer of defense in depth is to prevent the event from occurring, that is, implementing preventive controls such as authentication and so on. The second layer is containment, that is, to isolate and minimize the impact. The third layer is reaction, that is, incident response procedures, and the next layer is the recovery and restoration procedure, that is, backup arrangements.

9. What does the effectiveness of an information security program primarily depend on?

    A. The availability of a documented security policy and procedures

    B. Senior management commitment

    C. Periodic awareness training

    D. Developing an information security management system

    Answer: B. Senior management commitment

    Explanation: The most important element for an effective information security program is support and commitment from senior management. If senior management is committed to robust information security for the organization, there will no constraints for the security budget and resources. The other options are secondary aspects.

Information security program objectives

A security manager should understand the following objectives of a security program while implementing the program:

- To provide maximum support to business functions

- To minimize operational disruption

- To implement the strategy in the most cost-effective manner

After establishing the objectives, **key goal indicators** (**KGIs**) to reflect these objectives need to be developed. The next step is to determine the current state of security. The current state should be compared with established objectives and identified gaps should be addressed to improve the security processes.

Key aspects from a CISM exam perspective

The following are some of the key aspects from an exam perspective:

Question	Possible answer
What should the security policy be closely aligned with?	Organizational needs
What is the best method to evaluate the return on security investment?	Determining the extent of support for business objectives
What is the most important step before implementing a security policy?	Obtaining sign-off from stakeholders

Table 6.2 – Key aspects from the CISM exam perspective

Questions

1. The security manager notes that senior management is dissatisfied with the current state of information security. To address this, what is the most important consideration?

    A. Industry benchmarks

    B. Business strategy

    C. Technology advancement

    D. User awareness

    Answer: B. Business strategy

    Explanation: The security framework and security policy should closely align with the organizational needs. Policies must support the needs of the organization. For alignment of the security program, the security manager should have an understanding of the business strategy, plans, and objectives. Effective strategic alignment of the information security program requires regular interaction with business owners.

2. What should the security policy be most closely aligned with?

A. Industry-recognized practices

B. Organizational needs

C. International standard organization

D. Legal requirements

Answer: B. Organizational needs

Explanation: The security framework and security policy should closely align with the organizational needs. Policies must support the needs of the organization. The other options are secondary aspects.

3. Before implementing a security strategy, it is most important to do what?

A. Communicate with the IT department.

B. Train all the end users.

C. Determine the technology to be used.

D. Obtain sign-off from the stakeholders.

Answer: D. Obtain sign-off from the stakeholders

Explanation: Before implementing a framework and security policy, sign-off should be obtained from all relevant stakeholders to ensure that the policy is supporting the objectives and expectations of the business. The other options are secondary aspects.

Information security framework components

Frameworks are structures or outlines that support the implementation of an information security strategy. They provide the best practices for a structured security program. Frameworks are flexible structures that any organization can adopt as per their environment and requirements. Governance frameworks such as COBIT 5 and ISO 27000 are widely accepted and implemented frameworks for security governance.

Generally, a security framework has the following components:

- **Technical components**: This means the part of the framework that covers the technical and IT aspects of security. Examples of technical aspects include the configuration, monitoring, and maintenance of technical components such as a firewall, IDS, SIEM, and so on. It is very important to have assigned ownership for each technical asset to ensure proper risk treatment and compliance with security policies.

- **Operational components**: This means the part of the framework that covers ongoing management and administrative activities to ensure the required level of security assurance. Examples of operational components include preparing SOPs, patch management, log analysis, change management and other routine types of activities to support security, and so on. Each of these activities should be assigned to an individual who has the requisite authority and knowledge.

- **Management components**: This means the part of the framework that covers oversight functions. Examples of management components include the availability of a security policy, adequate resources for security, regulator monitoring of key aspects of information security, and so on.

- **Administrative components**: This means the part of the framework that covers support functions such as human resources, finance, and other functions. Examples of administrative components include personnel job descriptions, performance management, budget preparation, calculating return on investment, and so on.

- **Educational and informational components**: This means the part of the framework that covers education, awareness, and training requirements for enhancing the security posture of the organization.

Framework – success factor

A security framework should be designed and developed considering the business objectives and goals. It is important to have the consensus of business units for a security framework. On a lighter note, most security managers will find themselves in the situation depicted in the following diagram:

Figure 6.2 – Information security framework

A security manager should consider the following factors for successful implementation of the framework:

- To get the framework approved, the security manager should demonstrate a positive return on security investment. The best method to evaluate the return on security investment is to determine the level of support information security provides for the achievement of the business objectives.

- The most important thing when developing a framework for an information security program is to determine the desired outcome. If the desired outcome is not considered at the time of developing the framework, it will be difficult to determine a strategy, control objectives, and logical architecture.

- The security manager should consider the advantages and disadvantages of centralized as well as decentralized security functions. It is more convenient to monitor and control a centralized function. A decentralized function makes it easier to promote security awareness and ensures a faster turnaround for security requests as it is closer to business units. A decentralized unit is more responsive to business unit needs.

- The security framework and security policy should closely align with organizational needs. Policies must support the needs of the organization. For alignment of the security program, the security manager should have an understanding of business plans and objectives. Effective strategic alignment of the information security program requires regular interaction with business owners.

- Before implementing the framework and security policy, sign-off should be obtained from all relevant stakeholders to ensure that the policy is supporting the objectives and expectations of the business.

- Support from senior management is critical for an effective information security program.

- The framework should also define the process for handling exceptions to the policy and procedures. Inherent authority to grant an exception to the information security policy should reside with the authority that has approved the policy.

- While implementing a framework, policy, and controls, the most important consideration is the safety of human life.

Information security management needs to ensure that the framework supports the business objectives.

Key aspects from a CISM exam perspective

The following are some of the key aspects from an exam perspective:

Question	Possible answer
What is the best method to evaluate the return on security investment?	Determining the extent of support for business objectives
What is the advantage of a centralized security function?	It's easy to manage and control: • Improved compliance with organizational policies and standards. • Reduction of the total cost of ownership.
What is the advantage of a decentralized security function?	• It's more responsive to the requirements of business units. • It provides a faster turnaround for security requests as it is closer to business units. • It's easier to promote security awareness.

Table 6.3 – Key aspects from the CISM exam perspective

Questions

1. A security manager can determine the return on security investment by evaluating what?

    A. Extent of support for business objectives

    B. Number of security metrics developed

    C. Industry standards

    D. Process maturity model

    Answer: A. Extent of support for business objectives

    Explanation: To get the framework approved, the security manager should demonstrate a positive return on security investment. The best method to evaluate the return on security investment is to determine how information security supports the achievement of business objectives. The other options do not directly help to determine the return on investment.

2. The security manager notes that privileged access was granted to the entire HR team. What should the security manager do first?

    A. Revoke privileged access for all.

    B. Report to senior management.

    C. Talk to the data owners to understand the business needs.

    D. Implement a procedure to grant emergency access.

    Answer: C. Talk to the data owners to understand the business needs.

    Explanation: The first step is to determine the business needs for granting privileged access to all the team members. Access to all team members may be a business process requirement. Without understanding the business requirements, the security manager should not revoke or report to senior management.

3. What is the first step in the development of a well-defined information security program?

    A. Determine the security budget.

    B. Determine the strategic requirements.

    C. Determine the desired outcomes.

    D. Determine the security architecture.

    Answer: C. Determine the desired outcomes.

    Explanation: The most important thing when developing a framework for an information security program is to determine the desired outcome. If the desired outcome is not considered at the time of developing the framework, it will be difficult to determine a strategy, control objectives, and security architecture.

4. What is the benefit of a centralized information security organization structure?

    A. Comparatively easy to promote security requirements

    B. Comparatively easy to manage and control

    C. More responsive to business unit needs

    D. Enables a quick turnaround time for security requests

    Answer: B. Comparatively easy to manage and control

    Explanation: Due to centralized control, it is easy to manage the security functions as compared with decentralized functions. A decentralized function is more convenient and it is easier to promote security awareness and ensure a faster turnaround for security requests as it is closer to business units. A decentralized unit is more responsive to business unit needs.

5. What is the main advantage of a decentralized security function?

    A. Easy to manage and control

    B. Increased compliance with policies and procedures

    C. Better alignment of security to business needs

    D. Reduction in security budget

    Answer: C. Better alignment of security to business needs

    Explanation: A decentralized unit is more responsive to business unit needs as it is closer to business units. The other options are the advantages of centralized functions, that is, centralized management is easy to manage and control, ensures increased compliance, and reduces the cost of security.

6. The security manager notes that compliance to a particular set of standards is weak. What should be their first step?

    A. Remove that standard from the policy.

    B. Update the policy to address the risk.

    C. Enforce a penalty for non-compliance.

    D. Perform a risk assessment.

    Answer: D. Perform a risk assessment.

    Explanation: The first step is to conduct a risk assessment and determine the impact of non-compliance. On the basis of the potential impact, subsequent action should be determined.

7. How can the strategic alignment of a security program best be achieved?

    A. Active benchmarking with industry

    B. Increasing the security budget

    C. Regular interaction with business owners

    D. Addressing culture differences

    Answer: C. Regular interaction with business owners

    Explanation: The security framework and security policy should closely align with the organizational needs. Policies must support the needs of the organization. For alignment of the security program, the security manager should have an understanding of the business plans and objectives. Effective strategic alignment of the information security program requires regular interaction with business owners.

8. The security manager has received a request for an exception from the standard configuration of an operating system. What should be the security manager's first step?

A. Reject the request for an exception.

B. Determine the risk and identify the compensating controls.

C. Seek guidance from senior management.

D. Determine the industry practice.

Answer: B. Determine the risk and identify the compensating controls.

Explanation: The first step for the security manager is to determine the risk involved in granting the exception and evaluate whether any compensatory controls are in place to address the risk. On the basis of the perceived risk, the other options can be considered.

Defining an information security program road map

For effective implementation of a security program, it is recommended to develop a road map covering different stages with a clear objective to be achieved during each stage. The initial stage of program development is to talk to concerned stakeholders such as business units, legal, HR, finance, and other units. This will help the security manager to determine the security requirements of different units.

In the second stage, security requirements should be formalized to draft a basic security policy and approval should be obtained from senior management. A security steering committee consists of officials from different business functions. It plays an important part in the finalization of security requirements. In the third stage, members of the security steering committee emphasize the promotion of security awareness of the policy and conduct a security review to see whether they are in compliance. In the fourth stage, gaps identified during the security review should be addressed and a continuous monitoring process should be developed. Gradually, the security manager can start developing a consensus around roles and responsibilities, processes, and procedures in support of the policy.

A road map for the development of a security program should evolve around the security strategy of the organization. A road map should consider objectives, resources, and constraints. A road map should include various milestones in terms of KGI.

In the absence of a well-defined strategy, there can be a risk that a security program may not be integrated or prioritized as per the requirements of the organization. Most of the information security development efforts will evolve around the design, development, and implementation of the controls.

Gap analysis

A security manager should conduct gap analysis at periodic intervals to determine the gap between the control objectives and the performance of existing controls. Identified gaps should be addressed for improvement. It is also important to develop a procedure for monitoring the control effectiveness. This will help the security program to evolve and mature. On a lighter note, the following diagram depicts root cause analysis for security gaps:

Figure 6.3 – Gap analysis

Thus, the final objective of gap analysis is not only to identify the gap but also to address it for the improvement of security processes.

Value of a security program

A security program should provide value to the organization. A security manager should determine the cost of implementation of controls and the corresponding value of the assets to be protected. This will form the basis for determining that the information security program is delivering value. If the cost of control is higher than the value of the assets, then it does not provide any value.

Security program integration with another department

A security program should be integrated with the processes of other departments, such as IT, audit, risk management, quality assurance, HR, and so on. This helps to improve the effectiveness of the overall security program. The most important aspect is integration with information technology processes. Automated controls are considered to be more effective than manual controls. Automated controls are generally driven by the IT department. Also, IT is responsible for the implementation and operation of information processing systems. For any new IT project, the security department should be involved right from the feasibility stage to the implementation stage. In fact, the security department should be involved throughout the **system development life cycle (SDLC)** process. The security manager should be well versed in information technology in order to make informed decisions about technology risk.

A security program should also be integrated with HR processes. For example, in the event of the termination of an employee, details should immediately be made available to the security team so they can revoke all the access rights of that employee.

Also, when an employee is transferred to another department, it is very important to review and update their access rights to ensure that any access no longer needed is removed and appropriate access for the new position is granted.

Key aspects from a CISM exam perspective

The following are some of the key aspects from an exam perspective:

Question	Possible answer
What is the initial stage of information security program development?	To determine the security needs and requirements on the basis of discussion with concerned stakeholders such as business units, legal, HR, finance, and other units
What is the basis for determining whether a security program is delivering value?	Comparing the cost of achieving control objectives and the value of the assets protected
Who should provide the final approval of security patch implementation?	Business asset owner
For any new IT project, at what stage should the security department be involved?	From the beginning, that is, the feasibility stage
What is the basis of providing user access authorization?	Mapping the business needs

Question	Possible answer
What are the main project activities undertaken in developing an information security program?	Control design and deployment
What is the primary basis for the prioritization of security spending and budgeting?	Level of risk

Table 6.4 – Key aspects from the CISM exam perspective

Questions

1. How can value delivery by an information security program best be determined?

    A. Count of controls implemented

    B. Cost of achieving the control objectives

    C. Count of controls monitored

    D. Results of control testing

    Answer: B. Cost of achieving the control objectives

    Explanation: A security program should provide value to the organization. The security manager should determine the cost of implementation of control and the corresponding value of the assets to be protected. This will form the basis for determining whether the information security program is delivering value. If the cost of control is higher than the value of the assets, then it does not provide any value. The other options are secondary aspects.

2. Who should provide final approval for security patch updating hours?

    A. System administrator

    B. Business asset owner

    C. Security manager

    D. Business continuity manager

    Answer: B. Business asset owner

    Explanation: It is very important to take approval from the business asset owner for patch updating timings as patch updating may lead to unexpected problems and can interrupt business processes. Generally, the business asset owner will prefer non-working hours for patch updating.

3. While selecting the controls to meet the business objectives, what should the security manager primarily do?

    A. Focus on role-based access controls

    B. Focus on key controls

    C. Focus only on financial applications

    D. Focus on preventive controls

    Answer: B. Focus on key controls

    Explanation: The security manager should primarily focus on key controls to reduce the risk and protect the information assets. Role-based control may be one of the key control areas. Focusing only on financial applications is not justifiable as protection of other data (for example, customer data) may be equally critical. Key controls need not necessarily be only preventive controls.

4. What should an information security program primarily be integrated with?

    A. Audit department

    B. Risk management department

    C. Information technology

    D. Quality assurance

    Answer: C. Information technology

    Explanation: A security program should be integrated with the processes of other departments, such as IT, audit, risk management, quality assurance, HR, and so on. This helps to improve the effectiveness of the overall security program. The most important aspect is integration with information technology processes. Automated controls are considered to be more effective than manual controls. Automated controls are generally driven by the IT department. Also, IT is responsible for the implementation and operation of information processing systems. The other options are secondary aspects.

5. To protect and control the mobile devices issued by the organization, which of the following activities carried out by HR should be monitored?

    A. Issuing a termination notice

    B. Conducting background checks

    C. Releasing a paycheck

    D. Conducting a security awareness program

Answer: A. Issuing a termination notice

Explanation: In the event of termination of an employee, details should be immediately made available to the security team so they can revoke all the access rights of that employee, including de-provisioning of mobile devices. The other options are not as significant as the termination process.

6. For a new IT project, at which stage should the information security department be involved?

   A. Feasibility stage

   B. Implementation stage

   C. Design stage

   D. Post-implementation stage

   Answer: A. Feasibility stage

   Explanation: For any new IT project, the security department should be involved right from the feasibility stage till the project completion stage. In fact, the security department should be involved throughout the SDLC process. Security considerations will affect feasibility. Involving the security team only at later stages may not be an effective and efficient option.

7. What is the best way for the data owner to determine what access and authorization should be provided to users?

   A. The system administrator should have the authority to provide access.

   B. Access should be provided on the basis of user requests.

   C. Access should be provided on the basis of hierarchical preferences.

   D. Access should be provided by mapping to business needs.

   Answer: D. Access should be provided by mapping to business needs.

   Explanation: Access should be provided on a need-to-know basis, that is, by mapping to business needs. The other options are not justifiable if users do not require data to perform their duties.

8. If an employee is transferred to another department, what is the most important aspect?

   A. Reviewing and updating their access rights

   B. Updating the job profile document

   C. Conducting training for the new assignment

   D. Reviewing their performance in their last profile

Answer: A. Reviewing and updating their access rights

Explanation: When an employee is transferred to another department, it is very important to review and update the access rights to ensure that any access no longer needed is removed and appropriate access for the new position is granted. The other options are secondary aspects.

9. An information security manager should have a thorough understanding of information technology primarily for what reason?

    A. To ensure that IT staff cannot mislead the security manager

    B. To implement new IT technology

    C. To understand the IT budget

    D. To understand the IT issues for achieving adequate information security

    Answer: D. To understand the IT issues for achieving adequate information security

    Explanation: The security manager should be well versed in information technology in order to make informed decisions about technology risk. Technology knowledge will help the security manager to understand the IT issues for achieving adequate information security. The security manager is not expected to implement IT technology or adhere to the IT budget.

Policy, standards, and procedures

A security program is implemented through a specific set of policies, standards, and procedures. Let's understand how each one of these operates:

- **Policies**: A policy is a set of ideas or strategies that are used as a basis for decision making. They are the high-level statements of direction by management.

    There can be multiple policies at the corporate level as well as the department level. It should be ensured that department-level policies are consistent and aligned with corporate-level policies.

- **Standards**: A standard is a mandatory requirement to be followed in order to comply with a given policy or framework or certification or regulation. A standard provides detailed directions to comply with the policy.

    A standard helps to ensure an efficient and effective process, resulting in reliable products or services. Standards are updated as and when required to incorporate new processes, technology, and regulatory requirements.

A standard is a dynamic document and is changed if control objectives are not achieved or on the basis of the result of risk assessments.

- **Procedures**: Procedures are detailed steps and actions that help to support the policy and standards. Generally, procedures are changed more frequently as compared to policies and standards.

- **Guidelines**: In some cases, guidelines are required to implement procedures. Guidelines include information such as examples, suggestions, requirements, and other details for executing procedures.

Policies, standards, procedures, and guidelines should be available in the documented format.

Reviewing and updating documents

All the previously mentioned documents – that is, policies, standards, procedures, and guidelines – should be reviewed at periodic intervals to address new and emerging risks. The appropriate version history should be maintained. The security manager should check for currency.

The last review date confirms the currency of the documents and helps to determine that management has reviewed the standards to meet and address the current business environment.

The security manager should also consider the applicability of policies, standards, procedures, and guidelines to third-party vendors and service providers and their adherence to said documents.

Key aspects from a CISM exam perspective

The following are some of the key aspects from an exam perspective:

Question	Possible answer
Which document contains a high-level statement indicating the direction of the management?	Policy
Who should approve an exception to the information security policy?	The policy approver

Table 6.5 – Key aspects from the CISM exam perspective

Questions

1. "All computers are required to have the Windows 10 operating system and all servers are required to have Windows 2008." What is this statement an example of?

    A. A policy

    B. A guideline

    C. A standard

    D. A procedure

    Answer: C. A standard

    Explanation: A standard is a mandatory requirement to be followed to comply with a given policy or framework or certification or regulation. A standard helps to ensure an efficient and effective process, which results in reliable products or services. A policy is a high-level statement of management intent and it does not cover this type of requirement. Guidelines and procedures provide detailed dos and don'ts to support the organization's policies.

2. Which of the following is a function that should be exclusively performed by the information security department?

    A. Monitoring the performance of an operating system

    B. Implementing user access of operating systems

    C. Approving operating system access standards

    D. Setting firewall rules to protect an operating system

    Answer: C. Approving operating system access standards

    Explanation: Approving the standards should be performed by the information security team. The security team should ensure that standards meet the requirements of the security policy. Implementation of the approved standard is to be performed by the IT department. The other options are generally performed by the IT department.

3. Procedures are correctly linked to security policies through which of the following?

    A. Standards

    B. Audit

    C. Maturity model

    D. Guidelines

Answer: A. Standards

Explanation: Standards are the set of minimum requirements to be followed to comply with the requirements of the security policy. Standards (minimum requirement) are included in procedures to ensure that they comply with the intent of policies. Guidelines are generally detailed descriptions of the procedures. A maturity model is adopted to ensure continuous improvement in the security process.

4.   What is the most appropriate document to ensure compliance with a specific regulatory requirement?

A. Policies

B. Standards

C. Procedures

D. Guidelines

Answer: B. Standards

Explanation: A standard is a mandatory requirement to be followed to comply with a given framework or certification or regulation. Standards help to ensure an efficient and effective process, which results in reliable products or services. A policy is a high-level statement of management intent and it does not cover specific regulatory requirements. Guidelines and procedures provide detailed dos and don'ts to support the organization's policies and standards.

5.   The information security standard should primarily include what?

A. Date of creation

B. Author of the document

C. Approval of the document

D. Last review date

Answer: D. Last review date

Explanation: The most important element is the last review date, which helps to ensure the currency of the standard and provides assurance that the document is reviewed and updated to address the current issues.

6. Which of the following documents will be updated most frequently?

    A. Database hardening procedures

    B. Password complexity standard

    C. Information security policy

    D. Document retention standard

    Answer: A. Database hardening procedures

    Explanation: Generally, procedures are changed more frequently as compared with policies and standards. As an operating system changes, procedures for hardening also need to be changed. Policies and standards should be more static and less subject to frequent change.

7. What is the best way to relate a standard to a policy?

    A. A policy provides detailed directions to comply with the standard.

    B. Both policies and standards have the same content.

    C. A standard provides detailed directions to comply with the policy.

    D. A standard is a standalone document without a relationship to any particular policy.

    Answer: C. A standard provides detailed directions to comply with the policy.

    Explanation: A policy is a high-level statement of management intent and it does not cover specific requirements or actions. A standard is a mandatory requirement to be followed to comply with a given framework or policy. A standard provides detailed directions to comply with a policy.

8. An information security standard is most likely to be changed because of which of the following?

    A. Change in the effectiveness of controls

    B. Change in information security procedures

    C. Change in security budgets

    D. Change in the result of a periodic risk assessment

    Answer: D. Change in the result of a periodic risk assessment

    Explanation: A standard is a mandatory requirement to be followed in order to comply with a given framework or certification or policy. If the results of a risk assessment are not encouraging, then the standard should be updated to ensure that it appropriately addresses the organization's security objectives. The other options will not directly impact the standard.

9. An information security standard is most likely to be changed because of which of the following?

A. Reduction in security budget

B. Change in security procedure

C. Change in security guidelines

D. Control objectives not being met

Answer: D. Control objectives not being met

Explanation: A standard is a mandatory requirement to be followed in order to comply with a given framework or certification or policy. If the current standard does not help to achieve the intended control objectives, the standard should be modified to ensure that it appropriately addresses the organization's security objectives. The other options will not directly impact the standard.

10. Who is ultimately responsible for ensuring that information policies are consistent with laws and regulations?

A. Quality assurance team

B. Head of audit

C. Board of directors

D. Head of technology

Answer: C. Board of directors

Explanation: The final responsibility resides with the board of directors for compliance with laws and regulations. The other options will support the board to execute the security policy.

11. An exception to the information security policy can be granted by which of the following?

A. Process owner

B. Security manager

C. Policy approver

D. Audit manager

Answer: C. Policy approver

Explanation: A framework should define the process for handling exceptions to the policy and procedure. The inherent authority to grant an exception to the information security policy should reside with the authority that has approved the policy.

Security budget

Budgeting plays a significant role in the effective implementation of an information security program. The availability of adequate security personnel and other security resources is dependent on the security budget. The information security manager should be familiar with the budgeting process and methods used by the organization.

Primarily, the security budget is derived from and supported by the information security strategy. Before seeking approval for the budget, the security manager should ensure that senior management has approved the strategy and other business units have a consensus on the security strategy. This is a key element in a successful budget proposal.

Apart from routine expenditure, the budget should also consider unanticipated costs. Generally, in the area of incident response, it is difficult to predict the expenditure. The security manager may require obtaining external services to support the incident response processes where an organization does not have the necessary skills or bandwidth. The best approach to the budget for this kind of situation is to use historical data of incidents and related expenditure. If this information is not available, the security manager may rely on statistics from peer organizations to arrive at a reasonable budget.

Getting a security budget approved is a dream for every security manager, as depicted in the following diagram:

Figure 6.4 – Information security budget

Adequate funding for information security is the biggest challenge for a security manager. When funds are inadequate, the best option is to allocate available resources to areas of highest risk and at the same time educate management about the potential impact of underfunding.

Key aspects from a CISM exam perspective

The following is a key aspect from an exam perspective:

Question	Possible answer
What is the primary basis for the prioritization of security spending and budgeting?	Level of risk

Table 6.6 – Key aspect from the CISM exam perspective

Questions

1. Security spending and budgeting are prioritized primarily on the basis of what?

   A. Identified levels of risk

   B. Incident trends

   C. Discretion of the security manager

   D. Industry benchmarking

   Answer: A. Identified levels of risk

   Explanation: On the basis of the risk assessment, areas of high risk should be identified. Priority should be given to these areas of high risk. Security investment should be prioritized on the basis of the level of risk. Prioritization should not be based on trends or the discretion of the security manager and industry benchmarking.

2. Awareness for security funding should be raised by which of the following?

   A. Chief financial officer

   B. Chief information officer

   C. Information security manager

   D. Business process management

   Answer: C. Information security manager

   Explanation: Responsibility for raising awareness for sufficient and adequate funds for security initiatives resides with the information security manager. Even though the chief information officer, business process owner, and chief audit officer do play important roles in the final approval of funds, the information security manager has the ultimate responsibility to raise awareness for adequate security funds.

3. What is the best approach for a security manager who does not have adequate funding for a security program?

    A. Discontinue low-priority security controls.

    B. Ask management to accept the unaddressed risk.

    C. Prioritize risk mitigation and educate management.

    D. Reduce reliance on technology and perform more manual processes.

    Answer: C. Prioritize risk mitigation and educate management.

    Explanation: When funds are inadequate, the best option is to allocate available resources to areas of highest risk and at the same time educate management about the potential impact of underfunding. The other options are secondary factors.

Security program management and administrative activities

Information security program management includes activities to direct, monitor, and control the procedures related to information security. It includes both short-term and long-term planning for the achievement of security objectives. The security manager should ensure that the security program supports the requirements of management. In most organizations, the security manager is responsible for executing the security program. The information security steering committee, which consists of senior leadership from relevant functions of the organization, is responsible for ensuring that security objectives are aligned with business objectives. Senior management represented in the security steering committee is in the best position to support and advocate for the information security program. The role of the steering committee, as well as the security manager, is of utmost importance to ensure that security resources are utilized in an optimized manner. It is the responsibility of the CEO and senior management to support the security initiatives and provide adequate resources and authority to ensure that objectives are achieved.

A security program should be aligned with the program of other assurance functions to ensure that roles and responsibilities are not overlapping and at the same time there are adequate controls to protect the information assets of the organization.

An information security manager is required to be well versed in major security frameworks and international standards such as ISO 27001 and COBIT and be able to implement them as per the requirements of the organization. A framework is generally dependent on the structure, culture, business objectives, and so on of the organization.

The most effective way for an information security manager to perform their responsibilities is to act as a facilitator or consultant to help address the issues that impact the business objectives. They should be able to understand the impact of security on the performance level. There is no use in implementing heavy security if it degrades the performance drastically. The security manager is required to resolve competing objectives between security and performance. As a facilitator and consultant, the security manager is likely to achieve support from senior management and this will improve the effectiveness of the security program.

Information security team

For effective implementation of a security program, the most important element is the availability of skilled personnel resources. An information security team generally includes security engineers, quality assurance and testing specialists, access controllers, project managers, security architects, ethical hackers, security trainers, security auditors, and so on. Each team member should have the appropriate technical and administrative skills in accordance with their job functions. Skills can be in the form of education, expertise, and experience held by the individual. These skills should be mapped with the required job functions. On a lighter note, the following diagram depicts why relevant skills are important:

Figure 6.5 – Information security skills

A security manager should ensure that each security team member possesses and maintains relevant skills.

Roles and responsibilities

A role is a designation assigned to an individual in accordance with their job function. Responsibilities mean the set of actions an individual is required to perform. For example, system administrator is a role, and their responsibilities include assigning access to the system, monitoring system performance, ensuring backup schedules, and so on.

A clear and documented detail of roles, responsibilities, and accountability is necessary to ensure the effective implementation of an information security program.

Role-based access control is very important from a security perspective. An individual is assigned different access on the basis of their role. This will help to ensure that various accesses are provided on a need-to-know basis only.

External resources

Many organizations obtain the services of external resources to manage their information security program. It is of utmost importance to conduct a cost-benefit analysis before appointing external resources. External resources are generally preferred where a skill is required for a short time or for specific projects.

Acceptable usage policy

An **acceptable usage policy** (**AUP**) is a summary of the information security policy and procedures and includes details in a user-friendly manner about the acceptable usage of information resources. It helps to effectively communicate the dos and don'ts for improving the security posture of the organization.

Security managers need to ensure that the AUP is made available to all end users and it is read and understood. An AUP generally includes information about access control, information classification, document handling, incident reporting procedures, and other requirements related to end users. An AUP provides a general security baseline for the entire organization.

Documentation

Documentation of security policies and procedures helps to ensure that security procedures are repeatable and sustainable. A security manager is required to provide oversight over the creation and maintenance of security-related documentation. For better handling of documents, it is recommended to assign an owner for each document. The document owner is responsible for updating the documents as per defined procedures of approval and review. The document owner is also responsible for safeguarding the document in accordance with the classification level of the document.

A defined process should be in place for the creation, approval, change, maintenance, distribution, and retirement of a document. Each document should have appropriate classification and labeling to ensure that the document is handled and distributed in a secured manner.

Also, document version control is an important element to ensure the integrity of the document and to ensure that all recipients are using current documentation.

Project management

A security manager should ensure that security-related projects are appropriately managed in accordance with generally accepted project management techniques. Each major project should have defined goals, completion timelines, a process of measuring the progress and adherence to budget, assigned responsibilities, and other elements of project management. This will increase the effectiveness of security-related projects.

In the case of a large organization with multiple projects, the security manager should have a documented portfolio of the projects to determine the progress of each project. A project's portfolio will help to determine the priorities for each project and ensure that projects do not overlap, resources are appropriately allocated, and progress is continuously monitored.

Program budgeting

Budgeting plays a significant role in the effective implementation of an information security program. The availability of adequate security personnel and other security resources is dependent on the security budget. The information security manager should be familiar with the budgeting process and methods used by the organization.

Primarily, the security budget is derived from and supported by the information security strategy. Before seeking approval for the budget, the security manager should ensure that senior management has approved the strategy and other business units have a consensus on the security strategy. This is a key element in a successful budget proposal.

Apart from routine expenditure, the budget should also consider unanticipated costs. Generally, in the area of incident response, it is difficult to predict the expenditure. The security manager may need to obtain external services to support the incident response processes where an organization does not have the necessary skills or bandwidth. The best approach to budget for this kind of situation is to use historical data of incidents and related expenditure. If this information is not available, the security manager may rely on statistics from peer organizations to arrive at a reasonable budget.

Adequate funding for information security is the biggest challenge for a security manager. When funds are inadequate, the best option is to allocate available resources to areas of highest risk and at the same time educate management about the potential impact of underfunding.

Plan – do – check – act

To ensure the effective and efficient management of an information security program, a security manager should implement the following four elements of **total quality management (TQM)**:

- **Plan**: Structured planning is the most important element for the success of any program. Planning includes developing a strategy to achieve the program objective and scheduling different activities of the program.

- **Do**: Execute the strategy as per the plan.

- **Check**: Monitor the progress of the program and determine the areas of improvement. This requires the development of various metrics that indicate the progress or otherwise of the program.

- **Act**: Take action and address the risks and other irregularities identified by the monitoring processes.

The preceding TQM approach will help in the effective and efficient management of security processes with continuous improvement.

Security operations

A security manager should consider the following aspects of security operations to improve the effectiveness and efficiency of an information security program:

- A security manager should ensure that security monitoring processes such as scanning, testing, audit, and so on do not interrupt any running production process.

- Patches need to be applied as and when important updates are released after being tested. The patch management process should include an appropriate process of testing and approvals.

- It is highly recommended to update the anti-virus signature files on a daily basis. New attack patterns are introduced almost on a daily basis. If signature files are not updated on a daily basis, an organization is exposed to new types of attacks. The effectiveness of anti-virus software primarily depends on virus signatures stored in definition files.

The most effective way to verify that all critical systems are utilizing up-to-date virus signature files is to check sample systems and ensure that signature files installed are the latest ones.

For anti-virus software to be effective, it must be easy to maintain and updated frequently to address new viruses.

- A security manager should take adequate steps to protect the wireless network. Strong encryption is the most effective method to secure a wireless network as a point of entry into a corporate network.

- Implementation of monitoring products such as firewall, IDS, anti-virus, and so on may slow down the performance of the systems and networks. It can create a major impact as a system overhead for servers and networks.

- Overhead means excess or indirect utilization of computation time, memory, bandwidth, and other resources. A security manager should consider this aspect when evaluating products to monitor security across the organization. Monitoring products should support the business processes and should not become a cause of unnecessary interruptions.

- The most important element for the success of an information security program is support and commitment from senior management. If senior management is committed to the robust information security of the organization, there will no constraint for security budget and resources.

Thus, security operations should support the business operations in the most effective and efficient manner.

Key aspects from a CISM exam perspective

The following are some of the key aspects from an exam perspective:

Question	Possible answer
What is the most appropriate frequency for updating anti-virus signature files for anti-virus software?	On a daily basis
What does the effectiveness of virus detection software most depend on?	Virus definition files (signature files)
What is the best way to prevent accidental system shutdown from the console or operations area?	Use protective switch covers
What is the best method for securing data on USB drives or other mobile devices?	Strong encryption

Question	Possible answer
Who should be part of an information security steering committee?	Senior management from different departments such as IT, HR, business, marketing, and so on
What is the main reason for obtaining external resources to execute the information security program?	A cost-effective way to get the expertise that is not available internally
What is the most effective method to ensure the protection of data upon termination of employment?	Ensure that all logical access of the terminated employee is removed
What is the most important reason for formally documenting security procedures?	Ensuring that processes are repeatable and sustainable
When should a risk assessment of a new project be carried out?	Throughout the project life cycle

Table 6.7 – Key aspects from the CISM exam perspective

Questions

1. What is the most important aspect of the use of a vulnerability scanner?

    A. Not to use open source tools.

    B. Scan only critical servers.

    C. Adhere to the security budget.

    D. Not to interrupt the production process.

    Answer: D. Not to interrupt the production process.

    Explanation: The most important aspect is to ensure that the scan process does not interrupt the production process. There is no harm in using industry-recognized open source tools. The scan should concentrate on all the servers within a network because if any of the servers is compromised then the entire network is in danger. Adherence to the budget is not a major concern.

2. The effectiveness of an information security program can be best ensured by which of the following?

    A. Chief information officer

    B. Head of audit

    C. Steering committee

    D. Chief operating officer

    Answer: C. Steering committee

    Explanation: A security steering committee consists of senior officials from different business functions. It plays an important part in the finalization of security requirements. A security steering committee is in the best position to support the establishment of an information security program.

3. When should anti-virus signature files be updated?

    A. On a daily basis

    B. On a weekly basis

    C. During the hardware maintenance schedule

    D. After the occurrence of a major incident

    Answer: A. On a daily basis

    Explanation: New attack patterns are introduced almost on a daily basis. If signature files are not updated on a daily basis, an organization is exposed to new types of attacks. The other options are not effective.

4. The effectiveness of anti-virus software primarily depends on which of the following?

    A. Operating systems

    B. Updated patches

    C. Application upgrades

    D. Definition files

    Answer: D. Definition files

    Explanation: The effectiveness of anti-virus software depends on virus definition files. If definitions are not updated on a frequent basis, anti-virus software will not be able to control the new types of attacks. The other options are secondary aspects.

5. What is the most important criterion for the selection of anti-virus software?

    A. Availability of security budget

    B. Ability to integrate with a firewall and IDS

    C. Automatic alert notification feature

    D. Ease of maintenance and frequency of updates

    Answer: D. Ease of maintenance and frequency of updates

    Explanation: For anti-virus software to be effective, it must be easy to maintain and updated frequently to address new viruses. The other options are secondary factors.

6. What is the best way to reduce the risk of accidental system shutdown through the power button?

    A. Use redundant power supplies.

    B. Use protective switch covers.

    C. Set system down alarms.

    D. Install biometric readers.

    Answer: B. Use protective switch covers.

    Explanation: Installing protective switch covers will help to reduce the instances of an individual accidentally pressing the power button and shutting down the system. A redundant power supply will not prevent accidental system shutdown. Shutdown alarms will be after the fact. Biometric readers are generally used for granting access to the system and not for powering on or off the system.

7. An information security steering committee should consist of which of the following?

    A. External penetration testers

    B. Representations from regulatory bodies

    C. Board members

    D. Leadership from IT, business management, and human resources

    Answer: D. Leadership from IT, business management, and human resources

Explanation: The role of a steering committee is to ensure that the security initiatives are in harmony with the organization's mission and objectives. The steering committee monitors and facilitates the deployment of security resources for specific projects in support of business plans. The steering committee should consist of key executives and representatives from user management, which includes leadership from IT, business management, HR, and other departments.

8. What is the most important consideration for implementing system monitoring devices?

    A. Product documentation

    B. Ease of configuration

    C. Ease of available support

    D. System overhead

    Answer: D. System overhead

    Explanation: Overhead means excess or indirect utilization of computation time, memory, bandwidth, and other resources. Monitoring products can have a significant impact on system overhead for servers, applications, and networks. A security manager should ensure that monitoring devices do not degrade the performance of servers, applications, and networks. The other options are secondary aspects.

9. An organization is using a digital certificate along with a secure socket layer to authenticate a web server. What is the organization still vulnerable to?

    A. IP spoofing

    B. A man-in-the-middle attack

    C. Repudiation

    D. A Trojan program

    Answer: D. A Trojan program

    Explanation: If a computer is infected with a Trojan program, an attacker can take full control of the system and hijack, copy, or modify the information after authentication is done by the user. IP is not used for authentication and hence IP spoofing will not work. SSL along with a digital certificate will prevent a man-in-the-middle attack. A digital certificate will prevent the risk of repudiation.

10. What is the most effective way to ensure compliance with an information security policy?

    A. To circulate copies of a policy to all employees

    B. To perform periodic reviews for compliance

    C. To charge a heavy penalty for non-compliance

    D. To establish a dedicated helpdesk to support employees

    Answer: B. To perform periodic reviews for compliance

    Explanation: The best method is to conduct periodic reviews and determine the status of compliance. Gaps, if any, should be addressed appropriately. The other options are secondary factors.

11. What is the main advantage of using external resources for managing an information security program?

    A. It is a cost-effective way to gain expertise not available internally.

    B. It is the most effective way to delegate responsibility for maintaining the security program.

    C. It helps to reduce dependency on internal resources.

    D. It helps to adhere to the security budget.

    Answer: A. It is a cost-effective way to gain expertise not available internally.

    Explanation: The primary driver for obtaining the services of external resources is that it helps to contribute cost-effective expertise that is generally not available internally. The other options are secondary factors.

12. A server containing an accounting database is maintained by a database administrator. Who should determine the appropriate level of classification?

    A. Database administrator

    B. Finance department

    C. Security department

    D. IT department

    Answer: B. Finance department

    Explanation: The responsibility for determining the appropriate level of classification resides with the data owner. In this case, the finance department is the owner of the accounting data and hence the finance department should determine the level of classification for the server.

13. A particular module is accessible to all the members of the development team. The module is used to test the business data. From a security perspective, which of the following is the best option?

    A. Restrict the access as read-only.

    B. Capture and review logs for all the access.

    C. Implement two-factor authentication.

    D. Suspend the module and activate only as and when required.

    Answer: A. Restrict the access as read-only.

    Explanation: The best way is to allow read-only access for the module. The developer should not have the right to modify or download base data. The other options will not be as effective as read-only access.

14. The involvement of which of the following groups is very important in the design of security processes to make them accurate and functional?

    A. Audit management

    B. Compliance management

    C. Operational units

    D. Legal management

    Answer: C. Operational units

    Explanation: The most effective way to optimize the security program is to embed security processes with operational processes. The involvement of operational units is of utmost importance to ensure the security process is accurate and functional.

15. Which of the following roles should not be given the right to update a database access control list to ensure proper segregation of duties?

    A. Team member of the department owning the data

    B. Data custodian

    C. System programmer

    D. Security administrator

    Answer: C. System programmer

    Explanation: A system programmer should not have the privilege to update an access control list as it enables them to have unlimited control over the system. The data owner, data custodian, or security administrator may need to carry out the updating of access control lists as per their defined job responsibilities.

16. As a business requirement, an application programmer requires access to production data. What is the best way to ensure that production data is used only for authorized purposes?

    A. Make the application programmer a privileged user.

    B. Log all of the application programmer's activity for review by their manager.

    C. Take a non-disclosure agreement letter from the application programmer.

    D. Conduct a regular audit of the application.

    Answer: B. Log all of the application programmer's activity for review by their manager.

    Explanation: The best way to mitigate the situation is to capture the log for the activities of the programmer, and it needs to be reviewed by their manager. This will help to detect any inappropriate action on the part of the application programmer. The other options will not be as effective as log capturing and review.

17. What is the most important step upon the termination of employment?

    A. Take back the identity card.

    B. Take back the company-provided laptop.

    C. Delete all of the employee's folders.

    D. Remove all logical access provided to the employee.

    Answer: D. Remove all logical access provided to the employee.

    Explanation: The most important step is to remove all the logical access provided to the employee. Upon termination, an employee should not be able to access the organization's data. Taking back the identity card and laptop does not prevent the employee from logging in from external machines. Deleting an employee's folder needs to be considered after analyzing the nature of the data.

18. What is the main objective of documenting the security procedure?

    A. To ensure the process is repeatable and sustainable

    B. To comply with the requirements of the policy

    C. To ensure alignment with business objectives

    D. To ensure evidence is available for audit

Answer: A. To ensure the process is repeatable and sustainable

Explanation: The primary objective of documenting the security processes is to ensure that processes are repeatable and sustainable. This helps to ensure that security processes are performed correctly and consistently.

19. What should a process document for the use of a cryptography document primarily include?

    A. Various circumstances where cryptography should be used

    B. Type of cryptographic algorithms and key lengths

    C. Handling procedures of cryptographic keys

    D. Technical aspects of cryptographic solutions

    Answer: A. Various circumstances where cryptography should be used

    Explanation: The objective of a process document is to support the users to ensure the process is followed in a consistent and correct manner. The most important aspect that should be included in a process document is about circumstances where cryptography should be used. The other options are generally automated and system-driven and hence users may not be required to be involved much.

20. When should the risk assessment for a new process be conducted?

    A. Before the start of the process

    B. Throughout the entire life cycle of the process

    C. During the post-implementation review

    D. During the development of the business case

    Answer: B. Throughout the entire life cycle of the process

    Explanation: Risk assessment is not a one-time activity. It should be conducted at every stage of the newly implemented process for the most effective result.

21. The security manager notes that employees of the marketing department are sending some critical customer data through email. What should the security manager do first?

    A. Discuss the finding with the marketing manager to evaluate the risk and impact.

    B. Report the finding to the audit committee.

    C. Report the finding to the incident management team for further investigation.

    D. Conduct awareness training for the marketing department.

Answer: A. Discuss the finding with the marketing manager to evaluate the risk and impact.

Explanation: The first step for the security manager is to discuss the finding with the marketing manager and determine the risk and impact of such an act. Input from business unit management is very important in deciding the next step. The finding should not be directly highlighted to the audit committee without understanding the risk and impact. The other options are subsequent actions.

22. The security manager has obtained commitment and approval from senior management for the establishment of an information security program. What should be their next step?

    A. Develop metrics for measuring effectiveness.

    B. Conduct a risk assessment.

    C. Conduct a gap analysis.

    D. Obtain security resources.

    Answer: B. Conduct a risk assessment.

    Explanation: The first step is to conduct a risk assessment to identify the current needs and requirements of the organization and accordingly develop a security strategy. The other options are subsequent steps.

23. The security manager is creating security procedures for the entire organization. Which department should be given priority to write the procedure?

    A. Security department

    B. Legal department

    C. HR department

    D. Operations department

    Answer: D. Operations department

    Explanation: Most of the critical processes and data of the organization are generally handled by the operations department. The operations department has first-hand knowledge about the organization's processes and responsibilities and will help to ensure that written procedures are sound, repeatable, and sustainable.

24. What is the best method to address the risk of sending confidential information in an email attachment?

A. To implement content filtering

B. To conduct an email audit

C. To perform security training

D. To encrypt the attachment

Answer: A. To implement content filtering

Explanation: Content filtering is the best tool to address the issue as it has the ability to examine the content of an attachment and prevent information containing specific words or phrases from being sent out of the organization. Encryption will not be effective because it does not prevent confidential information from going out; in fact, content filtering will not be able to read encrypted information. Email audit and security training will not be as effective as content filtering.

Privacy laws

Privacy is the right of the individual to demand the utmost care is taken of their personal information that has been shared with any organization or individual. Individuals can demand that the use of their information should be appropriate, legal, and for a specific purpose for which information is obtained. On a lighter note, nowadays, users are well aware of their privacy rights as depicted in the following diagram:

Figure 6.6 – Privacy laws

The **Information Systems Audit and Control Association (ISACA)** describes several privacy principles that can be considered as a framework for privacy audits. The following are some of the privacy principles:

- Organizations should obtain appropriate consent before the transfer of personal information to another jurisdiction.

- Organizations should specify the purposes for which personal information is collected.

- Organizations are required to retain personal information only as long as necessary.

- Organizations should have appropriate security safeguards for protecting personal information.

- Organizations should have an appropriate process for reporting compliance with the privacy policy, standards, and laws.

- Organizations should have an appropriate governance mechanism over the third-party service provider processing privacy data on behalf of the organization.

- Organizations should comply with applicable data protection regulations for the transfer of personal information across country borders.

Questions

1. A privacy statement primarily includes which of the following?

   A. Privacy budget of the organization

   B. Notification about the accuracy of the information

   C. Notification about what the company will do with the information it collects

   D. Notification about the information classification process

   Answer: C. Notification about what the company will do with the information it collects

   Explanation: Generally, all privacy laws mandate the disclosure of how the information collected will be used. The privacy budget is generally not included in a privacy statement. Notification about the accuracy of information is included in a website disclaimer. Information classification is not part of a privacy statement.

Summary

In this chapter, we discussed information security program development management. This chapter will help CISM candidates understand important methods, tools, and techniques to develop a security program in an effective and efficient manner. This chapter will help CISM candidates to determine the budget requirements to run a security program. They will also have a basic idea about privacy laws and their impact on an information security program.

In the next chapter, we will discuss information security infrastructure and architecture.

7
Information Security Infrastructure and Architecture

In this chapter, we will discuss information security infrastructure and architecture and learn about methods, tools, and techniques for the development of robust information security programs. This chapter will help the **CISM** aspirant to understand security architecture in line with industry best practices. The CISM aspirant will gain basic knowledge of access control requirements, including biometrics and factors of authentication.

The following topics will be covered in this chapter:

- Information security architecture
- Architecture implementation
- Access control
- Virtual private networks
- Biometrics

- Factors of authentication
- Wireless networks
- Different attack methods

Let's discuss each one of these topics in detail.

Information security architecture

Just as conventional architecture defines the rules and standards for the construction of buildings, information security architecture addresses the design and implementation of the security posture of the organization. Security architecture helps to integrate different components of information security in an effective manner. Security architecture also defines the minimum level of security for the infrastructure.

Security architecture generally addresses the following security aspects:

- Where to place and deploy security tools such as **firewalls, intrusion detection system (IDS), anti-malware**, and more
- How to configure the security of applications and servers
- How to build the overall security environment

An architecture helps to integrate different components of information security in an effective manner. A structured architecture provides the framework to manage the complex security environment. As the size and complexity of the organization grow, a well-defined architecture helps the security manager to monitor and control all aspects of security. Security architecture provides the framework within which many large projects can be managed effectively and efficiently.

In the absence of well-designed security architecture, there can be a lack of integration, haphazard project management, and other weaknesses and vulnerabilities in the security environment. **Enterprise information security architecture (EISA)** was developed as a part of an overall enterprise IT system design. The following are some of the objectives of EISA:

- To manage the security process and performance
- To establish a common language for security within the organization
- To serve as a program development roadmap
- To ensure strategic alignment between business and security
- To support the business strategy
- To implement security policies and strategies

Security practitioners should ensure that the preceding objectives are achieved to improve the effectiveness of information security architecture.

Key learning aspects from the CISM exam perspective

The following table covers some of the key learning aspects from the CISM exam perspective:

Question	Possible answer
Security architecture should be aligned with what?	The business objectives and goals.
What is the best method for the effective integration of the different components of information security infrastructure?	Developing an architecture.

Table 7.1 – Key aspects from the CISM exam perspective

Questions

1. What should security architecture be aligned with?

    A. Industry accepted frameworks.

    B. The IT strategy.

    C. The IT budget.

    D. The business objectives and goals.

    Answer: D. The business objectives and goals.

    Explanation: The prime objective of security architecture is to support the business objectives and goals. The other options are secondary factors.

2. What is the most effective way to integrate the different components of information security infrastructure?

    A. Develop a business plan.

    B. Develop an architecture.

    C. Develop a system specification.

    D. Conduct a system audit.

    Answer: B. Develop an architecture.

    Explanation: Just as conventional architecture defines the rules and standards for the construction of buildings, information security architecture addresses the design and implementation of the security posture of the organization. An architecture helps to integrate the different components of information security in an effective manner.

3. What is the minimum level of security requirement for the infrastructure defined by?

    A. The available security budget.

    B. The information security guidelines.

    C. The information security strategy.

    D. The information security architecture.

    Answer: D. The information security architecture.

    Explanation: Just as conventional architecture defines the rules and standards for the construction of a building, information security architecture addresses the design and implementation of the security posture of the organization. An architecture helps to integrate the different components of information security in an effective manner. Security architecture also defines the minimum level of security for the infrastructure.

Architecture implementation

The security manager should consider the following important factors during the implementation of the security architecture:

- **Termination process**: An effective employee termination process is one of the most important aspects of the information security process. A terminated employee can misuse their credentials for unauthorized activity. Hence, the termination process should ensure the timely revocation of all access at the time an employee is terminated or otherwise ceases to be employed by the organization.

- **Security rules**: The security manager should also ensure that rules related to security tools, such as firewalls, IDS, anti-malware software, **security information and event management** (**SIEM**), and so on, should be reviewed at periodic intervals. Rules should be simple and easy to implement. However, if too many security rules are implemented, they can become difficult to manage, and there is a chance that a particular rule may conflict with another, which may lead to a security vulnerability. Also, it becomes difficult to test an overly complex set of security rules.

- **Phishing**: Phishing is a social engineering attack with the objective to obtain user data in an unauthorized way. In a phishing attack, the attacker acts as a trusted entity and tries to lure the victim to part with confidential information. The best method to address the risk of phishing is to conduct periodic awareness training for the users. Educating users will help to address the risk of visiting untrusted websites or email links.

- **Steganographic techniques**: In steganography, secret data is hidden in an ordinary file or image to avoid its detection. An ordinary file or image is sent to a recipient along with the secret data. For highly confidential data, an organization may use this technique to protect confidential information from third parties. The advantage of sending messages using steganographic techniques, compared to encryption techniques, is that in the case of steganography the existence of the messages is itself unknown.

- **Middleware**: Middleware is software that acts as a link between the operating system and applications. It has the capability to provide additional services to applications that are not provided by the operating system. Some examples of the functions handled by middleware are data management, application services, messaging, authentication, and more. The major risk associated with middleware is that data integrity may be adversely affected if the middleware is corrupted.

Key aspects from the CISM exam perspective

The following table covers some of the key aspects from the CISM exam perspective:

Question	Possible answer
What is the most important element of the employee termination process from a security perspective?	The timely revocation of the access rights of the terminated employee.
Who is required to ensure that the appropriate level of information security is applied to a business application?	The process owner/system owner.
What is the best method to control a phishing attack?	User awareness training.
What is the prime objective of change management?	• To ensure that only authorized changes are carried out. • To ensure that modifications made system do not introduce new security exposures.
What is the major risk of excessive numbers of firewall rules?	One rule may conflict with another rule and create a security weakness.

Table 7.2 – Key aspects from the CISM exam perspective

Questions

1. How can unauthorized activity by a former employee be best controlled?

    A. Ensuring background verification.

    B. Regular user awareness training.

    C. Implementing user monitoring.

    D. Having an effective termination process.

    Answer: D. Having an effective termination process.

    Explanation: An effective termination process is one of the most important aspects of information security processes. A terminated employee may use their active credentials to access the system or data for some unauthorized activities. Therefore, it is of utmost importance to ensure the timely revocation of all access privileges held by the terminated employee. The other options are not effective to prevent this type of situation.

2. Who is responsible for implementing and maintaining the required level of security for a business application?

    A. System administrator.

    B. Quality analyst.

    C. Process owner.

    D. Security manager.

    Answer: C. Process owner.

    Explanation: The responsibility for implementing and maintaining the required level of security for a specific business application resides with the business process owner. Process owners have a thorough knowledge of the business's needs and the security requirements for the business application for which they are responsible.

3. Data owners are generally responsible for what?

    A. Carrying out change management procedures.

    B. Implementing security for database servers.

    C. Regular updating of the operating system patches.

    D. Determining the extent of the application security required.

    Answer: D. Determining the extent of application security required.

Explanation: The data owner is responsible for determining the extent of the application security required for their data. Data owners have a thorough knowledge of the business's needs and the information security requirements for their systems and processes. The other options are the responsibility of the system administrator.

4. What is the best method to protect against the risk of a phishing attack?

   A. System hardening.

   B. Email filtering.

   C. An intrusion detection system.

   D. User awareness training.

   Answer: D. User awareness training.

   Explanation: In phishing attacks, an attacker acts as a trusted entity and tries to lure the victim to part with confidential information. The best method to address the risk of phishing is to conduct periodic awareness training for the users. Educating users will help to address the risk of visiting the untrusted website or email links. The other options will not be as effective as user awareness.

5. Which of the following would be an area of major concern for an organizational security system?

   A. A locally managed file server.

   B. An enterprise-level data server.

   C. A centrally managed load balancer.

   D. A centrally managed data center.

   Answer: A. A locally managed file server.

   Explanation: The area of most concern will be the locally managed file server, as it is not subject to centralized oversight and monitoring. The other options are subject to close scrutiny and monitoring.

6. Which of the following will make the task of eradicating some malicious code more difficult?

   A. A patch is applied after the data is infected.

   B. An access rule is changed after the data is infected.

   C. Hardware is upgraded after the data is infected.

   D. A backup is taken after the data is infected.

Answer: D. A backup is taken after the data is infected.

Explanation: The backup of the infected file will increase the spread of the infected code. It will then become difficult to eradicate the malicious code. The other options do not significantly increase the level of difficulty.

7. What is the most effective method to reduce a social engineering attack?

    A. Implementing a strong password policy.

    B. Conducting periodic security awareness programs.

    C. Changing passwords on a frequent basis.

    D. Having an automatic lockout facility.

    Answer: B. Conducting periodic security awareness programs.

    Explanation: In a social engineering attack, an attacker acting as a trusted entity lures a victim into opening an email. Security awareness is the best method to address the risk of social engineering attacks such as phishing. Educating users will help to address the risk of visiting the untrusted website or email links. The other options are secondary aspects.

8. Who will be best able to determine that new vulnerabilities have not been introduced during a change management process?

    A. Internal auditor.

    B. System user.

    C. System administrator.

    D. Data security manager.

    Answer: B. System user.

    Explanation: Change management is the best way to ensure that modifications made in systems do not introduce new security exposures. System users will be in the best position to conduct user acceptance testing and determine if a change to the system has introduced any new exposures.

9. What is the advantage of steganographic control compared to encryption techniques?

    A. The existence of the message is not known.

    B. The steganographic technique does not require a key.

    C. It is not possible to "sniff" steganographic traffic.

    D. Steganographic traffic is not reliable.

Answer: A. The existence of the message is not known.

Explanation: In steganography, secret data is hidden in an ordinary file or image to avoid its detection. The ordinary file or image is sent to a recipient along with secret data. For highly confidential data, organizations may use this technique to protect the confidential information from third parties. The benefit of using steganographic techniques compared to encryption techniques is that, in the case of steganography, the existence of messages is itself unknown.

Steganographic techniques do require a key to view the hidden message. Steganographic controls can be sniffed. Steganography does not impact traffic reliability.

10. What is the major risk of middleware?

    A. It becomes difficult to update operating system patches.

    B. It becomes difficult to take system backups.

    C. Data integrity may be affected.

    D. End user authentication becomes difficult.

    Answer: C. Data integrity may be affected.

    Explanation: Middleware is software that acts as a link between the operating system and applications. It has the capability to provide additional services to applications that are not provided by the operating system. Some examples of functions handled by middleware are data management, application services, messaging, authentication, and more. The major risk associated with middleware is that data integrity may be adversely affected if middleware is corrupted. The other options are not relevant.

Access control

The main objective of the access control process is to ensure that only authorized users are granted access. To achieve this, it is very important for user activities to be uniquely identifiable for accountability purposes. The security manager should also consider the following categories of access control.

Mandatory access control

In **mandatory access control** (**MAC**), control rules are governed by an approved policy. Users or data owners cannot modify the access role. MAC ensures that files are shared only with authorized users as per the security classification of the file. This will ensure that users cannot share the file with unauthorized users.

Discretionary access control

In **discretionary access control (DAC)**, access control can be activated or modified by the data owner at their discretion.

MAC is considered to be more robust and stringent in terms of information security compared to DAC. To increase the effectiveness of DAC, it should be aligned with MAC.

Role-based access control

Role-based access control (RBAC) is a control technique to allow access to only authorized users. In RBAC, access is allowed on only a need-to-know basis. RBAC helps to simplify the security administration for large organizations having thousands of users and multiple permissions. The components of RBAC, such as role permissions, make it convenient and simple to allow access to authorized users. Though RBAC is different from the MAC and DAC frameworks, it can enforce these policies without any complications.

Also, RBAC is considered the most effective method for implementing the **segregation of duties (SoD)**. It requires the user to define the roles and corresponding access requirements. Access is provided on the basis of the roles.

The best method for implementing RBAC is to create a matrix of different roles and their corresponding work descriptions.

Degaussing (demagnetizing)

The right kind of data formatting is very critical to ensure that residual data from media cannot be recovered by an unauthorized person. To the greatest extent possible, the media should be physically destroyed in such a way that it cannot be reused. However, it may not always be economical to destroy the media, and hence for these cases, extreme care should be taken for the complete deletion of the data, and the data should not be recoverable by any tool or technique. One of these methods is to demagnetize the media record.

Demagnetization involves gradually increasing the alternating current field around the media from 0 to some maximum value and then back to 0, thereby leaving a very low residue of magnetic induction on the media. This process of demagnetization is also known as **degaussing**.

Key aspects from the CISM exam perspective

The following table covers some of the key aspects from the CISM exam perspective:

Question	Possible answer
What is the most effective access control framework for organizations that have a large number of employees with multiple roles?	RBAC.
What is the best approach for implementing role-based access control?	Creating a matrix of work functions.
What is the best way to erase data?	Physical destruction, demagnetization, or degaussing in case the media is to be reused.

Table 7.3 – Key aspects from the CISM exam perspective

Questions

1. What is the most effective way to ensure that temporary employees are not provided excess access rights?

   A. Do not provide access to temporary staff.

   B. Implement a virtual private network.

   C. Implement mandatory access control.

   D. Implement role-based access control.

   Answer: D. Implement role-based access control.

   Explanation: Role-based access control means granting access on the basis of the roles of the staff members. They should be provided with access on a need-to-know basis only. This will best ensure that employees are not provided with excessive access rights. VPNs help in secured connectivity from remote locations. Mandatory access control prevents the delegation of responsibility for granting access, but providing clearances for temporary employees by higher authorities is time-consuming and expensive.

2. What is the best way to ensure that temporary staff do not get access to sensitive information?

   A. Set expiry dates for access rights.

   B. Avoid granting system administration roles.

C. Conduct background checks.

D. Get them to sign a non-disclosure agreement.

Answer: B. Avoid granting system administration roles.

Explanation: Administration rights can equip temporary staff members with unlimited access privileges. Temporary staff should not be assigned any administrative role that can provide them with privilege rights. Administrative access rights, if misused, can have a huge impact on an organization. The other options are secondary considerations.

3. What is the best way to prevent users from sharing files with unauthorized users?

A. Mandatory access control.

B. Discretionary access control.

C. Role-based access control.

D. Installing an intrusion detection system.

Answer: A. Mandatory access control.

Explanation: MAC rules are governed by an approved policy. Users or data owners cannot modify the access role. Mandatory access control helps to control the access on the basis of the security classification of the file. This will prevent the users from sharing the files with unauthorized users. The other options are not as effective as MAC for the prevention of file sharing.

4. What is the most effective method for preventing users from using a USB drive to copy files from the organization's computers?

A. Restricting the available drive allocation on all personal computers.

B. Enabling role-based access control.

C. Performing periodic awareness training on USB-related risks.

D. Disabling the USB ports on all the organization's computers.

Answer: A. Restricting the available drive allocation on all personal computers.

Explanation: The most effective method is to restrict the drive allocation. This will ensure that users cannot allocate USB drives in their system. Also, the user cannot attach compact disc writers as these would not be recognized by the operating system. Disabling the USB port may not be practical, as the mouse and other essential peripherals depend on these ports. Role-based access control or periodic training will not be able to prevent the user from copying files via the USB ports.

5. What is the most appropriate access control approach for an organization that has more than 1,000 employees with multiple departments and roles?

    A. Mandatory access control.

    B. Discretionary access control.

    C. Ad hoc access control.

    D. Role-based access control.

    Answer: D. Role-based access control.

    Explanation: Role-based access control is a control technique to allow access to only authorized users. In RBAC, access is allowed on only a need-to-know basis. RBAC helps to simplify the security administration for large organizations that have thousands of users and multiple permissions. Other options will not be as effective for role based access control.

6. What is the most effective method for implementing SoD?

    A. Conducting background verification of employees.

    B. Implementing role-based access control.

    C. Implementing heavy penalties for non-compliance to SoD.

    D. Updating job profiles on a periodic basis.

    Answer: B. Implementing role-based access control.

    Explanation: RBAC is considered the most effective method for implementing SoD. It requires the senior management to define the roles and corresponding access requirements. Access is to be provided on the basis of the roles. The other options do support the proper implementation of SoD, but the most effective method is RBAC.

7. What is the most cost-effective access control framework for a large organization?

    A. Mandatory access control.

    B. Role-based access control.

    C. Discretionary access control.

    D. Rule-based access control.

    Answer: B. Role-based access control.

Explanation: Role-based access control allows access to only authorized users. In RBAC, access is allowed on only a need-to-know basis. RBAC helps to simplify the security administration for large organizations that have thousands of users and multiple permissions. Due to administrative convenience, RBAC is considered the most cost-effective method compared to the other options.

8. Which access control framework is preferable for an organization that has regular job rotation?

   A. Rule-based access control.

   B. Role-based access control.

   C. Discretionary access control.

   D. Mandatory access control.

   Answer: B. Role-based access control.

   Explanation: Role-based access control is a control technique to allow access to only authorized users. In RBAC, access is allowed on only a need-to-know basis. RBAC helps to simplify the security administration for large organizations that have thousands of users and multiple permissions. The other options are not as effective as RBAC.

9. When will access control processes be meaningful and effective?

   A. When they reduce administrative costs.

   B. When they ensure that all user activities are uniquely identifiable.

   C. When they use two-factor authentication.

   D. When they integrate access control across the organization.

   Answer: B. When they ensure that all user activities are uniquely identifiable.

   Explanation: The main objective of the access control process is to ensure that only authorized users are granted access. To achieve this, it is very important that user activities are uniquely identifiable for accountability purposes. The other options will not have any meaningful effect if users are not individually identifiable.

10. To determine whether access controls are appropriately applied for a critical application, what should the security manager refer to?

    A. The end user documentation.

    B. The business process flow.

C. The IT security standards.

D. Any legal requirements.

Answer: C. The IT security standards.

Explanation: The IT security standards define the minimum security requirements to be applied for each type of application. The security manager should ensure that access controls are implemented in line with the IT security standards.

11. What is the best way to protect the critical data of an organization?

A. Perform periodic security awareness sessions.

B. Obtain non-disclosure agreements from all the employees.

C. Remove all the logical access of employees leaving the organization.

D. Restrict access to data on a need-to-know basis.

Answer: D. Restrict access to data on a need-to-know basis.

Explanation: The most effective approach is to provide access to only those employees who are required to access data for their role functions. Access should not be allowed to anyone else. The other options are secondary aspects.

12. Which of the following is the most common reason for the introduction of vulnerabilities in security software?

A. Patch updating of security software.

B. Changing access rules for security software.

C. Upgrading hardware for security software.

D. Taking backups of files.

Answer: B. Changing access rules for security software.

Explanation: The most common area that exposes the security software is access rules. Major vulnerabilities generally happen when access rules are changed, as access may be provided to undesirable candidates. The other options do not have significant exposure.

13. What is the most effective method of removing data from tape media that is to be reused?

A. Multiple overwrites.

B. Erasing the tapes.

C. Burning the tapes.

D. Degaussing the tapes.

Answer: C. Degaussing the tapes.

Explanation: Degaussing or demagnetization involves gradually increasing the alternating current field from 0 to some maximum value and back to 0 and thereby leaving a very low residue of magnetic induction on the media. This process of demagnetization is also known as degaussing. The other options are not as secure as degaussing the tapes. Neither multiple overwrites nor erasing the tapes are foolproof methods of removing the data. Burning the tape will physically destroy the tape, and then it cannot be reused.

14. Role-based access control can be best implemented by which of the following?

A. Creating a matrix of work functions.

B. Creating specialized teams for access control.

C. Implementing two-factor authentication.

D. Using individual logon scripts.

Answer: A. Creating a matrix of work functions.

Explanation: RBAC is a control technique to provide access on a need-to-know basis. This is a simplified approach, where a matrix of work functions along with corresponding access requirements is created. RBAC helps to simplify the security administration for large organizations that have thousands of users and multiple permissions. The components of RBAC, such as role-permissions, make it convenient and simple to allow access to authorized users. RBAC does not require specialized teams. Factors of authentication are not relevant to RBAC. Using automated logon scripts for assigning permissions to individual accounts is contrary to the intent of RBAC.

15. What is the most effective method for the success of a data classification scheme?

A. Classification of data on the basis of its protection level.

B. Classification of data on the basis of the possibility of leakage.

C. Ensuring the same level of protection for all types of data.

D. Creating awareness of the benefit of data classification.

Answer: D. Creating awareness of the benefit of data classification.

Explanation: The success of the data classification scheme depends on the accurate data classification by the users, and for that, it is of utmost importance to create user awareness. Data is not classified on the basis of its protection level. In fact, data protection levels are based on the classification of the data. Data is classified based on its criticality and not on the basis of the possibility of leakage. Data classification does not require the same level of protection for all types of data. In fact, the objective of a data classification scheme is to ensure the appropriate level of protection is provided based on the criticality of data.

16. What is the objective of comparing logical access records with the physical attendance record maintained by the security department?

    A. To monitor a key risk indicator.

    B. To determine instances of tailgating.

    C. To evaluate the performance of the security department.

    D. To reconcile wage payout.

    Answer: A. To monitor a key risk indicator.

    Explanation: The difference between logical and physical records indicates the existence of a discrepancy. A discrepancy can be due to any reason. It can indicate piggybacking, sharing of passwords, unauthorized logical access, or any other risk. Hence, this monitoring can serve as a key risk indicator. Tailgating, lapses of the security department, and wrong payouts are all risks.

Virtual private networks

A **virtual private network** (**VPN**) is used to extend a private network through the use of the internet in a secure manner. It provides a platform for remote users to connect to the organization's private network.

With the help of VPN technology, remote users and branch offices can connect the resources and applications hosted in the private network of the organization. For enabling a VPN, a virtual point-to-point connection is established by way of dedicated circuits of tunneling protocols.

VPN technology ensures the safeguarding of critical data traveling over the internet.

VPNs – technical aspects

A VPN provides a platform to hide the information from a sniffer on the internet. Instead of using expensive, dedicated leased lines, a VPN relies on public IP infrastructure, which is cost-efficient. To protect the data, a VPN encrypts the packets with **IP Security (IPSec)** standards.

A VPN is enabled either through **IPSec tunnel mode** or **IPSec transport mode**. In IPSec tunnel mode, the entire packet (including the header) is encrypted, whereas in IPSec transport mode, only the data portion is encrypted. A VPN uses the data encapsulation or tunneling methods to encrypt the traffic payload for the secure transmission of the data.

Advantages of VPNs

The following are some of the advantages of a VPN:

- A VPN helps organizations to expand their corporate network in a cost-efficient way.
- A VPN provides a platform to authorized remote users in terms of a secure and effective way of connecting to corporate networks.
- A VPN provides a platform for secure communication with business partners.
- A VPN provides a platform for efficient and effective supply chain management.

VPNs – security risks

The following are some of the risks associated with the use of a VPN:

- The risk of **malware** entering the network through remote access.
- If a remote computer is compromised, an intruder may send malicious code through a VPN to enter the organization's private network.
- The risk of poor configuration management.

Virtual desktop infrastructure environment

Another method for remote connection is the use of a **virtual desktop infrastructure (VDI)** environment. In a VDI setup, each user has their own dedicated **Windows**-based system which can be configured to their liking. Users can connect to virtual desktops from any location with any device.

In a VDI setup, all processing is done on the host server. Also, the data resides on the host server rather than the users' devices. It helps to safeguard the data if an endpoint device is lost or compromised.

Also, it establishes the segregation of personal and organizational data while using a remote PC. A user cannot download or copy data from the virtual desktop to their personal computer. This serves as a control against unauthorized copies of business data on a user's PC.

Key aspects from the CISM exam perspective

The following table covers some of the key aspects from the CISM exam perspective:

Question	Possible answer
What is the advantage of using a VDI from a security perspective?	It establishes the segregation of personal and organizational data while using a remote PC. This serves as a control against unauthorized copies of business data on a user's PC.
What is the benefit of VPN tunneling?	It provides a secure communication channel.

Table 7.4 – Key aspects from the CISM exam perspective

Questions

1. What is the most effective method for ensuring confidentiality in a wireless access point?

    A. Deploying a wireless intrusion prevention system.

    B. Prevent broadcasting of the **service set identifier** (**SSID**).

    C. Deploy wired equivalent privacy (WEP) authentication.

    D. Enforce a VPN over a wireless network.

    Answer: D. Enforce a VPN over a wireless network.

    Explanation: Deploying a VPN over a wireless network is the best method to ensure confidentiality. A VPN is used to secure the wireless network. It provides a platform for remote users to connect to the organization's private network. Deploying a wireless intrusion prevention system would not prevent sniffing of the information. Preventing broadcasting of the SSID is a good control, however, it does not prevent sniffing of the information. WEP authentication is a compromised protocol.

2. What is the most effective way to ensure the confidentiality of data transmitted over the internet?

A. A VPN.

B. An intrusion prevention system.

C. Routers.

D. Two-factor authentication.

Answer: A. A VPN.

Explanation: A VPN is used to extend a private network through the use of the internet in a secure manner. It provides a platform for remote users to connect to the organization's private network. To enable a VPN, a virtual point-to-point connection is established by way of dedicated circuits of tunneling protocols. VPN technology ensures the safeguarding of critical data traveling over the internet. The other options do not impact the confidentiality of data transmission over the internet.

3. What is the benefit of VPN tunneling?

A. It ensures secured communication.

B. It ensures strong authentication.

C. It ensures strong passwords.

D. It ensures strong network connectivity.

Answer: A. It ensures secured communication.

Explanation: VPN tunneling helps to hide the IP address and encrypt the messages, thereby securing the communication channel. The other options are not relevant for VPN tunneling.

4. What is the function of a VPN?

A. To implement security policies.

B. To compress data traveling in the network.

C. To hide data traveling in the network.

D. To verify the content of the data packet.

Answer: C. To hide data traveling in the network.

Explanation: The objective of a VPN is to hide data from the sniffer. A VPN uses data encapsulation or the tunneling method to encrypt the traffic payload for the secure transmission of the data.

5. Which of the following ensures security in a VPN?

    A. Data diddling.

    B. Data encapsulation.

    C. Data hashing.

    D. Data compression.

    Answer: B. Data encapsulation.

    Explanation: A VPN uses data encapsulation or the tunneling method to encrypt the traffic payload for the secure transmission of the data. A VPN is enabled either through IPSec tunnel mode or IPSec transport mode. In IPSec tunnel mode, the entire packet (including the header) is encrypted, whereas in IPSec transport mode, only the data portion is encrypted. Mere data hashing and compression will not ensure data confidentiality. Data diddling is an attack method.

6. What is the benefit of using VDI from a security perspective?

    A. It helps to reduce the IT resource budget.

    B. It helps to segregate personal and organizational data while using a remote computer.

    C. It helps to wipe data remotely.

    D. It waives the requirement of anti-malware software for the remote computer.

    Answer: B. It helps to segregate personal and organizational data while using a remote computer.

    Explanation: Through VDI, users can connect to their desktop from a remote location. Users can connect to virtual desktops from any location with any device. In a VDI setup, all processing is done on the host server. Also, data resides on the host server rather than on users' devices. It helps to safeguard the data if an endpoint device is lost or compromised.

    VDI establishes the segregation of personal and organizational data while using a remote PC. A user cannot download or copy data from a virtual desktop to their personal computer. This serves as a control against unauthorized copies of business data on a user's PC. Remote data wiping is not possible through VDI. Also, anti-virus software is recommended, even for a VDI environment.

Biometrics

Biometric verification is a process through which a person can be uniquely identified and authenticated by verifying one or more of their biological features. Examples of these biometric identifiers include a palm, hand geometry, fingerprints, retina and iris patterns, voice, and DNA.

Biometrics – accuracy measure

The accuracy of a biometric system determines how well a system meets the objective. Accuracy measures determine the success factor of the biometric system. In this section, we will discuss a few biometrics accuracy measures.

False acceptance rate

The **false acceptance rate** (**FAR**) is the rate of acceptance of unauthorized users. For example, biometric controls will not restrict unauthorized people.

For example, if biometrics allows access to an unauthorized person, then it is referred to as a *false acceptance.*

False rejection rate

The **false rejection rate** (**FRR**) is the rate of rejection of the correct person (that is, an authorized person). For example, the biometric controls will reject even an authorized person.

In this scenario, if the biometric controls do not allow access to an authorized person, then it is referred to as a *false rejection.*

Cross error rate or equal error rate

The **cross error rate** (**CER**) or **equal error rate** (**EER**) is the rate at which the FAR and FRR are equal. A biometric system with the lowest CER or EER is the most effective system. A biometric system with the highest CER or EER is the least effective system.

Relation between FAR and FRR

It must be noted that both the FAR and FRR are inversely proportionate. An increase in the FAR will result in a decrease in the FRR and vice versa. Also, if the FRR increases, the FAR will decrease. The CER or EER is an adjustment point where both the FAR and FRR are equal.

The most reliable biometric identifiers

Among the current biometric identifiers, a retina scan is considered the most accurate and reliable identifier with the lowest FAR. An iris scan is also considered a very reliable biometric feature.

Biometric sensitivity tuning

A biometric control can be generally tuned in the following three ways:

- **High false rejection rate**: This provides the most stringent access control. Here, the biometric matching criteria are set extremely high and in a few cases, even valid users are rejected. But overall, it provides good protection for a critical database.

- **High false acceptance rate**: Here, access control is not rigorous. Biometric matching criteria are set at a low level. Sometimes even unauthorized users are accepted.

- **Equal error rate**: This is a moderate type of access control. Here, sensitivity is tuned in such a way that the FRR is equal to the FAR (that is, there is neither high false rejection nor high false acceptance).

Thus, a critical database security manager would always prefer a high FRR. That is, biometric matching criteria that are set at a high level.

Control over the biometric process

Due to its immense benefit and ease of use and maintenance, biometric recognition is being widely used in large organizations for employee identification and authentication. Organizations are trying to increase the use of biometric features, as depicted in the following (lighthearted) illustration:

Figure 7.1 – Biometric reader

The security manager should verify that appropriate controls are in place to protect the biometric information of the users. The following are some of the important security aspects of biometrics:

- Biometric information should be securely stored.
- Access to biometric information should only be available to authorized staff.
- The data flow between biometric devices and the server should be encrypted.
- User access should be revoked immediately on employee resignation or termination.

The information security manager should be aware of the different types of biometric access.

Types of biometric attacks

The CISM aspirant should be aware of the following attacks to exploit the weaknesses in biometric controls:

- **Replay attack**: In a replay attack, an intruder attempts to use residual biometric characteristics (for example, residual fingerprints left on a biometric device) to gain unauthorized access.

- **Brute force attack**: In a brute force attack, the attacker sends numerous biometric samples with the objective of causing a malfunction in the biometric device.

- **Cryptographic attack**: In a cryptographic attack, an attacker attempts to obtain information by targeting algorithms or the encrypted information transmitted between biometric devices and access control systems.

- **Mimic attack**: In a mimic attack, the attacker attempts to reproduce a fake biometric feature of a genuine biometric user. For example, imitating the voice of an enrolled user.

Questions

1. Which of the following is considered the most accurate and reliable biometric identifier with the lowest FAR?

    A. Voice wave.

    B. Face identification.

    C. Hand geometry.

    D. Retina scan.

    Answer: D. Retina scan.

    Explanation: Of the current biometric identifiers, a retina scan is considered to be the most accurate and reliable, with the lowest FAR.

2. Which of the following biometric performance indicators should the information security auditor be most concerned about?

    A. False rejection rate (FRR)

    B. False acceptance rate (FAR)

    C. Cross error rate (CER)

    D. Equal error rate (ERR)

Answer: B. False acceptance rate (FAR)

Explanation: The information security auditor should be most concerned about the FAR as one of the critical performance indicators. This is because the FAR indicates the risk of unauthorized access to the systems.

3. Which of the following is considered the most important overall quantitative performance indicator for a biometric system?

    A. The percentage of employees enrolled.

    B. The false rejection rate (FRR).

    C. The false acceptance rate (FAR).

    D. The equal error rate (EER).

    Answer: D. The equal error rate (EER).

    Explanation: To evaluate the overall quantitative performance of a biometric system, it is important to consider the equal error rate (EER) or cross error rate (CER).

4. Which of the following is considered the most effective biometric system?

    A. That with the highest equal error rate (EER)

    B. That with the lowest equal error rate (EER)

    C. That with the highest false acceptance rate (FAR)

    D. That with the lowest false acceptance rate (FAR)

    Answer: B. That with the lowest equal error rate (EER)

    Explanation: The equal error rate (EER) is the rate at which the false acceptance rate (FAR) is equal to the false rejection rate (FRR). The biometric system with the lowest EER (or CER) is the most effective system. The biometric system with the highest EER (or CER) is the least effective system.

5. What is the accuracy of a biometric system evaluated by?

    A. The server utilization rate.

    B. The network connection rate.

    C. The system response rate.

    D. The FAR.

    Answer: D. The FAR.

Explanation: The FAR, FRR, and CER are the three main accuracy measures for a biometric control. The other options are more related to performance measures.

6. The effectiveness of a biometric system can be best measured by evaluating which of the following?

    A. The false acceptance rate (FAR).

    B. The cross error rate (CER).

    C. The staff enrolled rate.

    D. The false rejection rate (FRR).

    Answer: A. The false acceptance rate (FAR).

    Explanations: The FAR is the rate of acceptance of unauthorized users. For example, a *false acceptance* is when a biometric device provides access to an unauthorized person. For critical systems, the FAR should be nil or very low. In the case of a high FAR, the biometric control may not be considered effective.

7. An information security auditor is reviewing biometric controls for an organization's data center. Which of the following is the area of most concern?

    A. The use of a VPN for biometric access.

    B. Not all restricted areas are protected through biometric controls.

    C. Data in transit between biometric devices and the control server is not encrypted.

    D. Biometric controls were last reviewed over a year ago.

    Answer: C. Data in transit between biometric devices and the control server is not encrypted.

    Explanation: It is of utmost importance to implement a secure encrypted tunnel to protect the confidentiality of biometric data transmitted from biometric devices to the access control system. The other options are not as critical as the transmission of unencrypted data.

8. The information security auditor should review which of the following biometric life cycle stages first?

    A. The termination process.

    B. The enrollment stage.

C. The storage process.

D. The identification process.

Answer: B. The enrollment stage.

Explanation: The process of biometric control starts with the enrollment of the users and then is followed by the storage, verification, identification, and termination processes. The first step is to get the user enrolled in the device. The enrollment process involves an iterative process of getting biometric samples from the user, extracting the data from the sample, validating the data, and developing a final template, which is stored and used subsequently to authenticate the user.

9. Which of the following is considered the most effective access control mechanism?

   A. Session-based password.

   B. Iris scan.

   C. Password.

   D. Photo ID card.

   Answer: B. Iris scan.

   Explanation: Among all the features, iris scans are considered the most reliable for authentication. Intruders find it very difficult to duplicate iris scans for bypassing biometric controls. The other options are not as reliable as iris scan.

10. Which of the following is considered the most effective access control mechanism?

    A. Fingerprint scanner.

    B. Password.

    C. Cipher lock.

    D. Electronic access card.

    Answer: A. Fingerprint scanner.

    Explanation: Of all the options, the fingerprint scanner can be considered the most reliable control. A fingerprint is a biometric control that is very difficult to break. It is very difficult for the intruder to duplicate the fingerprint of the user, as no two fingerprints are identical (or, the chance of this happening is very rare), so authentication can be made with confidence. The other options are not as reliable as the fingerprint scanner.

11. An attack with the unauthorized use of residual biometric information is known as which of the following?

    A. A brute force attack.

    B. An encrypted attack.

    C. A mimic attack.

    D. A replay attack.

    Answer: D. A replay attack.

    Explanation: In a replay attack, the attacker makes use of a residual biometric characteristic (such as fingerprints left on a biometric device) to gain unauthorized access.

12. An attack in which the attacker attempts to reproduce the characteristics of a genuine biometric user is known as which of the following?

    A. A mimic attack.

    B. A cryptographic attack.

    C. A replay attack.

    D. A brute force attack.

    Answer. A. A mimic attack.

    Explanation: In a mimic attack, an attacker attempts to reproduce a fake biometric feature of a genuine biometric user. For example, imitating the voice of an enrolled user.

13. An attack in which data transmitted between a biometric device and an access control server is targeted is known as which of the following?

    A. A mimic attack.

    B. A brute force attack.

    C. A cryptographic attack.

    D. A replay attack.

    Answer: C. A cryptographic attack.

    Explanation: In a cryptographic attack, the attacker attempts to obtain information by targeting an algorithm or the encrypted information that is transmitted between a biometric device and an access control system.

14. An attack in which numerous biometric samples are sent to a biometric device is known as which of the following?

    A. A mimic attack.

    B. A brute force attack.

    C. A cryptographic attack.

    D. A replay attack.

    Answer: B. A brute force attack.

    Explanation: In a brute force attack, an attacker sends numerous biometric samples with the objective of causing a malfunction in the biometric device.

15. An organization is implementing biometric controls for access to its critical server. What will this do?

    A. Help to completely eliminate false acceptance.

    B. Require the enrollment of all users that access the critical server.

    C. Require separate passwords for access to biometric devices.

    D. Help to completely eliminate false rejections.

    Answer: B. Require the enrollment of all users that access the critical server.

    Explanation: For setting up a biometric control, the relevant users need to enroll themselves through the registration of their biometric feature. Options *A* and *D* are incorrect, as the risk of false acceptance as well as false rejection cannot be eliminated completely. Option *C* is not correct as the biometric reader is not required to be protected by a password.

16. The security manager generally desires following levels of sensitivity for a biometric access control for protecting a critical database?

    A. A high FRR.

    B. A high FAR.

    C. Equal error rate

    D. Below equal error rate

    Answer: A. A high FRR.

    Explanation: A biometric control can be generally tuned in the following three ways:

    High FRR: This is the most stringent access control. Here, biometric matching criteria are set as extremely high and in a few cases, even valid users are rejected. But overall, it provides good protection for a critical database.

High FAR: Here, access control is not rigorous. The biometric matching criteria are set at a low level. Sometimes even unauthorized users are accepted.

Equal error rate: This is a moderate type of access control. Here, sensitivity is tuned in such a way that the FRR is equal to the FAR. That is, there is neither high false rejection nor high false acceptance.

Thus, for a critical database, the security manager would always prefer a high FRR. That is, the biometric matching criteria are set at a high level.

Factors of authentication

There are three **authentication factors** that can be used for granting access:

- **Something you know**: For example, a password, PIN, or some other personal information

- **Something you have**: For example, a token, one-time password, or smart card

- **Something you are**: For example, biometric features, such as a fingerprint, iris scan, or voice recognition

Similarly, **two-factor authentication** means the use of two authentication methods from the preceding list. For critical systems, it is advisable to use more than one factor of authentication for granting access. The following illustration indicates the implementation of two-factor authentication in a lighthearted way:

Figure 7.2 – Two-factor authentication

From the user's perspective, two-factor authentication will require additional effort, and therefore the security manager should strike a balance between ease of access and control.

Password management

Strong and complex passwords should be one of the important requirements of an organization's password policy. The security manager should also ensure that the password policy is properly implemented. The most effective way to ensure compliance with password policy is to enable system-enforced password configuration.

Many organizations prefer implementing automatic password synchronization for administrative convenience. Password synchronization facilitates the synchronization of user passwords across different devices so a user needs to remember only a single password (instead of multiple passwords for different devices or machines).

This helps to reduce the administrative workload of resetting passwords. The following illustration indicates password management from the user's perspective:

Figure 7.3 – Password management

Frequent guidance and regularly raising awareness are key in promoting the requirements of the organization's password policy. This helps to persuade end users to comply.

Key aspects from the CISM exam perspective

The following table covers some of the key aspects from the CISM exam perspective:

Question	Possible answer
What is the best way to ensure that users comply with the password policy?	Enable system-enforced password configuration.
What is the prime benefit of implementing automated password synchronization?	Automated password synchronization decreases the overall administrative workload.

Table 7.5 – Key aspects from the CISM exam perspective

Questions

1. Which of the following provides the strongest authentication control for the logon to a corporate network?

    A. Biometrics.

    B. Encryption keys.

    C. **Secure socket layer (SSL)**.

    D. Two-factor authentication.

    Answer: D. Two-factor authentication.

    Explanation: Two-factor authentication is a more secure method of authentication as it requires more than one type of authentication. Apart from the password requirement, the user also needs to have an additional authentication factor to gain access. A biometric control alone is a single factor of authentication. Encryption is more relevant to the confidentiality of the information and is not concerned with authentication. SSL is used to establish encrypted links between the browser and web server and is not relevant for authentication.

2. How can you improve the password strengths of all the users in a large organization?

    A. Enable single sign-on.

    B. Conduct password audits.

    C. Discuss password policy with users.

    D. Install automatic strong password settings.

Answer: D. Install automatic strong password settings.

Explanation: Password strength can be best improved by installing automatic controls to allow only strong passwords, such as requiring the inclusion of numbers, special characters, and upper case letters. Single sign-on by itself does not ensure strong passwords. Conducting password audits and discussing the password policy will not be as effective as automatic password controls.

3. What is the best method for sharing passwords of a confidential file?

    A. Email the password along with a digital signature.

    B. Email the password and file together.

    C. Share passwords through an out-of-band channel.

    D. Enable delivery path tracing.

    Answer: C. Share passwords through an out-of-band channel.

    Explanation: Generally, passwords should not be shared through the same channel. It is risky to send the password to a file by the same channel as the file was sent. An out-of-band channel, such as the telephone, reduces the risk of interception. Digital signatures prove the identity of the sender of a message but do not ensure confidentiality. Delivery path tracing helps in the identification of the route used but does not confirm the identity of the sender.

4. The security manager noted that an application does not comply with one of the requirements of the password policy of the organization. What should they do?

    A. Report the non-compliance to the steering committee.

    B. Perform a risk assessment to quantify the risk.

    C. Separate the system from the corporate network.

    D. Accept the risk of non-compliance.

    Answer: B. Perform a risk assessment to quantify the risk.

    Explanation: The most important aspect for the security manager is to determine the impact of non-compliance by conducting a risk assessment. The effectiveness of the other options can be determined only after conducting a risk assessment.

5. What is the most effective method for ensuring that end users comply with the password requirements?

    A. Requirements for password complexity should be included in the security policy.

    B. Requesting acknowledgment from the users of compliance.

    C. Implementing a heavy penalty for non-compliance.

    D. Enabling system-enforced password configuration.

    Answer: D. Enabling system enforced password configuration.

    Explanation: Strong and complex passwords should be a requirement of the password policy. The security manager should also ensure that the password policy is properly implemented. The most effective way to ensure compliance with the password policy is to enable system-enforced password configuration. The other options are not as effective as system enabled control.

6. A critical device with a single user ID needs to be accessed by multiple users. What is the most efficient way to ensure that all access to the device is authorized?

    A. Enable access through a different device that requires adequate authentication.

    B. Change the password after each use.

    C. Purchase multiple versions of the device.

    D. Review access logs to detect the unauthorized users.

    Answer: A. Enable access through a different device that requires adequate authentication.

    Explanation: Authentication through a separate device helps to prevent unauthorized access and at the same time the sharing of the user ID is prevented. It also helps to capture the logs for the user access. Purchasing multiple devices and changing the password after each user is not feasible and cost-effective. Analyzing the log will not be effective, as there is only one user ID.

7. What is the primary benefit of automated password synchronization?

    A. It decreases the overall administrative workload.

    B. The availability of a permanent password.

    C. It increases security between multi-tier applications.

    D. Compliance with the information security policy.

Answer: A. It decreases the overall administrative workload.

Explanation: Many organizations prefer implementing automatic password synchronization for administrative convenience. Password synchronization facilitates the synchronization of user passwords across different devices so a user needs to remember only a single password in place of multiple passwords for different devices or machines. Password synchronization facilitates the smooth administration of password management, as it reduces the workload of resetting the passwords. Password synchronization by itself does not improve the security between multi-tier applications.

8.   What is the best way to improve the effectiveness of the password policy?

A. Conduct password audits.

B. Implement a single sign-on system.

C. Conduct frequent security awareness programs.

D. Implement a heavy penalty for non-compliance.

Answer: C. Conduct frequent security awareness programs.

Explanation: Frequent guidance and awareness is a key factor in promoting the requirements of the password policy and helps to persuade end users to comply. The other options will not be as effective as having frequent security awareness programs.

Wireless network

A network connection not involving the use of a cable or wire is known as a **wireless network**. A wireless network supports the communication between devices without the use of wires or cables. Cell phone networks and **wireless local area networks** (**WLANs**) are examples of wireless networks.

CISM aspirants should be aware of the following controls regarding the protection of wireless (**Wi-Fi**) security:

- Enabling encryption
- Enabling MAC filtering
- Disabling the SSID
- Disabling DHCP

Let's discuss each of these in detail.

Enabling encryption

Encryption is the process of converting data into an unreadable form. The process of encryption helps to scramble the data we send over the wireless network into a code. Encryption is an effective way of restricting intruders when it comes to accessing the wireless network. **Wi-Fi Protected Access (WPA)** and **WEP** are the two main types of encryption for wireless networks. For wireless connection, **WPA 2** is the strongest encryption standard. These encryption methods only protect data in transit and not data on the device.

Enabling MAC filtering

Each system/PC/laptop/mobile has a unique identification number, which is known as the **MAC address**. This control will help us to allow access to only selected and authorized devices. Hence, the router will restrict other unauthorized devices in terms of accessing the network. Blacklist features can be used to specifically reject some MAC addresses.

MAC addresses can be easily sniffed and then spoofed to gain unauthorized access, and hence MAC address filtering alone is not considered a good security mechanism.

Disabling the SSID

The **SSID** is the name of the wireless network. The SSID is also known as the **network ID**. If not disabled, this name is viewable to anyone with a wireless device within reachable distance of the network.

Such open broadcasting is not required or necessary unless it is purposefully done to promote the Wi-Fi network, as in the case of a hotel/restaurant/lounge/mall, and so on.

Disabling DHCP

Dynamic Host Configuration Protocol (DHCP) is a network management tool. It automatically assigns an IP address to each device connected to the network, which will help the devices to communicate with other IP networks. If DHCP is disabled, then the IP address can be configured manually – that is, using **static IP addresses**, and this helps to reduce the risk of unauthorized access.

Common attack methods and techniques for a wireless network

The following are some common attack methods for wireless networks.

Rogue access point

A **rogue access point** is installed by a hacker on a secure network to gain unauthorized access. A rogue access point facilitates a wireless backdoor for unauthorized users. Rogue access points can bypass the network firewalls and other monitoring devices and expose a network to attack. A rogue access attack specifically occurs on wireless networks.

War driving

War driving is a technique used by a hacker to search wireless networks from a moving car or vehicle by using a laptop or other wireless device with hacking tools or software. The same technique is used by information security auditors to test the wireless security of an organization.

War walking

War walking is a similar process to war driving, where hackers search wireless networks by walking with their devices instead of driving. This is commonly done in public areas, such as malls, hotels, and city streets.

War chalking

War chalking is a technique of drawing a mark or symbol in a public area indicating the existence of an open wireless network. These symbols are subsequently used by others to exploit weak wireless networks.

Key aspects from the CISM exam perspective

The following table covers some of the key aspects from the CISM exam perspective:

Questions	Possible answer
Which technique is used by hackers to search wireless networks from a moving car or vehicle by using hacking tools and software? (The same technique is used by information security auditors to test wireless security).	War driving.
Which is the strongest encryption standard for wireless connections?	WPA 2 (Wi-Fi Protected Access).

Table 7.6 – Key aspects from the CISM exam perspective

Questions

1. What is the most effective way to implement a secure wireless network?

   A. Enable MAC address filtering.

   B. Enable the WPA 2 protocol.

   C. Enable the WEP protocol.

   D. Two-factor authentication

   Answer: B. Enable the WPA 2 protocol.

   Explanation: Currently, the most secure protocol for wireless networks is the WPA 2 protocol. MAC filtering is a good practice, however, it can be easily sniffed with technical tools. WEP is no longer a secure encryption mechanism. Two-factor authentication will not address the issue of network sniffing.

2. Which of the following exposures is introduced specifically by the use of WLAN technology?

   A. Buffer overflows.

   B. Data spoofing.

   C. Rogue access points.

   D. Session hijacking.

   Answer: C. Rogue access points.

   Explanation: A rogue access point is installed by a hacker on a secured network to gain unauthorized access. A rogue access point facilitates wireless backdoors for unauthorized user access. Rogue access points can bypass the network firewalls and other monitoring devices and expose a network to attack. Rogue access attacks specifically occur on wireless networks, whereas the other options do not depend on the use of WLAN technology.

Different attack methods

The CISM aspirant should be aware of the following methods and techniques for information system attacks:

- **Alteration attack**: In this type of attack, alteration or modification of the data or code is done without authorization. Cryptographic code is used to prevent alteration attacks.

- **Botnets**: Botnets are compromised computers, also known as *zombie computers*. They are primarily used to run malicious software for **distributed denial of service (DDoS)** attacks, adware, or spam.

- **Buffer overflow**: A buffer overflow is also known as a buffer overrun. They are normally due to a software coding error, which can be exploited by an attacker to gain unauthorized access to the system. A buffer overflow occurs when more data is fed to the buffer than it can handle and excess data overflows to adjacent storage.

  Due to this, the attacker gets an opportunity to manipulate the coding errors for malicious actions.

  A major cause of buffer overflows is poor programming and coding practices.

- **Denial of service attack (DOS)**: In a DOS attack, a network or system is flooded with an enormous amount of traffic with an objective to shut down the network or the system.

- **Data diddling**: In a data diddling attack, data is modified as it enters a computer system.

  This is done mostly by a data entry clerk or a computer virus.

  Data is altered before computer security can protect the data.

  Data diddling requires very limited technical knowledge.

  Apparently, there are no preventive controls for data diddling, and as a result, organizations need to rely on compensatory controls.

- **Dumpster diving**: In a dumpster diving attack, an attempt is made to retrieve confidential information from the trash or a garbage bin.

  To address the risk of dumpster diving, employees should be made aware of this kind of risk by way of frequent security awareness training.

  A document discarding policy should be in place that defines the appropriate method of discarding various types of information. One example is the use of shredders to destroy documents. The following illustration indicates a dumpster diving attempt:

In a dumpster diving attack, intruders look for critical information in a garbage bin.

Figure 7.4 – Dumpster diving

- **War dialing**: War dialing is a technique in which tools are used to automatically scan lists of telephone numbers to determine the details of computers, modems, and other machines.

- **War driving**: In a war driving attack, attempts are made to locate and get unauthored access to wireless networks with the use of specialized tools.

  An intruder drives or walks around the building with specialized tools to identify unsecured networks.

  The same technique is used by information security auditors to identify unsecured networks and thereby test the wireless security of an organization.

- **Eavesdropping**: Through eavesdropping, an intruder gathers the information flowing in the network through unauthorized methods.

  Using different tools and techniques, sensitive information including emails, passwords, and even keystrokes can be captured by the intruder.

- **Email bombing**: In this technique, attackers repeatedly send an identical email to a particular address.

- **Email spamming**: In this attack, unsolicited emails are sent to thousands of users.

- **Email spoofing**: In this attack, an email source is spoofed. It is often used to trick the user into giving out sensitive information.

- **Flooding**: This is a type of DOS attack that brings down a network by flooding it with a huge amount of traffic, and the host's memory buffer cannot handle this traffic.

- **Interrupt attack**: In this type of attack, the operating system is invoked to execute a particular task, thereby interrupting the ongoing task.

- **Juice jacking**: In this type of attack, data is copied from a device attached to a charging port (frequently available in public places).

  Charging points double as a data connection point. The following figure indicates a juice jacking attempt:

Juice Jacking – High risk at public charging points

Figure 7.5 – Juice jacking

- **Malicious codes**:

  - **Trojan horse**: In this attack, malicious software is disguised as some legitimate software. Once installed, it starts taking control of the system.

  - **Logic bomb**: A program is executed when a certain event happens. For example, a logic bomb can be set to delete files or a database at a future date.

  - **Trap door**: This is also known as back door. A back door is an unauthorized method to gain entry into a system or database.

- **Man-in-the-middle attack**: In this attack, the attacker interferes while two devices are establishing a connection.

  Alternately, the attacker actively establishes a connection between two devices and pretends to each of them to be another device.

  If In case any device asks for authentication, it sends a request to the other device, and then a response is sent to the first device.

  Once a connection is established, the attacker can communicate and obtain information as they wish.

- **Masquerading**: In this type of attack, an intruder hides their original identity and acts as someone else. This is done to access a system or data that is restricted.

  The impersonation can be by either a person or a machine.

  Two-factor authentication requires the individual to authenticate themselves twice, which reduces the risk of a masquerading attack. It provides an additional security mechanism over and above passwords alone.

- **IP spoofing**: In IP spoofing, a forged IP address is used to break a firewall.

  IP spoofing can be considered the masquerading of a machine.

- **Message modification**: In this type of attack, a message is captured and altered, and deleted without authorization.

  These attacks can have a serious impact. For example, a modified message to a bank to make a payment.

- **Network analysis**: In this type of attack, an intruder creates a repository of information about a particular organization's internal network, such as internal addresses, gateways, and firewalls.

  The intruder then determines what services and operating systems are running on the targeted system and how they can be exploited.

- **Packet replay**: In this type of attack, an intruder captures the data packet as data moves along a vulnerable network.

- **Pharming**: In this type of attack, the traffic of a website is redirected to a bogus website.

  This is done by exploiting a vulnerability in the DNS server.

  Pharming is a major concern for e-commerce websites and online banking websites.

- **Piggybacking**: In this type of attack, which refers to a physical security vulnerability, the intruder follows an authorized person through a secured door to gain unauthorized access.

The following illustration indicates a piggybacking attempt.

In piggybacking and tailgating, the intruder attempts to follow an authorized person to enter the gate.

Figure 7.6 – Piggybacking

- **Password sniffing**: In a password sniffing attack, tools are used to listen to all the traffic in the network's **TCP/IP** packets and extract the usernames and passwords. This tool is known as a *password sniffer*.

These passwords are then used to gain unauthorized access to the system.

- **Parameter tampering**: The unauthorized modification of web application parameters with a malicious aim is known as *parameter tampering*.

As the hidden files in the web page are not visible, a developer may feel safe to pass the data without proper validation. This creates a risk, as an intruder may intercept the hidden data and then modify the parameters for malicious purposes.

- **Privilege escalation**: In a privilege escalation attack, high-level system authority is obtained by an employee through some unauthorized methods by exploiting security flaws.

- **Race condition**: This is also known as a **time of check (TOC)** or **time of use (TOU)** attack.

In this attack, an intruder exploits a small time window between the point in time a service is accessed and the point in time a security control is applied.

The longer the gap between the TOU and the time of service, the higher the chances are of race condition attacks being successful.

- **Salami**: In this technique, a small amount of money is sliced from a computerized transaction and transferred to unauthorized accounts.

- **Social engineering**: In a social engineering attack, an attempt is made to obtain sensitive information from users by tricking and manipulating people.

  In social engineering attacks, the attacker does not require any technical tools and techniques to obtain information.

  Social engineering is generally conducted through dialogue, interviews, inquiries, and other social methods of interaction.

  The objective of social engineering is to exploit human nature and weaknesses for obtaining critical and sensitive information.

  By implementing adequate and effective security awareness training, the consequences of social engineering attacks can be minimized.

- **Shoulder surfing**: In shoulder surfing attacks, an intruder or a camera captures sensitive information by looking over the shoulder of the user entering their details, which are visible on the computer screen.

  Passwords entered should be masked on the computer screen to prevent shoulder surfing attacks. The following figure illustrates a shoulder surfing attack:

In a shoulder surfing attack, someone is watching your activity.

Figure 7.7 – Shoulder surfing

- **Traffic analysis**: In this attack, communication patterns between entities are studied and information is deduced.

- **Virus**: A virus is a type of malicious code that can self-replicate and spread from computer to computer.

  A virus can take control of a user's computer and can delete or alter sensitive files. It can also disrupt system functioning.

- **Worms**: Worms are destructive programs that can destroy sensitive data. However, worms do not replicate like a virus.

- **Biometric attacks**:

  - **Replay attack**: In replay attacks, the attacker makes use of residual biometric characteristics (such as fingerprints left on a biometric device) to gain unauthorized access.

  - **Brute force attack**: In brute force attacks, the attacker sends numerous biometric samples to a biometric device with an objective of making it malfunction.

  - **Cryptographic attack**: In cryptographic attacks, the attacker attempts to obtain information by targeting algorithms or the encrypted information that is transmitted between a biometric device and an access control system.

  - **Mimic attack**: In a mimic attack, the attacker attempts to reproduce fake biometric features of a genuine biometric user. For example, imitating the voice of an enrolled user.

The CISM aspirant should also understand the difference between active and passive attacks. A **passive** attack is an attack in which only information is captured but does not modify, insert, or delete the data traffic. Examples of passive attacks include traffic analysis, network analysis, and eavesdropping. In an active attack, damage is done by modifying or deleting the data.

Key aspects from the CISM exam perspective

The following table covers some of the key aspects from the CISM exam perspective:

Questions	Possible answer
An attack in which internet traffic appears to originate from the internal IP address of the organization is?	IP spoofing.
A hidden file on a web page can expose the risk of what?	Parameter tampering.

Questions	Possible answer
An attack that does not require any tools and techniques to obtain critical information is called what?	Social engineering.
What is a technique to reduce the risk of shoulder surfing?	Masking onscreen passwords.
What is an inherent risk in data entry processes, for which apparently there is no preventive control?	Data diddling.
What are examples of passive attacks?	Traffic analysis/network analysis/eavesdropping.
What technique is used to test wireless security?	War driving.
What is a technique to perform DDoS attacks, spamming, and other types of attacks by using other computers as zombies?	Botnet attack.
What is an attack that has the capability to circumvent two-factor authentication?	Man-in-the-middle attack.
What is a risk due to poor programming and coding practices?	Buffer overflows
What is a risk due to URL-shortening services?	Phishing.
What is the most effective defense to address the risk of a **structured query language** (**SQL**) injection attack?	Strict controls on input fields.
What is the most effective method for addressing the risk of masquerading attacks?	Two-factor authentication.
When a credit card is swiped on a **Point of Sale** (**POS**) machine, data is transferred from the card to the machine. What is the most important control for such a data transfer?	Encryption of data.

Table 7.7 – Key aspects from the CISM exam perspective

Questions

1. The use of hidden files on web pages to save information from client sessions can risk what?

   A. Race conditions.

   B. Parameter tampering.

   C. Flooding.

   D. Juice jacking.

   Answer: B. Parameter tampering.

   Explanation: The unauthorized modification of web application parameters with a malicious aim is known as parameter tampering. As the hidden files in the web page are not visible, the developer may feel safe to pass the data without proper validation. This creates a risk as the intruder may intercept the hidden data and modify the parameters for malicious purposes.

2. An attack in which internet traffic appears to originate from an internal IP address of the organization is known as what?

   A. A DDOS attack.

   B. Parameter tampering.

   C. IP spoofing.

   D. Port scanning.

   Answer: C. IP spoofing.

   Explanation: In IP spoofing, a forged IP address is used to break a firewall. In this type of attack, the intruder hides their original identity and acts as someone else. The intruder generally makes use of a spoofed internal IP address to get access to a system or data which is restricted for outside IP addresses. IP spoofing can be considered the masquerading of a machine.

3. Which of the following can be considered a significant risk for **voice over internet protocol (VoIP)** infrastructure?

   A. DDOS attacks.

   B. Social engineering.

   C. Juice jacking.

   D. Premium rate fraud.

Answer: A. DDOS attacks

Explanation: In DDOS attacks, a network or system is flooded with enormous amounts of traffic with the objective of shutting it down. DDOS attacks are considered a significant risk for VoIP infrastructure. Premium rate fraud occurs when a phone system is compromised and used for making long-distance calls. However, a more significant risk is a DDOS attack. Juice jacking and social engineering do not directly have any impact on VoIP infrastructure.

4. In which of the following attacks do employees run the task scheduler without authorization to access restricted applications?

A. Privilege escalation.

B. Race condition.

C. Social engineering.

D. Buffer overflow.

Answer: A. Privilege escalation.

Explanation: In a privilege escalation attack, high-level system authority is obtained by some unauthorized methods by exploiting security flaws. In this example, a security flaw in the task scheduler is exploited by an employee to gain unauthorized access to restricted applications.

5. Which of the following attacks does not require any tools and techniques to obtain critical information?

A. Privilege escalation.

B. Race condition.

C. Social engineering.

D. Buffer overflow.

Answer: C. Social engineering.

Explanation: In social engineering attacks, an attempt is made to obtain sensitive information from users by tricking and manipulating people. In social engineering attacks, the attacker does not require any technical tools and techniques to obtain information. Social engineering is generally conducted through dialogue, interviews, inquiries, and other social methods of interaction.

6. What is the most effective way to reduce the consequences of social engineering attacks?

    A. Implement robust physical security.

    B. Implement robust logical security.

    C. Provide security awareness training.

    D. Prepare an information security policy.

    Answer: C. Provide security awareness training.

    Explanation: The objective of social engineering is to exploit human nature and weaknesses to obtain critical and sensitive information. By providing effective security awareness training, the consequences of social engineering attacks can be minimized. The other options will not help to directly address the impact of social engineering attacks.

7. Passwords should be masked onscreen to prevent what?

    A. Juice jacking.

    B. Tailgating.

    C. Shoulder surfing.

    D. Impersonation.

    Answer: C. Shoulder surfing.

    Explanation: In a shoulder surfing attack, the intruder or a camera captures sensitive information by looking over the shoulder of the user entering their details, which are visible onscreen. Passwords should be masked onscreen to prevent shoulder surfing attacks.

8. Mandatory processes of reading employee ID badges at the entrance are to prevent which of the following?

    A. Shoulder surfing.

    B. Piggybacking.

    C. Race condition.

    D. Dumpster diving.

    Answer: B. Piggybacking.

    Explanation: In this type of attack, the intruder follows an authorized person through a secured door to gain unauthorized access. Piggybacking is a physical security vulnerability.

9. Which of the following attacks is considered an inherent risk in data entry processes, for which apparently there is no preventive control?

    A. Shoulder surfing.

    B. Data diddling.

    C. Race condition.

    D. Dumpster diving.

    Answer: B. Data diddling.

    Explanation: In a data diddling attack, data is modified as it enters a computer system. This attack is generally carried out by a data entry clerk or a computer virus. Data is altered before computer security can protect the data. Data diddling only requires very limited technical knowledge. There are no preventive controls for data diddling, and hence organizations need to rely on compensatory controls.

10. Which of the following is considered a passive cybersecurity attack?

    A. Traffic analysis.

    B. Juice jacking.

    C. DOS.

    D. IP spoofing.

    Answer: A. Traffic analysis.

    Explanation: Passive attacks are attacks in which information is collected but not modified. Examples of passive attacks include traffic analysis, network analysis, and eavesdropping. The other options are examples of active attacks.

11. A password sniffing attack can do which of the following?

    A. Help intruders to impersonate another user.

    B. Help intruders to bypass physical security.

    C. Help intruders to gain unauthorized access to a system.

    D. Help to launch DDOS attacks

    Answer: C. Help intruders to gain unauthorized access to a system.

    Explanation: In a password sniffing attack, tools are used to listen to all of the traffic in the network's TCP/IP packets and extract usernames and passwords. This tool is known as a *password sniffer*. This password can then be used to gain unauthorized access to the system.

12. Which technique is used to test the wireless security of an organization?

    A. War driving.

    B. Juice jacking.

    C. War dialing.

    D. Social engineering.

    Answer: A. War driving.

    Explanation: War driving is a technique for locating and gaining access to wireless networks with the use of specialized tools. An attacker drives or walks around the building to identify unsecured networks. The same technique is used by information security auditors to identify unsecured networks and thereby test the wireless security of an organization.

13. Which of the following is used for DDOS attacks?

    A. Phishing techniques.

    B. Logic bombs.

    C. Botnets.

    D. Social engineering.

    Answer: C. Botnets.

    Explanation: A botnet is a network of zombie computers controlled by an attacker. Botnets can be used to perform DDOS attacks, spamming, and other types of attacks.

14. Wireless infrastructure increases which of the following risks?

    A. Port scanning.

    B. War driving.

    C. War dialing.

    D. Back door.

    Answer: B. War driving.

    Explanation: War driving is a technique used to identify weaknesses in wireless infrastructure. War driving is a technique for locating and getting access to a wireless network with the use of specialized tools, such as wireless ethernet cards. The intruder drives or walks around the building to identify unsecured networks.

15. In which of the following attacks is residual biometric information used to gain unauthorized access?

    A. Brute force attacks.

    B. Encrypted attacks.

    C. Mimic attacks.

    D. Replay attacks.

    Answer: D. Replay attacks.

    Explanation: In replay attacks, the attacker makes use of residual biometric characteristics (such as fingerprints left on a biometric device) to gain unauthorized access.

16. Which of the following attack methods has the capability to circumvent two-factor authentication?

    A. DDOS attacks.

    B. Man-in-the-middle attacks.

    C. Juice jacking.

    D. Brute force attacks.

    Answer: B. Man-in-the-middle attacks.

    Explanation: In this attack, an attacker interferes while two devices are establishing a connection. If any device asks for authentication, it sends a request to the other device and then the response is sent to the first device. Once a connection is established, the attacker can communicate and obtain information as they wish, thus circumventing two-factor authentication.

17. Which of the following risks increases due to poor programming and coding practices?

    A. Juice jacking.

    B. Social engineering.

    C. Buffer overflows.

    D. Brute force attacks.

    Answer: C. Buffer overflows.

Explanation: Buffer overflows are also known as buffer overruns. They normally occur due to a software coding error, which can be exploited by an attacker to gain unauthorized access to the system. Buffer overflows occur when more data is fed to the buffer than it can handle. As a result, excess data overflows to adjacent storage.

Due to this, an attacker gets an opportunity to manipulate the coding errors for malicious actions. A major cause for buffer overflows is poor programming and coding practices.

18. Which of the following risks increases due to URL-shortening services?

    A. Social engineering.

    B. Phishing.

    C. Vishing.

    D. DDOS attacks.

    Answer: B. Phishing.

    Explanation: URL-shortening services convert long URLs (web addresses) into short versions. A hacker can attempt to fool users by using URL-shortening services for the creation of URLs resembling a genuine website. This is done to spread malicious software or collect sensitive data by way of phishing.

19. Social engineering can succeed due to which of the following?

    A. Technical errors.

    B. Poor judgment.

    C. Highly qualified intruders.

    D. Computer errors.

    Answer: B. Poor judgment.

    Explanation: Social engineering can succeed due to the poor judgment of an employee who provides sensitive information to the intruder. The intruder can build a level of trust with the user/employee and take advantage of this.

20. Which of the following attacks is used to gather information about encrypted data being transmitted over a network?

    A. DDOS attacks.

    B. IP spoofing.

C. Traffic analysis.

D. Masquerading.

Answer: C. Traffic analysis.

Explanation: In traffic analysis, an intruder attempts to capture and analyze the nature of a traffic flow between hosts – for example, the frequency of messages, the length of messages, the session lengths, and other relevant information. With this technique, the intruder can attempt to gain valuable information from the traffic, even when the content of the messages is encrypted.

21. Which of the following is the most effective way to reduce the risk of dumpster diving?

    A. Security awareness training.

    B. A documented data discarding policy.

    C. Placing CCTV above bins.

    D. Purchasing high-speed shredders.

    Answer: A. Security awareness training.

    Explanation: Dumpster diving is the technique in which the intruder attempts to gather sensitive information from bins and other areas where documents are not properly discarded. Users should be appropriately trained in how to discard materials that contain sensitive information. In the absence of security awareness training, the other options may not be effective at preventing the risk of dumpster diving.

22. What is the best way to prevent intruders masquerading as authorized users and connecting to the corporate network?

    A. Encrypting the network traffic.

    B. Deploying an intrusion prevention system.

    C. Two-factor authentication.

    D. Use of digital signatures.

    Answer: C. Two-factor authentication.

    Explanation: Two-factor authentication requires the individual to authenticate themselves twice, which reduces the risk of masquerading. It provides an additional security mechanism over and above passwords alone. The other options are not relevant for authentication and access.

23. What is the most important aspect of securing credit card data when using the card with the POS device?

    A. Authorization.

    B. Authentication.

    C. Encryption.

    D. Digital signature.

    Answer: C. Encryption.

    Explanation: The data communication from the card to the POS device should be encrypted to protect the confidentiality of the data. Strong encryption of data should be used to protect the cardholder data. The other options will not prevent the reading of data by the intruder.

24. An SQL injection attack can be best prevented by which of the following?

    A. An intrusion prevention system.

    B. An intrusion detection system.

    C. Periodic audits.

    D. Periodic security awareness.

    Answer: A. An intrusion prevention system.

    Explanation: In an SQL injection attack, an SQL query is injected or inserted in the input field of the application. By entering a command in an input field of the web page, the hacker tries to bypass the authentication requirements. SQL injection attacks occur at the application layer. Most intrusion prevention systems will detect at least basic sets of SQL injections and will be able to stop them. The other options will not be effective.

25. Man-in-the-middle attacks between two computers can be prevented by which of the following?

    A. Using two-factor authentication.

    B. Establishing connections through an IP security v6 VPN.

    C. Conducting periodic security audits.

    D. Deploying IDS.

    Answer: B. Establishing connections through an IP security v6 VPN.

Explanation: IP security v6 is resilient to man-in-the-middle attacks. It includes the source and destination IP address within the encrypted portion, and hence effectively prevents man-in-the-middle attacks. The other options are not effective for preventing man-in-the-middle attacks.

26. The risk of tailgating/piggybacking can be best addressed by which of the following?

    A. Access cards.

    B. Photo identity cards.

    C. Awareness training.

    D. Biometric readers.

    Answer: C. Awareness training.

    Explanation: Piggybacking/tailgating is when an intruder follows authorized users to enter a restricted area. The best method for preventing piggybacking is to provide training to all authorized employees to be careful when entering restricted areas. Authorized users should challenge such intruders.

27. A form-based authentication control requiring the user to input their user ID and password can be bypassed by which of the following?

    A. Use of a weak password.

    B. SQL injection attacks.

    C. Lack of an account lockout facility.

    D. Lack of a session time-out facility.

    Answer: B. SQL injection attacks.

    Explanation: By entering a command in an input field of the web page, the hacker tries to bypass the authentication requirements. SQL injection attacks occur at the application layer. Most intrusion prevention systems will detect at least basic sets of SQL injections and will be able to stop them. After gaining access, the intruder can read the confidential data, modify the database by updating or deleting the data, or execute the administration operations on the database. The best way to protect against SQL injection attacks is to implement input controls so that programming commands can be rejected. The other options, though areas of weakness, will not lead to the bypassing of authentication requirements.

28. Which of the following exposures is introduced by the use of the **simple network management protocol v2 (SNMP v2)**?

    A. Slow network bandwidth.

    B. Unstable processing.

    C. Cleartext authentication.

    D. Cross-site scripting.

    Answer: C. Cleartext authentication.

    Explanation: The objective of SNMP is to monitor network behavior. SNMP collects and organizes the information about managed devices on the network. SNMP is also used to change the device's behavior. Devices such as routers, modems, switches, servers, printers, workstations, and more support SNMP.

    One of the security-related vulnerabilities associated with the use of SNMP is that it uses cleartext passwords for authentication. Passwords can be easily sniffed and reused.

29. What is the best way to prevent brute force attacks?

    A. Implement a maximum password age.

    B. User education.

    C. Install automatic strong password settings.

    D. Enable system lockout on multiple wrong password attempts.

    Answer: D. Enable system lockout on multiple wrong password attempts.

    Explanation: A brute force attack uses trial-and-error to guess the password of the targeted user. In a brute force attack, the attacker submits many passwords with the hope of eventually guessing a password correctly. The attacker systematically checks all possible passwords until the correct one is found. The best way to prevent brute force attacks is to enable system lockout when multiple wrong attempts are recorded. Generally, three attempts should be allowed, and the system should be locked after the fourth wrong attempt.

Summary

In this chapter, we discussed the infrastructure and architecture of information security. This chapter will help the CISM candidate to understand important methods, tools, and techniques to develop security programs in an effective and efficient manner.

We also learned about security architecture in line with industry best practices. We discussed access control requirements, including biometrics and factors of authentication.

In our next chapter, we will discuss the practical aspects of developing and managing information security programs.

8
Practical Aspects of Information Security Program Development Management

In this chapter, we will discuss the practical aspects of information security program development management and look at the methods, tools, and techniques for the development of an information security program. This chapter will help CISM aspirants understand the different types of cloud computing services. We will also discuss the different types of controls.

The following topics will be covered in this chapter:

- Cloud computing
- Controls and countermeasures
- Penetration testing

- Security program metrics and monitoring
- Common information security program challenges

Let's look at each one of the preceding topics in detail.

Cloud computing

Cloud computing is the process of utilizing the servers hosted on the internet for storing and processing data instead of a personal computer or local server. Cloud computing enables the user to access computer resources through the internet from anywhere without worrying about the physical availability of the resources. The following are some of the characteristics of cloud computing:

- It provides the capability for organizations to access data or applications from anywhere, anytime, and from almost any device.
- It provides the capability for the organization to scale IT resources as per the business requirements at the optimum cost.
- It provides the capability to monitor, control, and report usage of the resources.

Resources such as storage, processing power, memory, network bandwidth, and virtual machines can be used through cloud computing.

Cloud computing – deployment models

The following are the important details of the deployment models of cloud computing.

The private cloud

A private cloud is used for the exclusive benefit of the organization. A private cloud is considered the most secure type of deployment as it can be controlled and centralized by the organization. A cloud server is either deployed on-premises or off-premises.

The public cloud

The public cloud is open to all on the basis of pay per use. The public cloud is considered highly scalable as services can be reduced or increased as per the requirements of the organization.

It is very important to consider the following requirements for the use of the public cloud:

- Legal and regulatory compliance (such as data localization)
- Backup
- Right to audit
- Security requirements

The community cloud

Cloud services are used by specific communities of consumers who have shared concerns. A community cloud can be managed by one of the organizations or by a third party. An area of concern when using a community cloud is that data may be stored in the same cloud as the data of a competitor.

The hybrid cloud

The hybrid cloud is a combination of the private and the public cloud. An organization initially uses the private cloud and then, for additional requirements, the public cloud is used. It makes cloud storage complex as more than one model is used.

Types of cloud services

A CISM aspirant should understand the following types of cloud service models:

- **Infrastructure as a Service (IaaS):**

  - In this type of cloud service, services such as data storage, processing capability, memory, and network resources are provided to the user as per their requirements.

  - This helps the user to utilize computing resources without having to own or manage their own resources.

  - The end users or IT architects will use **virtual machines** (**VMs**) as per their requirements.

  - The user is not required to maintain or manage the physical servers as they are managed by service providers.

  - Some examples of infrastructure service providers are Google Compute Engine, **Amazon Web Services** (**AWS**), OpenStack, and so on.

- **Software as a Service (SaaS):**

  - With the help of SaaS, an end user can access an application through the internet.

  - Instead of local storage and processing, the application is hosted on a cloud managed by a third-party service provider.

  - Users are not required to maintain or control the application development platform and related infrastructure.

  - For example, users can make their own Word document in Google Docs online without having installed Office software, or edit a photo online on `pixlr.com` without installing any editing software.

- **Platform as a Service (PaaS):**

  - In PaaS, users can develop and deploy an application on a development platform made available by the service provider.

  - In the traditional method, an application or software is developed in local machines and hosted in a local server.

  - In PaaS, the application or software is developed online instead of on a local machine.

  - For example, applications such as Google App Engine, Windows Azure compute, and so on provide tools to develop applications.

Cloud computing – the security manager's role

Today, cloud computing is considered to be a solution to all computing problems and an end user may have many misunderstandings, as depicted in the following figure. The role of a security manager is to address all the misunderstandings so that security is not compromised:

Figure 8.1 – Cloud services

A security manager should consider the following risks and security controls for a cloud arrangement:

- Ensure compliance with relevant laws, regulations, and standards.

- Ensure compliance with privacy laws that restrict the movement of personal data to an offshore location.

- Ensure the availability of information systems and data on a continuous basis.

- Evaluate the business continuity and disaster recovery plan of the cloud service provider.

- Evaluate implemented controls for safeguarding the confidentiality, integrity, and availability of the data.

- Ensure that the SLA includes clauses with respect to the ownership and custody of the data and the security administration of cloud-related services.

- Ensure the inclusion of right to audit clauses in the SLA.

Key aspects from a CISM exam perspective

The following are some of the key aspects from an exam perspective:

Question	Possible answer
What is the benefit of cloud computing as compared to local hosting?	Ability to expand storage and bandwidth on demand

Table 8.1 – Key aspects from the CISM exam perspective

Questions

1. Which of the following is the best way to verify a cloud service provider's physical security arrangements?

   A. Verify the service provider's physical security policy and make sure that it is aligned with the organization's security policy.

   B. Verify a copy of independent security reviews or audit reports of the cloud service provider.

   C. Bind the service provider through a contract to align with the organization's security policy.

   D. Verify the service provider's disaster recovery plans and make sure that they include the necessary arrangements to protect the assets of the organization.

   Answer: B. Verify a copy of independent security reviews or audit reports of the cloud service provider.

   Explanation: The best way is to obtain and verify independent security reviews or audit reports of the cloud service provider. The other options are not sufficient in themselves to verify the physical security arrangements.

2. Which of the following is the most important clause in a contract with a cloud service provider?

   A. The contract should specify that upon contract expiration, a mandatory data wipe will be carried out in the presence of a representative of the enterprise.

   B. The contract should also include a non-compete clause.

   C. The contract should include a "right to audit" clause.

D. The contract should restrict the movement of data within the territory allowed as per the relevant law or regulation.

Answer: D. The contract should restrict the movement of data within the territory allowed as per the relevant law or regulation.

Explanation: It is very important to validate and verify whether the regulations of the location (where the infrastructure is located) is aligned with the enterprise's requirements. The contract should include terms to restrict the movement of assets within approved locations. The other options are also important, but option D should be considered to be the most important clause in a contract with a cloud service provider.

3. An information system auditor is reviewing the terms of the contract with a cloud service provider. Which of the following is the most important consideration?

    A. Clarity with respect to data ownership, data custody, and IPR-related requirements

    B. Clarity with respect to non-disclosure requirements

    C. Clarity with respect to data backup requirements

    D. Clarity with respect to data access requirements

    Answer: A. Clarity with respect to data ownership, data custody, and IPR-related requirements

    Explanation: It is very important that a contract has proper clarification with respect to data ownership, data custody, and other IPR-related requirements.

4. Which of the following would be of the most concern to the information system auditor with respect to the storage of personal customer information in a cloud environment?

    A. Inadequate disaster recovery procedure

    B. The data in the multi-tenancy environment being accessed by competitors

    C. Inadequate incident management procedure

    D. Inadequate business continuity arrangements

    Answer: B. The data in the multi-tenancy environment being accessed by competitors

    Explanation: The most important concern about the storage of personal data in a cloud environment is unauthorized access by competitors. Data leakage may have serious consequences.

5. An IS auditor is reviewing the terms of contract with a cloud service provider. Which of the following is the most important consideration?

    A. Physical security

    B. Compliance with legal requirements

    C. Data disposal policy

    D. Application disposal policy

    Answer: B. Compliance with legal requirements

    Explanation: The most important consideration is legal requirements, laws, and regulations. The other options are also important but option B should be considered to be the most important clause in a contract with a cloud service provider.

6. Which cloud deployment method is considered to be the most secure and to have very little chance of data leakage?

    A. Public cloud

    B. Private cloud

    C. Community cloud

    D. Hybrid cloud

    Answer: B. Private cloud

    Explanation: A private cloud is considered to be the most secure deployment method.

7. Which of the following is a benefit of cloud computing as compared to local hosting?

    A. Ability to expand storage and bandwidth on demand

    B. No training requirements for end users

    C. Ability to encrypt data

    D. Ability to enforce proper access control

    Answer: A. Ability to expand storage and bandwidth on demand

    Explanation: The main benefit of cloud computing is flexibility in obtaining the storage and bandwidth capacity as per the business requirements. This is very difficult to manage in a locally hosted environment. End user training is required irrespective of a cloud or local environment. Encryption and access control can be established in both a local and cloud environment.

Controls and countermeasures

Control is one of the important elements of an information security program. A major part of security management is the development, implementation, testing, and monitoring of controls. The objective of implementing a control is to address risks by preventing, detecting, or correcting undesirable events. Effective control provides reasonable assurance that business objectives will be achieved.

Countermeasures

Countermeasures are a type of control that is implemented to address specific threats. The objective of general controls is to protect information assets from all kinds of threats whereas countermeasures are put in place in response to a specific threat. Countermeasures are generally expensive and need to be implemented when existing general controls cannot mitigate specific threats. Countermeasures can be either technical or non-technical. The following are some examples of countermeasures:

- Disabling certain operating system commands to address a specific type of ransomware attack.

- Filtering all incoming emails may be impractical and expensive. In such a scenario, the countermeasure could be email filtering for known spammers.

- It may not be possible to restrict mobile phones on the premises. In such a scenario, the countermeasure could be cell phone jammers in sensitive areas.

- Countermeasures can also be non-technical, such as offering incentives for providing information with respect to a specific attack.

- Arranging specific security training sessions for employees who failed in a phishing exercise.

General controls and application-level controls

IT controls can be categorized as **IT general controls (ITGCs)** and **IT application controls (ITACs)**. ITGCs protect the overall information technology, which includes monitoring the network through firewalls and Intrusion Detection System (IDS), updating operating systems, the security of computer operations, and facility security. ITGCs support the entire organization in a centralized manner.

ITACs are designed specifically for an application. Examples of ITACs include transaction processing controls, user access controls, and other application-specific controls.

A security manager must ensure the appropriate deployment of ITGCs and ITACs in such a way that both should complement each other and not overlap. The limitations of ITGCs should be addressed by ITACs and vice versa. When general controls are weak, more emphasis needs to be placed on application-level control.

Control categories

A security manager should evaluate the current control environment to determine the effectiveness, efficiency, and adequacy of the controls implemented. For effective control management, a security manager should determine the following:

- Whether controls are adequate
- Whether controls have any scope for bypassing
- Whether controls are reviewed and tested
- Whether segregation of duties is maintained

A security manager should be aware of the following control categories:

Control category	Description
Preventive	The objective is to prevent an event from occurring. Examples include locked doors, user authentication, encryption, and so on.
Detective	The objective is to detect an event. Examples include audit, IDS, CCTV cameras, checksum, and so on.
Corrective	The objective is to correct error or omissions. Examples include data backup, forward error control, and so on.
Deterrent	The objective is to deter an event by providing a warning. Examples include warning signs and so on.
Directive	The objective is to mandate the behavior aspect by specifying dos and don'ts. Examples include an acceptable use policy.
Compensating	The objective is to address the absence of control or a weak control in a particular domain. Examples include compensating for a weak physical control by having a stringent logical access control.

Table 8.2 – Control categories

Failure mode – fail closed or fail open

A control can be designed to either fail closed or fail open. The failure mode of the control impacts safety, confidentiality, and availability. For example, in the event of the failure of an automatic door, an organization can opt for fail open (the door should remain open) or fail closed (the door should remain closed). In the case of fail open, confidentiality and integrity may be compromised, and in the case of fail closed, availability may be compromised. In such a situation, the risk should be determined for each element and a decision taken accordingly.

However, the safety of human life is always considered first. For example, even if a data center has highly confidential data, physical access controls should not fail closed and prevent an emergency exit.

Continuous monitoring

Continuous monitoring is the process of monitoring compliance on an ongoing basis. The prime objective of continuous monitoring is to provide immediate feedback about the performance of servers, networks, and cloud environments, which helps to enhance the operational, security, and business performance.

A security manager should understand that implementing continuous monitoring is expensive. Use of continuous monitoring may not be always feasible or practical so it should be used in areas where the risk is at its greatest level. Continuous monitoring is best deployed in areas where incidents may have a high impact and frequency.

Key aspects from a CISM exam perspective

The following are some of the key aspects from an exam perspective:

Question	Possible answer
Who is required to perform the day-to-day duties required to ensure the protection and integrity of data?	Data custodian (generally system administrator)
What is the most effective way to identify an application's back door?	Source code review
What is the risk of "fail open" in the event of a control failure?	Confidentiality and integrity may be compromised
What is the risk of "fail closed" in the event of a control failure?	Risk of availability

Question	Possible answer
What is the most important activity in the development of an information security program?	Control design and deployment
In which situation is continuous monitoring more cost-effective?	Areas where risk is high, that is, incidents may have high impact and frequency

Table 8.3 – Key aspects from the CISM exam perspective

Questions

1. What is the objective of corrective control?

    A. To decrease the number of adverse events

    B. To detect vulnerability

    C. To mitigate the impact

    D. To adhere to policy

    Answer: C. To mitigate the impact

    Explanation: Corrective controls are implemented to reduce the impact once a threat event has occurred and support the quick restoration of normal operations. Examples of corrective controls include the following:

    - Business continuity planning

    - Disaster recovery planning

    - Incident response planning

    - Backup procedures

2. Who is responsible for performing the routine duties required to ensure the protection of information?

    A. Data owner

    B. End users

    C. Audit team

    D. Data custodian

    Answer: D. Data custodian

Explanation: The data custodian is required to provide and implement adequate controls for the protection of the data. The data owner is required to classify the level of protection required for their data.

3. What is the most effective method to identify and remove an application back door?

    A. Internal audit

    B. Penetration test

    C. Source code review

    D. Anti-virus software

    Answer: C. Source code review

    Explanation: The most effective method to identify and remove an application back door is to conduct a review of the source code. The other options will not be as effective as a source code review.

4. What is the most effective deterrent control against employees misusing their privileges?

    A. Internal audit

    B. Log capturing and monitoring

    C. Signed acceptable use policy

    D. Two-factor authentication

    Answer: C. Signed acceptable use policy

    Explanation: The purpose of a deterrent control is to give a warning signal to deter or discourage the threat event. When an employee signs the acceptable use policy, they are aware of the consequences if the acceptable usage policy is not followed. This acts as a deterrent control. Two-factor authentication will not be able to prevent the activities of authorized users. Internal audit and log capturing are after the fact and may not be effective.

5. An external security attack can be prevented by doing what?

    A. Analyzing the system access log

    B. Conducting a background verification of temporary staff

    C. Network address translation

    D. Internal audit

Answer: C. Network address translation

Explanation: External security threats can be prevented by the use of network address translation as they have internal addresses that are non-routable. The other options are not as effective as network address translation.

6. A data backup policy primarily includes which of the following?

    A. Criteria for data backup

    B. Responsibility for data backup

    C. Procedure for data backup

    D. Data backup schedule

    Answer: A. Criteria for data backup

    Explanation: A policy is a high-level statement indicating the intent of the management. With respect to backup, it will include criteria for data backup. The criteria will help the user to determine which data is to be considered critical and accordingly at what frequency data backup is to be taken. The other options are generally included in procedure documents.

7. A security manager is involved in the development of a system. In which phase should they finalize the access control and encryption algorithm?

    A. Feasibility stage

    B. Procedural design

    C. System design specifications

    D. Software development

    Answer: C. System design specifications

    Explanation: System specifications with respect to the type of access control and encryptions are considered in the system design specifications. The feasibility phase includes a cost benefit analysis of the system development. In the procedural design phase, structured components are converted into procedural descriptions. The system development stage is too late as in this stage, the system is already being coded.

8. What is the most effective method of removing data from tape media that is to be reused?

    A. Multiple overwriting

    B. Erasing the tapes

C. Burning the tapes

D. Degaussing the tapes

Answer: D. Degaussing the tapes

Explanation: Degaussing is the best way to erase data from a disk. In the degaussing process, an alternating current field is increased gradually from 0 to some maximum value and again reduced to 0, thus leaving a very low residue of the magnetic induction on the device. This is known as demagnetization or degaussing. The other options are not as secure as degaussing the tapes. Multiple overwriting and erasing the tapes are not foolproof methods of removing the data. Burning the tapes will physically destroy the tapes and they cannot be reused.

9. Which of the following is an area of concern when implementing native database auditing?

   A. Native database auditing may interfere with event logging.

   B. Native database auditing impacts the production database performance.

   C. Native database auditing increases the security budget.

   D. Native database auditing makes configuration management more complex.

   Answer: B. Native database auditing impacts the production database performance.

   Explanation: With respect to database security, a *native audit* means tools and techniques that help the administrator to perform an audit of database activities. However, enabling the native audit may lead to performance degradation of the database. This is a major concern. The other options are less significant.

10. Enabling a database audit log function will result in which of the following?

    A. Risk of degradation of the performance

    B. Risk of database confidentiality

    C. Risk of database integrity

    D. Risk of configuration issues

    Answer: A. Risk of degradation of the performance

    Explanation: Enabling an audit log function may create a burden on database processing and it may result in degradation of the database performance. The more elaborate logging becomes, the slower the performance. It is important to strike a balance. The other options will not be impacted by enabling an audit log function.

11. Which of the following is an example of corrective control?

    A. To divert incoming traffic during a denial-of-service attack

    B. To filter network traffic

    C. To conduct a network audit

    D. To log network administrator activity

    Answer: A. To divert incoming traffic during a denial-of-service attack

    Explanation: The prime objective of corrective control is to reduce the impact of an event once it has occurred and to ensure restoration to normal operations. The process of diverting incoming traffic helps to correct the situation and hence it is a corrective control. Filtering network traffic is a preventive control. Audits and logging are detective controls.

12. When should application-level control be implemented?

    A. When general controls are weak

    B. When detective controls are to be implemented

    C. When preventive controls are to be implemented

    D. When corrective controls are to be implemented

    Answer: A. When general controls are weak

    Explanation: Application controls are controls implemented for a particular application whereas general system controls are controls implemented for the overall environment. An application is protected by a combination of application controls as well as general controls. When general controls are weak, more emphasis needs to be placed on application-level control. Detective, preventive, and corrective controls exist at both the general and application level.

13. A system administrator is entrusted to analyze network events, take appropriate action, and provide a report to the security team. Which of the following additional controls will be more relevant for a risk-based review of network activities?

    A. The activity of the system administrator should be monitored by a separate reviewer.

    B. The system administrator should also conduct audits of their activity on a monthly basis.

    C. Monitoring should be done by members of the security team only.

    D. Monitoring should be done by members of the steering committee.

Answer: A. The activity of the system administrator should be monitored by a separate reviewer.

Explanation: The activity of the system administrator needs to be monitored to ensure that their performance is in accordance with the information security program. Monitoring by a third party will be more effective than a self-audit. It is not necessary for monitoring to be done only by a member of the security team. The steering committee is not involved in routine monitoring.

14. Which risk will be applicable to a control that fails closed (secured)?

    A. Risk of confidentiality

    B. Risk of non-repudiation

    C. Risk of integrity

    D. Risk of availability

    Answer: D. Risk of availability

    Explanation: Controls can be designed either to fail closed or fail open. For example, in the event of the failure of an automatic door, an organization can opt for fail open (door should remain open) or fail closed (door should remain closed). In the case of fail open, confidentiality and integrity may be compromised, and in the case of fail closed, availability may be compromised. In such a situation, the risk needs to be determined for each element and a decision taken accordingly.

15. Which of the following primarily determines how a control is implemented?

    A. Security budget

    B. Measuring capabilities

    C. Training capabilities

    D. Failure modes

    Answer: D. Failure modes

    Explanation: Failure modes means in which mode controls operate when they fail, that is, whether a control fails open or fails closed. The failure mode of the control impacts safety, confidentiality, and availability. For example, in the event of the failure of an automatic door, an organization can opt for fail open (door should remain open) or fail closed (door should remain closed). In the case of fail open, confidentiality and integrity may be compromised, and in the case of fail closed, availability may be compromised. In such a situation, the risk needs to be determined for each element and a decision taken accordingly.

16. An organization is using an **electronic data interchange** (EDI) system to get orders from its distributors. What is the most effective way to ensure the authenticity of the orders received?

    A. Conduct a background check of all distributors.

    B. Conduct a reasonableness check for orders received from a distributor.

    C. Acknowledge the receipt of orders.

    D. Verify the sender's identity and determine whether orders are in accordance with contract terms.

    Answer: D. Verify the sender's identity and determine whether orders are in accordance with contract terms.

    Explanation: In an EDI environment, there are primarily two challenges with respect to the receipt of an order. The first challenge is to ensure that the order received is from a trusted partner and the second is to ensure that the order quantity is correct. Hence, controls should be available for the verification of a sender's identity and to determine the correctness of the quantity. The other options will not be as effective as option D.

17. What is the objective of segmenting a network?

    A. To limit the consequences of a compromise

    B. To reduce vulnerability

    C. For better administrative vulnerability

    D. To implement a data classification scheme

    Answer: A. To limit the consequences of a compromise

    Explanation: Segmentation means to divide the network into parts. Segmentation limits the consequences of an attack by constraining the scope of impact. Segmentation by itself does not reduce vulnerability. Segmentation may result in complex administration. Segmentation is not implemented primarily to support the data classification scheme.

18. Which of the following should a control policy primarily consider?

    A. Risk of control failure

    B. Safety of human life

C. Control monitoring process

D. Existing vulnerabilities

Answer: B. Safety of human life

Explanation: When implementing a framework, policy, and controls, the most important consideration is the safety of human life. Compared to human life, the other options are secondary aspects.

19. What is the most important activity in the development of an information security program?

A. Development of the security organization

B. Development of the security architecture

C. Development of a security team

D. Control design and development

Answer: D. Control design and development

Explanation: Control design and development is the prime activity in the development of an information security program. Most of the program development activities will evolve when designing, testing, and implementing controls. The other options are secondary aspects.

20. Where can continuous monitoring best be employed?

A. In areas where an incident may have a high impact and high frequency

B. In areas where an incident may have a low impact and high frequency

C. In areas where regulation requires strong security controls

D. In areas where the business is driven by an online system

Answer: A. In areas where an incident may have a high impact and high frequency

Explanation: A security manager should understand that implementing continuous monitoring is expensive. The use of continuous monitoring may not always be feasible or practical so it should be used in areas where the risk is at its greatest level. Continuous monitoring is best deployed in areas where incidents may have a high impact and frequency.

Penetration testing

In penetration testing, the tester uses the same techniques as used by hackers to gain access to critical systems/data. This helps the auditor to determine the security environment of the organization. Penetration testing helps to identify the risk relevant to the confidentiality, integrity, and availability of information systems. The objective of penetration testing is to verify the control environment of the organization and to take corrective action if a deficiency is noted. Penetration testing needs to be conducted only by a qualified and experienced professional.

Aspects to be covered within the scope of the test

From a risk perspective, the following aspects need to be covered within the scope of penetration testing:

- Precise details of IP addresses need to be included in the scope of the audit. Details of the testing technique (SQL injection/DoS/DDoS/social engineering, and so on) should be provided.

- The day and time of the attack (that is, either during office hours or after office hours) should be included.

- It is the responsibility of the penetration tester to provide an appropriate warning prior to the simulation so as to avoid false alarms being raised with law enforcement bodies.

Types of penetration tests

The following are some of the penetration tests that can be used to evaluate the security environment of an organization.

External testing

In external testing, a penetration attack is performed on the target's network from an outside network, that is, mostly from the internet.

Internal testing

In internal testing, an attack is conducted on the target from within the perimeter. This is done to determine the security risk if an actual intruder happens to be within the organization.

Blind testing

In blind penetration testing, the tester is not provided with any information or details about the network. Here, the tester is regarded as blind as they do not have any knowledge of the target environment. Such a test is expensive because detailed analysis, study, and research is required for an attack.

Double-blind testing

Double-blind testing is the extended version of blind testing where even the administrator and other information security staff of the target entity are not aware of the test. Both the tester and security team are blind as no one is aware of the test details. It simulates a real kind of attack. Double-blind testing helps to determine the incident handling and response capability of the target organization.

Targeted testing

In targeted testing, the organization's IT team as well as the penetration tester are aware of the testing scenario. The penetration tester is aware of the target details and network structure.

White box testing and black box testing

A CISM aspirant should also understand the difference between a white box penetration test and a black box penetration test. In white box penetration testing, relevant details of the infrastructure are made available to the tester in advance. They need not spend time gathering the information. This helps the tester to concentrate on exploitation.

In a black box approach, no information is provided about the infrastructure to the tester and it simulates an actual hacking attempt.

Risks associated with penetration testing

The following are some of the risks associated with penetration testing:

- A penetration test attempt by an unqualified auditor may have an adverse impact on the target's system.
- Sensitive information relating to the target environment gathered during penetration testing can be misused by the tester.
- Inappropriate planning and timing of the attack may cause the system to fail.
- This is a simulation of a real attack and may be restricted by law or regulations. Such attacks without appropriate approvals may have an adverse impact.

Key aspects from a CISM exam perspective

The following are some of the key aspects from an exam perspective:

Question	Possible answer
What is the main objective of performing a penetration test?	To identify weaknesses in network and server security
What is the most important action prior to contracting a third party to perform a penetration test against an organization?	<ul><li>To ensure that goals and objectives are clearly defined</li><li>To ensure that rules of engagement are clearly defined</li></ul>
What is the advantage of the white box penetration approach?	More time is spent in exploitation rather than discovering and information gathering
What is the most effective method to determine that a network is adequately secured against an external attack?	To perform periodic penetration testing
What is the primary area of interest for a penetration tester when conducting a penetration test?	Network mapping

Table 8.4 – Key aspects from the CISM exam perspective

Questions

1. The aggregated risk of linked vulnerabilities can be assessed by which of the following?

   A. System audits

   B. Penetration tests

   C. Auditing the code

   D. Vulnerability analysis

   Answer: B. Penetration tests

Explanation: Aggregated risk means a significant impact caused by a large number of minor vulnerabilities. Such minor vulnerabilities individually do not cause a major impact but when all these vulnerabilities are exploited at the same time, they can cause a huge impact. The goal of risk aggregation is to identify a significant overall risk from a single threat vector. Penetration testing is the best way to assess the aggregate risk by exploiting them one by one. Risk aggregation provides a good measurement for prioritizing risk.

2. What is the main objective when conducting a penetration test?

    A. Determine weaknesses in network and server security

    B. Determine improvement in the incident management procedure

    C. Determine the capability of threat vectors

    D. Determine the strength of the security team

    Answer: A. Determine weaknesses in network and server security

    Explanation: The objective of a penetration test is to identify weaknesses in network and server security. On the basis of the results of a penetration test, identified weaknesses are addressed to improve the security posture of the organization.

3. What is the prime reason for getting a penetration test conducted by an external company?

    A. To adhere to the security budget

    B. To provide training to internal users

    C. To get an independent view of security exposures

    D. To determine a complete list of vulnerabilities

    Answer: C. To get an independent view of security exposures

    Explanation: The main objective of engaging an external company to perform penetration testing is to get an independent view of security exposure. Even though the organization may have the necessary skills and resources to conduct a penetration test, third-party penetration testing is recommended to get an independent view from external experts. The other options are secondary aspects.

4. What is the most important aspect when appointing a penetration tester?

    A. To ensure that a demonstration has been obtained on a test system

    B. To ensure that goals and objectives are clearly defined

    C. To instruct security monitoring staff to prepare for the test

    D. To instruct IT staff to prepare for the test

    Answer: B. To ensure that goals and objectives are clearly defined

    Explanation: It is very important to establish a clear understanding of the scope of testing. In the absence of a defined scope, the tester may cause a system outage or other major damage. Sometimes, testing may have an adverse impact on business processes if the organization is not well prepared. The other options are secondary aspects. In the case of a blind penetration test, IT and security monitoring staff are not informed about the proposed test in order to determine their readiness with respect to any attack. A demonstration of the test system will reduce the spontaneity of the test.

5. What is the most important aspect when appointing a penetration tester?

    A. Ask for the tools to be used in testing.

    B. Instruct IT staff to prepare for the test.

    C. Instruct security monitoring staff to prepare for the test.

    D. Establish clear rules of engagement.

    Answer: D. Establish clear rules of engagement.

    Explanation: It is very important to establish a clear understanding of the scope of testing. In the absence of a defined scope, the tester may cause a system outage or other major damage. Sometimes, a test may have an adverse impact on business processes if the organization is not well prepared. The other options are secondary aspects. In the case of a blind penetration test, IT and security monitoring staff are not informed about the proposed test in order to determine their readiness with respect to any attack.

6. What is the most important requirement before conducting a black box penetration test?

    A. Clear scope of the test

    B. Documented incident response plan

C. Recommendation from the internal audit team

D. Proper communication to the incident management team

Answer: A. Clear scope of the test

Explanation: In a black box testing kind of attack scenario, the tester is provided with limited or no knowledge about the target's information systems. Inappropriate planning and timing of the attack may cause the system to fail. It is very important that the tester is very experienced and aware of the clear scope of the test. The other options are not as significant as a clear scope of the test.

7. What is the advantage of white box penetration testing, that is, where information about the infrastructure to be tested is provided in advance to the tester?

A. More time is spent in exploitation rather than discovering and information gathering.

B. Helps to simulate a situation exactly like actual hacking.

C. Test can be conducted with less cost.

D. No need to use penetration testing tools.

Answer: A. More time is spent in exploitation rather than information gathering and discovering.

Explanation: In the case of white box penetration testing, relevant details of the infrastructure are made available to the tester in advance. They need not spend time gathering the information. This helps the tester to concentrate on exploitation. A black box approach, where no information is provided, better simulates an actual hacking attempt. Cost is a secondary aspect. Penetration testing tools will be required for both white box as well as black box penetration testing.

8. What is ethical hacking generally used for?

A. Testing the alternate processing site

B. As an alternative to substantive testing

C. For control assessment of legacy applications

D. To determine the requirement for cyber insurance

Answer: C. For control assessment of legacy applications

Explanation: Ethical hacking involves the use of tools and techniques available with actual hackers to penetrate the network of an organization. The objective of ethical hacking is to find vulnerabilities in the existing controls and to address the loopholes. Ethical hacking is not directly relevant for the other options.

9. What is the most effective method to ensure that an organizational network is adequately secured against an external attack?

A. Implement an intrusion detection system.

B. Implement a security baseline.

C. Change the vendor default setting.

D. Conduct periodic penetration testing.

Answer: D. Conduct periodic penetration testing.

Explanation: The most effective way to ensure that an organization's network is properly secured against an external attack is to conduct a penetration test at regular intervals. The results of the penetration test determine the effectiveness of the security posture. Any loopholes identified during penetration testing should immediately be rectified. The other options are not as effective as penetration testing.

10. Which of the following is an area of primary interest for a penetration tester?

A. Nature of the data

B. Network mapping

C. Data analytics

D. Intrusion detection system

Answer: B. Network mapping

Explanation: The first step that a penetration tester conducts is to analyze the network mapping. Network mapping is the process of understanding the target network topology. It helps to determine the points of attack in a network. IDS is a secondary aspect. The nature of the data or data analytics is not relevant for a tester.

Security program metrics and monitoring

A metric is a measurement of a process to determine how well the process is performing. Security-related metrics indicate how well the controls are able to mitigate the risk. For example, the system uptime metric helps us to understand whether the system is available to the user as per the requirements. The following are some examples of security-related metrics:

- Percentage of critical server for which the penetration test is conducted
- Percentage of high-risk findings closed within a month
- Percentage of deviation from the information security policy

- Percentage of computers having unsupported operating systems
- Percentage of computers with updated patches
- Average response time to handle the incident

Objective of metrics

On the basis of effective metrics, an organization evaluates and measures the achievement and performance of various processes and controls. The main objective of a metric is to help management in decision making and to facilitate and track continuous improvement in the security posture.

Metrics should be able to provide relevant information to the recipient so that informed decisions can be made.

Monitoring

Metrics should be designed and developed in such a way that the results of the controls should be monitorable. If controls cannot be monitored, it leads to unacceptable risk and should be avoided. Monitoring helps to enable proper goal settings, progress tracking, benchmarking, and prioritizing. Monitoring of metrics is a fundamental aspect for a successful security program.

Attributes of effective metrics

CISM aspirants should understand the following attributes for effective metrics:

- **Meaningful**: A metric should be meaningful for the recipient and should provide a basis for sound decision making.
- **Consistent**: A metric should provide consistent results to make them comparable over a period of time. They should provide the same result under the same conditions each time they are measured.

    In the absence of a consistent method, the results of the metrics cannot be compared and trends can be misleading. Consistency is important to have reasonably accurate and reliable results.
- **Reliable**: The source of the input data and information should be genuine and reliable.
- **Accurate**: Appropriate controls should be in place to ensure the accuracy of metrics.

- **Timely**: A metric should be useful when it is available to the user on a timely basis and support them in their decision making.

- **Predictive**: To the extent possible, a metric should be able to indicate future events.

- **Unambiguous**: It is better not to have any information rather than have unclear information.

Information security objectives and metrics

The main goal of defining information security objectives is to measure the effectiveness of a security program. A security manager should consider designing metrics for each of the security objectives. In the absence of metrics, it will be difficult to determine the achievement of the objective. The success of an information security program is determined on the basis of the achievement of the security objectives.

Primarily, metrics should be based on security objectives so they can provide the measure to evaluate the effectiveness and efficiency of an information security program and its objectives.

Defined metrics help to measure the current state of affairs for different security objectives. This trend can be used to determine the improvement in the security program over time. If an organization is unable to take measurements over time that provide data regarding key aspects of its security program, then continuous improvement is difficult to monitor.

The main objective of implementing security control is to minimize the adverse impact from incidents. A reduction in the impact from security incidents indicates that security controls are effective.

Useful metrics for management

Management is generally interested in metrics that indicate the overall effectiveness of the security program. They need to determine whether the security program is headed in the right direction. They need to know the overall trend of security compliance to provide appropriate oversight.

Executive management will be more interested in the achievement of control objectives as they are directly linked to business objectives. Achievement of control objectives is the best metric for executive management to evaluate the effectiveness of a security program.

Key aspects from a CISM exam perspective

The following are some of the key aspects from an exam perspective:

Question	Possible answer
What is the prime objective of a metric?	Decision making (on the basis of effective metrics, an organization evaluates and measures the achievement and performance of various processes and controls. Effective metrics are primarily used for security-related decision making).
What is the main objective of defining the information security objectives?	To measure the effectiveness of a security program
What is the most significant attribute of a good information security metric?	The metric should be meaningful to the recipient
What is the best indicator that security controls are performing effectively?	A reduction in impact from security issues
In which phase of the **system devlopment life cycle (SDLC)** should metrics be designed to assess the effectiveness of the system over time?	Design phase
What is the best metric for an information security manager to use to support a request to fund new controls?	Incident trends and their impact
What is the most useful metric to determine the effectiveness of the log monitoring process?	Percentage of unauthorized penetration attempts investigated

Table 8.5 – Key aspects from the CISM exam perspective

Questions

1. The effectiveness of the incident response process is best indicated by which of the following?

    A. Increase in incident response team size

    B. Reduction in number of open incidents

    C. Reduction in the average response time to an incident

    D. Increase in number of incidents handled per year

    Answer: C. Reduction in the average response time to an incident

Explanation: Early response time helps to minimize the impact of the incident. Hence, to determine the effectiveness of the incident response team, the best indicator is a reduction in the average response time per incident. The other options are not direct indicators of the effectiveness of the incident response team.

2. What is the prime goal of defining the information security objectives?

    A. To measure the effectiveness of a security program

    B. To compare with industry standards

    C. To gain management support

    D. To justify the security budget

    Answer: A. To measure the effectiveness of a security program

    Explanation: Defined objectives can be used to measure the effectiveness of an information security program. The success of a program is determined by the achievement of the security objectives. The other observations are secondary aspects.

3. What is the most important aspect to improve the effectiveness of a continuous improvement program?

    A. Program metrics

    B. Adhering to the security budget

    C. Aligning the organization's security standards with international standards

    D. Complying with regulatory requirements

    Answer: A. Program metrics

    Explanation: Program metrics measure how well a process is doing in terms of its goals and objectives. Defined metrics help to measure the current state of affairs for different security objectives. This trend can be used to determine the improvement in a security program over time. If an organization is unable to take measurements over time that provide data regarding key aspects of its security program, then continuous improvement is difficult to monitor. The other options are secondary aspects.

4. What is the most important characteristic of an effective information security metric?

    A. It is meaningful to the recipient.

    B. It is complete and accurate.

C. It is consistent.

D. It is cost-effective.

Answer: A. It is meaningful to the recipient.

Explanation: A metric should be meaningful to the recipient and should provide a basis for sound decision making. Unless it is meaningful to the recipient, all of the other attributes are of no use.

5. The effectiveness of security controls can be best indicated by which of the following?

    A. Reduction in the impact from security issues.

    B. Reduction in the cost of implementing controls.

    C. A high percentage of staff have attended a security training program.

    D. Audit report without significant findings.

    Answer: A. Reduction in the impact from security issues.

    Explanation: The main objective of implementing security controls is to minimize the adverse impact from incidents. A reduction in the impact from security incidents indicates that security controls are effective. The other options do not directly indicate the effectiveness of security controls.

6. To determine the effectiveness of security controls, a review of which of the following should be conducted?

    A. Information security policies

    B. Risk management policies

    C. Security metrics

    D. User access rights

    Answer: C. Security metrics

    Explanation: Security metrics measure how well a process is doing in terms of its goals and objectives. Defined metrics help to measure the current state of affairs for different security objectives. This trend can be used to determine the improvement in a security program over time. The other options are secondary aspects.

7. Which of the following will executive management be more interested in?

    A. Trends showing the number of servers compliant with security requirements

    B. Number of servers compliant with security requirements

    C. Count of security patches applied

    D. Trends showing the count of security patches applied

    Answer: A. Trends showing the number of servers compliant with security requirements

    Explanation: The overall trend of security-compliant servers indicates the level of effectiveness of an information security program as compared to a standalone count. The trend or count of patch updating would be less relevant as it depends on the number of vulnerabilities. A high patch update rate need not necessarily indicate the effectiveness of a security program.

8. Which of the following will executive management be more interested in?

    A. Total count of controls applied

    B. Percentage of control objectives achieved

    C. Count of control objectives included in the policy

    D. Number of reported security incidents

    Answer: B. Percentage of control objectives achieved

    Explanation: Executive management will be more interested in the achievement of control objectives as they are directly linked to business objectives. The achievement of control objectives is the best metric for executive management to evaluate the effectiveness of a security program. The other options are secondary aspects.

9. During which phase of system development should information security metrics be developed?

    A. Implementation

    B. Testing

    C. Design

    D. Feasibility

    Answer: C. Design

    Explanation: Security metrics are developed during the design phase of system development. Metrics should be developed before the testing and implementation phase. The feasibility stage is too early for the development of security metrics. In the feasibility phase, the possibility of implementing a project is determined.

10. What is the most effective metric to be conveyed to senior management for security funding?

    A. Adverse incident trend reports

    B. Internal audit observations

    C. Vulnerability assessment reports

    D. Penetration test reports

    Answer: A. Adverse incident trend reports

    Explanation: Adverse incident trend reports indicate the impact on business objectives. Security incidents occur because either a control failed or there was no control in place. This will be taken seriously by the management to fund an appropriate budget for information security. The other options are secondary aspects.

11. What is the most important consideration for the development of an effective information security metric?

    A. Correct reporting time

    B. Relevance to the recipient

    C. Correct and complete measurement

    D. Cost of measuring the metrics

    Answer: B. Relevance to the recipient

    Explanation: Metrics should be meaningful for the recipient and should provide a basis for sound decision making. Unless it is meaningful to the recipient, all of the other attributes are of no use. The other options are secondary aspects.

12. What is the best way to determine whether a security program is achieving its objectives?

    A. Reduction in incident impact.

    B. Budget approval by senior management.

    C. Employees are adhering to the security policy and procedure.

    D. Decrease in incident reporting.

    Answer: A. Reduction in incident impact.

    Explanation: The prime objective of any security program is to reduce the impact of incidents. A reduction in incident impact indicates the security program is effective and achieving its objective. The other options do not directly indicate the achievement of security objectives.

13. What is the best method to resolve non-compliance with information security standards?

    A. Conduct regular audits of non-compliant areas.

    B. Conduct continuous vulnerability scanning.

    C. Conduct regular security awareness training.

    D. Present non-compliance reports to executive management at regular intervals.

    Answer: D. Present non-compliance reports to executive management at regular intervals.

    Explanation: Presenting reports to executive management will create performance pressure on business units and this will motivate them to address the non-compliant area at the earliest opportunity. The other options are secondary aspects.

14. What is the most accurate method to determine the **return on investment (ROI)** for security investment?

    A. Using only quantifiable risks

    B. Developing cost-effective processes

    C. Measuring monetary value in a consistent manner

    D. Considering investment amount as profit

    Answer: C. Measuring monetary value in a consistent manner

    Explanation: In the absence of a consistent method, the results of the metrics cannot be compared and trends can be misleading. Consistency is important to have reasonably accurate and reliable results. It is not practical to simply exclude qualitative risk because of the difficulties in measurement. Developing cost-effective processes and considering investment amount as profit are not relevant for the calculation of ROI.

15. What is the most useful metric to determine the effectiveness of the log monitoring process?

    A. Percentage of penetration attempts investigated

    B. Number of logs captured

    C. Number of log reports generated

    D. Number of staff engaged in the review of logs

Answer: A. Percentage of penetration attempts investigated

Explanation: The objective of capturing a log is to do a follow-up investigation for suspected attempts. Investigation helps to take various preventive and corrective actions. Merely capturing the logs or generating the reports will not serve the ultimate purpose. Hence, the most useful metric for measuring the success of log monitoring is to determine the percentage of suspected attempts investigated. If organizations do not investigate and keep only capturing the log, the ultimate objective of log capturing is not achieved.

16. For measuring and monitoring an information security program, what should metrics be based on?

   A. Financial risk

   B. Operational risk

   C. Security objectives

   D. Industry standards

   Answer: C. Security objectives

   Explanation: Primarily, metrics should be based on security objectives so they can provide the measure to evaluate the effectiveness and efficiency of an information security program and its objectives. Financial risk and operational risk can be one of the security objectives. Industry standards may or may not be aligned with the security objectives of the organization.

17. What is the main objective in developing security-related metrics?

   A. To identify security weakness

   B. To adhere to the security budget

   C. To enable continuous improvement

   D. To improve security awareness

   Answer: C. To enable continuous improvement

   Explanation: The main objective of a security-related metric is to measure the performance and facilitate and focus on continuous improvement in a security program. Metrics may indicate weakness but they do not directly identify the security weakness. The other options are secondary aspects.

18. What is the most effective approach to improve the information security management process?

    A. Perform security audits.

    B. Conduct penetration testing.

    C. Define and monitor the security metrics.

    D. Increase the security budget.

    Answer: C. Define and monitor the security metrics.

    Explanation: Metrics help to determine the level of performance over a period of time. They indicate the trend of the security performance by comparing against the baseline. This helps to identify areas of improvement. The other options are secondary aspects.

19. Metrics for measuring the effectiveness of anti-virus software are primarily relevant to which of the following?

    A. Steering committee

    B. Board of directors

    C. IT managers

    D. Information security manager

    Answer: D. Information security manager

    Explanation: Metrics are generally relevant to the owner of the control. Metrics for measuring the effectiveness of anti-virus software are primarily relevant to the information security manager. It helps them to determine the current state of control. If control is not performing as per expectations, the security team can investigate and address the issue.

Summary

In this chapter, we discussed the practical aspects of information security program development management. This chapter will help CISM candidates understand important methods, tools, and techniques to develop a security program in an effective and efficient manner. We also discussed how CISM candidates can design security metrics for effective monitoring of security controls.

In the next chapter, we will discuss information security monitoring tools and techniques.

9
Information Security Monitoring Tools and Techniques

In this chapter, we will discuss the methods, tools, and techniques for monitoring information security. We will discuss the technical aspects of implementing firewalls, as well as how **intrusion prevention systems (IPSes)** and **intrusion detection systems (IDSes)** function. We will also discuss some important aspects of digital signatures, **public key infrastructure (PKI)**, and asymmetric encryption, which are very important from the CISM exam's perspective.

The following topics will be covered in this chapter:

- Firewall types and their implementation
- IDSes and IPSes
- Digital signature
- Elements of PKI
- Asymmetric encryption

Let's understand each of these topics in detail.

Firewall types and their implementation

A firewall is a device that's used to monitor and control network traffic. It is generally placed in-between an enterprise's internal network and the internet to protect the system and infrastructure of the organization.

Security management should understand the following types of firewalls, as well as how they should be structured to protect information assets. CISM aspirants need to understand the following types and implementations of firewalls:

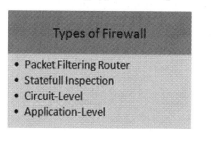

Figure 9.1 – Types of firewalls

Next, let's look at the different types of firewalls.

Types of firewalls

The following are the basic characteristics of the different types of firewalls.

Packet filtering router

A packet-filtering router is the most simple and initial version of a firewall. It tracks the IP address and port number of both the destination and source and takes action (either to allow or deny the connection) as per the defined rules. A packet-filtering router functions at the network layer of the OSI model.

Stateful inspection firewall

A stateful inspection firewall monitors and tracks the destination of each packet that is being sent from the internal network. Stateful inspection firewalls only allow incoming messages that are in response to the request that went out from the internal network. A stateful inspection firewall operates at the network layer of the OSI.

Circuit-level firewall

A circuit-level firewall operates on the concept of a bastion host and proxy server. It provides the same proxy for all services. It operates at the session layer of the OSI.

Application-level firewall

Here are a few characteristics of application-level firewalls:

- An application-level firewall is regarded as the most secure type of firewall.
- It operates at the application layer of the OSI.
- It controls applications such as FTP and HTTP.
- It also works on the concept of the bastion host/DMZ and proxy server, but it provides a separate proxy for each service.

Now, let's understand what bastion host/DMZ and proxy server are.

Bastion host/DMZ and proxy

CISM aspirants should understand the concept of the bastion host, proxies, and **Demilitarized Zone (DMZ)**.

What is a proxy?

The following diagram shows the concept of a proxy:

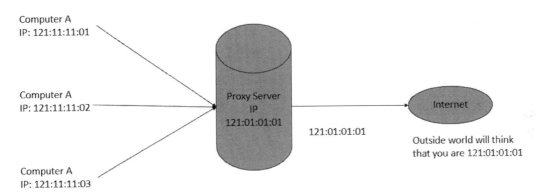

Figure 9.2 – Proxy server

The following are the features of a proxy server:

- A proxy can be regarded as a middleman. A proxy stands in between the internal and external networks.
- No direct communication will be allowed between the internal and external networks. All communication will pass through the proxy server.

- The outside world will not have the addresses of the internal networks. It can only recognize proxy servers.

- Proxy technology operating at the session layer is known as a circuit-level proxy, while proxy technology operating at the application layer is referred to as an application-level proxy.

Now, let's understand what demilitarized zones and bastion hosts are.

Demilitarized Zone (DMZ)/bastion host

DMZ is an area that can be accessed by an external network. The objective of setting up a DMZ is to prevent external traffic from having direct access to the critical systems of the organization. All the systems that are placed in DMZ should be hardened and all the required functionalities should be disabled. Such systems are also referred to as bastion hosts.

The firewall ensures that traffic from the outside is routed into the DMZ. Nothing valuable is kept in a DMZ because it is subject to attack and can be compromised.

Now, let's understand proxies, bastion hosts, and DMZ by looking at a simple example.

Your office has a receptionist. The receptionist has a phone number that is available in the phone dictionary. You and your colleagues have been given specific extension numbers. Only your receptionist and the internal staff know about this extension:

- **Proxy**: You cannot directly call outside your extension. First, you need to call your receptionist and request an outside connection. Your receptionist will do all the due diligence and then get you connected. The outsider will only know the receptionist's phone number. They will not be able to track your extension. This is known as a proxy.

- **Bastion host/demilitarized zone**: Similarly, the outsider cannot directly contact you on your extension. They need to call the receptionist first. The receptionist will do the necessary due diligence and then pass the call on to you. Since your receptionist is beautiful and has direct contact with outsiders, she is more vulnerable. You need to ensure that she does not possess any sensitive or critical data. This is known as a bastion host or demilitarized zone.

Now, let's discuss how the different types of firewalls are implemented.

Types of firewall implementation

CISM aspirants need to understand the following types of firewall implementation.

Dual-homed firewall

A dual-homed firewall includes one packet filtering router and one bastion host with two **Network Interface Cards (NICs)**.

The following diagram illustrates the concept of a dual-homed firewall:

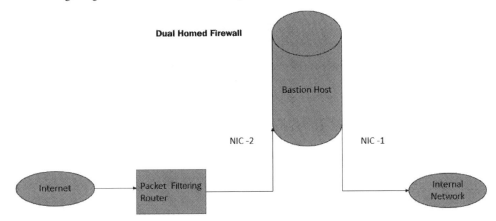

Figure 9.3 – Dual homed firewall

Screened host firewall

A screened host firewall includes one packet filtering router and one bastion host.

The following diagram illustrates the concept of a screened host firewall:

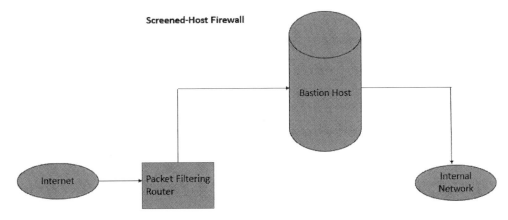

Figure 9.4 – Screened host firewall

Screened subnet firewall (demilitarized zone)

The following are the characteristics of a screened subnet firewall:

- A screened subnet firewall consists of two packet filtering routers. It also has one bastion host.

- Of the preceding firewall implementations, a screened subnet firewall (demilitarized zone) is regarded as the most secure type of firewall implementation.

The following diagram illustrates the concept of a screened subnet firewall:

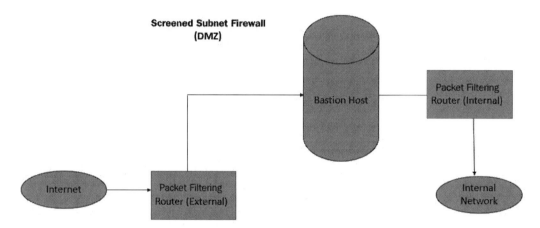

Figure 9.5 – Screened subnet firewall

Generally, servers that interact with the internet (extranet) are placed in a demilitarized area as this area is separate from internal servers and properly hardened. Also, generally, IDS is placed on a screened subnet, which is a decentralized zone.

Placing firewalls

A firewall should be placed in a hardened server with minimal services enabled. It is not recommended to place a firewall and IDS on the same physical server. A firewall should be implemented on a domain boundary to monitor and control incoming and outgoing traffic.

The most effective way to ensure that firewall rules are adequate is to conduct penetration tests periodically. Any gaps that are identified during the penetration test should be addressed immediately. This will help to improve the security posture of the organization.

Source routing

A firewall, by default, should be able to reject traffic with IP source routing. Source routing lets you get information about all the routers a packet transmits. This could potentially be used to bypass firewalls and hence is a security threat. If the firewall permits source routing, it is possible to conduct spoofing attacks by capturing the IP address of the organization.

Firewall and the corresponding OSI layer

CISM aspirants should have a basic understanding of the OSI layer for each type of firewall. The following table illustrates the different types of firewalls and their corresponding OSI layers:

Firewall	OSI Layer
Packet Filtering Firewall	Network Layer (3rd Layer)
Stateful Inspection Firewall	Network Layer (3rd Layer)
Circuit-Level Firewall	Session Layer (5th Layer)
Application-Level Firewall	Application Layer (7th Layer)

Figure 9.6 – Firewalls and OSI layers

The functionality of the firewall improves with the increase in layers. An application-level firewall that operates at the seventh layer is regarded as the most robust firewall.

Key aspects from the CISM exam's perspective

The following are some of the key aspects from an exam perspective:

Question	Possible Answer
What is the objective of a firewall?	To connect only authorized users to trusted networks (thereby restricting unauthorized access).
What is the most secure type of firewall?	The application-level firewall (as it works on the highest layer; that is, the application layer of the OSI model).
What is the most secure implementation technique?	Screened subnet firewall.
What is the most stringent and robust configuration setting in the firewall?	To reject all traffic and allow only specific traffic.

Question	Possible Answer
What firewall only permits traffic from external sources if it is in response to traffic from internal hosts?	Stateful inspection.
Where should an internet-facing server (extranet) be placed?	Screened subnet (demilitarized zone).
Where should the intrusion detection system ideally be placed?	Screened subnet (demilitarized zone).
What is the best technique to validate the adequacy of firewall rules?	To perform penetration testing regularly.
What is the primary disadvantage of using password-protected ZIP files to email files across the internet?	A mail filter or firewall may quarantine the password-protected file as it cannot verify whether the file contains malicious code.
What is the major risk when there is an excessive number of firewall rules?	One rule may override another rule and create a loophole.

Table 9.1 – Key aspects from the CISM exam perspective

Questions

1. What is the most robust firewall rule?

    A. The rule to permit all traffic and deny specific traffic.

    B. The rule to deny all traffic and permit only specific traffic.

    C. The rule to decide dynamically based on the nature of traffic.

    D. To provide discretion to the network administrator to permit or deny the traffic.

    Answer: B. The rule to deny all traffic and permit only specific traffic.

    Explanation: From all these options, the most robust firewall configuration is to deny all traffic and permit only specific traffic. This will be the most effective method to prevent unknown traffic from going to the organization's network.

2. At which of the following OSI layers does a packet filtering firewall operate?

    A. The packet filtering firewall operates at the network layer.

    B. The packet filtering firewall operates at the application layer.

    C. The packet filtering firewall operates at the transport layer.

D. The packet filtering firewall operates at the session layer.

Answer: A. The packet filtering firewall operates at the network layer.

Explanation: CISM aspirants should note that packet filtering and stateful inspection operate at the network layer (the third layer). The circuit-level firewall operates at the session layer (the fifth layer), and the application-level firewall operates at the application layer (the seventh layer).

3. What is the most robust and secure firewall system implementation?

    A. Screened host firewall

    B. Screened subnet firewall

    C. Dual-homed firewall

    D. Stateful inspection firewall

    Answer: B. Screened subnet firewall.

    Explanation: A screened subnet firewall (demilitarized zone) is regarded as the safest type of firewall implementation. A screened subnet firewall includes two packet filtering routers. It also has one bastion host. The screened subnet firewall acts as a proxy and does not allow direct communication between external and internal networks. A demilitarized zone and a screened subnet firewall function in the same way. It must be noted that with a screened subnet firewall, there are two packet filtering routers, while with a screened host firewall, there is only one packet-filtering firewall.

4. What firewall provides the most robust and secure environment?

    A. Stateful inspection

    B. Packet filter

    C. Application gateway

    D. Circuit gateway

    Answer: C. Application gateway.

    Explanation: An application-level firewall is considered the most secure kind of firewall. It functions at the highest level of the open system interconnection (OSI) model; that is, the application layer. It also works on the concept of bastion hosts and proxy servers, but it provides a separate proxy for each service. It controls applications such as FTP and HTTP. The application firewall functions at the application layer of OSI, whereas the circuit gateway functions at the session layer. The application gateway operates in a more granular aspect compared to other firewalls.

5. Which of the following firewall structures will best protect a network from internet attacks?

    A. Screened subnet firewall

    B. Screened host firewall

    C. Packet filtering router

    D. Circuit-level gateway

    Answer: A. Screened subnet firewall.

    Explanation: A screened subnet firewall (demilitarized zone) is regarded as the safest kind of firewall implementation. A screened subnet firewall includes two packet filtering routers. It also has one bastion host. A screened subnet firewall acts as a proxy and does not allow direct communication between external and internal networks. A demilitarized zone and a screened subnet firewall function in the same way. It must be noted that with a screened subnet firewall, there are two packet filtering routers, while with a screened host firewall, there is only one packet-filtering firewall.

6. Which of the following firewalls has been configured to permit external traffic only if it is in response to traffic from an internal host?

    A. Application-level gateway firewall

    B. Stateful inspection firewall

    C. Packet filtering router

    D. Circuit-level gateway

    Answer: B. Stateful inspection firewall.

    Explanation: A stateful inspection firewall monitors and tracks the destination of each packet that is being sent from the internal network. It makes sure that the incoming message is in response to the request that went out from the internal network. A stateful inspection firewall functions at the network layer of the OSI.

7. Which of the following firewalls will not allow a file to be downloaded through file transfer protocol (FTP)?

    A. Stateful inspection

    B. Application gateway

    C. Packet filter

    D. Circuit gateway

Answer: B. Application gateway.

Explanation: An application-level firewall is regarded as the most secure type of firewall. It functions at the application layer of the OSI model. It also works on the concept of bastion hosts and proxy servers, but it provides a separate proxy for each service. It controls applications such as FTP and HTTP. The application firewall operates at the application layer of OSI, whereas the circuit gateway operates at the session layer. The application gateway operates in a more granular aspect compared to other firewalls.

8. Which of the following firewalls will safeguard the most against hacking attempts?

    A. Stateful inspection

    B. A remote access server

    C. Application-level gateway

    D. Packet filtering

    Answer: C. Application-level gateway.

    Explanation: An application-level firewall is regarded as the most secure type of firewall. It functions at the application layer of the OSI model. It also works on the concept of bastion hosts and proxy servers but it provides a separate proxy for each service. It controls applications such as FTP and HTTP. The application firewall operates at the application layer of OSI, whereas the circuit gateway operates at the session layer. The application gateway operates in a more granular aspect compared to other firewalls.

9. What area is of most concern for a risk practitioner while reviewing a firewall implementation?

    A. The availability of a documented security policy.

    B. The availability of an updated firewall infrastructure with the most secure algorithm.

    C. The effectiveness of the firewall in enforcing compliance with information security policies.

    D. The technical skills of end users.

    Answer: C. The effectiveness of the firewall in enforcing compliance with information security policies.

Explanation: If the firewall is not able to enforce the requirements of the security policy, then that is a major loophole. The availability of a good security policy is important but it will be of little value if the same is not effectively implemented. Other options are not as significant as the effectiveness of the firewall.

10. Which of the following is the most common type of error while setting a firewall configuration?

    A. Incorrect configuration of the access lists.

    B. Inadequate protection of the administrator password.

    C. End users are not trained on firewall configuration.

    D. Anti-virus software is not updated at frequent intervals.

    Answer: A. Incorrect configuration of the access lists.

    Explanation: Accurately updating the current access list is a major challenge that's faced by most organizations. Hence, incorrectly configuring an access list is the most common type of error while setting a firewall configuration. The other options are not relevant to firewall configuration.

11. Which of the following is the first step of implementing a firewall in a big organization?

    A. To develop a security policy

    B. To conduct a gap analysis

    C. To review the access control list

    D. To set firewall configuration rules

    Answer: A. To develop a Security Policy.

    Explanation: The security policy specifies which firewall rules are to be configured. In the absence of a security policy, firewall rules will be ad hoc and may not support the objective of the organization. The other options are subsequent steps.

12. What is the most significant job of a firewall?

    A. Providing a routing service to connect different networks.

    B. Supporting load balancing.

    C. Connecting authorized users to a trusted network.

    D. Improving the network's performance.

Answer: C. Connecting authorized users to a trusted network.

Explanation: The prime function of a firewall is to connect authorized users to a trusted network, thereby preventing unauthorized access to the server. The other options are secondary factors.

13. What area is of the most concern for a security manager reviewing the firewall infrastructure?

    A. The firewall administrator has not been trained on the security aspects.

    B. The firewall rules are not reviewed at periodic intervals.

    C. The firewall configuration is not approved by the security manager.

    D. The implementation of a firewall above the commercial operating system with all the installation options enabled.

    Answer: D. The implementation of a firewall above the commercial operating system with all the installation options enabled.

    Explanation: When a firewall is placed on top of a commercial operating system without blocking the installation options, firewall security can be compromised. The other options are not as significant as option D.

14. What is the most effective way to ensure that firewall is configured as per the security policy?

    A. To conduct a review of the security policy

    B. To conduct a review of the reported incident.

    C. To conduct a review of the access control list

    D. To conduct a review of the parameter settings

    Answer: D. To conduct a review of the parameter settings.

    Explanation: Reviewing the parameter settings helps us understand the configuration. This can then be compared with the requirements of the security policy. The other options are not as significant as reviewing the parameter settings.

15. The primary function of a firewall is to address which of the following issues?

    A. Unauthorized attempts to access the network outside the organization.

    B. Unauthorized attempts to access the network within the organization.

    C. Slow bandwidth.

    D. Input processing error.

Answer: A. Unauthorized attempts to access the network outside the organization.

Explanation: The primary function of the firewall is to protect the network from external resources. The other options are not the objective of implementing a firewall.

16. What is the primary objective when installing two parallel firewalls attached directly to the internet and the same demilitarized zone?

    A. To establish a multi-layer defense

    B. To distinguish the test and production environments

    C. To allow for traffic load balancing

    D. To control denial of service risks

    Answer: C. To allow for traffic load balancing.

    Explanation: Two parallel firewalls with two separate entries are useful to allow traffic load balancing. A multi-level defense will only be established if firewalls are installed in a series; that is, one behind another. If the firewalls are deployed in parallel, then they provide concurrent paths for compromise and do not provide a multi-layer defense. Both firewalls are connected to the same demilitarized zone, so they cannot separate the test and production environments. Firewalls generally cannot control denial of service risks.

17. Where should an internet-facing server (extranet) be best placed?

    A. Before the firewall

    B. Outside the router

    C. On a screened subnet

    D. On the firewall server

    Answer: C. On a screened subnet.

    Explanation: Generally, servers that interact with the internet (extranet) are placed in a demilitarized area as this area is separate from internal servers and properly hardened. Placing the server before the firewall or outside the router would make it defenseless. The firewall should be placed in a hardened server with a minimum service enabled. It is not recommended to place anything else on the firewall server.

18. Where should an intrusion detection system (IDS) be placed?

    A. Before the firewall

    B. Outside the router

C. On a screened subnet

D. On the firewall server

Answer: C. On a screened subnet.

Explanation: Generally, IDS is placed on a screened subnet, which is a decentralized zone. The demilitarized area is separate from internal servers and properly hardened. Placing the IDS before the firewall or outside the router is not recommended as the IDS will generate alerts on all malicious traffic, even though the majority of such traffic will eventually be blocked by the firewall and never reach the internal network. The firewall should be placed in a hardened server with minimal services enabled. It is not recommended to place anything else on the firewall server.

19. Where is the best place to deploy a firewall?

A. On the database server

B. On the web server

C. On the IDS server

D. On the domain boundary

Answer: D. On the domain boundary.

Explanation: A firewall should be placed on a domain boundary to monitor and control incoming and outgoing traffic. The firewall should be placed in a hardened server with minimal services enabled. It is not recommended to place the firewall along with other services such as an IDS, database, or web server.

20. What is the most effective method to ensure that firewall rules and settings are adequate?

A. To survey the IT team members.

B. To periodically analyze the system logs to determine any abnormal activities.

C. To conduct penetration tests frequently.

D. To conduct system audits frequently.

Answer: C. To conduct penetration tests frequently.

Explanation: The most effective way to ensure that firewall rules are adequate is to conduct penetration tests periodically. Gaps that have been identified during the penetration test should be addressed immediately. This will help improve the security posture of the organization. The other options are not as effective as penetration testing.

21. What is one disadvantage of emailing a password-protected ZIP file?

    A. They do not use strong encryption

    B. The firewall administrator can read the file

    C. They may be quarantined by the firewall or mail filters

    D. They utilize high network bandwidth

    Answer: C. They may be quarantined by the firewall or mail filters.

    Explanation: Generally, firewall or mail filters would quarantine the password-protected ZIP files as the filter (or the firewall) will not be able to determine if the file contains malicious code. ZIP files can use strong encryptions. Generally, the firewall will not be able to read the password-protected file. A Password-protected file, by itself, does not increase network bandwidth.

22. What area is of the main concern for a security manager reviewing the firewall configuration?

    A. The firewall allows source routing

    B. The firewall server is standalone

    C. The firewall rules are reviewed on an ad hoc basis

    D. The firewall allows unregistered ports

    Answer: The firewall allows source routing,

    Explanation: Firewalls, by default, should be able to reject traffic with IP source routing. Source routing lets you get information about all the routers a packet transmits. This could potentially be used to bypass firewalls and hence is a security threat. If source routing is allowed by the firewall, the intruder can attempt spoofing attacks by stealing the internal IP addresses of the organization. Deploying a firewall in a standalone server is a good practice. The firewall should be placed in a hardened server with minimal services enabled. Firewall rules should be reviewed in a structured way periodically. Allowing unregistered ports is not recommended but does not necessarily pose a significant security risk.

23. What is the best way to prevent external individuals to access and modify the critical database of the organization?

    A. A screened subnet

    B. An acceptable usage policy

    C. Role-based access controls

D. An intrusion detection system

Answer: A. A screened subnet.

Explanation: In a screened subnet, one bastion host is deployed along with two packet filtering routers. It is considered the most secured type of firewall implementation. It acts as a demilitarized zone. An acceptable usage policy and role-based access will not have an impact on external users. Intrusion detection systems will be able to identify invalid attempts, but they will not be able to prevent attempts.

24. What device can be normally placed in a demilitarized zone?

    A. Financial database

    B. Web server

    C. Operational database

    D. Print server

    Answer: B. Web server.

    Explanation: A demilitarized zone is a separate area that is exposed to an external-facing untrusted area. Generally, servers that interact with the internet are placed in a demilitarized area as this area is separate from internal servers and hardened properly. Servers and resources placed in DMZ are isolated and are not directly connected to the internal network. The database should not be placed in a DMZ as it is exposed to an external connection.

25. Generally, where is an intranet placed?

    A. On the internal network

    B. Outside the firewall

    C. On a demilitarized zone

    D. On the external router

    Answer: A. On the internal network.

    Explanation: An intranet server is not required to communicate with external networks as external people do not need to access the same one. So, for security purposes, it should be placed on an internal network. Placing the intranet server outside the firewall or on a demilitarized zone or an external router will expose it to external threats.

26. What area is of major concern when there is an excessive number of firewall rules?

    A. One rule may conflict with another rule and create a loophole

    B. High expenditure for maintaining the rules

    C. It may impact network performance

    D. The firewall may not able to support excessive rules

    Answer: A. One rule may conflict with another rule and create a loophole.

    Explanation: Firewall rules should be simple and easy to implement. In the case of an excessive rule, it is difficult to manage the same and there is a chance that a particular rule may conflict with another rule, which may result in a loophole. Also, it becomes complex to test a high number of rules, so the operating effectiveness of the rule cannot be determined. High expenditure and network performance is a secondary concern. Next-generation firewalls can handle any number of rules.

IDSes and IPSes

Monitoring security events is a very important aspect of information security. Two important monitoring tools are IDS and IPS.

Intrusion detection system

IDS helps monitor a network (network-based IDS) or a single system (host-based IDS) to recognize and detect an intrusion activity.

Network-based and host-based IDS

The following table differentiates between network-based and host-based IDSes:

Network-Based IDS	Host-Based IDS
It monitors the activities of a full network.	It monitors the activities of a single system or host.
Comparatively, network-based IDSes have high false positives (that is, a high rate of false alarms).	Host-based IDSes have low false positives (that is, a low rate of false alarms).

Network-Based IDS	Host-Based IDS
Network-based IDSes are generally used to detect attacks from outside.	Host-based IDSes are the preferred choice for detecting attacks from the inside.
Network-based IDSes inspect the content and header information of all the packets moving across the network and identifies any irregular behavior.	Host-based IDSes detect activities on host computers such as files being deleted, programs being modified, and so on.

Table 9.2 – Difference between network-based and host-based IDSes

Components of IDS

The following table shows the various components of the IDS:

Components	Description
Sensors	The sensors collect data. Data may be in the form of IP packets, log files, and so on.
Analyzers	The analyzer analyzes the data and determines the intrusion activity.
Administration console	The administration console helps the administrator control and monitor IDS rules and functions.
User interface	The user interface lets the user view the results and carry out the required task.

Table 9.3 – Components of IDS

Limitations of IDS

The following are some of the limitations of IDS:

- IDS operates based on the policy's definition. The weakness of the policy definition weakens how IDS functions.

- IDS cannot control application-level vulnerabilities.

- IDS cannot control the backdoor into an application.

- IDS cannot analyze the data that is tunneled into an encrypted connection.

Types of IDS

The following are the types of IDS:

Type	Descriptions
Signature-based	• In signature-based IDS, IDS looks for specific predefined patterns to detect intrusions. • Patterns are stored as signatures and are updated frequently. • They are also known as rule-based IDS. • Signature-based intrusion detection systems are not capable of identifying new types of attacks where signatures are not available yet.
Statistical-based	• Statistical-based IDS attempts to identify abnormal behavior by analyzing the statistical algorithm. • Any abnormal activity is flagged as an intrusion. For example, if normal logon hours are between 7 A.M. to 5 P.M. and if someone logs in at 11 P.M., it will raise this as an intrusion. • Statistical IDS generates the most false positives compared to other types of IDS.
Neural network	• Neural networks work on the same principle as statistical-based IDS. • However, they have advanced functionality; that is, self-learning. • Neural networks keep updating the database by monitoring the general pattern of the activities. • Neural networks are most effective when addressing problems that can be solved by analyzing a large number of input variables.

Table 9.4 – Types of IDS

Tuning is the most important element for successfully implementing IDS. Tuning is the process of adjusting the criteria to determine abnormal behavior. If the criteria are not tuned properly, IDS may generate false alarms or may not identify the actual abnormality. The most effective way to determine whether IDS has been tuned properly is to simulate various attack scenarios and review the performance of the IDS.

Placing IDS

Network-based intrusion detection systems can be installed either between the firewall and the external network (that is, the internet) or between the firewall and the internal network.

If an IDS is installed between the firewall and the external network, it will be able to identify all the intrusion attempts, irrespective of whether any intrusion packets bypassed the firewall or not:

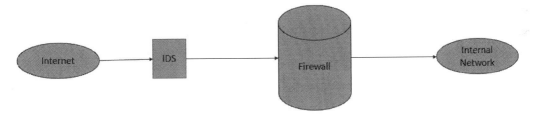

Figure 9.7 – IDS placed before the firewall

If an IDS is installed between the firewall and the internal network, it will be able to detect only those attempts that bypassed the firewall rules:

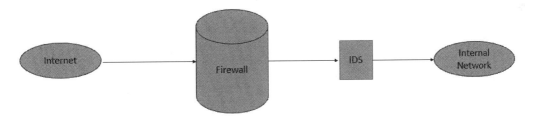

Figure 9.8 – IDS placed after the firewall

Next, let's understand the IPS.

Intrusion prevention system

IPSes can not only detect intrusion attempts but also prevent the impact of intrusion attacks.

Difference between IDS and IPS

IDS only monitors, records, and provides alarms about intrusion activities, whereas the intrusion prevention system also prevents intrusion activities.

Honeypots and honeynets

A honeypot is a decoy system that's been set up to attract hackers and intruders. The purpose of setting up a honeypot is to capture the details of intruders to proactively strengthen the security controls. High interaction honeypots provide a real environment to attack, whereas low-interaction honeypots provide limited information.

A honeynet is a combination of linked honey pots. Honeynets are used for large network setups.

Key aspects from the CISM exam's perspective

The following are some of the key aspects from the exam's perspective:

Question	Possible Answer
What is the objective of installing an IDS?	To identify attacks on the internal network.
What is the disadvantage of a statistical-based IDS?	Generate false alarms, even for minor abnormalities.
What is the disadvantage of a signature-based IDS?	Unable to detect new attack methods.
Which IDS can update its database and perform self-learning?	Neural network-based IDS.
What component of IDS collects data?	Sensor.
What IDS has the highest false alarms?	Statistical-based IDS.
What can be set up to capture the information of an intruder to proactively strengthen the security controls?	Honeypot.

Question	Possible Answer
What is the first action that should be taken to prepare for a system attack?	To gather information.
Which type of IDS is effective to mitigate a denial or distributed denial of service attack?	• Statistical-based or anomaly-based. • Neural network-based.
What will happen if an IDS is set with a low threshold value to determine an attack?	Increase in the number of false positives.

Table 9.5 – Key aspects from the CISM exam perspective

Questions

1. Which intrusion detection system observes the general pattern of activities and updates its database?

    A. Neural network-based IDS

    B. Statistical-based IDS

    C. Signature-based IDS

    D. Role-based IDS

    Answer: A. Neural network-based IDS.

    Explanation: Neural networks work on the same principle as statistical-based IDS. However, they have the advanced functionality of self-learning. Neural networks keep updating the database by monitoring the general pattern of the activities.

2. Which part of an IDS collects data?

    A. The console

    B. The sensor

    C. The analyzer

    D. The interface

    Answer: B. The sensor.

    Explanation: The sensor's job is to collect data. Data may be in the form of IP packets, log files, and so on. The analyzer's job is to analyze the data and determine the intrusion activity. The administration console helps the administrator control and monitor IDS rules and functions. The user interface lets the user view the results and carry out the required task.

3.   Which intrusion detection system has the highest false alarms?

A. Neural network-based IDS

B. Statistical-based IDS

C. Signature-based IDS

D. Host-based IDS

Answer: B. Statistical-based IDS

Explanation: Statistical-based IDS attempts to identify abnormal behavior by analyzing the statistical algorithm. Any abnormal activity is flagged as an intrusion. For example, if the normal logon hours are between 7 A.M. to 5 P.M. and if someone logs in at 11 P.M., it will raise this as an intrusion. Statistical IDS generates the most false positives compared to the other types of IDSes.

4.   What is the major concern for an auditor verifying an intrusion detection system (IDS)?

A. The number of false alarms

B. Not being able to identify the intrusion activity

C. Using an automated tool for log capturing and monitoring

D. The IDS is placed between the internal network and the firewall

Answer B. Not being able to identify the intrusion activity.

Explanation: If the IDS is not able to identify and detect the intrusion activity, then this will be the area of most concern. It defeats the core purpose of installing the IDS. Attacks will remain unnoticed if they're not identified by the IDS, so no corrective and preventive action needs to be taken for such attacks. The number of false alarms is not as significant as IDS not being able to detect the intrusion attack. Options C and D are not areas of concern.

5.   Where is the best place to put an intrusion detection system that detects intrusions that bypass firewalls?

A. Between the firewall and the external network

B. Between the firewall and the internal network

C. Between the external network and the internal network

D. Alongside the firewall

Answer: B. Between the firewall and the internal network.

Explanation: If an IDS has been installed between the firewall and the internal network, it will be able to detect only those attempts that bypassed the firewall rules. If an IDS is installed between the firewall and the external network, it will be able to identify all the intrusion attempts, irrespective of whether the intrusion packets bypassed the firewall or not.

6. Which of the following is a characteristic of an intrusion detection system (IDS)?

    A. To collect evidence on intrusive activity

    B. To route the traffic as per the defined rule

    C. To block restricted websites

    D. To act as an access control software

    Answer: A. To collect evidence on intrusive activity.

    Explanation: The intrusion detection system helps monitor a network (network-based IDS) or a single system (host-based IDS) to recognize and detect an intrusion activity. The function of IDS is to analyze the data and determine the intrusion activity. IDS does not provide features as per the other options.

7. What is the most frequent problem regarding an intrusion detection system (IDS)?

    A. False rejection rate

    B. False acceptance rate

    C. False positives

    D. DDoS attacks

    Answer: C. False positives.

    Explanation: Identifying false positives is one of the routines and frequent issues when implementing IDS. IDS operates based on policy definitions. The weakness of policy definitions is that they weaken how IDSes function. The false acceptance rate and the false rejection rate are associated with biometric implementations. DDoS is a type of attack and is not an issue regarding how IDSses operate.

8. Intrusion attacks and network penetration can be detected based on unusual system behavior from which of the following?

    A. Hub

    B. Packet filters

    C. Switch

    D. Intrusion detection system (IDS)

Answer: D. Intrusion detection system (IDS)

Explanation: IDS attempts to identify abnormal behavior by analyzing the statistical algorithm presented. Any abnormal activity is flagged as an intrusion. Hubs and switches are the networking devices for routing. A packet filter is a type of firewall that restricts blocked traffic.

9. Which of the following is the most important control for detecting intrusions?

    A. Access control procedures

    B. Automatically logging off inactive computers

    C. Monitoring unsuccessful login attempts

    D. Account lockout after a specified number of unsuccessful logon attempts

    Answer: C. Monitoring unsuccessful login attempts.

    Explanation: The most important control for identifying and detecting intrusions is to actively monitor unsuccessful login attempts. The other options will not directly help detect the intrusion.

10. Which of the following is the most important concern regarding intrusion detection systems?

    A. Many false alarms are generated by statistical-based IDSes.

    B. A firewall is installed between the intrusion detection system and the external network.

    C. The intrusion detection system is used to detect encrypted traffic.

    D. Zero-day threats are not identified by signature-based IDSes

    Answer: A. Many false alarms are generated by statistical-based IDSes.

    Explanation: Many instances of false alarms indicate that the IDS configuration needs to be tuned further. A poorly configured IDS would impact business processes or systems that need to be closed due to false alarms. It can harm business profitability. An IDS cannot read encrypted traffic; however, it can be compensated by a next-generation firewall. The other options are not as significant at blocking critical services and systems.

11. What is the most important factor that impacts the effectiveness of a neural network?

    A. The neural network detects all the known types of intrusion.

    B. The neural network flags all activities that are not normal.

C. The neural network monitors the general pattern of activities, creates a database, and addresses the complex problems involving input variables from different sources.

D. The neural network solves problems where a large database is not required.

Answer: C. The neural network monitors the general pattern of activities, creates a database, and addresses the complex problems involving input variables from different sources.

Explanation: Neural networks work on the same principle as statistical-based IDSes. However, they have advanced functionality regarding self-learning. Neural networks keep updating the database by monitoring the general pattern of the activities. They are most effective at addressing problems that can be solved by analyzing a large number of input variables.

12. An organization that wishes to protect the public-facing website on its server should install the network intrusion detection system where?

A. In a demilitarized zone

B. On the same web server where the website is hosted

C. Between the firewall and the external network

D. In the organization's internal network

Answer: A. In a demilitarized zone.

Explanation: Public-facing websites are placed in demilitarized zones to safeguard the internal network from external attacks. The IDS should be placed in the same demilitarized zone. The IDS will monitor the network traffic to detect any intrusions. A network-based intrusion would not be installed in a web server, just like a host-based IDS. Placing the IDS outside the firewall would not help protect the website.

Placing an IDS in an internal network is good to ensure that the website is not prone to internal attacks. However, an IDS would normally be placed in a demilitarized zone.

13. To prevent a rootkit from being installed on a web server hosting an application, which of the following should be installed?

A. Packet filtering

B. A network-based intrusion detection system

C. The latest operating system patch

D. A host-based intrusion prevention system

Answer: D. A host-based intrusion prevention system.

Explanation: The most recommended option is to install a host-based intrusion prevention system. A host-based IPS will prevent the activities on the host computer or server such as files being deleted, programs being modified, and so on. A network-based IDS will be able to detect irregular traffic but if signatures are not updated or traffic is encrypted, it may bypass the IDS. Regular OS patch updates address such vulnerabilities, but host IPSes are more effective at preventing unauthorized installation. A network based intrusion detection system will not able to prevent rootkit installation. A packet-filtering firewall will not able to restrict the rootkit if the incoming IP is correct.

14. Which of the following helps capture information to proactively strengthen the security controls?

    A. Honeypot

    B. Proxy server

    C. IDS

    D. IPS

    Answer: A. Honeypot.

    Explanation: A honeypot is a decoy system that's set up to attract hackers and intruders. The purpose of setting up a honeypot is to capture the details of intruders to proactively strengthen your security controls.

15. Which of the following systems can block a hacking attempt?

    A. Intrusion prevention system

    B. Router

    C. Switch

    D. Intrusion detection system

    Answer: A. Intrusion prevention system.

    Explanation: Intrusion prevention systems can not only detect intrusion attempts but also prevent the impact of an intrusion attack. Intrusion detection systems only monitor, record, and provide alarms about intrusion activities, whereas intrusion prevention systems prevent intrusion activities. Router and switch are devices that are used for network routing.

16. Which of the following is the first action you should perform when preparing for a system attack?

    A. Capture information

    B. Erase the evidence

    C. Gain access

    D. Launch a DoS attack

    Answer: A. Capture information.

    Explanation: The first step that an intruder takes is capturing and gathering relevant information about the target environment. Based on this information, they attempt various techniques to gain access. Once the objective has been accomplished, they try to erase the evidence.

17. After the firewall, which of the following is considered the next line of defense for network security?

    A. Anti-malware software

    B. Router

    C. Switch

    D. Intrusion detection system

    Answer: D. Intrusion detection system.

    Explanation: Network-based intrusion detection systems are considered the next line of defense after firewalls. Intrusion detection systems monitor, record, and provide alarms about intrusion activity that bypasses the firewall. IDSes can identify abnormal traffic easier compared to anti-malware software. Router and switch are devices that are used for network routing.

18. What is the major concern regarding a poorly configured intrusion prevention system?

    A. The administrator has to verify high instances of alarms

    B. Critical services or systems are blocked due to false alarms

    C. The network is slowed down

    D. The cost of the intrusion prevention system is high

    Answer: B. Critical services or systems are blocked due to false alarms.

Explanation: A poorly configured firewall would largely impact business processes or systems that need to be closed due to false alarms. It can harm business profitability. The other options are not as significant as blocking critical services and systems.

19. What is the most important aspect to consider while deploying an intrusion detection system?

    A. Tuning

    B. Patch updating

    C. Logging

    D. Change management

    Answer: A. Tuning.

    Explanation: Tuning is the most important element for successfully implementing IDSes. Tuning is the process of adjusting the criteria to determine abnormal behavior. If the criteria are not tuned properly, the IDS may generate false alarms or may not identify the actual abnormality. Patch updates are more related to the operating system. Logging and change management are not as relevant as tuning.

20. Statistical-based IDSes are not as popular as signature-based IDSes due to which reason?

    A. They are more expensive than signature-based IDSes

    B. They require specialized staff to monitor

    C. They generate false alarms from different user or system actions

    D. They are not capable of detecting new types of attacks

    Answer: C. They generate false alarms from different user or system actions.

    Explanation: Statistical-based IDSes attempt to identify abnormal behavior by analyzing the statistical algorithm. Any abnormal activity is flagged as an intrusion. For example, if normal login hours are between 7 A.M. to 5 P.M. and if someone logs in at 11 P.M., it will raise this as an intrusion. Statistical IDSes generate the most false alarms compared to other types of IDS. Statistical-based IDSes can identify new attacks while signature-based IDSes cannot. Statistical-based IDSes may be more expensive and may require specialized staff, but the more important aspect is that they can detect false alarms.

21. What is the main disadvantage of signature-based intrusion?

    A. High instances of false alarms

    B. Unable to detect new attack methods

    C. High cost of maintenance

    D. Use of high network bandwidth

    Answer: B. Unable to detect new attack methods.

    Explanation: In signature-based IDSes, the IDS looks for specific predefined patterns to detect intrusions. These patterns are stored as signatures and are updated frequently. They are also known as rule-based IDSes. Signature-based IDSes are not capable of identifying new types of attacks that signatures are not available for yet. The other options are not relevant.

22. What is the most effective way to determine the deployment of an intrusion detection system?

    A. Simulate various attack scenarios and review the performance of the IDS

    B. Deploy a honeypot to determine any abnormal activity

    C. Review the configuration of the IDS

    D. Compare the IDS rules to the industry benchmark

    Answer: A. Simulate various attack scenarios and review the performance of the IDS.

    Explanation: The most effective way to determine whether the IDS has been tuned properly is to simulate various attack scenarios and review the performance of the IDS. The other options are secondary aspects.

23. What is the main objective of deploying an intrusion detection system?

    A. To comply with the information security policy

    B. To comply with regulatory requirements

    C. To determine the patterns of suspicious access

    D. To identify the attacks on internal networks

    Answer: D. To identify the attacks on internal networks.

    Explanation: The main objective of an IDS is to identify the attacks on an internal network and provide alerts for immediate countermeasures, thereby minimizing the impact of the attack. The other options are secondary aspects.

24. Which of the following is very important to ensure that the intrusion detection system can view all the traffic in DMZ?

    A. Placing the IDS before the firewall.

    B. Ensuring that all the end devices are connected to the IDS.

    C. Ensuring encrypted traffic is decrypted before being processed by the IDS.

    D. Ensuring the appropriate network bandwidth is being used.

    Answer: C. Ensuring encrypted traffic is decrypted before being processed by the IDS.

    Explanation: IDSes cannot read encrypted traffic. Encryption should be terminated before it is processed by the IDS. Encryption should be terminated at the secure socket layer or a VPN server to allow all traffic to be monitored. Placing an IDS before the firewall will generate a high number of alerts that will be eventually blocked by the firewall. The end devices don't need to be connected to IPS. Network bandwidth is not relevant.

25. What is the most effective way to detect an intruder who has successfully penetrated a network?

    A. Perform periodic audits

    B. Perform periodic penetration testing

    C. Establish vendor-provided default settings

    D. Install a honeypot on the network

    Answer: D. Install a honeypot on the network.

    Explanation: A honeypot is a decoy system that's set up to attract hackers and intruders. The purpose of setting up a honeypot is to capture the details of intruders to proactively strengthen your security controls. As honeypots are closely monitored, any unauthorized attempts are more likely to be detected before significant damage is inflicted. The other options will not directly help detect the intruder.

26. Denial or **distributed denial of service (DDoS)** attacks can be mitigated by which of the following?

    A. Signature-based detection

    B. An external router

C. Anti-virus software

D. Anomaly-based detection

Answer: D. Anomaly-based detection.

Explanation: Anomaly-based detection works based on the statistics of normal traffic patterns. It is also known as a statistic-based IDS. Anything different from the normal traffic range will be considered as deviation and an alert will be generated. In a DDoS attack, incoming traffic increases tremendously, so it is detected by anomaly-based detection. The other options will not be effective in detecting DDoS attacks.

27. What is the most effective way to lure hackers and get their information without exposing the information assets?

A. Set a firewall

B. Set a proxy

C. Set a decoy file

D. Set a router

Answer: C. Set a decoy file.

Explanation: A decoy file is also known as a honeypot. A honeypot is a decoy system that's set up to attract hackers and intruders. The purpose of setting up a honeypot is to capture the details of intruders to proactively strengthen your security controls. The other options are used to keep the hacker out of the internal network.

28. What will happen if an IDS is set with a low threshold value to determine an attack?

A. An increase in the number of false positives

B. An increase in the number of false negatives

C. Logs will not be captured

D. Active monitoring will be ignored

Answer: A. An increase in the number of false positives.

Explanation: Intrusion detection systems use different logs such as firewall logs, system logs, and application logs. These logs are analyzed to determine the trends and patterns of attacks. A threshold is an acceptable deviation from the normal pattern. A low threshold value means anything outside that value will be considered as an attack. Even genuine business traffic will be considered an attack if it is above the threshold. A low threshold value generally increases the number of false positives.

Digital signature

A digital signature is a process wherein a digital code is attached to an electronically transmitted document to validate the integrity of the document and the identity of the sender.

Creating a digital signature

A digital signature can be created by performing two steps:

1. Create a hash (message digest) of the message.

2. Encrypt the hash with the private key of the sender.

The following table shows how to create a digital signature:

Steps description	Step Results
Step 1: Creating hash value (message digest) of given message.	4526dee03a36204cbb9887b3528fac4e
Step 2: Encryption of above hash (message digest)	4xxxxxxxxxxxxxxxxxxxxxxxxxxxxxxxxxxxe ↑

Digital Signature

Figure 9.9 – Digital signature

Now, let's discuss hash values and message digests.

What is a hash or message digest?

A hash function is a mathematical algorithm that provides a unique fixed string for any given message. Note that the hash value will be unique for each message. Let's understand this by looking at the following table:

Message	Hash Value
Meeting at 8 AM	4526dee03a36204cbb9887b3528fac4e
Meeting at 8 PM	10ca8c76ec6b2b34a9a06505da298ed8

Figure 9.10 – Hash values

The following software shows the hash value of the message `Meeting at 8 AM`:

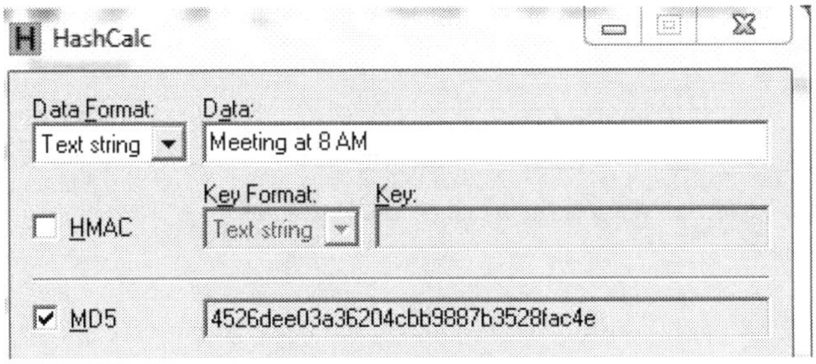

Figure 9.11 – Hash software

The following software shows the hash value of the message `Meeting at 8 PM`:

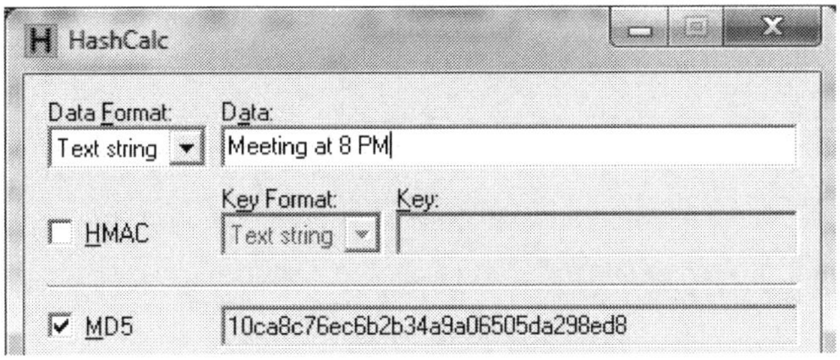

Figure 9.12 – Hash software

The hash value of the first message is for 8 A.M., while the second is for 8 P.M. As you can see, the hash value has changed, even though only one letter has changed in our message:

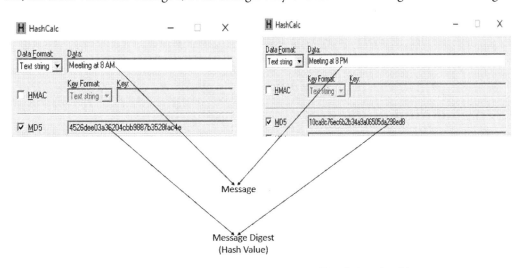

Hash value changes with slightest change in message. Thus it helps to validate the integrity of the message.

Figure 9.13 – Matching hash value

Let's look at how the message flows from sender A to recipient B:

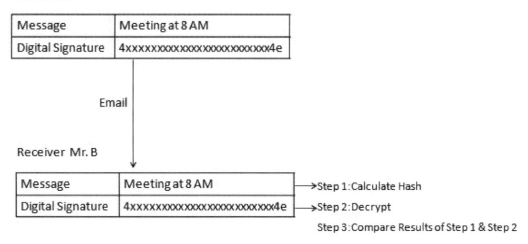

Figure 9.14 – Verifying the digital signature

Receiver Mr. B will perform the following steps:

1. First, he will independently calculate the hash value of `Meeting at 8 AM`. The hash value will be `4526dee03a36204cbb9887b3528fac4e`.

2. Then, he will decrypt the digital signature – that is, `4xxxxxxxxxxxxxxxxxxxxxxxxx4e` – using the public key of sender Mr. A. (This proves authentication and non-repudiation.)

3. Finally, he will compare the value derived from *Step 1* with the value derived from *Step 2*. If both tally, this proves the integrity of the message.

Thus, a digital signature is used to verify the following properties:

*   Integrity (that is, a message has not been tampered with)

*   Authentication (that is, a message has been sent by the sender)

*   Non-repudiation (that is, the sender cannot later deny sending the message)

However, a digital signature does not provide confidentiality

Key aspects from the CISM exam's perspective

The key aspects regarding digital signatures are as follows:

- In any given scenario, a digital signature ensures the integrity of the message (that is, the message hasn't been altered), the authentication of the message (that is, the message has been sent by the sender), and non-repudiation (that is, the sender cannot deny that they sent the message in a court of law).

- When creating a digital signature, only the hash of the message is encrypted (and not the entire message). Hence, the digital signature does not provide confidentiality or privacy.

- When encrypting the hash of the message, the private key of the sender should be used.

- Non-repudiation provides the best evidence about the occurrence of specific actions or transactions. The initiator of the transaction cannot deny that transaction.

Questions

1. A hash function is used to ensure what?

   A. The confidentiality of the message

   B. The integrity of the message

   C. The availability of the message

   D. The compression of the message

   Answer: B. The integrity of the message.

   Explanation: A digital signature is used to validate the integrity, authentication, and non-repudiation of messages. However, it does not ensure message confidentiality. A digital signature includes an encrypted hash total of the message. This hash value would change if the message was subsequently altered, thus indicating that the alteration had occurred. Hence, it helps to ensure message integrity. Digital signatures will not able to address and support any of the other options.

2. A digital signature addresses which of the following concerns about electronic messages?

   A. The authentication and integrity of data

   B. The authentication and confidentiality of data

C. The confidentiality and integrity of data

D. The authentication and availability of data

Answer: A. The authentication and integrity of data.

Explanation: A digital signature is used to validate the integrity, authentication, and non-repudiation of electronic messages. It does not ensure message confidentiality or the availability of data. A digital signature can be created by performing the following two steps:

Step 1: Create a hash value (message digest) of the message.

Step 2: Encrypt the hash with the private key of the sender.

3. A digital signature addresses which of the following concerns about electronic messages?

A. Unauthorized archiving

B. Confidentiality

C. Unauthorized copying

D. Alteration

Answer: D. Alteration.

Explanation: The hash value of a message is used to create the digital signature. Each message has a unique hash. If the message changes, the hash also changes. Thus, the hash value will not be the same if the message is altered afterward. A digital signature will not address other concerns.

4. Which of the following is used to address the risk of a hash being compromised?

A. Digital signatures

B. Message encryption

C. Email password

D. Disabling an SSID broadcast

Answer: A. Digital signatures

Explanation: A digital signature is created by encrypting the hash of the message. An encrypted hash cannot be altered without knowing the public key of the sender.

5. A digital signature provides which of the following?

    A. Non-repudiation, confidentiality, and integrity

    B. Integrity, privacy, and non-repudiation

    C. Integrity, authentication, and non-repudiation

    D. Confidentiality, privacy and non-repudiation

    Answer: C. Integrity, authentication, and non-repudiation.

    Explanation: A digital signature is used to validate the integrity, authentication, and non-repudiation of electronic messages. It does not ensure message confidentiality or the availability of data.

6. The *MAIN* reason to use digital signatures is to ensure data is what?

    A. Private

    B. integral

    C. Available

    D. Confidential

    Answer: B. Integral

    Explanation: Digital signatures provide integrity because the hash of the message changes if any unauthorized changes are made to the data (file, mail, document, and so on), thus ensuring data integrity.

7. The strongest evidence of the occurrence of a specific action is provided by which of the following?

    A. Proof of delivery

    B. Non-repudiation

    C. Proof of submission

    D. Authorization

    Answer: B. Non-repudiation.

    Explanation: Non-repudiation assures that the sender of the message or initiator of the transactions can later deny the fact of sending the message or initiating the transaction. Non-repudiation is the most effective way to validate that a specific action occurred. Digital signatures are used to provide non-repudiation.

8. A sender's authenticity can be best ensured by which of the following?

A. The use of the sender's private key to encrypt the hash of the message.

B. The use of the receiver's public key to encrypt the entire message.

C. The use of the sender's public key to encrypt the hash of the message.

D. The use of the receiver's private key to encrypt the entire message.

Answer: A. The use of the sender's private key to encrypt the hash of the message.

Explanation: The sender encrypts the hash of the message with their private key. If the recipient is successful in decrypting the message with the public key of the sender, then it proves authentication – that is, the message was sent from the sender. It ensures non-repudiation – that is, the sender cannot repudiate having sent the message. For authentication, the entire message doesn't need to be encrypted. Encrypting the entire message would involve more cost and time, so only encrypting the hash is necessary.

9. In an e-commerce transaction, an organization is validating the customer through a digital signature when they receive communication from the customer. How can this be done?

A. A hash of the message can be transmitted and encrypted with the organization's private key.

B. A hash of the message can be transmitted and encrypted with the customer's private key.

C. A hash of the message can be transmitted and encrypted with the customer's public key.

D. A hash of the message can be transmitted and encrypted with the organization's public key

Answer: B. A hash of the message can be transmitted and encrypted with the customer's private key.

Explanation: A digital signature can be created as follows:

Step 1: Create the hash (message digest) of the message.

Step 2: Encrypt the hash with the private key of the sender.

In the question, the sender is the customer. So, the hash is to be encrypted with the customer's (sender's) private key.

10. Digital signatures help with what?

    A. Detecting spam.

    B. Providing confidentiality.

    C. Adding to the workload of gateway servers.

    D. Decreasing the available bandwidth.

    Answer: A. Detecting spam.

    Explanation: By using a digital signature, a sender can be tracked. A digital signature helps authenticate the sender. The recipient will be able to set the configuration to their system to delete messages automatically from specific senders. The file size of the digital signature is only a few bytes and will not have any impact on bandwidth. There will be no major impact on the workload of gateway servers.

11. What is the basic difference between hash and encryption regarding a hash value?

    A. It cannot be reversed.

    B. It can be reversed.

    C. It is concerned with integrity and security.

    D. It creates an output of a bigger length than the original message.

    Answer: A. It cannot be reversed.

    Explanation: Let's understand the outcome of hashing, as well as encryption:

    For the `Meeting at 8 AM` message, the hash value is `4526dee03a36204cbb9887b3528fac4e`.

    For the `Meeting at 8 AM` message, the encryption value is `Mxxxxxx xx x xM`.

    Now, from the `4526dee03a36204cbb9887b3528fac4e` hash value, we cannot derive the message, but from `Mxxxxxx xx x xM`, we can derive the original message via decryption.

    Hashing operates in a one-way fashion; it cannot be reversed. We can create a hash from the message, but it is not possible to create a message from that particular hash. Thus, the hash value is irreversible, whereas encryption is. This is the major difference between encryption and hash values.

12. An organization is sharing critical information with vendors via email. Organizations can ensure that the recipients of emails (that is, vendors) can authenticate the identity of the sender (that is, employees) by doing what?

    A. Having employees digitally sign their email messages.

    B. Having employees encrypt their email messages.

    C. Having employees compress their email messages.

    D. Password protecting all email messages.

    Answer: A. Have employees digitally sign their email messages.

    Explanation: When an employee digitally signs their email messages, the receiver will be able to validate the integrity or authenticity by checking the digital signature.

13. A digital signature ensures that the sender of the message cannot deny generating and sending the message. This is known as what?

    A. Integrity

    B. Authentication

    C. Non-repudiation

    D. Security

    Answer: C. Non-repudiation.

    Explanation: Non-repudiation provides the best evidence about the occurrence of a specific action or transaction. The sender of the email or initiator of the transaction cannot deny that transaction. Digital signatures are used to provide non-repudiation.

14. In an e-commerce transaction, which of the following should be relied on to validate the occurrence of the transaction?

    A. Proof of delivery

    B. Authentication

    C. Encryption

    D. Non-repudiation

    Answer: D. Non-repudiation.

    Explanation: Non-repudiation provides the best evidence about the occurrence of a specific action or transaction. The initiator of the transaction cannot deny that transaction. Digital signatures are used to provide non-repudiation.

15. Mr. A has sent a message containing the encrypted (by A's private key) hash of the message to Mr. B. This will ensure which of the following?

    A. Authenticity and integrity

    B. Authenticity and confidentiality

    C. Integrity and privacy

    D. Privacy and non-repudiation

    Answer: A. Authenticity and integrity.

    Explanation: In this case, the message is not encrypted (only the hash is encrypted), so it will not ensure privacy or confidentiality. Encrypting the hash will ensure authenticity and integrity.

16. To implement a digital signature, which of the following is required?

    A. The signer must have the public key of the sender, while the receiver must have the private key of the sender.

    B. The signer must have the private key of the sender, while the receiver must have the public key of the sender.

    C. Both the signer and receiver should possess a public key.

    D. Both the signer and receiver should possess a private key.

    Answer: B. The signer must have the private key of the sender, while the receiver must have the public key of the sender.

    Explanation: A digital signature can be created as follows:

    Step 1: Create a hash (message digest) of the message.

    Step 2: Encrypt the hash with the private key of the sender.

    On the recipient's end, the hash is decrypted using the public key of the sender.

17. What is the objective of including a hash value (message digest) in a digital signature?

    A. Ensuring the integrity of the message

    B. Defining the encryption algorithm

    C. Confirming the identity of the originator

    D. Compressing the message.

    Answer: A. Ensuring the integrity of the message.

    Explanation: A digital signature is created by calculating the hash value for the given message. Recalculating the hash of the original message should provide the same hash value. Thus, it helps to ensure message integrity.

18. What is the best way to ensure that the information that is transmitted over the internet is genuine and transmitted by the known sender?

    A. Use a steganographic technique

    B. Use an encryption technique

    C. Use two-factor authentication

    D. Use an embedded digital signature

    Answer: D. Use an embedded digital signature.

    Explanation: A digital signature is used to determine the identity and integrity of the data. The other options are not relevant for determining whether the message and sender are genuine.

19. What is the most effective way to ensure non-repudiation?

    A. Encryption

    B. Hash

    C. Symmetric encryption

    D. Digital signatures

    Answer: D. Digital signatures.

    Explanation: A digital signature is used to validate the integrity, authentication, and non-repudiation of electronic messages. Non-repudiation is the process of ensuring that the sender of the message or initiator of the transaction is not in a position to deny the message. Encryption and symmetric encryption provide confidentiality but not non-repudiation. Hash provides integrity but not non-repudiation.

20. What is the most effective way to ensure that a data file has not changed?

    A. Validate the last modified date of the file

    B. Encrypt the file

    C. Provide role-based access control

    D. Create a hash value of the file, then compare the file hashes

    Answer: D. Create a hash value of the file, then compare the file hashes.

    Explanation: The best way is to create the hash of the original file and then compare it with the suspected file to ensure that both files are the same. If the hash has changed, then it indicates that the file has been modified. The last modified date can also be fabricated. File encryption and role-based access control are good forms of access control but they do not prevent the file from being corrupted or modified by a valid user.

21. What is the most effective way to validate the password that's entered by a user?

    A. Packet filtering

    B. Encryption

    C. System hardening

    D. Hashing

    Answer: D. Hashing.

    Explanation: Hashing is the process of converting a given password into another value. The result of a hash function is known as a hash value. When a user enters the password, it is converted into a hash and compared with the stored hash. If the hash matches, then access is granted. The actual password cannot be generated from the hash (because it is a one-way algorithm), so the actual password remains the same.

Elements of PKI

A **public key infrastructure** (**PKI**) is a set of rules and procedures for creating, managing, distributing, storing, and using a digital certificate and public key encryption.

PKI terminologies

CISM aspirants should have a basic understanding of the following terms regarding public key infrastructure:

- **Digital certificate**: A digital certificate is an electronic document that proves the ownership of a public key. The digital certificate includes details about the key, details about the owner, and detail about the digital signature of the issuer of the digital certificate. It is also known as a public key certificate.

- **Certifying Authority** (**CA**): A certification authority is an entity that is responsible for issuing digital certificates.

- **Registration Authority** (**RA**): A registration authority is an entity that verifies user requests for digital signatures and recommends the certificate authority to issue them.

- **Certificate Revocation List** (**CRL**): CRL is a list of digital certificates that have been revoked and terminated by the certificate authority before their expiry date. These certificates should no longer be trusted.

- **Certification Practice Statement (CPS)**: A certification practice statement is a document that prescribes the practice and process of issuing and managing digital certificates by certifying authority. It includes details such as the controls that are in place, the method for validating applicants, and using certificates.

- **Public Key Infrastructure**: PKI is a set of roles, policies, and procedures for issuing, maintaining, and revoking public key certificates.

Now, let's discuss the process of issuing a PKI.

The process of issuing a PKI

Issuing a public key involves the following process:

1. The applicant applies for a digital certificate to be issued to CA.

2. The CA delegates the verification process to RA.

3. RA verifies the correctness of the information provided by the applicant.

4. If the information is correct, then RA recommends CA for issuing the certificate.

5. CA issues the certificate and manages the same throughout its life cycle. CA also maintains details of certificates that have been terminated or revoked before their expiry dates. This list is known as CRL. CA also maintains a document called a CPS that contains the **standard operating procedure (SOP)** for issuing and managing certificates.

CA versus RA

The following table shows the differences between CA and RA:

CA	RA
The CA is responsible for issuing and managing digital certificates.	The RA verifies the correctness of the information provided by applicants.
The CA delegates some of the administrative functions, such as verifying the information provided by applicants.	Once the application's information has been authenticated, the RA recommends that the CA issue a certificate.
The CA authenticates and validates the holder of the certificate after issuing the certificate.	The RA authenticates the information of the applicant before issuing the certificate.

Table 9.6 – Differences between CA and RA

Single point of failure

The private key of a certificate authority is used to issue the digital certificate to all the parties in the public key infrastructure. If the private key of CA is compromised, it will lead to a single point of failure for the entire PKI infrastructure because the integrity of all the digital certificates is based on this private key.

Functions of RA

A registration authority does the following:

- Verifies and validates the information provided by the applicant.
- Ensures that the applicant owns a private key and that it matches the public key that was requested for a certificate. This is known as **proof of possession** (**POP**).
- Distributes physical tokens containing private keys.
- Generates shared secret keys during the initialization and certificate pickup phase of registration.

Key aspects from the CISM exam's perspective

The following table covers some important aspects from the CISM's exam perspective:

Questions	Possible Answers
Which authority manages the life cycle of a digital certificate?	Certifying Authority
In which document is a procedural aspect for dealing with a compromised private key prescribed?	Certification Practice Statement
Where are the contractual requirements between the relying parties and the certificate authority prescribed?	Certification Practice Statement

Table 9.7 – Key aspects from the CISM exam perspective

Questions

1. Which of the following functions manages the life cycle of a digital certificate?

   A. **Registration Authority (RA)**

   B. **Certifying Authority (CA)**

   C. Public key authority

   D. Private key authority

   Answer: B. **Certifying Authority (CA)**.

   Explanation: A CA is an entity that is responsible for issuing digital certificates. The CA is responsible for issuing and managing digital certificates.

2. Which of the following is the function of the **Registration Authority (RA)**?

   A. To issue the digital certificate

   B. To manage the certificate throughout its life cycle

   C. To document and maintain certificate practice statements

   D. To validate the information of the applicants for the certificate

   Answer: D. To validate the information of the applicants for the certificate.

   Explanation: A registration authority has the following functions:

   - To verify and validate information provided by the applicant.

   - To ensure that the applicant owns a private key and that it matches the public key requested for a certificate. This is known as **proof of possession (POP)**.

   - To distribute physical tokens containing private keys.

   - To generate shared secret keys during the initialization and certificate pickup phase of registration.

3. Which of the following authorities manages the life cycle of a digital certificate to ensure the existence of security in the digital signature?

   A. **Certificate Authority (CA)**

   B. **Registration Authority (RA)**

   C. Certification practice statement

   D. Public key Authority

Answer: A. **Certificate Authority (CA)**.

Explanation: A CA is an entity that issues digital certificates. The CA is responsible for issuing and managing digital certificates.

4. A certificate authority can delegate which process?

    A. Certificate issuance

    B. Certificate life cycle management

    C. Establishing a link between the applicant and their public key

    D. Maintaining the certificate revocation list

    Answer: C. Establishing a link between the applicant and their public key.

    Explanation: CA delegates some of the administrative functions such as verifying the information provided by applicants. RA is delegated with the function of verifying the correctness of information provided by applicants. RA verifies that the applicant owns a private key and that it matches with the public key requested for the certificate. This is known as proof of possession (POP).

5. Which of the following is considered a weakness in a public key infrastructure process?

    A. The certificate authority is in a centralized location

    B. The transaction can be executed from any device.

    C. The user organization is also the owner of the CA

    D. The availability of multiple data centers to manage the certificate

    Answer: C. The user organization is also the owner of the CA.

    Explanation: This indicates that there is a conflict of interest as the user and owner of the certificate are the same. The independence of the certifying authority will be impaired in this scenario, and this is considered a major weakness.

6. Which of the following is the function of the Registration Authority?

    A. Issuing certificates.

    B. Validating the information provided by the applicant.

    C. Signing the certificate to achieve authentication and non-repudiation.

    D. Maintaining the certificate revocation list.

    Answer: B. Validating the information provided by the applicant.

Explanation: A Registration Authority has the following functions:

- To verify and validate information provided by the applicant.

- To ensure that the applicant owns a private key and that it matches the public key requested for a certificate. This is known as **proof of possession (POP)**.

- To distribute physical tokens containing private keys.

- To generate shared secret keys during the initialization and certificate pickup phase of registration.

7. The procedural aspect of dealing with a compromised private key is prescribed in what of the following?

    A. Certificate practice statement

    B. Certificate revocation list

    C. Certificate disclosure statement

    D Applicant disclosure form

    Answer: A. Certificate practice statement.

    Explanation: A certification practice statement is a document that prescribes the practice and process of issuing and managing digital certificates by certifying authority. It includes details regarding the controls in place, the method for validating applicants, and the usage of certificates.

8. Which of the following is a function of a certifying authority?

    A. To ensure the availability of a secured communication network based on certificates.

    B. To validate the identity and authenticity of the certificate owner.

    C. To ensure that both communicating parties are digitally certified.

    D. To host the private keys of subscribers in the public domain.

    Answer: B. To validate the identity and authenticity of the certificate owner.

    Explanation: A registration authority has the following functions:

    - To verify and validate information provided by the applicant.

    - To ensure that the applicant owns a private key and that it matches the public key requested for a certificate. This is known as **proof of possession (POP)**.

    - To distribute physical tokens containing private keys.

    - To generate shared secret keys during the initialization and certificate pickup phase of registration.

9. When is a certificate authority not required in a public key infrastructure?

    A. When users are not related to each other

    B. When two-factor authentication is used

    C. When users attest to each other's identities

    D. When role-based access control is used

    Answer: C. When users attest to each other's identities.

    Explanation: The objective of the certificate authority is to support the identification of the key holder. If the users have already attested to each other's identity, the certificate authority may not be required. The certificate authority is relevant for the other options.

10. In a public key infrastructure, the contractual relationship between parties is provided in which of the following?

    A. Certificate revocation list

    B. Digital certificate

    C. Non-repudiation certificate

    D. Certification practice statement

    Answer: D. Certification practice statement.

    Explanation: A **certification practice statement** (**CPS**) is a document that prescribes the processes for issuing and managing the digital certificates of the certifying authority. It also provides the contractual requirements between the relying parties and the certificate authority. It includes details such as the controls that should be in place, the method for validating applicants, and how certificates are used.

11. What is the role of the certificate authority in public key infrastructure?

    A. It supports the accuracy and integrity of the transferred data.

    B. It prevents repudiation of transactions.

    C. It attests to the validity of a user's public key.

    D. It reduces the cost of data transfers.

    Answer: C. It attests to the validity of a user's public key.

    Explanation: The certifying authority is responsible for issuing and managing digital certificates. The certifying authority authenticates and validates the holder of the certificate after issuing the certificate. The other options are not the function of a certificate authority.

12. What is the single point of failure in PKI?

   A. The public key of the certificate authority (CA)

   B. The private key of the holder of a digital certificate

   C. The private key of the certificate authority

   D. The public key of the holder of a digital certificate

   Answer: C. The private key of the certificate authority.

   Explanation: The private key of a certificate authority is used to issue the digital certificate to all the parties in public key infrastructure. If the private key of CA is compromised, it will lead to a single point of failure for the entire PKI infrastructure. This is because the integrity of all the digital certificates is based on this private key. If the private key of a holder is compromised, it will affect only that holder. The public key is published and poses no risk.

Asymmetric encryption

Cryptography is defined as the art or science of writing secrets using techniques such as encryption. Encryption is the process of converting data into unreadable code so that it cannot be accessed or read by unauthorized people. This unreadable data can be converted into a readable form via decryption. Different types of algorithms are available for encryption and decryption.

Symmetric encryption vis a vis asymmetric encryption

There are two types of encryption: symmetric encryption and asymmetric encryption. The following table shows the difference between the two terms:

Symmetric Encryption	Asymmetric Encryption
A single key is used to encrypt and decrypt the messages.	Two keys are used – one for encryption and the other for decryption.
It is known as a symmetric key because both the encryption and decryption keys are the same.	It is known as asymmetric encryption because both the encryption and decryption keys are different. A message encrypted by a private key can be decrypted only with the corresponding public key. Similarly, a message encrypted with a public key can be decrypted only with the corresponding private key.

Symmetric Encryption	Asymmetric Encryption
Comparatively faster computation and processing.	Comparatively slower computation and processing.
Comparatively, the symmetric encryption process is cheaper.	Comparatively, a symmetric encryption process is costlier.
A major disadvantage of symmetric encryption is that the key is shared with another party.	No such challenge is faced in asymmetric encryption as two separate keys are used.
For large key distributors, symmetric encryption is not preferred as scaling will result in complex distribution and storage problems.	For large key distributors, asymmetric encryption is preferred as scaling is more convenient.

Table 9.8 – Differences between symmetric and asymmetric encryption

Now, let's discuss the different types of encryption keys.

Encryption keys

In an asymmetric environment, a total of four keys are available with different functions. The following table indicates who possesses the different keys:

Type of Key	Availability
Sender's private key	This key is only available to the sender.
Sender's public key	This key is available in the public domain. Public keys can be accessed by anyone.
Receiver's private key	This key is only available to the receiver.
Receiver's public key	This key is available in the public domain. Public keys can be accessed by anyone.

Table 9.9 – Different types of key and their functions

Using keys for different objectives

The aforementioned keys are used to achieve the following objectives:

- Confidentiality

- Authentication and non-repudiation

- Integrity

Let's discuss these further.

Confidentiality

In asymmetric encryption, two keys are used – one for encryption and another for decryption. Messages that are encrypted by one key can be decrypted by another key. These two keys are known as private keys and public keys. A private key is only available to the owner of the key; a public key is available in the public domain.

Messages can be encrypted with the following keys:

- **Receiver's public key**: If a message is encrypted using the public key of the receiver, then only the receiver can decrypt the same as they are the only one who has access to that private key. This will ensure message confidentiality as only the owner of the private key can read the message.

- **Receiver's private key**: The sender will not own the receiver's private key and hence this option is not feasible.

- **Sender's public key**: If a message is encrypted using the public key of the sender, then it can only be decrypted using the private key of the sender. The receiver will not own the sender's private key, so this option is not feasible.

- **Sender's private key**: If a message is encrypted using the private key of the sender, then anyone with a public key can encrypt the same. The public key is available in the public domain, so anyone can encrypt the message. This will not ensure the confidentiality of the message.

So, regarding message confidentiality, the receiver's public key is used to encrypt the message, while the receiver's private key is used to decrypt the message.

Authentication

Authentication is ensured by verifying and validating some unique features of the sender. Normally, we validate a document by verifying the signature of the sender. This signature is unique for everyone. Similarly, for digital transactions, a private key is unique for each owner. Only the owner owns their unique private key. Each private key has a corresponding public key. A third person can authenticate the identity of the owner by using a public key. When the objective is to authenticate the sender of the message, the sender's private key is used to encrypt the hash of the message. The receiver will try to decrypt the same by using the sender's public key. If it's successfully decrypted, this will indicate that the message is genuine and that the sender has been authenticated.

So, to authenticate a message, the sender's private key is used to encrypt the message, while the sender's public key is used to decrypt the message.

Non-repudiation

Non-repudiation refers to a situation wherein the sender cannot take on the responsibility of the digital message or transaction. Non-repudiation is established once the sender has been authenticated. Hence, for non-repudiation, the same concept of authentication will apply.

Hence, for non-repudiation of the message, the sender's private key is used to encrypt the message, while the sender's public key is used to decrypt the message.

Integrity

Integrity refers to the correctness, completeness, and accuracy of the message/data. To achieve integrity, the following steps must be performed:

- The sender will create a hash of the message.
- This hash is encrypted using the sender's private key.
- The message, along with an encrypted hash, is sent to the receiver.
- The receiver will do two things. First, they will decrypt the hash value using the sender's private key. Then, they will calculate the hash of the message that was received.
- The receiver will compare both hashes and if both hash values are the same, the message is considered correct, complete, and accurate.

The following table shows the process of using different keys to achieve each of these objectives:

Objective	Use of Keys	What to Encrypt
Confidentiality	Receiver's public key	Full message
Authentication/ non-repudiation	Sender's private key	The hash of the message
Integrity	Sender's private key	The hash of the message
Confidentiality and authentication/ non-repudiation	For confidentiality: Use the receiver's public key to encrypt the full message.	
	For authentication (non-repudiation): Use the sender's private key to encrypt the hash of the message.	
Confidentiality, integrity, and authentication/ non-repudiation	For confidentiality: Use the receiver's public key to encrypt the full message.	
	For integrity, authentication, and non-repudiation: Use the sender's private key to encrypt the hash of the message.	

Table 9.10 – Process of using different keys

Key aspects from the CISM exam's perspective

The following are some of the key aspects from the exam's perspective:

Question	Possible Answer
In asymmetric encryption, message confidentiality can be ensured by doing what?	Using the receiver's public key for encryption and using the receiver's private key for decryption.
In asymmetric encryption, message authentication can be ensured by doing what?	Using the sender's private key to encrypt the message or hash and using the sender's public key to decrypt the message or hash.
In asymmetric encryption, message non-repudiation can be ensured by doing what?	Using the sender's private key to encrypt the message or hash and using the sender's public key to decrypt the message or hash.

Question	Possible Answer
In asymmetric encryption, message integrity can be ensured by doing what?	Using the sender's private key to encrypt the hash and using the sender's public key to decrypt the hash.
What is the most effective security measure for protecting data held on mobile computing devices?	Encrypt the stored data.
What is the most effective way to protect a Wi-Fi (wireless) network as a point of entry into an enterprise network?	Strong encryption.

Table 9.11 – Key aspects from the CISM exam perspective

Questions

1. What is the best way to secure customer communication in an e-commerce application?

    A. Data encryption

    B. Multiple authentication methods

    C. Digital signature

    D. Maximum password age

    Answer: A. Data encryption.

    Explanation: The best method is to encrypt the communication, which will ensure the confidentiality of the transactions. Multiple authentications, maximum password age, and digital signatures may help with strong authentication, but they will not help maintain the confidentiality of data in transit.

2. What is the most commonly used protocol to safeguard the confidentiality of data that's transmitted in an e-commerce application?

    A. Secure Socket Layer

    B. Dynamic Host Configuration Protocol

    C. Secure Shell

    D. Telnet

    Answer: A. Secure Socket Layer.

Explanation: **Secure Socket Layer** (**SSL**) is the protocol that operates at the transport layer. It is used for privacy and data security while communicating over the network. SSL makes use of cryptographic functions to protect the confidentiality, reliability, and integrity of private documents traveling through the internet. **Dynamic Host Configuration Protocol** (**DHCP**) is a protocol that's used to manage the network configuration. A DHCP assigns an IP address and other network configuration parameters to every device on a network so that they can communicate with other IP networks. **Secure Shell** (**SSH**) and Telnet are remote terminal control protocols. Through these protocols, a user can connect to a terminal from a remote location.

3. What is the most effective way to protect the data on a mobile computing device?

A. To conduct a data integrity check

B. To encrypt the data stored on the mobile

C. To enable a screensaver for the device

D. To enable biometric access control

Answer: B. To encrypt the data stored on the mobile.

Explanation: Encryption is the most effective way to safeguard the data stored on mobile devices. Encryption converts the data into an unreadable format. It can only be read by the person possessing the encryption key. The other options are good controls but they are not as effective as encrypting the data.

4. For a large number of key distributions, why is public key encryption preferred compared to symmetric key encryption?

A. Computation is more efficient in public key encryption

B. Scaling is comparatively more convenient in public key encryption

C. The maintenance cost is less in public key encryption

D. Public key encryption provides greater encryption

Answer: B. Scaling is comparatively more convenient in public key encryption.

Explanation: One of the limitations of the symmetrical key is that it requires a key for each pair of individuals who wish to have communicated privately, resulting in an exponential increase in the number of keys. This, in turn, results in complex distribution and storage problems. Public key encryption does not have this issue. Public key encryption requires more computation efforts and maintenance costs compared to symmetric keys. A public key by itself does not provide greater encryption strength.

5. Which of the following is more likely to cause an internal attack on a network?

    A. No minimum timeframe defined for password expiry

    B. Security training is not given in a structured manner

    C. User passwords are not encrypted

    D. All PCs are placed in a single subnet

    Answer: C. User passwords are not encrypted.

    Explanation: If passwords are sent over an internal network in plain text, they can be easily sniffed. Passwords should be encrypted for adequate security. The other options do not present significant exposure.

6. What is the most effective way to prevent a database administrator from reading sensitive data from a database?

    A. Capture the log for database access

    B. Implement application-level encryption

    C. Implement a DLP solution

    D. Provide security awareness training to the database administrator

    Answer: B. Implement application-level encryption.

    Explanation: Encryption makes the database unreadable for DBA and other staff. This helps the DBA perform this routine function without reading the data in cleartext. The other options cannot prevent the DBA from reading the data in a database.

7. In a public key infrastructure, the public key of the other party is required to do what?

    A. Authorize the user

    B. Create the digital signature

    C. Authenticate the sender

    D. Compress the file

    Answer: C. Authenticate the sender.

    Explanation: The public of the other party is used to decrypt the message and if the message is successfully decrypted, it helps authenticate the user; that is, the owner of the corresponding private key. Authorization and compression are not functions of PKI. A private key is used to create a digital signature.

8. What is the best way to secure a wireless network as a point of entry into an organization's network?

   A. Intrusion detection system

   B. Strong encryption

   C. Two-factor authentication

   D. Packet filtering router

   Answer: B. Strong encryption.

   Explanation: The most effective way to secure a wireless network is to provide strong encryption. IDSes and routers will not offer any protection from local attacks. Two-factor authentication is for access control and will not protect data from being sniffed.

9. What is the best way to secure data on a USB device?

   A. Authentication-based access

   B. Only read data on the USB device

   C. Encrypt the USB device

   D. Restrict the use of the USB device

   Answer: C. Encrypt the USB device

   Explanation: Encryption is the most effective way to safeguard the data stored on mobile devices. Encryption converts the data in the USB in an unreadable format. It can only be read by the person who possesses the encryption key. The other options are good controls but they are not as effective as encrypting the USB device.

Summary

In this chapter, we discussed various information security monitoring tools and techniques such as firewalls and various types of IDSes and IPSes. Hopefully, this chapter has helped you understand the important methods, tools, and techniques for developing a security program effectively and efficiently. We also discussed digital signatures and encryption technology from an information security perspective.

In the next chapter, we will provide an overview of incident management procedures.

Section 4: Information Security Incident Management

This part provides an overview and framework of incident management. It covers 19% of the CISM exam certification.

This section contains the following chapters:

- *Chapter 10, Overview of Information Security Incident Manager*
- *Chapter 11, Practical Aspects of Information Security Incident Management*

10
Overview of Information Security Incident Manager

In this chapter, we will provide an overview of information security incident management and understand the advantages of a structured and effective incident management process. In this chapter, CISM aspirants will be able to gain an understanding of different aspects of incident management.

The following topics will be covered in this chapter:

- Incident management overview
- Incident response procedure
- Incident management metrics and indicators
- The current state of the incident response capabilities
- Developing an incident response plan

Let's understand each of these topics in detail.

Incident management overview

Incident management is defined as the process of handling disruptive events in a structured manner to minimize the impact of a business process. In most of the organization, the responsibility of developing and testing incident management lies with the information security manager.

Objectives of incident management

Security managers need to understand the following objectives of the incident management process:

- Detecting incidents early
- Accurately investigating the incident
- Containing and minimizing damage
- Being able to restore services early
- Determining the root cause and addressing the same to prevent reoccurrence

All these activities will lead to minimizing the impact the incident has on the organization.

Phases of the incident management life cycle

It is very important to have a structured and well-defined process to manage the incident. The following life cycle is recommended for effective incident management.

Phase 1 – Planning and preparation

The first phase is to prepare an incident management policy, assign roles and responsibilities, develop communication channels, create user awareness, and develop systems and procedures to manage the incidents.

An incident response plan is a very important document that includes a step-by-step process to be followed, along with assigned roles and responsibilities. An incident response plan helps the security manager handle incidents.

Phase 2 – Detection, triage, and investigation

The second phase is about detection techniques and processes such as the **intrusion detection system (IDS)**, **intrusion prevention system (IPS)**, and **security information and event management (SIEM)** tools and their implementation. Timely detection is of the utmost importance for an effective incident management process. A security manager needs to verify and validate the incident before any containment action is taken.

Triage means to decide the order of treatment based on its urgency. It is very important to prioritize the impact based on its possible impact. Quickly ranking the severity criteria of an incident is a key element of incident response. To determine the severity of an incident, it is recommended to consult the business process owner of the affected operations.

Phase 3 – Containment and recovery

The next phase is executing the containment process for the identified incident. Containment means taking some action to prevent the expansion of the incident. Incident response procedures primarily focus on containing the incident and minimizing damage. For example, when a virus is identified in a computer, the first action should be containing the risk; that is, disconnecting the computer from the network so that it does not impact other computers.

After successful containment, forensic analysis must be performed, ensuring a proper chain of custody. Chain of custody is a legal term that requires that evidence is handled properly to ensure its integrity. In the case of major incidents, the recovery procedure should be executed as per the business continuity plan and disaster recovery plan.

Phase 4 – Post-incident review

This phase will help evaluate the cause and impact of the incident. It also helps you understand the loopholes in the processes. It provides you with the opportunity to improve based on lessons learned.

Phase 5 – Incident closure

This phase is about evaluating the effectiveness of the incident management process. The final report is submitted to management and other stakeholders.

In the next section, we will discuss the relationship between incident management, business continuity, and disaster recovery.

Incident management, business continuity, and disaster recovery

The security manager should understand the relationship between incident management, business continuity, and disaster recovery. The incident management process is generally the first step when an adverse incident is identified. The goal of an incident management process is to prevent incidents from becoming disasters. Incidents vary in nature, extent, and impact.

Minor incidents can be effectively handled by the incident management process. However, there can be incidents that lead to major business disruptions and, in such cases, the organization needs to activate their **business continuity plan (BCP)** and **disaster recovery plan (DRP)** processes. Responsibility for declaring a disaster should be entrusted to an individual at the senior level who has enough experience to determine the impact of the incident on business processes. This responsibility for declaring a disaster should be determined when the incident response plan is established. The business continuity and disaster processes involve activating an alternate recovery site.

Incident management and service delivery objective

Service delivery objective (SDO) is the service level required to be maintained during a disruption. For example, during the normal course of operations, an organization provides a service to 100 clients. The organization wants to provide a continuous service to the top 20 clients, even during business disruption. In this case, the service delivery objective is the top 20 clients. The SDO should be sufficient to sustain the credibility of the organization.

The primary focus of incident response is to ensure that the defined service delivery objectives are achieved. The acceptability of partial system recovery after a security incident is most likely based on the SDO. The SDO also has a direct impact on the level and extent to which data restoration is required.

Maximum tolerable outage (MTO) and allowable interruption window (AIW)

The **maximum tolerable outage (MTO)** is the maximum time that an organization can operate from an alternate site. Various factors affect the MTO, such as location availability, resource availability, raw material availability, or electric power availability at an alternate site, as well as other constraints. The RTO is determined based on the MTO.

For example, a disaster occurred on January 1, and from January 2 onward, the service was made available to 20% of the clients (that is, the SDO) from an alternate site. However, the organization can only operate from an alternate site for 2 months due to location constraints. These 2 months are considered the MTO.

The **allowable interruption window** (**AIW**) is the maximum time for which normal operations of the organization can be down. After this point, the organization starts to face major financial difficulties that threaten its existence. Let's continue with the preceding example where, if, within 2 months of a disaster, the main site is not made operational, the organization will not be able to sustain itself due to financial scarcity. This indicates that the organization only has financial capabilities for 2 months. These 2 months are considered the AIW.

The security manager should try to ensure that the MTO is equal to or higher than the AIW. Generally, the MTO should be as long as the AIW to minimize the risk to the organization. This means that arrangements for an alternate site should be made at least until the organization has financial stability.

Key aspects from the CISM exam's perspective

The following are some of the key aspects from the exam's perspective:

Question	Possible Answer
What is the best time to determine who should be responsible for declaring a disaster?	At the time of preparing the incident response plan.
What is the objective of containment?	To reduce the impact of the incident.
What should be the highest priority when designing an incident response plan?	Safety of human life.
What is the primary objective of incident response?	To minimize the business impact (incident response procedures primarily focus on containing the incident and minimizing damage).
Who can best determine the severity of the incident?	The business process owner of the affected operational areas.
The acceptability of partial system recovery after a security incident is most likely based on what?	The service delivery objective.
What is the MTO?	The MTO is the maximum time that an organization can operate from an alternate site due to resource constraints.

Question	Possible Answer
What is The AIW?	The AIW is the maximum time that the normal operations of the organization can be down for. After this point, the organization starts to face major financial difficulties that threaten its existence.
What should be the relationship between the MTO and AIW?	The MTO should be equal to or higher than the AIW. Generally, the MTO should be as long as the AIW to minimize the risk to the organization.
On what basis is the prioritization of incident response determined?	It is based on the business impact analysis.

Practice questions

1. Which of the following plans will best support the security manager in handling a security breach?

    A. Change management plan

    B. Business continuity plan

    C. Incident response plan

    D. Disaster recovery plan

    Answer: C. Incident response plan.

    Explanation: The incident response plan includes a detailed procedure for handling the incident. It also includes detailed roles and the responsibilities of different teams to handle the incident. A security breach can be best handled by using an incident response plan. The BCP and DRP will be applicable when an incident becomes a disaster and an alternate site must be activated. The change management plan is used to manage the changes and does not directly impact how a security breach is handled.

2. The security manager has been informed about a fire in the facility. What should be his course of action?

    A. To check the facility access log

    B. To call a meeting with the emergency response team

C. To activate the business continuity plan

D. To activate alternate site operations

Answer: A. To check the facility access log.

Explanation: The first step should be to check the facility access log and determine the number of employees in the facility. They should be evacuated on an emergency basis. The safety of people should always come first. The other options are secondary actions.

3. What is the most effective way to address the risk of network **denial of service (DoS)** attacks?

A. Regularly updating operating system patches

B. Installing a packet filtering firewall to drop suspect packets

C. Employing NAT to make the internal address non-routable

D. Employing load balancing devices

Answer: B. Installing a packet filtering firewall to drop suspect packets.

Explanation: In a DoS attack, numerous packets are sent to a particular IP address to disrupt the services. Installing a packet filtering firewall will help drop the suspected packets and thus reduce network congestion caused by the DoS attack. Patching the OS will not affect network traffic. Implementing NAT or load balancing would not be as effective in addressing the DoS attack.

4. An incident was reported about a stolen laptop. What should be the first course of action of the security manager?

A. To determine the impact of the information loss

B. To remove the stolen laptop from the inventory list

C. To ensure compliance with reporting procedures

D. To remove access for the user immediately

Answer: C. To ensure compliance with reporting procedures.

Explanation: The first step is to initiate the reporting process, as defined in the incident response procedure. The incident response procedure may include submitting a report to the police authorities, wiping out data remotely, removing users, and so on. Determining the impact and removing the item from the inventory list are subsequent actions.

5. When should the person responsible for declaring the disaster be established?

    A. At the time the plan was established

    B. After the incident is confirmed by the security team

    C. After the incident management plan has been tested

    D. After the incident management plan has been approved

    Answer: A. At the time the plan was established.

    Explanation: Roles and responsibilities should be assigned at the time of preparing the plan. An unclear plan will have an adverse impact when executing the plan. Without assigned roles and responsibilities, testing and approval will not be effective.

6. Apart from backup data, an offsite site should also store what?

    A. The contact details of the key supplier

    B. Copies of the business continuity plan

    C. Copies of key service-level agreements

    D. The contact details of key employees

    Answer: B. Copies of the business continuity plan.

    Explanation: The BCP contains a step-wise process to ensure continuity of the business from an alternate site. Without a copy of the BCP, recovery efforts may not be effective. Generally, the BCP includes contact details of key employees, suppliers, and key service-level agreements.

7. When an incident is reported, what should be the priority of the security manager?

    A. Investigation

    B. Documentation

    C. Restoration

    D. Containment

    Answer: D. Containment.

    Explanation: Containment means taking some action to prevent the expansion of the incident. Incident response procedures primarily focus on containing the incident and minimizing damage. For example, when a virus is identified in a computer, the first action should be containing the risk; that is, disconnecting the computer from the network so that it does not impact other computers. The other options are subsequent actions.

8.   What area is of the most concern for a security manager?

   A. Logs are not captured for the production server.

   B. The access rights of a terminated employee are not deactivated.

   C. An increase in incident reporting concerning phishing emails.

   D. A Trojan horse installed on the system administrator's computer.

   Answer: D. A Trojan horse installed on the system administrator's computer.

   Explanation: A Trojan horse is a type of illegitimate software that is often disguised as legitimate software. It is a type of malware. Trojans are used by intruders to attempt to gain unauthorized access to an organization's network and systems. Finding a Trojan horse in an administrator's computer is a major concern as the administrator will have privileged access, which can be exploited. The other options are serious issues but not as significant as a Trojan horse.

9.   What area is of most concern for a security manager?

   A. Anti-malware software is updated daily.

   B. Security logs are reviewed after office hours.

   C. It takes 24 hours to update patches after their release.

   D. It takes 6 days to investigate the security incidents.

   Answer: D. It takes 6 days to investigate the security incidents.

   Explanation: A delay in an investigation is of major concern as it can have a major impact on business processes. The other options do not pose significant risks.

10. Management's requirement for a quick incident resolution _____.

   A. always gives positive results

   B. often clashes with effective problem management

   C. increases the attrition rate of the security team

   D. supports the forensic investigation

   Answer: B. often clashes with effective problem management.

   Explanation: One of the most important objectives of problem management is to understand the root cause of the incident and address the same so that the same type of incident does not reoccur. Merely restoring the service at the earliest juncture is not the solution. Hence, if the incident is to be closed within a strict timeline, then this aspect may be missed. Quick resolution may not always give positive results. Forensics is concerned with evidence, analysis, and preservation from a legal perspective and is not concerned with service continuity.

11. The security manager has noted that a network attack is in progress. What should be his course of action?

    A. Disconnecting all network access points

    B. Analyzing the event logs

    C. Isolating the impacted network

    D. Monitoring the attack to trace the perpetrator

    Answer: C. Isolating the impacted network.

    Explanation: The most important action is to isolate the network and contain the spread of the attack. Disconnecting all the network access points will impact business processes and should be the last resort. Analyzing and monitoring are subsequent actions.

12. The emergency response plan should primarily concentrate on what?

    A. Protecting sensitive data

    B. Protecting the infrastructure

    C. The safety of personnel

    D. Activating the recovery site

    Answer: C. The safety of personnel.

    Explanation: The safety of human life is of the topmost priority for any emergency response plan.

13. What is the most important aspect of an incident response policy?

    A. Details of the key supplier

    B. Escalation criteria

    C. Communication process

    D. Backup requirements

    Answer: B. Escalation criteria.

    Explanation: The escalation criteria include specific actions to be followed, as per the predefined timelines. It also includes the defined roles and responsibilities of individual team members. To smoothly execute incident response, it is of the utmost importance to follow the escalation criteria.

14. The security manager has noted a security incident. What should be his next course of action?

    A. Inform senior management

    B. Determine the impact of a compromise

    C. Report the incident to the stakeholders

    D. Investigate the root cause of the security breach

    Answer: B. Determine the impact of a compromise.

    Explanation: The first course of action is to determine how much of an impact this will have on the organization. Even while reporting to senior management and other stakeholders, the extent of compromise needs to be submitted.

15. The security manager has noted that a computer has been infected with a virus. What should be their first course of action?

    A. Determine the source of the virus infection

    B. Scan the entire network to determine whether another device is infected

    C. Disconnect the computer from the network

    D. Format the hard disk

    Answer: C. Disconnect the computer from the network.

    Explanation: The first step is to contain the spread of the virus by disconnecting the infected computer. The other options are subsequent steps.

16. What is the main objective of incident response?

    A. To provide the status of the incident to senior management

    B. To evaluate the evidence

    C. To minimize business disruptions

    D. To support authorities in their investigation

    Answer: C. To minimize business disruptions.

    Explanation: The main objective of incident response is to contain the incident, thereby minimizing damage. The other options are not the primary objectives of incident response.

17. The security manager has noted that the email server has been compromised at the administrative level. What is the best way to make the system secure?

    A. To change the administrative password of the system

    B. To configure 2-factor authentication

    C. To rebuild the system from the original media

    D. To isolate the server from the network

    Answer: C. To rebuild the system from the original media.

    Explanation: Due to a compromise at the administrative level, malware may be installed on the server. The best way is to rebuild the email server from the original media. This will address the risk of the presence of any hidden malware. Isolation is a temporary solution. Changing the password and 2-factor authentication will not be able to address the hidden virus in the email server.

18. A business continuity program is primarily based on what?

    A. The cost of building an offsite recovery site

    B. The cost of the unavailability of the system

    C. The cost of the incident response team

    D. The cost of the disaster recovery team

    Answer: B. The cost of the unavailability of the system.

    Explanation: Unavailability of the system due to a disaster may result in a loss to the organization. Loss due to the unavailability of a system increases daily. A business continuity program is considered based on this loss. Based on the unavailability of the system. RTO, RPO, and recovery sites are finalized. The other options do not directly impact the business continuity program.

19. Which of the following documents is the most important to include in the computer's incident response team manual?

    A. Results of risk analysis

    B. Incident severity criteria

    C. Details of key suppliers

    D. Call tree directory

    Answer: B. Incident severity criteria.

Explanation: It is very important to prioritize the impact based on its possible effect. Quickly ranking the severity criteria of an incident is a key element of incident response. The other details are not included in the computer incident response team manual as they will be included in the BCP.

20. The security manager has noted that a server is infected with a virus. What is the most important action to take here?

    A. Immediately isolate the server from the network

    B. Determine the possible impact of the infection

    C. Determine the source of virus entry

    D. Determine a security loophole in the firewall

    Answer: A. Immediately isolate the server from the network.

    Explanation: The most important action is to isolate the server and contain any further spread of the virus. The other options are subsequent actions.

21. What is the primary purpose of the incident response procedure?

    A. Containing incidents to reduce damage

    B. To determine the root cause of the incident

    C. To implement corrective control to prevent reoccurrence

    D. To maintain records of the incident

    Answer: A. Containing incidents to reduce damage.

    Explanation: Containment means taking some action to prevent the expansion of the incident. Incident response procedures primarily focus on containing the incident and minimizing damage. The other options also lead to minimizing damage.

22. What is the most important objective of incident management?

    A. To contain

    B. To conduct root cause analysis

    C. To eradicate

    D. To control the impact

    Answer: D. To control the impact.

    Explanation: The main objective of incident management is to minimize the damage to the organization. Containment, root cause, and eradication are the steps to minimize the damage.

23. The severity of the incident can be best determined by which of the following?

   A. Analyzing past incidents

   B. Benchmarking with a similar industry

   C. The value of the impacted asset

   D. Involving managers from affected operational areas

   Answer: D. Involving managers from affected operational areas.

   Explanation: The severity of the incident can be best determined based on the level of impact on the organization. The manager of the affected operational areas will be in the best position to determine the impact. Past incidents and benchmarking will not give an accurate impact. Valuation is based on the total business impact and not only on asset value.

24. The security manager is developing an incident response plan. What should be his first step?

   A. Determining the time required to respond to the incident

   B. Determining the escalation process

   C. Determining the resource requirement

   D. Determining the category of the incident based on its likelihood and impact

   Answer: D. Determining the category of the incident based on its likelihood and impact.

   Explanation: The first step should be to determine the various categories of the incidents based on their likelihood and impact. Based on the category, other options such as turnaround time, escalation process, and required resources can be determined.

25. What is the main objective of incident management and response?

   A. Restore the disruptive processes within a defined time frame

   B. Conduct a walk-through to recover from an adverse event

   C. Comply with the insurance coverage clause

   D. Address the event to control the impact within an acceptable level

   Answer: D. Address the event to control the impact within an acceptable level.

   Explanation: The main goal of an incident management process is to restrict the incidents from growing into problems and problems growing into disasters. Restoring disruptive processes is the objective of the disaster recovery procedure.

26. What is the most effective factor in any incident management process?

    A. The capability to detect the incident

    B. The capability to respond to the incident

    C. The capability to classify the incident

    D. The capability to document the incident

    Answer: A. The capability to detect the incident.

    Explanation: Timely detection is of the utmost importance for an effective incident management process. The other options are not as significant as the capability to detect the incident.

27. The security manager noted that incident reports from different business units are not consistent and correct. What should be his first course of action?

    A. To determine whether a clear incident definition and criteria for severity exist

    B. To implement a training program for all the employees of the organization

    C. To escalate the issue to senior management for appropriate action

    D. To impose a heavy penalty for an inconsistent approach

    Answer: A. To determine whether a clear incident definition and criteria for severity exist.

    Explanation: The first step is to determine whether an organizational-level incident management procedure exists. If not, this should be done on priority. The other options are secondary actions.

28. What is the best way to detect security violations in a timely and effective manner?

    A. To develop a structured communication channel

    B. To conduct a third-party audit of incident reporting logs

    C. To implement an automatic compliance monitoring system

    D. To enable anonymous reporting

    Answer: A. To develop a structured communication channel.

    Explanation: The organization should have well-defined communication channels for timely communication concerning incidents to different stakeholders and external parties. Channel should support two-way communication; that is, employees should be able to communicate with the incident management team and management should be able to communicate with employees. Having an ineffective communication process is a major challenge as incomplete or untimely communication will cause hurdles in the incident handling process. The other options are not as significant as the communication channel.

29. What is an area of major concern for a risk-based incident response program?

    A. Fraud due to collusion among employees

    B. Poor quality of investigations

    C. Reduction in false positive alerts

    D. Repeated low-risk events

    Answer: D. Repeated low-risk events.

    Explanation: In a risk-based approach, the focus is on high-risk events. Perpetrators may take advantage of this and concentrate on exploiting low-risk areas multiple times. Even though the impact of the event is small per incident, accumulated damages may be much higher. Hence, it is also important to review the possibility of the repeated occurrence of low-risk events.

30. The security manager has noted that a server has been compromised and sensitive data has been stolen. After confirming the incident, the next step is to do what?

    A. Report this to law enforcement

    B. Start containment

    C. Ensure the availability of backup data

    D. Disconnect the affected server

    Answer: B. Start containment.

    Explanation: Containment means taking some action to prevent the expansion of the incident. Incident response procedures primarily focus on containing the incident and minimizing damage. Disconnecting the server is part of the containment process. The other options are subsequent steps.

31. In which of the following plans is proactive security assessment and evaluation done for computing infrastructure?

    A. Business continuity plan

    B. Business impact analysis

    C. Incident management plan

    D. Disaster recovery plan

    Answer: C. Incident management plan.

Explanation: The objective of the incident management plan is to not only recover from an incident that has already occurred, but to take actions to prevent the incident. The incident management plan should include a proactive security assessment to improve the processes and reduce the chances of the incident occurring. The BCP and DRP concentrate on activities that deal with business interruption due to disaster. The BIA is used to determine the critical processes of the organization.

32. What is the most effective way to determine the impact of a denial-of-service attack?

    A. To determine the source of the attack

    B. To determine the number of hours that the attack was active for

    C. To determine the criticality of the affected services

    D. By reviewing the firewall logs

    Answer: C. To determine the criticality of the affected services.

    Explanation: The business impact can be best determined by knowing the criticality of the affected system. The other options will not help determine the impact.

33. What is the most effective way to monitor outsourced incident management functions?

    A. Frequently testing the plan and a dedicated team to provide any oversights

    B. The availability of the documented plan from the service provider

    C. A structured communication channel

    D. Frequently auditing the service provider's functions

    Answer: A. Frequently testing the plan and a dedicated team to provide any oversights.

    Explanation: Testing the plan will help you understand the capability of the service provider to address the incidents. Also, it is important to have an oversight team to monitor the activity of the service provider. Audits, structured communication channels, and documented plans are also important aspects, but in the absence of a tested plan, it is difficult to determine the capabilities of the service provider.

34. What is the most important aspect while defining the incident response procedures?

    A. Closing the incident within a defined timeline

    B. Minimizing the number of incidents

    C. Collecting evidence for the audit

    D. Meeting service delivery objectives

    Answer: D. Meeting service delivery objectives.

    Explanation: The incident response procedure should support the service delivery objective. This is the extent of the service's operational capability to be maintained during an incident. The other options are not as significant as supporting the service delivery objectives.

35. After an incident, the security manager has noted that full system recovery will take a longer time than normal. His efforts are concentrated on partially recovering the system. This level of partial system recovery is most likely based on what?

    A. The capability of the recovery manager

    B. The maximum tolerable outage

    C. The service delivery objective

    D. The availability of a recovery budget

    Answer: C. The service delivery objective.

    Explanation: The SDO is the extent of the service's operational capability to be maintained from an alternate site. The SDO is directly related to business needs and is the level of service to be attained during disaster recovery. This is influenced by business requirements. The MTO and available budget are determined based on the SDO.

36. The security manager has noted that the BCP has not been updated in the last 5 years and that the **maximum tolerable outage (MTO)** is much shorter than the **allowable interruption window (AIW)**. What should be their course of action?

    A. Take no action as the same has already been approved by business management

    B. Conduct a fresh business impact analysis and update the plan

    C. Increase the maximum tolerable outage

    D. Decrease the allowable interruption window

Answer: B. Conduct a fresh business impact analysis and update the plan.

Explanation: Generally, the MTO should be as long as the AIW. However, without conducting the business impact analysis, there is no way to determine whether the MTO or AIW is incorrect. Based on a fresh business impact analysis (**BIA**), the AIW will be arrived at. AIW is the maximum time that the normal operations of the organization can be down for. After this point, the organization starts facing major financial difficulties that threaten its existence. Based on the AIW, the MTO should be arrived at. The maximum tolerable outage is the maximum time that an organization can operate from an alternate site. Various factors affect the MTO, such as location availability, resource availability, raw material availability, or electric power availability at alternate sites, as well as other constraints. All these constraints should be addressed to ensure that the MTO is as long as the AIW.

37. Incident management supports the organization by doing what?

    A. Removing external threats

    B. Optimizing the risk management efforts

    C. Streamlining the recovery plans

    D. Structuring the reporting process

    Answer: B. Optimizing the risk management efforts.

    Explanation: Incident management is a component of risk management that focuses on preventing and containing the adverse impact of incidents. Incident management does not remove these threats. The other options are not the primary objective of incident management.

38. Which of the following is determined the priority of incident response activities?

    A. Disaster recovery plan

    B. Business continuity plan

    C. Security team structure

    D. Business impact analysis

    Answer: D. Business impact analysis.

    Explanation: The BIA determines the critical processes of the organization. Incident response activities primarily focus on protecting the critical processes of the organization. The other options do not impact the prioritization of incident response activities.

39. The data restoration plan is primarily based on what?

    A. Transaction processing time

    B. Backup budget

    C. Service delivery objective

    D. Data restoration software

    Answer: C. Service delivery objective.

    Explanation: The data restoration plan determines how much data will be restored within a predefined limit. The extent of data restoration is primarily based on the SDO. This is the extent of the service's operational capability to be maintained from an alternate site. The service delivery objective is directly related to business needs and is the level of service to be attained during disaster recovery. This is influenced by business requirements.

40. What is the most important factor for a global organization to ensure the continuity of a business in an emergency?

    A. Documenting delegation of authority at an alternate site

    B. Documenting key process documents at an alternate site

    C. Documenting the key service provider at an alternate site

    D. Support from senior management

    Answer: B. Documenting key process documents at an alternate site.

    Explanation: Continuity can be best ensured if personnel who have to resume the key processes are aware of the procedure. If procedural documents are not available at an alternate site, it will hamper the continuity arrangement. If the key process documents are made available at an offsite location, they can be utilized by employees operating from the offsite location during a disaster. This documentation will also support employees who may not typically be involved in performing those functions. The other options are not as significant as key process documents.

Incident response procedure

The most effective way to handle an incident is to lay down a structured process for incident management. On a lighter note, the following figure indicates the preparedness of the incident management team:

Figure 10.1 – Incident team

A well-defined incident management process will yield far better results in reducing business disruptions compared to unorganized incident management processes.

The outcome of incident management

The security manager should understand that good incident management will have the following outcome:

- The organization can effectively handle any unanticipated events.
- The organization will have robust detection techniques and processes for identifying incidents.
- The organization will have well-defined criteria for defining the severity of the incident and the appropriate escalation process.

- The availability of experienced and well-trained staff to effectively handle the incidents.

- The organization will have proactive processes to manage the risk of incidents in a cost-effective manner.

- The organization will have well-defined metrics to monitor the response capabilities and incident management's performance.

- The organization will have well-defined communication channels for timely communication concerning incidents for different stakeholders and external parties.

- The organization will have a well-defined process to analyze the root cause of the incident and address any gaps to prevent their reoccurrence.

The role of the information security manager

The extent to which the security manager is involved in managing incidents varies in different organizations. However, for any information security-related incident, the prime responsibility of handling the incident resides with the information security manager.

To manage security incidents, the information security manager should have a good conceptual understanding of the incident management procedures. They should also have a thorough understanding of the business continuity and disaster recovery processes. This will ensure that the incident management plan is integrated with the overall business continuity and disaster recovery plan.

Security Information and Event Management (SIEM)

A **Security information and event management (SIEM)** system collects data from various sources and analyses the same for possible security events.

The SIEM system can detect attacks by signature or behavior (heuristics)-based analysis. SIEM can perform granular assessments. SIEM can highlight the developing trends and can alert the risk practitioner for immediate response. SIEM is the most effective way to determine aggregate risk from different sources. SIEM is the best way to counter advanced persistent threats. On a lighter note, the importance of log capturing and monitoring can be seen from the following figure:

Figure 10.2 – SIEM

The following are some of the characteristics of an effective SIEM:

- It can consolidate and correlate inputs from different systems.
- It can identify incidents.
- It can notify staff.
- It can prioritize incidents based on the possible impact.
- It can track the status of each incident.
- It can integrate with other IT systems.

Thus, SIEM can provide information on policy compliance, as well as incident monitoring and other capabilities if they're deployed, configured, and tuned.

A properly installed SIEM system will help automate the incident management process and lead to considerable cost savings by minimizing the impact of the incidents. Though SIEM may be costly, it helps to save on the operating costs of manual processes (in place of SIEM) and recovery costs (by detecting incidents early).

SIEM helps to identify the incidents by way of log analysis based on predefined rules. One of the most important challenges of implementing SIEM is to reduce false-positive alerts. The most effective way to reduce false-positive alerts is to develop business use cases. The business use case documents the entire workflow, which provides the required results. The scenario business case would focus on the ability of SIEM to analyze the logs for known threats.

Key aspects from the CISM exam's perspective

The following are some of the key aspects from the exam's perspective:

Question	Possible Answer
What is the most effective way to reduce the false-positive alerts generated by SIEM?	Building business use cases.
What is the most important characteristic of SIEM?	To promote compliance with security policies (SIEM can provide information on policy compliance, as well as incident monitoring and other capabilities).

Practice questions

1. What is the best way to reduce the false-positive alerts of a security information and event management system?

    A. Build business cases

    B. Analyze the network traffic

    C. Conduct a risk assessment

    D. Improve the quality of logs

    Answer: A. Build business cases.

    Explanation: One of the most important challenges associated with implementing SIEM is to reduce the false-positive alerts. The most effective way to reduce false-positive alerts is to develop business use cases. The business use case documents the entire workflow, which provides the required results. In this scenario, the business case would focus on the ability of SIEM to analyze the logs for known threats. The other options are components for developing the business case.

2. What is the most effective way to utilize **security information and event management (SIEM)**?

   A. SIEM supports compliance with security policies.

   B. SEIM is used to reduce the residual risk.

   C. SEIM replaces the packet filtering firewall.

   D. SEIM promotes the compensating controls.

   Answer: A. SIEM supports compliance with security policies.

   Explanation: SIEM helps to identify the incidents by way of log analysis based on predefined rules. SIEM can provide information on policy compliance as well as incident monitoring and other capabilities if they're properly deployed, configured, and tuned. SIEM is not meant to reduce the residual risk, replace the firewall, or promote compensating controls.

3. Advanced persistent threats can be most effectively countered by which of the following?

   A. An intrusion detection system

   B. A security information and event management system

   C. An automated penetration test

   D. A comprehensive network management system

   Answer: B. A security information and event management system.

   Explanation: The SIEM system collects data from various sources and analyzes the same for possible security events. The SIEM system can detect attacks via signature or behavior (heuristics)-based analysis. SIEM can perform granular assessments. SIEM can highlight the developing trends and can alert the risk practitioner for an immediate response. SIEM is the most effective method for determining aggregate risk from different sources. The other options are not as effective as SIEM.

Incident management metrics and indicators

The effectiveness and efficiency of the incident management process can be best measured through various metrics. Metrics are measures that are used to track and compare the performance of various processes. Metrics are generally developed in the form of **key performance indicators (KPIs)** and **key goal indicators (KGIs)**.

Key performance indicators and key goal indicators

KPIs are generally quantifiable measures that are used to measure activity; for example, the percentage of incidents detected within 24 hours). KGIs can be either quantitative or qualitative, depending on the process. KGIs are intended to show the progress of a predefined goal. For example, a goal can be to install antivirus on all the systems within 1 month. This can be monitored daily. The KGI can be 5%, for day 1 10%, for day 2 20% for day 3, and so on. KPIs should be able to provide value to the process owner, as well as management. KPIs should not be too complex to understand, as shown in the following figure:

Figure 10.3 – KPIs

Defined KPIs and KGIs should be agreed upon by the relevant stakeholders and approved by senior management.

Metrics for incident management

The metrics for incident management help the security manager understand the capabilities of the incident management processes and further areas for improvement. The following are some of the metrics for measuring the performance of incident management processes:

- Number of reported incidents

- Number of detected incidents

- Average time to detect the incident

- Average time to close the incident
- Percentage of incidents resolved successfully
- Number of employees trained on security awareness
- Trends indicating the total damage over the period

These metrics should help the organization achieve defined objectives efficiently and cost-effectively. Defined KPIs and KGIs should be agreed upon by the relevant stakeholders and approved by senior management.

Reporting to senior management

Key metrics should be reported to senior management frequently. It helps senior management understand the capabilities of the incident management processes and their gaps (if any).

The current state of the incident response capabilities

Every organization has some sort of incident management capability, either structured or unstructured. The information security manager must determine the current state of this capability. This will help them understand the areas for further improvement. The information security manager can determine the current state in any of the following ways:

- The current state can be determined by surveying senior management, business managers, and IT employees. This will help them understand the perception and focus of the group on incident management capabilities.

- The current state can also be determined by way of self-assessment. This can be done by comparing current processes with some standard criteria. However, in this method, the views of the other stakeholders are ignored, and this can be a major challenge.

- The current state can be determined by way of external assessment or audit. This is the most comprehensive method as it involves interviews, simulations, benchmarking with best practices, and other aspects. This approach is generally used by an organization with adequate incident response capabilities that wants to improve its processes.

It is also important for the security manager to have a thorough understanding of the history of incidents.

History of incidents

Past incidents can provide valuable information about trends, business impacts, and incident response capabilities. This information can be used to prepare a strategy for future incidents.

Threats and vulnerabilities

The security manager should understand the basic difference between a threat and a vulnerability, as follows:

Threat	Vulnerability
A threat is what we're trying to protect against.	A vulnerability is a weakness in the system or process.
Examples of threats incude natural disasters, fire, hackers, and other unknown forces.	Examples of vulnerabilities include lack of antivirus, weak coding, and poor access control.
Threats are not under our control.	Vulnerabilities can be controlled by us.

Let's understand the responsibility of the security manager for threat and vulnerability assessment.

Threats

The key responsibility of a security manager is to ensure that various types of threats that can be applied to an organization are identified and documented. Threats that are not identified are more vulnerable than a threat that is well documented.

The following are some sources of threats:

- Environmental threats such as natural disasters
- Technical threats such as electric failure, fire, and IT issues
- Man-made threats such as corporate sabotage, disgruntled employees, and political instability

Sources of threat identification include past incidents, audit reports, media reports, information from national **computer emergency response teams** (**CERTs**), data from security vendors, and communication with internal groups. Risk scenarios are used at the time of the threat and vulnerability assessment to identify various events and their likelihood and impact.

Vulnerability

Vulnerabilities are security weaknesses. The existence of a vulnerability is a potential risk. It represents a lack of adequate controls. The security manager should conduct regular vulnerability assessments and bridge the gap before they are found by an adversary and exploited. Vulnerability management is a proactive way to ensure that incidents are prevented.

Developing an incident response plan

An **incident response plan** (**IRP**) is one of the most important components of incident management. The incident response plan determines the activities to be carried out in case of an incident. The incident response plan includes different processes for handling the incident, along with assigned roles and responsibilities for managing the incident.

Elements of an IRP

The security manager should understand the following stages when developing an incident response plan.

Preparation

Preparing the incident response plan in depth helps it execute smoothly. The following activities are carried out in the preparation phase:

- Defining processes to handle the incidents
- Developing criteria for deciding on the severity of the incident
- Developing a communication plan with stakeholders
- Developing a process to activate the incident management team

Identification and triage

In this phase, emphasis is put on the identification and detailed analysis of the incident. The following activities are carried out in the identification phase:

- Determining whether the reported incident is valid
- Assigning the incident to a team member
- Detailed analysis of the incident
- Determining the severity of the incident and following the escalation process

Triage means to decide on the order of treatment based on its urgency. It is very important to prioritize the impact based on its possible impact. Quickly ranking the severity criteria of an incident is a key element of incident response. To determine the severity of an incident, it is recommended to consult the business process owner of the affected operations.

Triage provides a snapshot of the current status of all incidents reported to assign resources according to their criticality.

Containment

In this phase, the incident management team coordinates with the business process owner to perform a detailed assessment and to contain the impact of the incident. The following activities are carried out in the containment phase:

- Coordination with the relevant business process owner

- Deciding on the course of action to limit the exposure

- Coordination with the IT team and other relevant stakeholders to implement the containment procedure

Eradication

After containment, the next phase of action is to determine the root cause of the incident and eradicate it. The dictionary meaning of eradication is *the complete destruction of something*. To ensure this destruction (which does not reoccur), determining the root cause of an incident and addressing the same is of the utmost importance. Hence, the incident response team addresses the root cause during the eradication process. The following activities are carried out in the eradication phase:

- Determining the root cause of the incident.

- Addressing the root cause.

- Improving the defenses by implementing further controls.

- In the case of a virus infection, existing viruses are eradicated, and further antivirus systems are implemented to prevent reoccurrence.

Organizations should have a defined and structured method for root cause analysis. Ad hoc processes may lead to the situation shown in the following figure:

Figure 10.4 – Root cause analysis

The objective of root cause analysis is to eliminate the reason for reoccurring incidents.

Recovery

In this phase, an attempt is made to restore the system to the degree specified in the SDO or BCP. This phase should be completed as per the defined RTO. The following activities are carried out in the recovery phase:

- Restoring the systems, as defined in the SDO
- Testing the system in coordination with the system owner

Lessons learned

In this last phase, lessons learned are documented to determine what has happened, details of the actions that were initiated, what went wrong, what went right, and areas for further improvement. The report should be submitted to senior management and other stakeholders.

Gap analysis

Gap analysis is the most effective way to determine the gap between the current incident management capabilities and the desired level. Once gaps have been identified, the security manager can work to address the same and improve the incident management processes. The gap analysis report is used to determine the steps needed for improvement.

Business impact analysis

Business impact analysis is conducted to determine the business impact due to potential incidents. Business impact analysis is done for all identified potential incidents. The following are the key elements of a business impact analysis:

- Analyzing business loss due to processes or assets not being available

- Establishing escalation criteria for prolonged incidents

- Prioritizing processes or assets for recovery

The objective of the BIA is to understand what impact an incident could have on the business and what processes or assets are critical for the organization. Participation from the business process owner, senior management, IT, risk management, and end users is required for an effective BIA. However, end users might have a different perspective of the BIA, as indicated in the following figure:

Figure 10.5 – Business impact analysis

Identifying critical processes, systems, and other resources is one of the important aspects of the BIA.

Goals of the BIA

The following are some of the primary goals of the BIA:

- To identify and prioritize critical business unit processes. The impact of an incident must be evaluated. The higher the impact, the higher its priority should be.

- The BIA is also used to estimate the MTD or MTO for the business. This helps with designing the recovery strategy.

- It also determines the longest period of unavailability of critical systems, processes, or assets until the time the organization starts facing a financial crisis; that is, the AIW.

- The BIA helps to allocate resources as per the criticality of the processes.

Steps in the BIA

The following are the steps for conducting the BIA:

1. The initial step is to identify the critical processes and assets of the organization.

2. The second step is to identify the dependencies of these identified critical processes.

3. The third step is to determine possible disruptions that can impact the critical processes or their dependencies.

4. The fourth step is to develop a strategy to restore the processes and assets in case of disruption.

5. The last step is to document the assessment results and create a report for business process owners and senior management.

Escalation process

The incident response plan should contain a structured process of escalation for various categories of incidents. The objective of the escalation process is to highlight the issue to the appropriate authority as per the risk perceived and the expected impact of the incident. For example, minor issues should be escalated to the manager, major issues should be escalated to the senior manager, and so on. Risk and impact analysis will be the basis for determining what authority levels are needed to respond to particular incidents.

The escalation process should also state how long a team member should wait for an incident response and what to do if no such response occurs. For each type of possible incident, a list of actions should be documented. Roles and responsibilities should be defined for each such action.

The incident response plan should also contain the names of official(s) who are authorized to activate the BCP and DRP in case of major disruptions.

The security manager should determine the escalation process in coordination with business management and it should be approved by senior management.

Help desk/service desk process for identifying incidents

The help desk/service desk is most possibly the first team to receive information about the incident. The help desk team should be trained to determine the severity of the incident and escalate it to the appropriate team for further action. Detecting an incident early and quickly activating the incident response plan is the key to effective incident management.

The security manager should have a well-defined process for the help desk team to differentiate a typical incident from a possible security incident. Help desk executives should have the relevant skills, as depicted in the following figure:

Figure 10.6 – Help desk management

Frequent security awareness training for end users, as well as help desk staff, is one of the most important factors for identifying and reporting an incident early.

Incident management and response teams

The incident response plan should determine the staff requirements for handling the incident. Each team should have predefined assigned responsibilities for managing the incident. They should have relevant experience and should be trained appropriately as per their responsibilities. The team's size may depend on the size and complexity of the organization. The defined roles and responsibilities of the incident response team increase the effectiveness of incident management. The following are some of the teams that are involved in handling incidents:

- **Emergency action team**: They are generally first responders that deal with incidents such as fire or other emergencies.

- **Damage assessment team**: They are qualified professionals who are capable of assessing the damage to infrastructure. They determine whether an asset is a complete loss or whether it can be restored.

- **Emergency management team**: They are responsible for making key decisions and coordinating the activities of other teams.

- **Relocation team**: They are responsible for smoothly relocating to an alternate site from an affected site.

- **Security team**: They are responsible for monitoring the security of information assets. They are required to limit the exposure of security incidents and resolve any security-related issues.

Incident notification process

Notifying the relevant stakeholders of the incident promptly is one of the key components of an effective incident management process. Having an effective notification process helps limit the potential loss and damage due to an incident.

Most detective systems have an automated notification process enabled that helps the concerned employee act immediately.

Challenges in developing an incident management plan

The security manager should also understand the challenges in developing the incident management plan:

- **Lack of management support and organizational consensus**: One of the key challenges for a security manager is to obtain support from senior management. Also, it is important to have a consensus with the business process owner on incident management processes.

    This can be best achieved by highlighting the benefits of incident management from the organization's perspective.

- **Incident management plan not aligned with the organization's goals**: Incident management can only be effective if it supports the goals of the organization. However, business processes change significantly over time. The security manager should ensure that the incident management processes are kept aligned as per business requirements.

- **Experienced and trained resources**: The most important challenge is the availability of experienced and well-trained staff to handle incidents.

- **Lack of communication process**: Having an ineffective communication process is a major challenge as incomplete or untimely communication will cause obstacles in the incident handling process.

- **Complex incident management plan**: The security manager should keep the incident management plan simple and meaningful for all stakeholders. Also, the plan should be realistic and achievable.

Key aspects from the CISM exam's perspective

The following are some of the key aspects from the exam's perspective:

Question	Possible Answer
What is the immediate next step once the incident is reported to the security manager?	Validate the incident.
Who is the best person to notify when a major vulnerability is identified?	System owner.
What are the most important factors when identifying an incident?	<ul><li>Security awareness training.</li><li>A well-defined communication channel.</li></ul>
Who should determine the members of the incident response team?	Information security manager.

Question	Possible Answer
What should be the content of the escalation process document?	The escalation process should state how long a team member should wait for an incident response and what to do if no such response occurs.
What does the triage phase indicate?	Triage provides a snapshot of the current status of all the incidents reported to assign resources as per their criticality.
What is the basis for developing escalation guidelines?	Risk and impact analysis.
In which phase of incident management is root cause analysis conducted? (That is, containment/eradication/lessons learned/ recovery?)	Eradication.
What is a slack space?	Slack space means the additional storage that is available on a computer's hard disk drive. Slack space is created when a computer file does not need all the space that has been allocated by the operating system. Slack space can be used to store hidden data. Verifying the slack space is an important aspect of computer forensics.

Practice questions

1. What is the relevance of slack space during an incident investigation?

    A. Slack space can be used to store hidden data.

    B. Slack space contains a password.

    C. Slack space is used to capture logs.

    D. Slack space contains investigation processes.

    Answer: A. Slack space can be used to store hidden data.

    Explanation: Slack space means the additional storage that is available on a computer's hard disk drive. Slack space is created when a computer file does not need all the space that has been allocated by the operating system. Slack space can be used to store hidden data. Verifying the slack space is an important aspect of computer forensics.

2. The information security has manager noted a security breach. What should be their immediate course of action?

    A. To confirm the incident

    B. To evaluate the impact

    C. To notify stakeholders

    D. To isolate the incident

    Answer: A. To confirm the incident.

    Explanation: The next step should be to confirm the incident to rule out any false positives. A security manager needs to verify and validate the incident before any containment action is taken. Once the incident has been confirmed, the next step should be to isolate the incident. The other options are subsequent steps.

3. The security manager noted a new type of attack in the industry wherein a virus is disguised in the form of a picture file. What should their first course of action be?

    A. Delete all the picture files stored on the file server

    B. Block all emails containing picture file attachments

    C. Block all incoming emails containing attachments

    D. Quarantine all the mail servers connected to the internet

    Answer: B. Block all emails containing picture file attachments.

    Explanation: The first step should be to block all emails containing picture files until the time signature files are updated. Deleting all the picture files and quarantining mail servers is not necessary. Also, blocking all the incoming emails will hamper the business process.

4. Who should be notified immediately when a vulnerability is discovered in a web server?

    A. System owner

    B. Forensic investigators

    C. Data owner

    D. Development team

    Answer: A. System owner.

Explanation: A vulnerability should be reported to the system owner to take appropriate corrective action. The system owner should, in turn, report to the data owner if the vulnerability is in a database arrangement. The system owner will coordinate with the development team for any development-related changes to address the vulnerability.

5. The security manager received a report about a customer database being breached by a hacker. What should be their first step?

    A. To confirm the incident

    B. To report to senior management

    C. To initiate containment

    D. To report to law authority

    Answer: A. To confirm the incident.

    Explanation: The first step should be to confirm the incident to rule out any false positives. A security manager needs to verify and validate the incident before any containment action is taken. Once the incident has been confirmed, the next step should be to contain the incident. The other options are subsequent steps.

6. Once the security incident has been confirmed, what should be the next task of the security manager?

    A. To determine the source of the incident

    B. To contain the incident

    C. To determine the impact of the incident

    D. To conduct the vulnerability assessment

    Answer: B. To contain the incident.

    Explanation: Once the incident has been confirmed, the next step should be to contain the incident. Containment means taking some action to prevent the expansion of the incident. Incident response procedures primarily focus on containing the incident and minimizing damage.

7. Which of the following is the most effective way to address the network-based security attacks that are generated internally?

    A. Implement two-factor authentication

    B. Implement static IP addresses

C. Capture the log at a centralized location

D. Install an intrusion detection system

Answer: D. Install an intrusion detection system.

Explanation: Installing an IDS will help the security manager identify the source of the attack. An IDS can be used to detect both internal as well as external attacks, depending on how it is placed. An IDS is used to monitor the network or systems for abnormal activities. IP addresses can be spoofed, and hence implementing a static IP may not be useful. If the attack is from an internal source, two-factor authentication may not be helpful. Capturing the log will only be meaningful if it is monitored through SIEM.

8. The security manager has noted a serious vulnerability in the installed firewall. What should be their next course of action?

A. To update operating system patches

B. To block incoming traffic until the time vulnerability is addressed

C. To obtain guidance from the firewall manufacturer

D. To conduct a penetration test

Answer: B. To block incoming traffic until the time vulnerability is addressed.

Explanation: The first course of action is to consult with the firewall manufacturer as they may have patches to address the vulnerability. They will also be in the position to suggest a workaround and compensating controls to address the issue. Blocking all incoming traffic may not be feasible as it will hamper the business processes. Updating OS patches and penetration tests will not help solve the vulnerability.

9. The security manager has noted that confidential human resource data is accessible to all the users of the human resource department. What should be their first step?

A. Recommend that the confidential data be encrypted

B. Disable access to confidential data for all users

C. Discuss the situation with the data owner

D. Provide security training to all HR personnel

Answer: C. Discuss the situation with the data owner.

Explanation: The first step should be to discuss the situation with the data owner and determine the requirement for data access on a need-to-know basis. Based on this discussion, access should be provided based on the relevant job function. Access for other users needs to be removed. Data encryption may not be feasible as the user may need to access data for further processing.

10. What is the most effective metric to justify the establishment of an incident management team?

    A. The business impact of past incidents

    B. Industry-wide monetary losses due to incidents

    C. Trends in improvement in security processes

    D. Possible business benefits from incident impact reduction

    Answer: D. Possible business benefits from incident impact reduction.

    Explanation: The best way to justify the establishment of an incident management team is to highlight the possible business benefit derived due to structured incident management processes. Trends of past incidents and industry losses may not directly impact future expected losses.

11. What is the most important factor for identifying security incidents early?

    A. A structured communication and reporting procedure

    B. Documented criteria for the incident's severity level

    C. Having an IDS installed

    D. Security awareness training for end users

    Answer: D. Security awareness training for end users.

    Explanation: Frequent security awareness training for end users, as well as help desk staff, is one of the most important factors for identifying and reporting an incident early. The availability of a well-structured communication and reporting procedure is also an important aspect, though it is only useful when the staff can identify the incident. An IDS will not be able to identify non-IT-related incidents. Determining the severity level is a subsequent step and will be useful once the incident has been identified.

12. What is the main objective of the incident response plan?

    A. Prevent the incident from occurring

    B. Streamline business continuity processes

C. Train users to deal with incidents

D. Promote business resiliency

Answer: D. Promote business resiliency.

Explanation: Business resilience means the capability of the organization to sustain the disruption. The main objective of the incident response plan is to minimize the impact of an incident by developing resilient processes. The incident response plan is a means to reduce the impact of the incident but it cannot prevent the occurrence of the incident. Business continuity processes are addressed by the business continuity plan, not by the incident response plan.

13. An end user has noted a suspicious file on a computer. They report the same to the security manager. What should be the security manager's first step?

    A. Isolate the file

    B. Report to senior management

    C. Verify whether the file is malicious

    D. Determine the source of the file

    Answer: C. Verify whether the file is malicious.

    Explanation: The first step should be to confirm whether the file is malicious to rule out any false positives. A security manager needs to verify and validate the incident before any containment action is taken. Once the incident has been confirmed, the next step should be to isolate the file. The other options are subsequent steps.

14. The members of the organization's information security response team are determined by which of the following?

    A. Board of directors

    B. Operations department

    C. Risk management department

    D. Information security department

    Answer: D. Information security department.

    Explanation: Generally, information security responses are handled by the information security manager and they should ensure that the team members consist of individuals that have the requisite knowledge and experience to handle the incidents.

15. The security manager received an alert from an IDS about a possible attack. What should be the security manager's first step?

    A. Determine the severity of the attack.

    B. Determine whether it is an actual incident.

    C. Isolate the affected machines.

    D. Activate the incident response plan.

    Answer: B. Determine whether it is an actual incident.

    Explanation: The first step should be to confirm the incident to rule out any false positives. A security manager needs to verify and validate the incident before any containment action is taken. Once the incident has been confirmed, the next step should be to isolate the file. The other options are subsequent steps.

16. After confirming the security breach related to customer data, the security manager should notify who first?

    A. Board of directors

    B. Affected customers

    C. Data owner

    D. Regulatory authority

    Answer: C. Data owner.

    Explanation: The data owner should be notified of who will be in the best position to determine the impact of the security breach. The data owner needs to coordinate another course of action with the computer incident response team. The other options are to be notified later, as required by the incident management policy.

17. The efficiency of the incident response team can be best improved by which of the following?

    A. Defined security policy

    B. Defined roles and responsibilities

    C. A structured communication channel

    D. Forensic skills

    Answer: B. Defined roles and responsibilities.

Explanation: The defined roles and responsibilities of the incident response team increase the effectiveness of incident management. Each team should have predefined assigned responsibilities for managing the incident. They should have relevant experience and should be trained as per their responsibilities. The other options are important but the most significant aspect is defined roles and responsibilities.

18. What is the main objective of the senior manager reviewing the security incident's status and procedures?

    A. To ensure that adequate corrective actions are implemented

    B. To comply with the security policy

    C. To determine the capability of the security team

    D. To demonstrate management commitment to security

    Answer: A. To ensure that adequate corrective actions are implemented.

    Explanation: The main objective is to ensure that incidents are closed by taking appropriate corrective action as per business requirements. A review by management will help align the security policy with the business objectives. The other options are not the objective of management review.

19. The response team noted that the investigation of an incident cannot be completed as per the timeframe. What should be their next action?

    A. Continue to work until the investigation is complete

    B. Escalate to the next level for resolution

    C. Ignore the current investigation and take up a new incident

    D. Change the incident response policy to increase the timeline

    Answer: B. Escalate to the next level for resolution.

    Explanation: The incident response policy and procedure will have defined escalation and timelines for each activity. If the activity is not completed within the defined timeline, then it should be escalated to the next level.

20. Which of the following is the most important factor for identifying a security incident promptly?

    A. Install an intrusion detection system.

    B. Perform frequent audits.

    C. A well-defined and structured communication plan.

D. Frequently reviewing network traffic logs.

Answer: C. A well-defined and structured communication plan.

Explanation: Two of the most important aspects when it comes to identifying incidents promptly are frequent security awareness training for end users and a well-defined communication plan. A well-defined and structured communication plan facilitates the information flows from the end user to the senior management in a time-bound manner so that incidents can be recognized, declared, and appropriately addressed. An IDS will not able to address non-technical incidents. An audit is generally detective in nature and may not be able to identify the incident promptly. Reviewing the network logs will help address only network-related incidents.

21. The incident escalation process should primarily state what?

    A. Timelines for response and what do to if no response occurs

    B. How to define the criticality of the incident

    C. How to communicate with the senior manager and other stakeholders

    D. How to calculate the impact of the incident

    Answer: A. Timelines for response and what do to if no response occurs.

    Explanation: The objective of the incident escalation process is to state how long a team member should wait for an incident response and what to do if no such response occurs. Defined timeframes are important steps of an effective escalation process. The communication process can also be part of the escalation process, but the most significant aspect is its timeframe. Determining severity and impact are not part of the escalation process.

22. By using the triage phase of the incident response plan, a security manager can determine what?

    A. The dashboard's current status of all the incidents reported

    B. The turnover time for the closure of each incident

    C. The appropriateness of the post-incident review procedure

    D. A strategic review of the incident's resolution

    Answer: The dashboard's current status of all the incidents reported.

Explanation: Triage means to decide the order of treatment based on its urgency. It is very important to prioritize the impact based on its possible effect. Triage provides a snapshot of the current status of all the incidents that are reported to assign resources as per their criticality. Triage does not focus on already resolved incidents and does not determine the appropriateness of the post-incident review procedure. Triage provides a view of both the tactical and strategic levels.

23. Escalation guidelines are mostly derived from which of the following?

    A. Management discretion

    B. Risk and impact analysis

    C. Audit reports

    D. The capability of the resource

    Answer: B. Risk and impact analysis.

    Explanation: The objective of the escalation process is to highlight the issue to the relevant authority, as per the risk perceived and the expected impact of the incident. This includes minor issues to be escalated to the manager, major issues to be escalated to the senior manager, and so on. A risk and impact analysis will be a basis for determining what authority levels are needed to respond to particular incidents.

24. The incident management program is considered most effective when what happens?

    A. It detects, assesses, and prevents the reoccurrence of the incidents.

    B. It follows the documentation of all the incidents.

    C. It has sufficient resources to deal with the incident.

    D. It provides a dashboard for management.

    Answer: A. It detects, assesses, and prevents the reoccurrence of the incidents.

    Explanation: The objective of the incident management program is to detect and contain the incident and also implement controls to prevent future occurrences. The other options are secondary aspects.

25. What is the best metric to determine the readiness of the incident response team?

    A. Time required to detect the incident

    B. Time between detection and reporting to management

    C. Time between detection and response

    D. Time between detection and documentation

    Answer: C. Time between detection and response.

Explanation: The readiness of the response team can be best determined by the time between the detection of the incident and the response provided. The time required to detect the incident determines the control's effectiveness. The response is more relevant compared to the documentation and reporting to senior management.

26. What area is of most concern for establishing an effective incident management program?

    A. The incident reporting to senior management is not structured.

    B. The details of the key process owner are not defined in the security policy.

    C. Not all the incidents are managed by the IT team.

    D. The escalation process is inadequately defined.

    Answer: D. The escalation process is inadequately defined.

    Explanation: In the absence of a structured escalation process, there can be a substantial delay in handling the incident. This can have a huge adverse impact on business processes. The IT team is only required to manage incidents related to IT processes. The security policy is a high-level statement and you do not need to include details of the key process owner. Unstructured reporting is not a major concern compared to an inadequate escalation process.

27. The security manager has noted that if a server fails for 3 days, it could cost the organization $100,000; that is, two times more than if it could be recovered in 1 day. This calculation is arrived at from which of the following?

    A. Incident management planning

    B. Business impact analysis

    C. Business continuity planning

    D. Alternate site planning

    Answer: B. Business impact analysis.

    Explanation: A BIA is conducted to determine the business impact due to potential incidents. The following are the key elements of a BIA:

    - Analyzing business losses due to processes or assets not being available

    - Establishing escalation criteria for prolonged incidents

    - Prioritizing processes or assets for recovery

    The other options do not directly consider the impact of the incident.

28. What is the most effective way of training the members of a newly established incident management team?

A. Formal training

B. Virtual training

C. On the job training

D. Mentoring

Answer: A. Formal training.

Explanation: As all the team members are new, it is advisable to conduct formal training. Formal training involves a structured way of learning, starting from basic concepts to advanced-level learning. This helps everyone, even if they are from different backgrounds. On-the-job training and mentoring will be more relevant when the team is already established and they have some senior and experienced members.

29. What is the best way to determine the effectiveness of the incident response team?

A. The percentage of incidents resolved within the defined time frame

B. The number of employees in the incident response team

C. The percentage of open incidents at the end of the month

D. The number of incidents arising from internal sources

Answer: A. The percentage of incidents resolved within the defined time frame.

Explanation: The effectiveness of the incident response team is best determined by the closure of incidents within the defined time frame. A timely resolution will help minimize the impact of the incident. The other options, by themselves, do not provide any indication of effectiveness.

30. In which of the following processes does the incident response team address the root cause?

A. Eradication

B. Containment

C. Reporting

D. Recovery

Answer: A. Eradication.

Explanation: The dictionary meaning of eradication is "*the complete destruction of something.*" To ensure such destruction (which does not reoccur), determining the root cause of an incident and addressing the same is of the utmost importance. Hence, the incident response team addresses the root cause during the eradication process.

Summary

In this chapter, we provided an overview of incident management. This chapter will help CISM candidates determine and document incident response procedures for effective incident management. This chapter will also help CISM candidates design incident management metrics and indicators. We also discussed how CISM candidates can determine the current state of an organization's incident response capability.

In the next chapter, we will discuss the practical aspects of information security incident management.

11
Practical Aspects of Information Security Incident Management

In this chapter, we will discuss the practical aspects of information security incident management. We will start by understanding the importance of building business resilient processes and the practical aspects of the business continuity plan and the disaster recovery plan. We will discuss the business continuity and disaster recovery process and learn about various aspects of testing the incident response, business continuity, and disaster continuity plans.

The following topics will be covered in this chapter:

- Business continuity and disaster recovery procedures
- Testing incident response, business continuity, and disaster continuity
- Executing a response and recovery plan
- Post-incident activities and investigation

Let's understand each of these topics in detail.

Business continuity and disaster recovery procedures

A **business continuity plan** (**BCP**) is defined as laid down processes to prevent, mitigate, and recover from disruption. A **disaster recovery plan** (**DRP**) is a subset of the overall BCP. While the goal of BCP is to prevent and mitigate the incident, the goal of DRP is to restore operations if business operations are down due to an incident. Thus, BCP is a continuous process of implementing various controls to prevent or mitigate the impact of an incident, whereas disaster recovery is only activated when preventive measures have failed and business processes are impacted due to an incident.

Even if an organization has a well-defined BCP plan, it may face the situation depicted in the following figure:

Figure 11.1 – Business continuity plan

It is of utmost importance that BCP and DRP plans, as well as their documents, are available at an offsite location as well.

Phases of recovery planning

The security manager should understand the following phases when implementing BCP and DR procedures:

- The initial phase is to conduct a risk assessment and business impact analysis to understand the critical processes and assets of the organization.

- Developing and documenting a response and recovery strategy.

- Training the staff on the response and recovery procedure.

- Testing the response and recovery plans.

- Auditing the response and recovery plans.

Before developing a detailed BCP, it is important to conduct a **business impact analysis (BIA)**. A BIA helps to determine the incremental cost of losing different systems. Based on the BIA, the recovery efforts required for the system are determined. For critical systems, the **recovery time objective (RTO)** will be low, so the recovery cost will be higher. Similarly, for non-critical systems, the RTO will be high and the recovery cost will be comparatively less.

Let's understand this with an example. The organization has two systems: system A and system B. System A is a critical system and the organization cannot afford the system to go down for more than 1 day. Hence, the RTO, in this case, is 1 day. To restore the system within 1 day, the organization needs to have a hot site equipped with all the required arrangements. This results in high recovery costs.

System B is noncritical. It will not have any impact, even if it is down for 10 days. Hence, the RTO is 10 days. Organizations can manage this through a cold site without much arrangement. So, comparatively, the recovery cost will be low.

In a nutshell, the critical system will have a low RTO and high recovery cost, whereas the non-critical system will have a high RTO and low recovery cost.

Recovery sites

In the event of an incident, a primary site may not be available for business operations. To address such similar scenarios, an organization should have an arrangement for resuming services from an alternate site to ensure the continuity of business operations. Many business organizations cannot afford the discontinuity of business processes, even for a single day, so they need to invest heavily in an alternate recovery site. These arrangements can vary according to the needs of the business organization.

From the perspective of the CISM exam, candidates should have an understanding of the following alternate recovery sites:

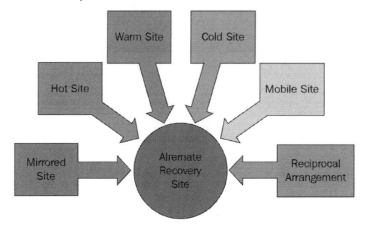

Figure 11.2 – Alternate recovery site

Let's look at each of the preceding alternate sites in detail.

Mirrored site

A mirrored site is regarded as a replica of the primary site. When arranging a mirrored site, the following components are already factored in:

- The availability of space and basic infrastructure

- The availability of all business applications

- The availability of an updated data backup

A mirrored site can be made available for business operations in the shortest possible timeframe as everything (in terms of systems and data) has already been considered and made available. It must be noted that the cost of maintaining a mirrored site is very high compared to the alternatives.

Hot site

A hot site is the second-best alternative after a mirrored site. The following components are already factored in while arranging a hot site:

- The availability of space and basic infrastructure

- The availability of all business applications

However, for a hot site to function, it also requires an updated data backup.

Warm site

The following components are already factored in while arranging a warm site:

- The availability of space and basic infrastructure
- The availability of a few business applications

However, for a warm site to function, it requires the following components:

- An arrangement regarding the required IT applications
- An arrangement for the required data

Cold site

The availability of space and basic infrastructure are already factored in while arranging a cold site:

However, for a cold site to function, it also requires the following components:

- An arrangement regarding the required IT applications
- An arrangement for the required data

Mobile site

In a mobile site, a moveable vehicle is used that is equipped with the required computing resources. A mobile site can be moved to any warm or cold site, depending on the requirements. The scale of business operations will determine the need for a mobile site.

Reciprocal agreement

In a reciprocal agreement, two organizations having similar capabilities and processing capacities agree to provide support to one another in case of an emergency. Reciprocal agreements are not regarded as very reliable. A reciprocal agreement is the least expensive as this relies solely on an arrangement between two firms.

The following table summarizes the characteristics of each alternative recovery site:

Parameters/Type of Alternate Sites	Mirrored Site	Hot Site	Warm Site	Cold Site
Space and basic infrastructure	Available	Available	Available	Available
IT equipment for processing	Available	Available	Only a few pieces of equipment available	Not available
Database	Available	Not available	Not available	Not available
Maintenance cost	Costliest	-	-	Cheapest
Recovery time	Fastest	-	-	Slowest

Figure 11.3 – Characteristics of an alternate recovery site

A mirrored site is the fastest mode of recovery, followed by a hot site. A cold site is the slowest mode of recovery. For a critical system, mirrored/hot sites are appropriate options, while for non-critical systems, a cold site is an appropriate option. A reciprocal agreement will have the lowest expenditure in terms of a recovery arrangement.

Factors impacting recovery site selection

Security managers need to consider the requirements of the organization, as well as the cost of maintaining the recovery site. The following factors impact which recovery site is selected.

Allowable interruption window (AIW)

The **allowable interruption window** (**AIW**) is the maximum time that the normal operations of the organization can be down for. After this point, the organization starts facing major financial difficulties that threaten its existence.

Recovery time objective (RTO)

The **recovery time objective** (**RTO**) is the extent of system downtime that an organization can tolerate. In other words, the RTO is the extent of acceptable system downtime. For example, an RTO of 2 hours indicates that an organization will not be overly impacted if its system is down for up to 2 hours.

The RTO is said to be achieved when the system is restored within the defined RTO.

Recovery point objective (RPO)

The **recovery point objective** (**RPO**) is the extent of acceptable downtime an organization can tolerate. For example, an RPO of 2 hours indicates that an organization will not be overly impacted if it loses data for up to 2 hours.

The RPO is used to determine the various factors of the backup strategy, such as the frequency and type of backup (that is, mirroring, tape backup, and so on).

Service delivery objective (SDO)

The **service delivery objective** (**SDO**) is the level of service and operational capability to be maintained from an alternate site. The service delivery objective is directly related to business needs and is the level of service to be attained during disaster recovery. This is influenced by business requirements.

Maximum tolerable outage (MTO)

The **maximum tolerable outage** (**MTO**) is the maximum time that an organization can operate from an alternate site. Various factors affect the MTO, such as resource availability, location availability, raw material availability, or electric power availability at the alternate site, as well as other constraints.

Apart from these factors, the following factors must be considered while selecting an alternate site:

- The recovery site should be an appropriate distance from potential hazards such as water bodies, chemical factories, or other areas that can cause significant risk to the recovery site.

- The recovery site should be away from the primary site so that both are not subject to the same environmental event.

- Operating from the recovery site should be feasible for longer durations as well. Major disruptions can make the primary site unavailable for several months. The maximum tolerable outage (that is, the arrangement to operate from the recovery site) should be planned for the allowable interruption window (that is, until the organization starts facing a financial crisis).

Continuity of network services

In today's business scenario, it is very important to arrange for redundant telecommunication and network devices to ensure the continuity of business operations. The following are network protection methods:

- Alternative routing, such as last-mile circuit protection and long-haul network diversity
- Diverse routing

Alternative routing

In alternative routing, information is routed through some alternative cables such as copper cable and fiber-optic cable.

The following are two types of alternative routing:

- **Last-mile circuit protection**: Last-mile circuit protection is used to have redundancy for local communication.
- **Long - haul network connectivity**: It is used to have redundancy for long-distance communication.

Diverse routing

This is a way to route information through split or duplicate cables:

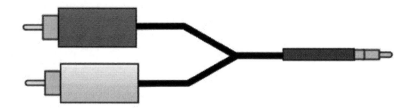

Figure 11.4 – Diverse routing

In diverse routing, a single cable is split into two parts, whereas in alternative routing, two entirely different cables are used.

Insurance

The security manager should consider insurance as one of the important factors to minimize the impact of loss due to an incident. Insurance can be obtained to recover damages. The following are some of the specific types of insurance coverage:

- Insurance to cover damage to IT equipment and facilities
- Insurance to cover damage to computer-related media
- Insurance to cover damage on account of cyberattacks
- Insurance to cover third-party claims and liability
- Insurance to cover loss of profit due to business disruptions
- Insurance to cover legal liability arising from errors and omissions
- Insurance to cover any financial loss that occurs as a result of fraud or dishonesty committed by the employees (fidelity insurance)
- Insurance to cover damage to media in transit

Key aspects from the CISM exam's perspective

The following are some of the key aspects from the exam's perspective:

Question	Possible Answer
What is the primary basis that a business continuity plan is developed on?	A recovery strategy approved by senior management.
What is the MTO?	The maximum tolerable outage is the maximum time that an organization can operate from an alternate site.
What is the primary factor for determining the MTO?	Available resources to operate the alternate site.
Which recovery site has the greatest chance of failure?	Reciprocal arrangement.
What is the most important factor for deciding the prioritization of the business continuity plan?	Business impact analysis.
What is the RTO?	The extent of acceptable system downtime.
What is the RPO?	The extent of acceptable data loss.

Question	Possible Answer
The backup strategy is primarily influenced by what?	RPO.
What is the most effective way to reduce the financial impact due to downtime caused by an incident?	Business interruption insurance.

Practice questions

1.   A business continuity plan is primarily based on which of the following?

A. Available alternate site

B. Available continuity budget

C. Strategy to cover all the applications of the organization

D. Strategy validated by senior management

Answer: D. Strategy validated by senior management.

Explanation: Senior management is in the best position to understand and adopt the strategy that is most beneficial for the organization's continuity. BCP is primarily based on the service delivery objective of management. A strategy that covers everything is not practical. If the objective of senior management is achieved, it will support the budget for the business continuity processes and alternative sites.

2.   Which of the following is an aspect of the business continuity program?

A. Detailed review of the technical recovery plan

B. Detailed testing of network redundancy

C. Updating the equipment at the hot site

D. Developing a recovery time objective for critical functions

Answer: D. Developing a recovery time objective for critical functions.

Explanation: While the goal of BCP is to prevent and mitigate an incident, the goal of DR is to restore operations in the event that business operations are down due to an incident. Developing an RTO directly relates to business continuity, whereas the other options are related to infrastructure disaster recovery.

3. MTO is primarily based on what?

   A. Available resources

   B. Service delivery objective

   C. Operational capabilities

   D. Size of the recovery team

   Answer: A. Available resources.

   Explanation: The maximum tolerable outage is the maximum time that an organization can operate from an alternate site. Various factors affect the MTO such as resource availability, location availability, raw material availability, or electric power availability at the alternate site, as well as other constraints. SDO and operational capability should be addressed while considering the available resources for the alternate site.

4. Which of the following is relevant to the recovery point objective?

   A. Extent of system downtime

   B. Before image restoration

   C. Maximum tolerable outage

   D. After image restoration

   Answer: B. Before image restoration.

   Explanation: RPO is the level of acceptable data loss. Whenever a database is corrupted, the recovery process only recovers completed transactions; any incomplete transactions are rolled back. This is before image processing occurs. The extent of system downtime is referred to as RTO.

5. Which of the following ensures the correct prioritization of operations in the event of disaster recovery?

   A. Business impact analysis

   B. Risk assessment

   C. Organization hierarchy

   D. Threat assessment

   Answer: A. Business impact analysis.

   Explanation: BIA is conducted to determine the critical processes of the organization and decide the recovery strategy during a disaster.

6. Which recovery arrangement has the highest chance of failure?

    A. Warm site

    B. Hot site

    C. Reciprocal arrangement

    D. Cold site

    Answer: C. Reciprocal arrangement.

    Explanation: In a reciprocal agreement, two organizations that have similar capabilities and processing capacities agree to provide support to one another in case of an emergency. Reciprocal agreements are not regarded as very reliable. They have many challenges, such as the same processing capabilities of both organizations, testing the plan, keeping the plan updated, and so on.

7. The RPO for an application is best determined by which of the following?

    A. Security manager

    B. Chief operating officer

    C. Risk management

    D. Internal audit

    Answer: B. Chief operating officer.

    Explanation: The RPO is best determined by the business process owner; that is, the chief operating officer. The chief operating officer has adequate knowledge to make this decision.

8. What is the objective of the recovery point objective?

    A. To determine the maximum tolerable period of data loss

    B. To determine the maximum tolerable downtime

    C. To determine the level of business resiliency

    D. To determine the type of alternate site

    Answer: A. To determine the maximum tolerable period of data loss.

    Explanation: The RPO is a measure of the user's tolerance to data loss. In other words, the recovery point objective is the extent of acceptable data loss. For example, an RPO of 2 hours indicates that an organization will not be overly impacted if it loses data for up to 2 hours.

9. When conducting business impact analysis, who is the best person to determine the recovery time and cost estimates?

    A. Business continuity manager

    B. Security manager

    C. Business process owners

    D. IT department

    Answer: C. Business process owners.

    Explanation: The business process owners will be in the best position to determine the impact of the unavailability of their system or processes and the appropriate recovery time and cost estimates.

10. What is the best way to ensure that a business continuity plan supports the organization's needs?

    A. To conduct an external audit of the business continuity plan

    B. To determine the size of the business continuity team

    C. To periodically test the plan on varied scenarios

    D. To update management regularly

    Answer: C. To periodically test the plan on varied scenarios.

    Explanation: You should conduct the test periodically and determine whether the plan supports the requirements of the business. The other options are not as effective as periodic tests.

11. When will the proximity factor be of most importance?

    A. While performing a business impact analysis

    B. While performing a BCP test

    C. While developing a disaster recovery procedure

    D. While selecting an alternate recovery site

    Answer: D. While selecting an alternate recovery site.

    Explanation: While selecting an alternate recovery site, it is of utmost importance to consider the site's proximity to hazards. The recovery site should be an appropriate distance from potential hazards, such as water bodies, chemical factories, or other areas that can cause significant risk to the recovery site. The recovery site should also be away from the primary site so that both are not subject to the same environmental event.

12. What is the most important factor to consider when designing the technical aspects of the disaster recovery site?

   A. Standby resource

   B. Recovery point objective

   C. Allowable interruption window

   D. Maximum tolerable outage

   Answer: C. Allowable interruption window.

   Explanation: **Allowable interruption window (AIW)** is the maximum time for which the normal operations of the organization can be down. After this point, the organization starts facing major financial difficulties that threaten its existence. The technical specification of the DR site will be based on this constraint. Based on AIW, the organization needs to choose between a mirrored, hot, warm, or cold site.

13. What is the most important factor when selecting an offsite facility?

   A. The primary and offsite facilities should not be subject to the same environmental threats

   B. The primary and offsite facilities should be in the same perimeter for ease of operation

   C. The maintenance cost of the offsite facility

   D. The facility to transport media at a lower cost

   Answer: A. The primary and offsite facilities should not be subject to the same environmental threats.

   Explanation: The offsite facility should also be away from the primary site so that both are not subject to the same environmental event. In the case of natural calamities, both sites will be impacted if they're in the same proximity.

14. What is the most important factor when selecting an offsite facility?

   A. The outcome of business impact analysis

   B. Adequate distance between the primary site and offsite so that the same disaster does not simultaneously impact both sites

   C. The location of the offsite facilities of other organizations in the same industry

   D. The applicability of regulatory requirements to an offsite location

   Answer: B. The adequate distance between the primary site and offsite so that the same disaster does not simultaneously impact both sites.

Explanation: The offsite facility should also be away from the primary site so that both are not subject to the same environmental event. In the case of natural calamities, both sites will be impacted if they're located in the same proximity. The other options are secondary factors.

15. The recovery time objective is said to be achieved when which of the following occurs?

    A. A disaster is declared

    B. A recovery of the backup is completed

    C. The systems are restored

    D. Normal functions have started

    Answer: C. The systems are restored.

    Explanation: The recovery time objective is the amount of time required to restore a system. Normal functioning may occur significantly later than the RTO. The recovery time objective is the minimum acceptable operational level and is generally lower than normal operations.

16. Which of the following indicates that the business continuity plan objective is being achieved?

    A. The test results show that the recovery time objective was not exceeded

    B. BCP testing is conducted consistently

    C. The test results show that the recovery point objective is inadequate

    D. Assets are assigned to the owners and an evaluation is done

    Answer: A. The test results show that the recovery time objective was not exceeded.

    Explanation: The recovery time objective is the extent of acceptable system downtime. A system should be restored within RTO. RTO is an important element of a business continuity plan. If RTO is achieved during testing, then it indicates that the business continuity plan objectives have been achieved. Conducting a BCP test and asset ownerships are not the core objectives of the business continuity plan.

17. The time required to restore a process is determined by which of the following?

    A. Recovery time objective

    B. Maximum tolerable outage

    C. Recovery point objectives

    D. Service delivery objectives

Answer: A. Recovery time objective.

Explanation: The recovery time objective is the length of time required to restore the system at a service level acceptable to the organization.

18. The security manager is required to ensure the availability of the key business processes at the offsite location. They should verify which of the following?

    A. Recovery point objective

    B. Operational hierarchy

    C. Staff requirements at the offsite

    D. End-to-end transaction flow

    Answer: D. End-to-end transaction flow.

    Explanation: If an organization can establish an end-to-end transaction flow from the offsite location, then it can be validated that the key business processes are available at the offsite location. The achievements of the RPO and staff requirements do not indicate the availability of the required support and processes at the offsite location.

19. The priority of actions in a BCP is determined by which of the following?

    A. Business impact analysis

    B. Risk evaluation

    C. Internal audit report

    D. Vulnerability analysis

    Answer: A. Business impact analysis.

    Explanation: Business impact analysis (BIA) is used to determine the critical process of the organization and decide on the priority level and recovery strategy during a disaster.

20. While conducting the business continuity test, the security manager noted that new software that is important for businesses is not included in the recovery strategy. This type of concern can be avoided in the future by doing what?

    A. Conducting periodic and event-driven business impact analysis to determine the need of the business

    B. All the new applications should be given priority for recovery

C. Business process should not be changed for a consistent recovery strategy

D. Conducting a thorough risk assessment before the acquisition of a new application

Answer: A. Conducting periodic and event-driven business impact analysis to determine the need of the business.

Explanation: This situation could have been controlled if the organization conducted BIA periodically and also based on some event (such as purchasing a new system). This helps update the recovery strategy as per the current requirement of the business.

21. The security manager is designing a backup strategy. What is the most important factor?

A. The quantum of data

B. Recovery point objective

C. Recovery time objective

D. Maximum tolerable outage

Answer: B. Recovery point objective.

Explanation: The recovery time objective is the extent of acceptable data loss. For example, an RPO of 2 hours indicates that an organization will not be overly impacted if it loses data for up to 2 hours. The recovery point objective is used to determine the various factors of the backup strategy, such as frequency and the type of backup (that is, mirroring, tape backup, and so on).

22. The recovery time objective is primarily based on which of the following?

A. Legal requirements

B. Business requirements

C. Recovery budget

D. Resource availability

Answer: B. Business requirements.

Explanation: The recovery time objective is the extent of acceptable system downtime. RTO is primarily based on business requirements. Generally, business requirements are inclusive of legal requirements.

23. An organization is in the process of acquiring a new recovery site as the old site is no longer adequate to support the business objectives. Until the new site is available, which of the following objectives for recovery will have to be changed?

A. Recovery budget

B. Recovery point objective

C. Service delivery objective

D. Business continuity test

Answer: C. Service delivery objective.

Explanation: The service delivery objective is the level of service and operational capability to be maintained from an alternate site. This is influenced by business requirements. Until the new offsite is available, SDO should be kept at a lower level. The other options do not directly impact the new recovery site.

24. A new security manager has noted that an organization has multiple data centers. They have arranged one of their own data centers as a recovery site instead of having a dedicated recovery site. Which area is of major concern?

A. Difficulty in establishing communication between data centers

B. Differences in processing capacity load between data centers

C. Difficulty in conducting BCP tests

D. Difference in system software versions between data centers.

Answer: B. Difference in processing capacity load between data centers.

Explanation: Due to differences in capacity, the data center may not able to handle the loads of other data centers during a disaster. This is an area of major concern. The other options can be addressed without much concern.

25. An organization has developed an automated tool to manage and store its business continuity plan. The security manager should be careful because of which reason?

A. To ensure the availability of the tool when a disaster occurs

B. To ensure that the maintenance cost is within the approved budget

C. To ensure the tool has the appropriate version control

D. To ensure that access is available to the authorized individual

Answer: A. To ensure the availability of the tool when a disaster occurs.

Explanation: The area of most importance is the availability of tools during a disaster. In the absence of such tools, it will be extremely difficult to implement business continuity procedures. These tools should be accessible from an offsite location also. The other options are not as serious as the unavailability of tools during a disaster.

26. The incident response team has activated a recovery site. Even though the processing capability is only half of that of the primary site's, the team notifies management that they have restored the critical system. This indicates that the team has achieved which of the following?

    A. The security budget

    B. The recovery point objective

    C. The service delivery objective

    D. The recovery time objective

    Answer: C. The service delivery objective.

    Explanation: The service delivery objective is the level of service and operational capability to be maintained from an alternate site. The service delivery objective is directly related to business needs and is the level of service to be attained during disaster recovery. The other options are linked to service delivery objectives.

27. What is the most effective way to ensure that incident response activities are aligned with the requirements of business continuity?

    A. To conduct a scenario-based structured walk-through

    B. To distribute an enterprise-wide incident response procedure

    C. To develop a working group represented by each department

    D. To benchmark an incident response procedure with the industry

    Answer: A. To conduct a scenario-based structured walk-through.

    Explanation: A structured walk-through will help you understand the capabilities of the incident response plan to support the requirements of business continuity. This walk-through should include team members from incident response and business continuity. It will help with identifying gaps or misalignments between the plans.

28. What is the most effective way to compensate for the financial impact of downtime caused due to disaster?

    A. Availability of offsite media storage

    B. Business interruption insurance

    C. Business continuity plan

    D. Disaster recovery plan

    Answer: B. Business interruption insurance.

    Explanation: Business interruption insurance is the best way to compensate for the loss that occurs due to business disruptions. The other options are more focused on restoring services early to minimize the downtime cost. However, they cannot compensate for losses that have already occurred.

29. "In the case of a disaster, the backup for the end of the previous day should be restored." Which of the following will be relevant to this statement?

    A. Recovery time objective

    B. Recovery point objective

    C. Allowable interruption window

    D. Service delivery objective

    Answer: B. Recovery point objective.

    Explanation: RPO is a measure of the user's tolerance to data loss. In other words, the recovery point objective is the level of acceptable data loss. For example, an RPO of 2 hours indicates that an organization will not be overly impacted if it loses data for up to 2 hours.

    The recovery point objective is used to determine the various factors of a backup strategy, such as its frequency and type of backup (that is, mirroring, tape backup, and so on).

30. The recovery point objective is determined based on which of the following?

    A. The extent of acceptable system downtime

    B. The available security budget

    C. The acceptable level of service

    D. The extent of acceptable data loss

Answer: D. The extent of acceptable data loss.

Explanation: The RPO is a measure of the user's tolerance to data loss. The recovery point objective is the level of acceptable data loss. For example, an RPO of 2 hours indicates that an organization will not be overly impacted if it loses data for up to 2 hours. The recovery point objective is used to determine the various factors of a backup strategy, such as its frequency and type of backup (that is, mirroring, tape backup, and so on). The extent of the acceptable system downtime is indicated by the recovery time objective. The acceptable level of service is determined by the service delivery objective.

31. What is the most important factor for successfully recovering a business?

    A. A copy of the disaster recovery plan is maintained offsite

    B. Separate ISPs for network redundancy

    C. The equipment required for the hot site is determined regularly

    D. Documented criteria for declaring a disaster

    Answer: A. A copy of the disaster recovery plan is maintained offsite.

    Explanation: If a copy of the plan is not available during the disaster, business recovery will be seriously impaired. The other options are generally addressed satisfactorily in the business continuity program.

32. The security manager noted that it was not possible to restore the data in the available time while considering various constraints. What solution should the security manager suggest?

    A. To increase the recovery time objective

    B. To decrease the security budget

    C. To adjust the maximum tolerable outage

    D. To adjust the allowable interruption window

    Answer: A. To increase the recovery time objective.

    Explanation: The recovery time objective means the time within which the system should be restored. If data is not available within the defined timeline, then the system will not be restored as per the RTO. In this case, it is advisable to increase the RTO. The allowable interruption window is based on the maximum time the organization can be down before major financial impacts occur. It cannot be adjusted. Adjusting the **maximum tolerable outage (MTO)** or decreasing the security budget will not have any effect on the situation.

33. Which of the following is not a characteristic of hot site provisioning?

    A. A hot site is situated in another city

    B. All the equipment at a hot site is provided at the time of disaster and is not available on the floor

    C. A hot site will be shared with multiple clients

    D. The equipment at a hot site will not be a replica of the original site as some equipment may be substituted for the equivalent model

    Answer: B. All the equipment at a hot site is provided at the time of disaster and is not available on the floor.

    Explanation: A hot site indicates that the site is already equipped with the required equipment and can be activated at any time. If the equipment is not available on the floor, then it does not meet the requirements of a hot site. A hot site can be arranged in another city as well. Many commercial providers arrange shared hot sites. Substituting the equivalent equipment is not a major concern.

Testing incident response, BCP, and DRP

Regular testing and exercises are very important in determining the continued adequacy and effectiveness of the BCP and DRP. It helps to validate the compatibility of the offsite facility to support the organization in case of a disaster. Testing the BCP will help to determine the effectiveness of the plan and identify any gaps therein. This provides an opportunity to improve the plan.

Types of test

The following are some of the important methods for testing the BCP and DRP.

Checklist review

This test is performed before a real test. A checklist is provided to all members of the recovery team for review and to ensure that the checklist is current and updated.

Structured walk-through

This includes a review of the BCP and DRP on paper. Team members review each step to evaluate the effectiveness of the DRP. Identified gaps, deficiencies, and constraints are addressed to improve the plan.

Simulation test

In this type of test, a roleplay is prepared for a disaster scenario and the adequacy of the DRP is determined. This does not include activating the recovery site.

Parallel test

In this type of test, the recovery site is activated to determine the readiness of the site. However, the primary site continues to operate normally.

Full interruption test

A full interruption test provides the information security manager with assurance because it is the closest test to an actual disaster. The primary site is completely shut down and operations are carried out from the recovery site, as per the DRP.

This type of test is the most expensive and potentially disruptive. It is advisable that testing should start with a simple exercise and once confidence is established, it should gradually expand to a full restoration test.

Tests should be scheduled in such a way that they will minimize disruptions to normal operations. Key recovery team members should be actively involved in test procedures. It is recommended to conduct full interruption tests annually once the test is performed satisfactorily.

Effectiveness of tests

Out of all these tests, the full interruption test is considered to be the most effective to determine the readiness of BCP and DRP.

In both parallel tests and simulation tests, normal business operations are not impacted. In parallel tests, the recovery site is activated, whereas a simulation test recovery site is not activated. When the objective of a test is not to disturb the normal business operations, then a parallel test is considered the most effective, followed by a simulation test.

Category of tests

The security manager should also understand the following categories of tests concerning the recovery process.

Paper test/desk-based evaluation

In this type of test, concerned staff have a walk-through of the BCP and discuss what might happen if a particular type of service disruption occurs. A paper test is conducted before the preparedness test.

Preparedness test

In this type of test, with the help of a simulated system crash, preparedness is verified in a localized environment. A preparedness test is the most cost-effective way to evaluate the adequacy of the plan. It helps to improve the plan gradually. A preparedness plan is considered a localized version of a full test. A preparedness test includes phase-wise simulation of the entire environment at a very reasonable cost and helps the recovery team understand the various challenges associated with the actual test scenario.

Full operational test

A full operational test is to be conducted once a paper test and preparedness test have been carried out. This test occurs before the full disruption test. A full operational test is a costly and time-consuming affair and involves many challenges.

Recovery test metrics

To determine the effectiveness of a plan, critical metrics should be evaluated during the test. These metrics should be based on the key objectives of the plan. On a lighter note, the following figure indicates the importance of test metrics:

Figure 11.5 – Test metrics

The following are some of the important metrics for the recovery plan:

- Whether the recovery processes are completed within predefined timelines.

- Whether the amount of work that's performed from the recovery site is within the service delivery objective.

- Whether the accuracy of the transactions that are performed from the recovery site is acceptable.

Success criteria for the test

The security manager should consider the following important factors when conducting a test:

- The results of the test should be documented and evaluated. It is not possible to evaluate the effectiveness of the BCP if the test results are not documented and analyzed properly.

- The success of a disaster recovery test depends on whether all the critical business functions were successfully recovered and reproduced.

- If a test is performed by a third-party service provider, the security manager needs to ensure that all the data and applications have the appropriate protection level. Data should be erased from the third-party infrastructure once the test is completed.

- Frequent testing and improving from lessons learned will help ensure that the incident management response plan is aligned with current business priorities.

- It is essential that testing should be conducted in a realistic condition after considering all the crises in an actual disruptive event.

- The security manager should understand the risk of untested plans. An untested plan may not work as expected and the organization could face severe consequences in the event of a disaster.

Key aspects from the CISM exam's perspective

The following are some of the key aspects from the exam's perspective:

Question	Possible Answer
Which type of test provides the most assurance of the effectiveness of BCP and DRP?	Full interruption test.
Which type of test provides the most assurance of the effectiveness of BCP and DRP without impacting the normal business operations?	• Parallel test (first preference) • Simulation test (second preference)
What is the most effective way to determine that disaster recovery planning is current?	Regular testing of the disaster recovery plan.
What is the best way to determine the ability of the organization to resume operation after a disaster?	Restoration testing.
What is the difference between a parallel test and a simulation test?	In a parallel test, the recovery site is activated, whereas in a simulation test, the recovery site is not activated.

Practice questions

1. When is a recovery test considered successful?

    A. A restoration is done with the help of data available from the recovery site

    B. The IT team and business owners are involved in the recovery test

    C. The critical business processes are recovered and duplicated within the defined time frame

    D. The recovery test results are documented and presented to senior management

    Answer: C. The critical business processes are recovered and duplicated within the defined time frame.

    Explanation: For a recovery test to be successful, it is very important to ensure that all the critical processes are successfully recovered and reproduced to support the business functions. This should be done within the defined time frame. The other options do not directly indicate the success of the test.

2. The organization is using the infrastructure of a third-party service provider to conduct a recovery test. After completing the test, the security manager should ensure which of the following?

   A. All the data and the applications from the devices of the service provider should be erased

   B. A meeting should be conducted at the site to evaluate the test results

   C. The assessment of the recovery site is to be discussed with the service provider

   D. The test is conducted within the security budget

   Answer: A. All the data and the applications from the devices of the service provider should be erased.

   Explanation: It is of utmost importance to ensure the security of the organizational data. After completing the test, all the data and applications from the devices of the service provider should be erased. The other options are not as significant as erasing all the data.

3. What is the most effective way to improve the performance of the incident response team?

   A. Training the incident response team about new threats

   B. Periodically testing and improving the plan from lessons learned

   C. To ensure that all the members of the incident response team have an expert level of IT knowledge

   D. To invite ideas from all the team members

   Answer: B. Periodically testing and improving the plan from lessons learned.

   Explanation: Periodic testing will help you understand the capability of the plan. Any deficiencies noted during the test should be addressed immediately. This will help you improve the effectiveness of the plan. The other options are not as significant as periodic testing.

4. Which test provides the most assurance about the effectiveness of the recovery plan?

   A. Walk-through test

   B. Tabletop exercise

   C. Full interruption test

   D. Simulation test

Answer: C. Full interruption test.

Explanation: A full interruption test provides the best assurance to the security manager because it is the closest test to an actual disaster. The primary site is completely shut down and operations are carried out from the recovery site, as per the DRP.

5. What is the most effective way to ensure that operational incident risks are managed effectively?

    A. Tested business continuity plan/disaster recovery plan

    B. Timely reporting incidents

    C. Incident management awareness

    D. Increase in security budget

    Answer: A. Tested business continuity plan/disaster recovery plan.

    Explanation: The best indicator of incident risk management is a detailed and structured plan that is tested periodically. The other options will not be as effective as tested recovery plans.

6. The organization wants to test the effectiveness of its business continuity plan. However, it does want to impact its normal business operations. Which of the following tests will give the most assurance?

    A. Checklist test

    B. Simulation test

    C. Walk-through test

    D. Full interruption test

    Answer: B. Simulation test.

    Explanation: Out of all these tests, a full interruption test is considered to be the most effective to determine the readiness of BCP and DRP. However, in a full interruption test, no business operations are impacted. In this simulation test, a roleplay is prepared for a disaster scenario and the adequacy of the DRP is determined. A simulation test is more effective compared to a checklist test or walk-through test.

7. The security manager has noted that the system administrator has failed to report an attempted attack. This situation can be prevented by doing what?

    A. Periodically testing the incident response plan

    B. Periodic vulnerability assessment

C. Mandatory training for all staff

D. Periodically auditing the incident response plan

Answer: A. Periodically testing the incident response plan.

Explanation: Periodically testing the incident response plan will help to determine the effectiveness of the plan and identify any shortcomings. It helps to improve the plan by plugging in the deficiency. The other options are good controls, but periodic testing will be more effective.

8. What is the most effective way to determine that the disaster recovery plan is current?

A. Perform periodic audits of the disaster recovery plan

B. Periodically train the disaster recovery team

C. periodically test the disaster recovery plan

D. Perform a periodic risk assessment

Answer: C. Periodically test the disaster recovery plan.

Explanation: Periodically testing the incident response plan will help determine the effectiveness of the plan and identify whether it supports the current business processes and objectives. It helps improve the plan by plugging in the deficiency. The other options are good controls, but periodic testing will be more effective.

9. Which of the following activities increases the chance of operations resuming after a disaster?

A. Restoration testing

B. Checklist review

C. Arranging for a warm site

D. Developing an incident response plan

Answer: A. Restoration testing.

Explanation: Restoration testing will help determine the capabilities of the organization to restore the data from the recovery site during a disaster. The success of the restoration test indicates that the organization is capable of recovering from disasters as data drives the majority of the business processes. The other options will not be meaningful if the data recovery process is questionable.

10. An organization does not want to disturb its continuous operations. Which test will be best to determine the effectiveness of the response and recovery process without impacting normal business operations?

A. Full interruption test

B. Simulation test

C. Parallel test

D. Structured walk-through

Answer: C. Parallel test.

Explanation: Out of all these tests, the full interruption test is considered to be the most effective to determine the readiness of BCP and DRP. However, in a full interruption test, no business operations are impacted. In both parallel tests and simulation tests, normal business operations are not impacted. In a parallel test, the recovery site is activated, whereas in a simulation, the test recovery site is not activated. When the objective of the test is not to disturb the normal business operations, the parallel test is considered the most effective, followed by the simulation test.

11. Which of the following demonstrates the difference between a parallel test and a simulation test?

A. In a parallel test, team members do a walk-through of the necessary recovery tasks. The same is not done in a simulation test.

B. In a parallel test, normal business operations are stopped; the same is not done in a simulation test.

C. In a parallel test, a fictitious scenario is used for the test; the same is not done in a simulation test.

D. In a parallel test, the recovery site is brought to operational readiness; the same is not done in a simulation test.

Answer: D. In a parallel test, the recovery site is brought to operational readiness; the same is not done in a simulation test.

Explanation: The difference between a parallel test and a simulation test is that in a parallel test, a recovery site is activated, whereas in a simulation test, a recovery site is not activated. In both, a test walk-through is done and fictitious scenarios are used. In both parallel tests and simulation tests, normal business operations are not impacted. When the objective of the test is not to disturb the normal business operations, a parallel test is considered the most effective, followed by a simulation test.

12. The security manager has reported a DRP test as a failure, even though all the essential services have been restored at the hot site. What is the main reason for this failure?

    A. The expenditure of the test exceeded the security budget

    B. The level of service exceeded the service delivery objective

    C. A few systems were updated with an old version of the operating system

    D. The aggregate recovery activities exceed the acceptable interruption window

    Answer: D. The aggregate recovery activities exceed the acceptable interruption window.

    Explanation: The allowable interruption window is based on the maximum time the organization can be down before major financial impacts occur. If restoration is not done within the AIW, then the test will not be considered a success. The **service delivery objective (SDO)** is the minimum level of service to be continued at a recovery site. If the level of the service exceeds the expected SDO, then it is a positive achievement. Using an old version of the OS might cause a delay but it is not a major issue.

13. What is the major challenge of an untested response plan?

    A. It may not contain up-to-date contact information

    B. It may not be approved by senior management

    C. It poses a risk that the plan will not work when needed

    D. It will not be possible to determine the budget for the recovery site

    Answer: C. It poses a risk that the plan will not work when needed.

    Explanation: A major challenge is that the untested plan may not work as expected when a disaster occurs. Testing the plan helps determine the effectiveness of the plan. The other options are secondary concerns.

14. The success of a disaster recovery test primarily depends on which of the following?

    A. Minimal interruption to normal business processes

    B. The predefined scope of the test

    C. Preparedness of the recovery site

    D. Active participation of business management

    Answer: D. Active participation of business management.

Explanation: The most important factor for the success of a test is active participation from business management. Business process owners have a thorough understanding of processes and recovery priorities. To conduct a test, sufficient resources are required, which may not be possible without the support of management. The other options are secondary concerns.

Executing response and recovery plans

Security managers need to consider various aspects regarding the execution of the plan. To smoothly execute the plan, it is very important to have defined roles and responsibilities for each individual. Regarding the overall management of the plan, there should be a facilitator or director who should be in charge of executing the plan. This role should be assigned to a senior executive who has sufficient authority to make decisions during a crisis.

The security manager should consider the following aspects when executing a plan:

- They must ensure that control procedures are implemented in such a way that risks are appropriately addressed. For example, just installing anti-malware is not sufficient. The virus signature file should be updated regularly (ideally, it should be automated to update daily). Any time gap between this updating can be subject to exposure.

- In the case of a malware-infected server, it is advisable to rebuild the server from the original media and update it with subsequent patches. This will address the risk of hidden malware.

- It is advisable to synchronize all the applications and servers with a common time server. This will help during a forensic investigation. The time server will provide a common time reference that will help accurately reconstruct the course of events.

- In the event of a security breach, the security manager should keep the senior management informed about the impact on the organization and details of the corrective actions that have been taken.

Key aspects from the CISM exam's perspective

The following are some of the key aspects from the exam's perspective:

Question	Possible Answer
What is the ideal frequency for updating a virus signature file for anti-malware software?	Ideally, it should be automated to update daily.
What information should be provided to senior management in the event of a security breach?	The impact on the organization and details of the corrective actions to be taken.

Practice questions

1. An organization has implemented automatic updates for its virus signature file every Saturday morning. What is the area of most concern?

    A. The unavailability of technical staff to support the update

    B. The applications are exposed to new viruses during the intervening week

    C. The systems are not tested once the signature file has been updated

    D. The failed batch can be rectified only on Monday

    Answer: B. The applications are exposed to new viruses during the intervening week.

    Explanation: As a prudent practice, virus signature files should be updated daily to address the risk of new viruses. In this case, files are updated every week, which makes the application vulnerable to new viruses during the intervening week. The other options are secondary concerns.

2. A compromised server has been isolated and appropriate forensic processes have been completed. What should be the next step?

    A. Reuse the server after scanning

    B. Discontinue the use of the server

    C. Use the server as a honeypot

    D. Rebuild the server with the original media and subsequent patches

    Answer: D. Rebuild the server with the original media and subsequent patches.

    Explanation: It is recommended to rebuild the server with the original media and update it with subsequent patches as the compromised server might have some hidden malicious files that cannot be detected through mere scanning. Discontinuing the use of the server or using it as a honeypot may not be a feasible option. There is no harm in using the server after rebuilding it with the original media.

3. The security manager has discovered that a hacker is analyzing the network perimeter. What action should they take?

    A. Reboot the firewall

    B. Check intrusion detection system logs and monitor for any active attacks

    C. Update the IDS version

    D. Initiate server trace logging

Answer: B. Check the intrusion detection system logs and monitor for any active attacks.

Explanation: The information security team should verify the **intrusion detection system (IDS)** logs and continue to monitor the situation. The other options are not relevant at this point. Updating the IDS could further cause temporary exposure until the updated version is tuned properly.

4. The security manager is investigating the breach by analyzing the logs from different systems. What will best support the correlation between these logs?

    A. Application server

    B. Domain name server

    C. Time server

    D. Database server

    Answer: C. Time server.

    Explanation: The time server provides a common time to all the connected servers and applications. The time element is very important during a forensic investigation. The other options will not directly assist in log reviews and their correlation.

5. A hacker was successful in gaining access to an application by guessing the password of a shared administrative account. The security manager can detect this breach by analyzing what?

    A. Router logs

    B. Invalid login attempts

    C. The password complexity rule

    D. Concurrent logins

    Answer: B. Invalid login attempts.

    Explanation: As a password was guessed, there will have been multiple attempts to gain access. These attempts are recorded in an invalid login log. Analyzing this log for invalid login attempts can lead to the discovery of this unauthorized activity. The other options will not directly indicate the unauthorized attempt. For shared accounts, concurrent use is common, so reviewing concurrent logins will not be helpful.

6. The security manager has discovered that a hacker is probing the organization's network. What should the security manager do?

A. Reboot the router connecting to DMZ

B. Switch off all the servers located on DMZ

C. Monitor the probe and isolate the affected segment

D. Initiate server trace logging

Answer: C. Monitor the probe and isolate the affected segment.

Explanation: In the case of a probe, it is advisable to monitor the situation and isolate the network under the probe. The other options are not warranted.

7. Once a security branch has occurred in the organization, what is the most important aspect to report to senior management?

A. Details of security logs indicating the source of the breach

B. Reports of similar incidents at the organization

C. A business case for an increase in security budget

D. The impact of the incident and the corrective action taken

Answer: D. The impact of the incident and the corrective action taken.

Explanation: Senior management is more interested in the impact caused by the breach and what corrective actions have been taken to minimize the damage and prevent further reoccurrence. The other options may not be relevant at this point.

8. Who should an incident with serious consequences be communicated to by the security manager?

A. To the appropriate regulatory body once the perpetrator has been identified

B. To management after determining the severity of the incident

C. To the insurance company to compensate for business disruption

D. To the legal department to initiate legal proceedings

Answer: B. To management after determining the severity of the incident.

Explanation: The security manager is required to communicate the details of the incident, along with its severity and impact, to management. Generally, communication with the regulators and insurance companies is handled by the legal and compliance team. Management will take calls for legal proceedings; the security manager is not expected to directly report to the legal department.

Post-incident activities and investigation

The objective of a post-incident review is to learn from each incident and improve the organization's response and recovery procedure. Lessons learned during incident management can be best used to improve the security posture of the organization, as well as the incident management process.

During a post-incident review, the overall cost of the incident is determined. This cost includes loss or damage to infrastructure, loss of business, cost of recovery, and cost of resources used to handle the incident. This cost provides useful metrics to justify the existence of the incident management team.

Identifying the root cause and corrective action

The information security manager should appoint an event review team. This team should be responsible for determining the root cause of the incident and suggest the appropriate action to prevent the reoccurrence of the incident.

Sometimes, the security manager obtains the services of third-party experts to independently and objectively review the root cause of the incidents.

Documenting the event

It is very important to have a structured process for documenting all the events related to the incident. This serves as a crucial set of evidence for further investigation. It can also be provided to authorities for forensic analysis. This process of recording the events should be entrusted to an employee who is well versed in forensic processes.

Documentation will also help you analyze the complete incident at the time of the post-incident review.

Chain of custody

The security manager should make sure that the appropriate chain of custody process is defined and documented for handling evidence. Chain of custody is a legal term referring to the order and manner in which evidence is handled to ensure the integrity of the evidence and its admissibility in a court of law.

The first step in any forensic investigation is to determine the process to ensure a chain of custody. This evidence handling procedure should be designed in consultation with the legal department, IT department, business process owners, and forensic experts. On a lighter note, the following figure indicates why it is important to have an expert for forensic investigations:

Figure 11.6 – Chain of custody and forensic experts

The security manager should use the following framework to establish the chain of custody:

- Evidence should only be handled by authorized officials. The expertise of employees is the most important factor in a forensic investigation.

- In the case of an ongoing incident, power should only be disconnected after consulting forensic experts as sudden power loss may result in information on the hard disk being corrupted. Other means of isolation and containment should be given first preference.

- Forensic tools should be used to create a bit-by-bit copy of the hard disk and other media to ensure legal admissibility. A bit-by-bit image will ensure that erased or deleted files and data in slack memory is also copied. Any further analysis or testing should be done on this copy. Original media should remain unchanged.

- A dedicated custodian should be appointed who is required to have safe custody of the evidence.

- Data from the original device should be copied using a cable with a write-protect diode (write block) to prevent writing on the original drive.

- Once data has been copied from the original media, the hash value of the original media and a copy should be calculated and compared to ensure that the copy is the exact image of the original media.

- The procedure that's followed to detect, extract, and analyze all the evidence should be recorded, along with details of the time, date, tools used, details of the forensic experts, and other relevant records. This will help establish that the investigation is fair, unbiased, and well documented.

These procedures should be well documented and frequent training should be given to concerned employees.

Key aspects from the CISM exam's perspective

The following are some of the key aspects from the exam's perspective:

Question	Possible Answer
What is the reason for consulting third-party teams when carrying out post-event reviews of incidents?	To independently and objectively review the root cause of the incidents.
What is the first step when initiating a forensic investigation?	Determining the process to ensure a chain of custody.
What is the most important objective of a post-incident review?	To document and analyze the lessons learned and to improve the process.
What is the best way to copy from media that is part of forensic evidence?	To create a bit-by-bit image of the original media source and turn it into new media.
What is the most important factor of forensic investigations that will potentially involve legal action?	Chain of custody.
What is the most important consideration when collecting and preserving admissible evidence during an incident response?	Chain of custody.
What is the reason for not immediately disconnecting power for an ongoing incident?	To avoid loss of data stored in volatile memory.

Question	Possible Answer
What is the best way to determine that the copy of the original media is complete, correct, and accurate?	Compare the hash images of both files.
What is the primary purpose for maintaining incident history?	To track and record the progress of the incident handling process.
What are the basic steps when investigating a suspected hard disk or server?	<ul><li>The first action is to create a bit-by-bit image of the original media.</li><li>The second step is to create and compare the hash of the original media and the copied media. This will help ensure that the copy is a replica of the original.</li><li>Start analyzing from the copied drive. Forensic analysis should not be performed on original media. It may impact the integrity of the evidence.</li></ul>

Practice questions

1. What is the main objective for involving a third-party team in a post-incident review?

    A. To have independent and objective reviews of the root cause of the incident

    B. To save on costs on the post-incident review

    C. To utilize the expertise of third-party teams

    D. To identify the lessons learned

    Answer: A. To have independent and objective reviews of the root cause of the incident.

    Explanation: It is always advisable to involve the third party for post-incident reviews to avoid conflicts of interest. The involvement of a third party will help the organization have an independent and objective review of the cause of the incident. Involving a third party will generally increase the cost. The availability of expert services is one of the advantages but not the prime factor for involving a third party. Lessons learned can be identified through the in-house team.

2. What is the most important element of a forensic investigation?

    A. A structured incident management system

    B. Defined roles and responsibilities for the incident management team

    C. The involvement of legal experts

    D. The expertise of the resources

    Answer: D. The expertise of the resources.

    Explanation: A forensic investigation is the process of gathering and analyzing all crime-related evidence to conclude an event. Investigators will analyze the hard drives, computers, or other technologies to establish how a crime took place. The most important element of a forensic investigation is the expertise of the employee doing the investigation. The other options are secondary aspects. The involvement of a legal expert depends on the nature of the investigation.

3. What is the most important aspect while collecting evidence for forensic analysis?

    A. Assign the job to a qualified person

    B. Request the end user to do an image copy

    C. Ensure evidence is stored at an offsite location

    D. Ensure that evidence is collected in the presence of law enforcement

    Answer: A. Assign the job to a qualified person.

    Explanation: A forensic investigation is the process of gathering and analyzing all crime-related evidence to conclude an event. Evidence will only be accepted in legal proceedings if it is proved that the integrity of the evidence has not been compromised. Hence, it is of utmost importance that evidence should only be handled by a qualified person. The end user is not qualified to take an image copy. Evidence can be stored anywhere, provided the appropriate controls are in place to safeguard its integrity. Involvement of law enforcement is not mandatory while collecting evidence.

4. What should be the first step while taking a forensic image of a hard drive?

    A. To determine the forensic software to take the image

    B. To establish the chain of custody log

    C. To enable a write blocker for the hard disk

    D. To create a cryptographic hash of the hard disk's content

Answer: B. The establish the chain of custody log

Explanation: Chain of custody is a legal term referring to the order and manner in which evidence is handled to ensure the integrity of the evidence and its admissibility in a court of law. The first step should be to determine and safeguard the integrity of the hard drive. The other options are important steps but they must be done after the chain of custody has been established.

5. What is the prime purpose of conducting a post-incident review?

    A. To determine the lessons learned to improve the process

    B. To ensure adherence to the security budget

    C. To review the performance of the incident response team

    D. To determine new incident management software

    Answer: A. To determine the lessons learned to improve the process.

    Explanation: The objective of a post-incident review is to learn from each incident and improve the organization's response and recovery procedure. Lessons learned during incident management can be best used to improve the security posture of the organization, as well as the incident management process. The other options are secondary aspects.

6. What is the prime purpose of conducting a post-incident review?

    A. To determine the integrity of evidence for legal proceedings

    B. To identify the lessons learned

    C. To identify the source of the incident

    D. To identify vulnerable areas

    Answer: B. To identify the lessons learned.

    Explanation: The objective of a post-incident review is to learn from each incident and improve the organization's response and recovery procedure. Lessons learned during incident management can be best used to improve the security posture of the organization, as well as the incident management process. The other options are secondary aspects.

7. The security manager has discovered that the original data was inadvertently altered while collecting forensic evidence. What should have been the action in the forensic investigation?

    A. Create a backup of all media that is to be used for the investigation

    B. Copy a bit-by-bit image from the original media to a new form of media

    C. Create a cryptographic hash of the hard disk's content

    D. Install an error checking program to ensure that there is no disk error

    Answer: B. Copy a bit-by-bit image from the original media to a new form of media.

    Explanation: The first step is to create a copy of the original media by copying a bit-by-bit image into new media. This is very important to ensure that all the analysis is performed on the copy drive, not the original drive. A simple backup may not be able to copy 100% of the data, such as erased or deleted files and data in slack space. The other options are subsequent steps.

8. What is the most important aspect to consider while collecting and preserving admissible evidence?

    A. Isolating the system

    B. Chain of custody

    C. Segregation of duties

    D. Time synchronization

    Answer: B. Chain of custody.

    Explanation: Chain of custody is a legal term referring to the order and manner in which evidence is handled to ensure the integrity of the evidence and its admissibility in a court of law. The first step should be to determine and safeguard the integrity of the hard drive. The other options are secondary aspects.

9. What is the most important aspect when evidence is to be used in legal proceedings?

    A. Whether the investigator is independent

    B. Whether the investigation was done timely

    C. Whether the perpetrator has been identified

    D. Whether the chain of custody is maintained

    Answer: D. Whether the chain of custody is maintained.

Explanation: Chain of custody is a legal term referring to the order and manner in which evidence is handled to ensure the integrity of the evidence and its admissibility in a court of law. The most important aspect is to determine the integrity of the evidence. The other options are secondary aspects.

10. What is the most important aspect when evidence is to be used in legal proceedings?

    A. Hard drives should be encrypted

    B. Use of generic audit software for data analytics

    C. Proven forensic processes are applied

    D. Use of automated log review software

    Answer: C. Proven forensic processes are applied.

    Explanation: Admissibility of evidence in a legal proceeding depends on what processes are used to collect, analyze, and preserve the evidence. Proven forensic processes help with admitting the evidence.

11. What should be the first step of the security manager after the aftermath of a distributed denial of service attack?

    A. To perform a penetration test to determine system vulnerabilities

    B. To conduct an assessment to determine the system's status

    C. To notify law enforcement

    D. To isolate the firewall

    Answer: B. To conduct an assessment to determine the system's status.

    Explanation: The first step should be to determine the status of the system in terms of damage and other impacts. This status will help the security manager determine further courses of action. Penetration tests and notifying law enforcement are subsequent actions. Isolating the firewall after the incident will not provide any benefit.

12. Which of the following is considered a violation of the chain of custody?

    A. The suspected hard drive was not removed in the presence of a law enforcement agency

    B. The suspected hard drive was kept in a tape library for further analysis

    C. The suspected hard drive was stored in a safe under a dual control

    D. The suspected hard drive was handed over to authorized independent investigators

Answer: B. The suspected hard drive was kept in a tape library for further analysis.

Explanation: If the hard drive is stored in a tape library, the chain of custody can't be verified as several individuals would have access to the library. It is not mandatory to remove the disk in the presence of a law enforcement agency. Storing the hard drive in a safe and handing it over to an authorized investigator does not violate the chain of custody.

13. A rootkit was installed in a server and the critical data of the organization was stolen. What should be the next step of the security manager to ensure the admissibility of evidence in legal proceedings?

    A. Proper documentation of events

    B. Timely notification of law enforcement

    C. Take an image copy of the media

    D. Scrap the affected server

    Answer: C. Take an image copy of the media.

    Explanation: The next step should be to take the image copy of the media. Analysis should be performed on the copy, not the original media. Preserving the evidence and maintaining the chain of custody is very important to ensure legal admissibility. Documenting and notifying law enforcement are subsequent steps. Scraping the server will result in the evidence being destroyed.

14. What is the most important aspect when evidence is to be used in legal proceedings?

    A. Timely detection of evidence

    B. Preserving the integrity of the evidence

    C. Isolating all IT equipment

    D. Documenting the sequence of events

    Answer: B. Preserving the integrity of the evidence.

    Explanation: It is of utmost importance to demonstrate the integrity of the evidence to ensure this is recognized in legal proceedings. The other options do help in the investigation process, but they are not relevant to the admissibility of the evidence.

15. What is the best source to analyze a compromised server for forensic investigation?

    A. A bit-level copy of the server

    B. The backup data of the server maintained offsite

C. Volatile memory data

D. Original compromised server

Answer: A. A bit-level copy of the server.

Explanation: Analysis should not be conducted on the original affected server. This may impact the integrity of the evidence. Analysis should be performed on a bit-level copy of the server. The bit-level copy image will support the integrity and quality of the forensic evidence that is admissible in a court of law. The other options will not provide quality and an exact image for the investigation work.

16. What is the main reason to conduct a post-incident review?

    A. To adhere to the incident management policy

    B. To preserve the forensic evidence

    C. To improve the response process

    D. To ensure proper documentation

    Answer: C. To improve the response process.

    Explanation: The objective of a post-incident review is to learn from each incident and improve the organization's response and recovery procedure. Lessons learned during incident management can be best used to improve the overall security posture of the organization, as well as the incident management process. The other options are secondary aspects.

17. What should be the priority during a forensic analysis of electronic information?

    A. Documenting the events

    B. Locating the evidence and preserving the integrity of the evidence

    C. Creating a forensic-quality image

    D. Identifying the perpetrator

    Answer: B. Locating the evidence and preserving the integrity of the evidence.

    Explanation: The priority should be locating the electronic evidence and preserving the integrity of the evidence. The other options are secondary aspects.

18. While handling the incident, what should be the most important aspect while interacting with the media?

    A. Using specially drafted messages by an authorized person

    B. Providing all the evidence under investigation

C. Denying any response until recovery

D. Reporting the impact and recovery status

Answer: A. Using specially drafted messages by an authorized person.

Explanation: It is always advisable to provide details that have been preapproved by senior management. Any unnecessary information may create havoc and impact the reputation of the organization.

19. What is the main reason for not disconnecting the power while analyzing the suspected behavior of a computer?

   A. To ensure the safety of the hard drive

   B. To contain the spread of exposure

   C. To prevent the loss of data in server logs

   D. To prevent the loss of data that's available in volatile memory

   Answer: D. To prevent the loss of data that's available in volatile memory.

   Explanation: Disconnecting the power may result in the data stored in volatile memory being lost. This data may be critical for the investigation and for understanding the impact of the incident. Disconnecting the power will generally not impact the safety of the hard drive or the loss of data in server logs. Disconnecting the power will help contain the spread. However, instead of disconnecting the computer, it should be isolated from the network.

20. When will data recovery from a specific file be the most challenging?

   A. When all the files in the directory have been erased

   B. When the disk has been formatted

   C. When the file's content has been overwritten multiple times

   D. When the partition table on the disk has been deleted

   Answer: C. When the file's content has been overwritten multiple times.

   Explanation: Overwriting the file makes it difficult to recover the data. Even highly specialized tools may not be able to recover overwritten files in a few instances. Deleted files that have not been overwritten can easily be retrieved using forensic tools. Formatted disks and partition tables can also be recovered.

21. The security manager has discovered an attempted SQL injection attack on an application but could not determine whether it was successful. Who should be in the best position to assess the possible impact of the attack?

    A. Application support team

    B. Incident response team

    C. Business process owner

    D. Network security team

    Answer: A. Application support team.

    Explanation: SQL injection is an application-based attack. The application support team will be in the best position to determine any unauthorized activity regarding the application database. The business process owner will only be able to discover the attack if it has a major impact on business processes. Since SQL injection is an application-based attack, the network security team or incident response team will not be able to assess the possible impact.

22. What is the most important advantage of implementing a systematic and methodological incident management program?

    A. It reduces the cost of incident management

    B. It makes incident management more flexible

    C. It helps the responder gain experience

    D. It provides evidence of due diligence to support legal and liability claims

    Answer: D. It provides evidence of due diligence to support legal and liability claims.

    Explanation: A structured process of incident management supports legal and liability claims as evidence is formally documented and handled methodically. The other options are secondary aspects.

23. Once a virus incident has been resolved, the security manager will be most interested in knowing about what?

    A. The configuration of anti-malware software

    B. The other organizations that have been impacted by this virus

    C. The path of entry for the virus

    D. The author of the virus

    Answer: C. The path of entry for the virus.

Explanation: The security manager needs to understand the entry path of the virus. The first step is to determine the entry path so that the investigation can identify what controls failed. This loophole is to be addressed as early as possible to prevent reoccurrence.

24. What is the objective of reviewing the observations of staff involved in a disaster recovery test?

    A. To determine the efficiency level of the staff

    B. To determine the lessons learned

    C. To determine the effectiveness of DRP training

    D. To identify resource requirements

    Answer: B. To determine the lessons learned.

    Explanation: Based on a discussion with the staff involved in disaster recovery, test areas of improvement can be determined. This helps improve the effectiveness of the test. The other options are secondary aspects.

25. The effectiveness of incident management is mostly dependent on which of the following?

    A. The criteria set for determining the severity level

    B. The capabilities of the intrusion detection system

    C. The capabilities of the help desk team

    D. An effective communication and reporting process

    Answer: D. An effective communication and reporting process.

    Explanation: A structured communication and reporting process is an important aspect to ensure that incidents are reported promptly to the incident response team. Timely reporting will help with prompt responses. IDS may not be able to detect and report anything other than IT incidents. The capabilities of the help desk team is also an important aspect but without reporting from end users, the help desk team will not be able to detect the incident. Determining the severity level is a secondary aspect compared to the communication and reporting process.

26. The security manager has taken a bit-by-bit copy image of the suspected hard drive. What should their immediate next step be?

    A. Encrypt the original as well as the image

    B. Start analyzing the content of the image

    C. Create hashes for the original and the bit-by-bit copy image

D. Validate the tool that was used to create the image

Answer: C. Create hashes for the original and the bit-by-bit copy image

Explanation: Once a bit-by-bit copy has been created, the next step is to generate a hash for both the original drive as well as the copied drive. A hash value is a fixed value derived from the content. If the content changes, the hash value also changes. Both hashes should be compared to ensure that the copy is complete, correct, and accurate. Analysis should start only after ensuring that the copy is a replica of the original. Tool validation should happen before initiating the copy. Encrypted images cannot be analyzed.

27. The security manager has identified a vulnerability in a server. What should their next step be?

A. Reporting

B. Eradication

C. Analysis

D. Containment

Answer: C. Analysis.

Explanation: The next step should be to analyze the vulnerability concerning the possibility of exposure, possible impact, applicable threat factors, and other relevant factors. Identifying a vulnerability does not necessarily mean that an incident has occurred. Containment and eradication are steps to be taken after the incident has occurred. Reporting is to be done after the analysis.

28. The best way to resolve the operational issues with a third-party service provider is to include what in the service-level agreement?

A. A penalty clause

B. Audit requirements

C. Jurisdiction for legal action

D. Defined responsibilities

Answer: D. Defined responsibilities.

Explanation: If the responsibilities of the service provider and service receiver are defined and documented, it will help with smoothly executing the process without much conflict. In the case of operational issues, responsibility ownership will help determine the course of action. The other options are secondary aspects for resolving operational issues.

29. Concerning a recent incident, the investigation revealed the involvement of an internal employee. The security team has confiscated their computer. What is the best next step?

A. Create a bit-by-bit image of the hard drive

B. Analyze the content of the original hard drive

C. Create a logical copy of the hard drive

D. Encrypt the data on the hard drive

Answer: A. Create a bit-by-bit image of the hard drive.

Explanation: To the best extent possible, forensic analysis should not be performed on original media. It may impact the integrity of the evidence. The best way is to create a bit-by-bit image of the original media. The bit-by-bit image will ensure that erased or deleted files and data in slack memory are also copied. A logical copy will only copy the files and folders and may not copy other necessary data to help with examining the hard drive for forensic evidence. Encryption is not required.

30. What is the most important aspect to ensure the admissibility of evidence in a legal proceeding?

A. The aging of the evidence

B. The media used to store the evidence should be write blocked

C. The evidence should be reviewed by an independent authority

D. Traceability of control

Answer: D. Traceability of control.

Explanation: Traceability of control means to demonstrate who had control of the evidence throughout the process. It indicates a proper chain of custody. The other options are secondary aspects.

31. What is the main objective of documenting the history of a security incident?

A. To maintain evidence for forensic investigation

B. To record the progress and document the exceptions

C. To assign a severity level to the incident

D. To determine the accountability of the incident response team

Answer: B. To record the progress and document the exceptions.

Explanation: Documenting the incident history helps you keep a record of the incident from its detection until the incident is closed. This helps determine whether all the related aspects of incident management are performed appropriately, as per the defined process and timelines. Exceptions, if any, are discussed and deliberated and appropriate actions are taken. The other options are secondary aspects.

32. The root cause of a security incident has indicated that one important process was not monitored. As a result, the monitoring process has been started. Monitoring will best help with which of the following?

    A. Compliance with the security policy

    B. Reduction in the security budget

    C. Improvement in identification

    D. Increase in risk appetite

    Answer: C. Improvement in identification.

    Explanation: A structured method of monitoring helps in detecting incidents early. In the absence of any monitoring process, the incident may go undetected and can have a major impact on business processes. Monitoring will help improve the identification of threats and vulnerabilities. Implementing a monitoring process may increase the security budget. Monitoring does not impact the risk appetite. Compliance with the security policy is a secondary aspect.

33. Concerning a forensic investigation, data is to be copied from the original drive for further analysis. Which of the following must be ensured?

    A. The disk model is the same as the original

    B. Two copies should be made available

    C. Generate a hash from both the original as well as the copy

    D. Conduct a restoration test

    Answer: C. Generate a hash from both the original as well as the copy.

    Explanation: Once a bit-by-bit copy has been created, the next step is to generate a hash for both the original drive as well as the copied drive. A hash value is a fixed value derived from the content. If this content changes, the hash value also changes. Both hashes should be compared to ensure that the copy is complete, correct, and accurate. Analysis should start only after ensuring that the copy is a replica of the original. It is not necessary to have the same disk model. It is good practice to have two copies, but a more important aspect is creating a hash. Restoration is not relevant while evaluating the evidence.

34. What should be your priority when evidence is to be used in legal proceedings?

    A. Notify law enforcement

    B. Prevent contamination of evidence

    C. Initiate an incident response plan

    D. Document the events sequentially

    Answer: B. Prevent contamination of evidence.

    Explanation: For legal proceedings, the integrity of the evidence is of utmost importance. Hence, the first step in such a situation is to prevent contamination or alteration of the evidence. The other options are subsequent steps.

Summary

In this chapter, we discussed the practical aspects of information security incident management. This chapter will help CISM candidates define resilient business processes and determine the different aspects of business continuity plans and disaster recovery plans. This chapter will also help CISM candidates test various plans and improve their effectiveness. We also discussed how CISM candidates can implement different post-incident activities and investigations.

In this book, we have discussed all four domains of the CISM Review Manual of the ISACA. This book will help CISM aspirants gain sufficient theoretical as well as practical understanding to pass the CISM exam.

`Packt.com`

Subscribe to our online digital library for full access to over 7,000 books and videos, as well as industry leading tools to help you plan your personal development and advance your career. For more information, please visit our website.

Why subscribe?

- Spend less time learning and more time coding with practical eBooks and Videos from over 4,000 industry professionals
- Improve your learning with Skill Plans built especially for you
- Get a free eBook or video every month
- Fully searchable for easy access to vital information
- Copy and paste, print, and bookmark content

Did you know that Packt offers eBook versions of every book published, with PDF and ePub files available? You can upgrade to the eBook version at `packt.com` and as a print book customer, you are entitled to a discount on the eBook copy. Get in touch with us at `customercare@packtpub.com` for more details.

At `www.packt.com`, you can also read a collection of free technical articles, sign up for a range of free newsletters, and receive exclusive discounts and offers on Packt books and eBooks.

Other Books You May Enjoy

If you enjoyed this book, you may be interested in these other books by Packt:

Cybersecurity Career Master Plan

Dr. Gerald Auger, Jaclyn "Jax" Scott, Jonathan Helmus, Kim Nguyen

ISBN: 978-1-80107-356-1

- Gain an understanding of cybersecurity essentials, including the different frameworks and laws, and specialties
- Find out how to land your first job in the cybersecurity industry
- Understand the difference between college education and certificate courses
- Build goals and timelines to encourage a work/life balance while delivering value in your job
- Understand the different types of cybersecurity jobs available and what it means to be entry-level
- Build affordable, practical labs to develop your technical skills
- Discover how to set goals and maintain momentum after landing your first cybersecurity job

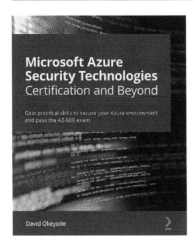

Microsoft Azure Security Technologies Certification and Beyond

David Okeyode

ISBN: 978-1-80056-265-3

- Manage users, groups, service principals, and roles effectively in Azure AD
- Explore Azure AD identity security and governance capabilities
- Understand how platform perimeter protection secures Azure workloads
- Implement network security best practices for IaaS and PaaS
- Discover various options to protect against DDoS attacks
- Secure hosts and containers against evolving security threats
- Configure platform governance with cloud-native tools
- Monitor security operations with Azure Security Center and Azure Sentinel

Packt is searching for authors like you

If you're interested in becoming an author for Packt, please visit `authors.packtpub.com` and apply today. We have worked with thousands of developers and tech professionals, just like you, to help them share their insight with the global tech community. You can make a general application, apply for a specific hot topic that we are recruiting an author for, or submit your own idea.

Share your thoughts

Now you've finished *Certified Information Security Manager Exam Guide*, we'd love to hear your thoughts! Scan the QR code below to go straight to the Amazon review page for this book and share your feedback or leave a review on the site that you purchased it from.

`https://packt.link/r/1801074100`

Your review is important to us and the tech community and will help us make sure we're delivering excellent quality content.

Index

B

W

Z

Made in the USA
Columbia, SC
17 April 2022

59113922R00337